HUMAN RIGHTS AND THE CONSTITUTION
Vision and the Reality

HUMAN RIGHTS AND THE CONSTITUTION
Vision and the Reality

Edited by
K.P. Saksena

Published under the auspices of
the Institute for World Congress on Human Rights
New Delhi

GYAN PUBLISHING HOUSE
NEW DELHI-110002

Human Rights and the Constitution : Vision and the Reality

(*Human Rights*)

Rs. 890

ISBN: 81-212-0819-X

Published in 2003 in India by
Gyan Publishing House
5, Ansari Road, Darya Ganj, New Delhi-110002
Phones : 23282060, 23261060, Fax (011) 23285914
E-mail : gyanbook@vsnl.com
Website : http://www.gyanbooks.com

Laser Typesetting at: Sharma Graphic, Delhi
Printed at: Mehra Offset Press, Delhi

Contents

Preface

In the short history of independent India, the most significant date is not 15th of August -- a date unilaterally set by Britain for quitting India -- but the 26th of January, 1950. That was the day when the constitutional framework, which the people gave themselves for governance became fully operative. It was the fulfilment of peoples solemn resolve to constitute a sovereign democratic republic, which would ensure to all its citizens (irrespective of one's religion, race, caste, sex or place of birth), social, economic and political justice; liberty of thought, expression, belief, faith and worship; equality of status and of opportunity; and to promote among ourselves fraternity ensuring respect for the dignity of the individual as a human being.

After 50 years and plus, where do we stand today in terms of promises made as enshrined in our Constitution? How the Constitution had worked, especially in the context of promotion and protection of human rights? What path have we traversed? What progress, if any, have we made and where we failed? What are the unfinished tasks and what was needed to carry on the movement towards the goal?

In commemoration of 50 years of India's Constitution, those of us concerned with human rights problems, considered it appropriate to do stock-taking in the context of issues noted above.

With this objective, the Centre for Human Rights Education and Research, Institute for World Congress on Human Rights (IWCOHR) in association with National Human Rights Commission (NHRC) and India International Centre (IIC) convened a two-day national seminar on "Human Rights and Fifty Years of India's Constitution" on 15th to 16th of December, 2000. This book has resulted from that national seminar and various chapters included here are the revised version of the text of the papers contributed to the seminar.

We hope that this volume will help contribute wider awareness of human rights issues and also help strengthen better understanding, advocacy and policy-making in regard to human rights problems in India. In preparation of this volume, we have had the benefit of support and cooperation of many individuals and organisations; I am indebted to them, although it is difficult to name them all.

We wish to place on record our appreciation and gratitude to the contributors, who despite having other pressing engagements, agreed to join us at the seminar and made invaluable contribution to the seminar-deliberations and to this volume. We also wish to extend our gratitude and appreciation to Mr. Justice J.S. Verma (Chairman, NHRC), who extended us NHRC's financial assistance towards the overall expenses of the seminar, to Mrs. Justice Sujata V. Manohar (Member, NHRC), who kindly agreed to deliver the inaugural address and made the text of her address available to us for inclusion in this publication, to Mr. Virendra Dayal (seniormost Member of NHRC), who could find time despite his other demanding preoccupations to chair one of the sessions of the seminar and also actively participated in the discussion on various issues. Our thanks are also due to Mr. N.N. Vohra (Director, IIC), who very kindly made available to us, conference room facilities at IIC, free of charge and could find time to chair the session on 'Human Rights and Law Enforcement' and actively participated in the discussion.

As convenor of this seminar and editor of this volume, I am also grateful to the members of the Board of Trustees of the Institute for their support and guidance and to the members of the editorial board of the Institute -- Mrs. Malti Singh, Prof. V.S. Mani and Dr. J.C. Batra.

Thanks are also due to Dr. R.S. Saini (HURITER, JNU), Ms. Una Gupta and Ms. Shilpa Johri, for providing valuable support and assistance in the organisational work of the seminar and in the preparation of this volume.

—*KPS*

Notes on Contributors

Justice Sujata V. Manohar	-	*Former Chief Justice Kerala and Bombay High Courts, former Judge of Supreme Court of India; she is Member, National Human Rights Commission (NHRC), New Delhi.*
V.S. Mani	-	*Professor of International Law, is Director, Centre for Promotion of Human Rights Teaching & Research (HURITER), Jawaharlal Nehru University (JNU), New Delhi. He is also a Life Member, Board of Trustees and Treasurer, Institute for World Congress on Human Rights (IWCOHR), New Delhi.*
Mool Chand Sharma	-	*Professor of International Law, Delhi University, Delhi and Adviser (Research), NHRC.*
J.C. Batra	-	*Barrister of Law and Senior Advocate, Supreme Court of India, New Delhi. He is also a Life Member, Board of Trustee, IWCOHR.*
N.R. Madhava Menon	-	*Well known jurist and exponent of International Human Rights Law, is Vice Chancellor, West Bengal University of Juridical Sciences, Kolkata.*
Abhishek M. Singhvi	-	*Ph.D. (Cantab), PIL (Harvard), an eminent Jurist and former Solicitor General of India, is Senior Advocate, Supreme Court of India, New Delhi.*
Chaman Lal	-	*Former Commander, Para-Military Forces, is a human rights activist, and presently Special Rapporteur, NHRC.*
K.P. Saksena	-	*Former Professor of International*

		Organisation and Founder-Director, HURITER, JNU, is a Life Member, Board of Trustee and Secretary General, IWCOHR and Director of IWCOHR Centre for Human Rights Education and Research, New Delhi.
Jayashree Gupta	-	*Director, Department of Consumers and Hony. Chairman, Human Rights Group, Ministry of Home Affairs, New Delhi.*
Smt. Pritam Arora	-	*Social Activist and Educationist, is Vice President, All India Mahila Congress (I), New Delhi.*
Imtiaz Ahmad	-	*Professor, JNU, New Delhi.*
R.M. Pal	-	*Formerly Senior Faculty Member, Rajdhani College, Delhi University, Dr. Pal is Editor, PUCL Bulletin, published by People's Union for Civil Liberties and of Radical Humanist.*
G.S. Bhargava	-	*Former Resident Editor, The Indian Express and Principal Information Officer, Government of India (1978-80), is an eminent Journalist, New Delhi.*
Justice Rajindar Sachar	-	*Former Chief Justice, Delhi High Court; UN Special Rapporteur, Member UN Sub-Commission on Human Rights; former President, People's Union of Civil Liberties (PUCL), is a Senior Advocate, Supreme Court of India, New Delhi.*
Abdulrahim P. Vijapur	-	*Ph.D. (JNU), LL.M (Essex, U.K.), author/editor of several published books on human rights issues, Dr. Vijapur is presently Reader, Department of Political Science, Aligarh Muslim University, Aligarh (U.P.).*

Introduction

K.P. Saksena

I

As a prefatory to the review of fifty years of the working of India's Constitution in the context of human rights, essayed in the pages that follow, a brief historical perspective is outlined here.

The Constitution of India was adopted by the Constituent Assembly on 26th November, 1949 and came into full force on 26th January 1950.[1] It was the culmination of the National Movement for social reform and freedom, which began in the 19th century, followed by protracted struggle against British Rule. Beginning the 1920s, the movement concretised by early 1930s, into three related objectives: (a) national independence and complete freedom from foreign yoke; (b) convening of a Constituent Assembly composed of the representative people of India to make out the constitutional framework for governance of the country[2]; and (c) to ensure democratic system of government which would guarantee fundamental rights and freedoms to the people without discrimination of caste, creed, descent, gender, race or religion and also ensure social welfare of the people in general and overall advancement of the tribal people and backward classes including the so-called "untouchables", in particular.

The first objective was reached by August 1947, though at a very heavy cost and in a diluted form. The country was partitioned on the basis of religion, resulting in two-way migration of people, killing and trauma of unprecedented sufferings and uprooting of more than 10 million people. Again, British government itself decided to quit India and offered us independence on a silver platter and thus robbed us of achieving independence of our own.

As regards the second objective, the Constituent Assembly, composed of the representatives of India, did come about and was convened on 9th of December, 1946, but could meet only for a short duration. It gained momentum in its work only after independence. Here again, we were denied the satisfaction of cultivating the fruits of our long struggle. The Constituent Assembly came into being under particular historical conditions and the British government had a hand in its birth. In the Cabinet Mission Plan of May 1946, the British government, for the first time, had conceded India's right to independence (to be "granted" by June 1948) and to draw its own Constitution. Under this Plan, a Constituent Assembly was to be set up consisting of 381 members representing all the provinces under British rule and "Indian States" on the basis of one member to represent approximately one million people. To speed-up the setting up of the Constituent Assembly, it was to be composed of representatives indirectly elected by a system of proportional representation from the then provincial legislators, who had themselves been elected, in 1945, on a restricted franchise, consisting of about 20-24 per cent of adult populace. Again, a significant section of the Constituent Assembly was to be non-elective also, i.e., 93 members nominated by the rulers of the Indian States.

In sum, unlike the constituent assemblies of the past, the Constituent Assembly of India was not a product of revolution, but a product of revolutionary political achievements. Further, the Constituent Assembly was created by the British to enable the Indian political leaders to draft the Constitution for "Royal Assent". Eventually, the assent was not needed since the transfer of power (full independence) took place much before the Constituent Assembly enacted the Constitution of India.

Again, the Constituent Assembly was initially intended to draft a constitution for the whole of India, but Mountbatten Plan June 3, 1947 predated the grant of independence by a year (on August 15, 1947), and more significantly, announced the partition of the country. Subsequently the Indian Independence Act, 1947 passed by the British Parliament partitioned India into two separate dominions of India and Pakistan. The Act also made a division of the Constituent Assembly and of its members.

At the time of its birth as a sovereign State (August 15, 1947), hurriedly decided by the erstwhile foreign rulers, the country was not strong enough to build a democratic edifice. India's revolution for the social and political change was not complete. It has not yet given shape to a united and strong nation. We were a badly divided and fragmented society. Such diversities and divisions in language, mode of living, religion etc. as not found in any other part of the world. What was most challenging was that a vast majority of the people were reeling under abject poverty; annual per capita income was approximately Rs. 290. On the other hand, there were individuals and families more rich than found anywhere else in the world.

Again, India at one time the most prosperous country in the world, lost the crucial period of nearly 200 years, thanks to British colonial rule, to keep pace with the rest of the world, in industrial development. In 1947, Indian economy had remained mainly agricultural; 72 per cent of its total working force was occupied in agriculture. The organised industry employed only 2 per cent of the working force, less than the number employed in civil services. 11 per cent were employed in all forms of small-scale and cottage industries and the remaining were small traders.

At that stage, only less than 12 per cent of the people in India could read and write. These 12 per cent were having among them highly educated people in every academic discipline, and included two Nobel Laureate - one in literature and the other in science.

Let us turn to another aspect. Territorial-wise, India was a sharply divided country. The so-called provinces ruled directly by British Indian Government (which had also pockets of so-called native states ruled by autocratic rulers) constituted around 50 per cent of India's territory and more than 65 per cent of its people. The other part of the territory had more than 500 native states (some of them larger than several of the European nations-states) ruled by autocratic princely rulers, who had special relationship with the British government referred to as "Paramountcy". On 15th of August, 1947, paramountcy was to lapse and these autocratic rulers of "native states" were free to join India or Pakistan or declare their independence. These states represented approximately 43 per cent of India's territory and 24 per cent of its population. With lapse of paramountcy, several of these native states, for example, Bhopal, Hyderabad, Mysore had declared their "intent" for "independence".[3]

There was more to the dicey situation. The remaining part of India having mountainous regions and thick forest areas were home of tribal people and the so-called "Adivasis". These areas were referred to as "Tribal and Excluded Areas", having special administrative arrangements under the British rule.

Throughout its history, Indian rulers adhering to the traditional Indian principle of "live and let live", had left these tribal people, to their own way of life. With the advent of British rule, these Tribal and Excluded Areas were brought under effective British control. The Church followed the British flag. It was not surprising that a large number of tribal people and "Adivasis" were converted to Christianity.

When India gained independence, one option was to follow the policy as practised by European settlers in North America and Australia – to seize their rich part of their land and then exterminate them, or force them to live in isolation in remote areas. The other alternative, which independent India adhered to, was to treat them as part of the Indian people, to promote their social welfare and to bring them to the mainstream of Indian civilisation.

With this background, one can well visualise the kind of challenging task the Constituent Assembly was confronted with. Fortunately, at that point of time (a rare occasion in India's history), the members, who got elected, to the Constituent Assembly, though with a very limited franchise, represented a galaxy of high statesmanship, social and political leadership. They eschewed narrow caste, religious, regional consideration and envisioned an India maintaining its territorial integrity, unity in diversity and bringing together all the people of India (what remains after partition) into a common fold ensuring basic human rights for all, irrespective of caste, colour, descent, gender, race, religion etc. and providing special safeguards for the rights of the minorities.

At the very first meeting of the Constituent Assembly (9th of December 1946), Jawaharlal Nehru moved the historic "Objectives Resolution", which inspired the shaping of the Constitution through its all-subsequent stages. It inter alia asserted "solemn resolve to proclaim India as an independent sovereign republic" and that "all powers and authority of the Sovereign Independent India, its constituent parts and organs of Governments are derived from the people" and that the Constitution shall "guarantee and secure to all the people of India, justice - social, economic and political; equality of status, of opportunity and before the law; freedom of thought and expression, belief, faith, worship, association and action, subject to law and public morality and "adequate safeguards" provisions "for minorities, backward and tribal areas, depressed and other backward classes."[4]

At the time when India gained independence, the concept of constitutionalism was not confined to governance of the State with political, diplomatic and police role. State was rather looked upon as a powerful instrument for removing social injustices, elimination of artificial inequalities and ensuring social welfare of the people.

Indeed, the guiding force of India's constitution-making was the objectives set during the National Movement for independence with the emphasis on elimination of social and economic injustices, equality of law (which was denied by the British government) and participation of the people through their representatives in the governance of the State.

The members of the Constituent Assembly did take advantage of learning from the experiences of the Constitution of other democratic countries, such as that of United States of America, Australia, Canada and Ireland. They attempted to fit those experiences to Indian conditions and socio-economic requirements.

What followed was a special Chapter, i.e., Part-III of the Constitution, which enumerated judiciable "Fundamental Rights" and following Chapter, i.e., Part-IV devoted to laying down of Principles, fundamental in the governance of the country.

The Fundamental Rights in the Constitution of India are more elaborate than those found in any other written constitution. The Constitution itself classifies the Fundamental Rights under seven groups: (a) Right to Equality; (b) Right to Particular Freedoms; (c) Right against Exploitation; (d) Right to Freedom of Religion; (e) Cultural and Educational Rights; (f) Right to Property; and (g) Right to Constitutional Remedies.

The Fundamental Rights were meant to ensure that no person shall be deprived of one's life, liberty or property, except in accordance with the law that no one will be denied equality before the law. All citizens were to have the right to freedom of religion, assembly, association and movement. In the special circumstances that prevailed before and at the time of independence, the Constitution also provided rights to minorities to protect and conserve their language and culture and various means are provided whereby the citizen can move the Supreme Court and other courts for Fundamental Rights.

Although the Fundamental Rights primarily protect individuals and minority groups from arbitrary and prejudicial State action, three of the Articles have been designed to protect the individual against the action of other citizens. Article 17 abolishes untouchability; Article 15(2) lays down that no citizen shall suffer any disability in the use of shops, restaurants, wells, roads and other public places on account of one's religion, race, caste, gender or place of birth; Article 23 prohibits forced labour, which was more commonly practised by the land-owners against poor peasants. Therefore, not only negative injunctions on the State not to interfere with certain liberties of the citizens but also obligates to protect the citizen rights from encroachment by society. In sum, the Fundamental Rights aims to foster the social revolution by creating a society egalitarian to the extent that all citizens were to be equally free from coercion or restriction by the State, or by society or by private citizen. Thus, ensuring that liberty was no longer to be the privilege of the few.

As an eminent Anglo-American scholar[5] aptly notes that the Indian Constitution is first and foremost a social document. He further adds that the majority of its provisions are either directly aimed at furthering the goals of social revolution or attempt to foster this revolution by establishing the conditions necessary for its achievements. In the Directive Principles, one finds an even clearer statement of social revolution. Unlike Fundamental Rights in Part-III, the Directive Principles are not judiciable but these principles are fundamental in the governance of the country (Article 38).

It was well realised by the framers of the Constitution that fundamental rights guaranteed, would be meaningless for majority of the people unless efforts are made to create socio-economic conditions for the upliftment of the common people and those because of social evils such as caste-system and untouchability or for other reasons (such as Tribal people/Adivasis) who were left behind.

As such, the next part of the Constitution, i.e., Part-IV included Directive Principles of State Policy. It was clearly spelled out that while fundamental rights are enforceable in court of law, certain ideals such as economic and social security and economic and social democracy which is pledged for in the Preamble and the State is directed to aim at securing by regulation of legislation and administrative policy.

It is neither the occasion nor possible, to go into the details, but to emphasise that the Constitution of India aimed at ensuring fundamental rights along with upliftment of the people, promotion of their social welfare and envisioned that one day the tree of true liberty would bloom in this country. The question is after fifty years and plus, how do we assess the situation? What promises our Constitution made then and where do we stand today? These and related issues constitute the thematic focus of the study.

II

To begin with, Mrs. Justice Sujata Manohar (Chapter-I) provides an overview and argues that fifty years of India's Constitution, in practice, leaves much to be desired, to say the least. The constitutional framework provided us institutions, she contends, "they have not failed us, we have failed the institutions", because we were "not able to put in these institutions men and women with ideals and principles who can run them as they should be run." She gives details to argue that solitary institution, "which still stands amidst the ruins, is the judiciary, which has used the mandate of our Constitution to protect human rights and our fundamental freedoms though there may have been some lapses."

In Chapter-II, Professor V.S. Mani presents a perceptive analysis of the ideals enshrined in the Preamble and critically assesses the extent to which they were embodied in Chapter-III and Chapter-IV of the Constitution. He further examines the ground realities as experienced during and on the completion of fifty years of the functioning of the Constitution. He also discusses the initiative to incept, by the Parliament, of various human rights institutions, i.e., National Human Rights Commission (NHRC), National Commission for Minorities, National Commission for Scheduled Castes and Scheduled Tribes and the National Commission for Women. He also analyses the functioning of these commissions, the role of the media and the extent to which they have made a difference in the overall situation in the context of protection of human rights of the individual and groups.

Prof. Mool Chand Sharma (Chapter-III) emphasises how in any framework of human rights, the judiciary has to play a crucial role in safeguarding against violation of human rights by states, individuals or society. Indeed, the Constitution of India, he contends, has assigned the judiciary a role as the guardian of the Constitution and also affirmed the rights of the citizens for judicial remedy (Article 13), which regretably got circumscribed by Parliament. Prof. Sharma cites instances how the activism of judiciary has provided expansive interpretation to fundamental rights such as right to life and liberty as enshrined in Article 21 and right to information as guaranteed under Article 19(1). However, he argues that judiciary should not overstep in the area reserved for the legislators and concludes that judiciary, in India, "except on certain occasions such as the emergency period (1975-77) has performed its role to protect human rights with fair degree of sensitivity and responsiveness". He further contends that in the last couple of decades the process of globalisation and role of Trans-national Corporations (TNCs) posit a serious challenge to the nation-state and also to the judiciary. As such, the judiciary has before it a challenging task to ensure that these new developments, including in the field of science and technology, are responsive to the needs of humanity and human development.

Dr. J.C. Batra (Chapter-IV) takes a critical look at one of the most innovative judicial phenomenon known as Public Interest Litigation (PIL), which allows individuals and groups (NGOs) to bring to the attention of the judiciary instances of gross violation of human rights needing judicial remedial action.

Prof. N.R. Madhava Menon (Chapter-V) concentrates on the state of economic and social rights and also reflects on the so-called "liberalisation" and economic reforms carried out in recent years and their impact on economic, social and cultural rights.

In the next chapter (Chapter-VI), Dr. Abhishek M. Singhvi takes up the most perennial problem of all times - inflicting torture upon individuals and human beings - one of the most insidious evils, which has continued from time immemorial until this supposedly modern age, which is widely regarded as recognition of respect the rights of all individuals.

To eliminate this most insidious evil, the United Nations has adopted several international instruments and specifically the Convention against Torture and other Cruel, Inhuman or Degrading Treatment or Punishment. Yet, in reality, the practice of inflicting torture continues unabated. One of the most glaring proofs of this evil is borne by the death of individuals while in police-custody.

Dr. Singhvi provides a perceptive analysis of this problem, with citation of its prohibition both under international and domestic laws and why it continues unabated. A significant part of Dr. Singhvi's paper is devoted to providing citation of cases and political, legal developments to deal with this evil. He follows a pragmatic approach by suggesting a remedial framework, which could substantially reduce, if not altogether eliminate, torture and other cruel, inhuman or degrading treatment or punishment.

In a broader framework, Mr. Chaman Lal (Chapter-VII) discusses the right to life and personal liberty in the context of law enforcement. He discusses various constitutional provisions to ensure right to life and personal liberty provided in international human rights law and also in the Indian legal system. He cites cases where this right is respected by law enforcement officials more in its breach than observance. He further elaborates on the safeguards recently provided by enunciation of more effective legal procedure and further elaborated and strengthened by the judicial decisions. However, that notwithstanding the constitutional guarantees reinforced by the specific provisions in substantive laws to protect peoples' right to life and liberty, all the wings of the system - police, prosecution, judiciary and prison administration, he contends, have registered an alarming fall in the standards of their performance and integrity and that practice of illegal arrests, custodial torture sometimes leading to death in custody and other gross violations of human rights by law enforcement officials are part of their day-to-day performances. He concludes that realisation of this most fundamental right could become a reality if the respect for human rights and human dignity gets in-built into professional ethics of law enforcement officials.

Chapter-VIII essays the evolution of the concept of the Right to Equality, in historical perspective, indicating how throughout the ages human beings were discriminated against on the basis of birth/ descent, gender, colour, race, religion, etc. and how the concept of equality gained universal recognition, at least in theory, in the mid-twentieth century. It also analyses the meaning and significance of the concept, its elaboration in international instruments and related provisions in the Constitution of India. It further examines the extent to which it is available to common people in our country.

Dr. Jayashree Gupta followed by Mrs. Pritam Arora, in their respective contributions (Chapter-IX and X), provide facts and figures to show that although right to womens equality finds a place of pride in our Constitution and equally progressive laws and judicial decisions to protect and promote that equality, but the reality is very different. Women are still discriminated against from birth to every walk of life. Dr. Gupta further contends that equality could become a reality only when women come out openly and unitedly to fight against injustices.

Prof. Imtiaz Ahmad (Chapter-XI) provides a trenchant analysis of the provisions of the Constitution and the intent of the Constitution-makers, especially in the context of right to equality and safeguards for the rights of the minorities. He contends that in principle decision-making whether by legislature, executive or judiciary and there are instances galore, if accepted, then in such a situation posits a fundamental threat. He believes that our Constitution and the law have provided our nation with unique freedom. With its abiding faith in law and constitutional rights, a free, egalitarian, prosperous and tolerant open society could be in the process of emergence. But ground realities are very different.

In Chapter XII, Dr. R.M. Pal, rightly laments that 50 years have passed, but Article 45 of the Constitution, which demanded of the Government to endeavour introduction of free and compulsory education to children upto the age of 14, still remains on paper. He also contends that in the priority list of human rights NGOs, schooling and education of children have not received due attention. The Government has spent time and money by way of setting up of commissions and committees which in turn have produced voluminous reports, which also did not move beyond paper work and the fact remains that increasing number of children (by way of population growth) are growing illiterates. In 1995, the Supreme Court verdict that right to education is a fundamental right has yet to get implemented.

Mr. G.S. Bhargava (Chapter XIII) succinctly makes a case for development of human rights culture, which calls for historical, psychological and traditional factors contributing to the milieu in which the constitution operates. If it is conducive to the achievements of liberal and egalitarian objectives and purposes, as enshrined in the Indian Constitution, it can be said to foster a human rights culture. He then examines the extent to which and the element of assurance in working of the Indian Constitution has lived up to the promise of ushering in a humane and human rights-prone society in the country.

Mr. Justice Rajinder Sachar (Chapter XIV) focuses on the international dimension of human rights and critically examines the question of implementation of international norms as spelled out in various international conventions and covenants, through domestic legislation and law-enforcement officials including the judiciary. In the same context, Dr. A.P. Vijapur specifically discusses the safeguards to protect the rights of the minorities as provided in the Indian Constitution and various international instruments. He believes that constitutional provisions provide the best safeguards but regrettably the practice leaves much to be desired.

III

As will be noted, in all the contributions by various authors contained in this volume, one common refrain is that although the constitutional framework requires some changes in the light of the experiences gained over the last 50 years and plus but it is not the Constitution that has failed us but the functionaries, who were expected to function within the constitutional framework and of implementing the guidelines enshrined in the Constitution for promotion and protection of human rights. Constitutional provisions have been followed by political and administration functionaries more in their breach than in observance. This is true more so in regard to the politicians and bureaucrats but also to some extent, the judiciary. As Justice M.N. Venkatachaliah succinctly contends that "the biggest and the most sinister violation of human rights in this country is the cynical and derisive attitude of those in authority to the issues of survival of this nation as a civilized country." Another inherent weakness, he points out, is that we have yet to develop the spirit of liberty within us as part of our political faith.[6]

Further, over the last 50 years, the Constitution has undergone such momentous changes by numerous amendments and counter-amendments, by the Parliament as also by scores of judicial decisions and interpretations.

Right from the beginning, conflict between the two principles, i.e., supremacy of Parliament including custodianship of the Constitution came into conflict with, what is referred to as guardianship of the Constitution given to the judiciary (High Courts and Supreme Court) to interpret the Constitution and to protect the rights of the individual. The judiciary performed its role admirably but then it came into conflict with what Parliament attempted to do to promote the objectives set in the Directive Principles. For instance, the judiciary in some of the cases interpreted Right to Private Property in a way which came into conflict with the legislations, adopted by the legislators to pursue Directive Principles.

Let us turn to amendments and counter-amendments, which

have very much distorted the fabric of Fundamental Rights as originally enshrined in the Constitution. Indeed, since the adoption of the Constitution, more than 90 amendments in a span of fifty years and plus have been made, which in itself tell the story.

Parliament adopted the First Amendment Act within a year of the Constitution coming into force. It was necessitated because a number of legislations adopted by the State Legislatures in pursuit of socio-economic reforms were declared ultravires of the Constitution by the High Courts. Hence, the 1st Amendment was effected to establish supremacy of the Parliament in the context of judicial review. By this Amendment, a new Schedule known as 9th Schedule was appended to the Constitution and consequently legislations adopted in pursuance of the Directive Principles were placed under the 9th Schedule and as such, beyond the reach of judicial review. Interpretation and implementation of such legislations were left in the hands of the bureaucracy. Over the period, some 389 legislative enactments adopted by State Legislatures and Parliament, which directly effect Fundamental Rights, one way or the other, placed in the 9th Schedule are beyond the reach of the judiciary for judicial review or interpretation.

It is not possible to discuss, within the limited space of this Introduction, all the Amendments in detail; a summarised version is included in the Appendix.[7] However, specific mention may be made here of two amendments, which attempted to bring about vital changes in the constitutional framework and that of Fundamental Rights.

The most significant changes were undoubtedly attempted during Indira Gandhi's emergency regime by adopting 42nd Amendment Act, 1976. Taking advantage of Emergency Powers which resulted in the control over the Union as well as the State Legislatures, the Amendment which amounted to drastic "revision", rather than amendment of the Constitution (i) it fettered the scope for judicial review of ordinary laws; (ii) practically obliviated the possibility of judicial review of any Act for amendment of the Constitution; (iii) it placed Directive Principles (Part-IV) to a fundamental status as to supersede Fundamental Rights in Part-III; (iv) it further jettisoned the Fundamental Rights by inserting a new Article (51A) laying down "Fundamental Duties" of citizens; (vi) it compromised federal character of the Constitution by giving the Centre power to send armed forces to a State, without the latter's request and by transferring legislative powers from the State List to the Concurrent List.

Then Janta Government came to power. It carried out 43rd and 44th Amendment (1977, 1978) in an attempt to wipe out provisions introduced by the 42nd Amendment and in the process resulted in total elimination of one of the Fundamental Rights - the Right to Property.[8]

Let us turn to judicial interpretations. The judiciary has undoubtedly played its part as the guardian of the Constitution and in widening the scope of Fundamental Rights. The Supreme Court and the High Courts have to a considerable extent remained independent and free of political pressure and corruption, although the same could not be said about the District Courts and Subordinate Courts. In interpreting provisions relating to Fundamental Rights, the Supreme Court has often shown more exuberance than discretion. This is quite revealing in a number of cases relating to bonded labour, child labour[9] etc.

This aspect is more glaringly demonstrated in the interpretation of the primordial right - right to life. Article 21 simply states in negative terms that "No person shall be deprived of his life and personal liberty except according to the procedure established by law." The Supreme Court added substance to this Article by elaborating in number of cases, such as the well-known *A.K. Gopalan V. State of Madras* 1950, the meaning of life and liberty. It also provided that Right to Life includes right to live with human dignity encompassing availability of socio-economic security.

Such an interpretation is in line with the rationale of the concept as progressively developed by UN bodies concerned with human rights. The (UN) Human Rights Committee, for instance, has maintained that right to life encompasses not merely protection against intentional or arbitrary deprivation of life but places on each State-parties to International Covenants the oligation to pursue such policies as to ensure access to the means for minimum socio-economic needs of every individual, measures to eliminate malnutrition and epidemics and to create better health conditions etc.[10]

But then it seems that judges of the Supreme Court as if vying against fellow judges to "improve" the interpretation have soared so high in the realm of idealism as to lose the ground reality.

Subsequent judgements went on to include "the right to live with human dignity and all that goes along with it..." Pray, what it means? It includes the Supreme Court asserts "the finer graces of human civilization which makes life worth living...It includes right to health which does not mean simply freedom from sickness but full healthy life maintained by nutritious food..." It includes roads in reasonable conditions for people living in remote areas...access to roads is access to life itself." Another Supreme Court judgement lays down that right to life includes the right to "all that gives meaning to man's life including the tradition, culture and heritage and protection of that heritage in full measure. In another judgement the apex Court laid down that right to life includes right to "shelter" -- not the kind of shelter, which animal needs but a residential place where individuals could live with dignity and which provides facilities of a "home" and livelihood. If government fails to do so, anyone is entitled to build "jhuggi and jhonpari" in public places and even on both sides of the railway tracks, on the pedestrian walks and open spaces around "posh" areas. That they cannot be removed from such places because by living in such "slums" they earn their living, i.e. right to life. They can be removed only if given compensation for vacating the public places (occupied illegally) and rehabilitated to places where they can earn their living at the same level as they did when they constructed "jhuggis" and "jhonparis" in posh areas.

That is not the end of the story of right to life. Another Supreme Court judgement goes on to assert that right to life, for Imams of Masjids, includes that they be paid adequate salary for their services so that they could live the life of economic security and human dignity. Should the Wakf Boards or Committees concerned with the administration of Masjids fail to pay adequate salary, these Imams are entitled to get the same from the Government.[11]

Such a right to life has not been talked about for priests of temples or clergies of churches. Ours is a secular democracy, indeed.

It seems that justices of the Supreme Court were more interested in propounding their social philosophy and ideals; indeed they had been vying against each other to be more loud, rhetorical and idealist in pronouncing judicious interpretations. In doing so, they have been ignoring ground realities and what lies in the realm of the practicable. As such, they were only raising false hopes among the people and, it seems, were more interested in getting publicity in bold headlines in the press.

While recalling some such flaws in the role of the judiciary, one cannot ignore the positive aspects; in many ways, judiciary has played an effective role to provide judicial remedies to the grievances of the people for violation of their Fundamental Rights. On the other hand, both Legislature and the Executive have failed and miserably so in living upto the responsibility which the Constitution assigned to them.

Indeed, the sad part of 50 years of India's democracy has been that right from the beginning (in 1952) and increasingly so since 1960s, people who won elections to the State Legislatures as also to the Parliament were those who were motivated not by the desire to serve the people, but to seek political and economic gains. Again, India is perhaps the only country in the world where democratic system was introduced in one go with adult franchise. It was indeed a right decision since for the first time every Indian got a sense of self-esteem and experienced that he/she is part of Indian social-political system. Where the system erred is that no qualifications especially in terms of education were laid down for the candidates to be elected. This led to the situation where illiterate persons and subsequently criminals got elected. As regards adult franchise granted to the people of whom, at the initial stage, 12 per cent could read and write and a vast majority of them were suffering from abject poverty, illiteracy, superstitions, etc. provided fertile grounds to those who could make use of money and muscle power to get elected. The result has been criminalisation of politics or one could say politicisation of criminals. It is estimated that around 700 members of State Legislatures and 40 in Parliament have a criminal background and some of them are facing trial on the charges of murder, extortion and similar heinous crimes. Another unfortunate part is that these facts are widely known, yet no effective steps have been taken to set rights the wrong being perpetuated. Dharam Vira Report (1980-81) first draw attention to this gruesome development, followed by Vohra Committee Report submitted almost two decades ago. Vohra Report recorded the findings that leaders of armed gangs of criminals are getting themselves elected to local bodies, State Assemblies and Parliament and that such elements have acquired political clout and are jeopardizing the functioning of the administration and the safety of life and property of the people. Similar references to the growing menace were made by the Law Commission Report in 1999.

In this sordid situation, not a single party, whether in power or in opposition, took a committed and constructive step; instead, placed the blame on "other" parties. Yet each of them continues to resort to this evil practice.

Dismayed, an NGO, "Association for Democratic Reforms" filed a Public Interest Litigation (PIL) in the Supreme Court demanding that under Article 19 the voters must have the necessary information about the candidates whom they were electing. The Supreme Court issued directives to the Election Commission (EC) to ensure that while accepting nomination for various elective posts, the Commission should seek full particulars of the candidate, for the information of the common man of this country, who is to represent him in Parliament, where laws to bind his rights and liberties, may be enacted. As per directives, the EC made it compulsory for the candidates to include information whether they were charge-sheeted or convicted of a criminal offence and also information on candidate's educational qualification and financial assets in terms of movable and immovable property. This provided a rare occasion when all political parties - in power as also the group of them, in opposition, displayed complete unanimity. Consequently, the Parliament unanimously adopted a legislation scuttling the directives of the Supreme Court/Election Commission.

Such development points a dismal future for democracy and rule of law in India and, therefore, for human rights.

Nonetheless, one could see some light through the dark tunnel. Over the period, despite linguistic, religious diversities, old caste and clan conflicts and abortive secessionist activities the concept of Indian nationhood has been strengthened: "India is my country and I am an Indian" is a sentiment much stronger today than what it was in 1947. Again, despite hot and cold wind blowing from both inside and outside the country, India, unlike most of the other Afro-Asian countries, has adhered to a democratic system of government and rule of law. Indeed, as of today, the Constitution of India, after that of United States of America and Republic of Ireland, is the oldest written Constitution in the world.

What is more significant is that increasingly a large section of the citizenry - both as individuals and in groups (NGOs) are coming forward to resist authority when abused and committing themselves to bring a better social and political environment. Literacy rate has gone up from less than 12 per cent in 1949 to more than 65 per cent. Innovations in information technology and media have opened things in a big way to create wider awareness of social and political issues. These developments have become a vital factor in exposing villainy and malevolent facets of politicians.

As a veteran human rights activist, Mr. Justice V.M. Tarkunde once observed: "In India, we have just 10 per cent of democracy and human rights but that is good enough to fight for the remaining 90 per cent of human rights."

References

1. The provisions relating to citizenship, elections, provisional Parliament, temporary transitional provisions were given immediate effect, i.e., from November 26, 1949, the rest of the Constitution came into force on 26 January, 1950 and the date is referred as the date of its commencement.

This date of January 26 was set, in commemoration of the pledge of "Purnea Swaraj" (complete independence) taken in Lahore on that date, in 1930.

2. In 1920s, a turning point came in the history of India's national movement with the demand that Indian people themselves should decide the constitutional framework and not the British Government. See in particular, Subhash C. Kashyap, Jawaharlal Nehru, the Constitution and the Parliament (New Delhi: Metropolitan Publishers, 1990), pp. 23-49.

3. However, before India's day of independence - August 15, 1947, all the Native States, except Junagarh, two small States under Muslim rulers in Kathiawar, Jammu-Kashmir and Hyderabad have acceded, thanks to Sardar Vallabh Bhai Patel, to India and only a couple of them to Pakistan. For details, see V.P. Menon, *The Story of Integration of Indian States* (Calcutta: Orient Longman's, 1956); Also Urmila Phadnis, *Towards the Integration of Indian States*: 1919-49 (New Delhi: Asian Publishing House, 1968).

4. The resolution was adopted on January 22, 1947.

5. Granville Austin, *The Indian Constitution* (London: The Oxford University Press, 1966), pp. 50-51.

6. "Human Rights in India: A Balance Sheet" in K.P. Saksena, ed., *Human Rights - Fifty Years of India's Independence* (New Delhi: Gyan Publishing House, 1998), p. 32.

7. For ready reference, Appendix II of this volume contains summarised versions of 85 Amendments gazetted by Government of India, until June 2002.

8. Durga Das Basu, *Introduction to the Constitution of India*, 10th edn., (New Delhi: Prentice Hall of India Pvt. Ltd., 1983), pp. 112-117.

9. See, for instance, "Recent Supreme Court Judgements on Child Labour: A Critique" in K.P. Saksena, ed. *Human Rights: Fifty Years of India's Independence* (New Delhi: Gyan Publishing House, 1999), pp. 73-77.

10. For elaborate details on this aspect, see, in particular, B.G. Ramacharan, ed. *Rights to Life in International Law* (Dordrecht, Martinus Nijhoff, 1985).

11. Excerpts from judicial decisions referred to here are from citations in Arun Shourie, *Courts and their Judgements* (New Delhi: Rup & Co., 2001), pp.144-197.

1
Human Rights and the Constituion : An Overview

Sujata V. Manohar

Nani Palkiwala dedicated his book *"We, the People of India"* to his countrymen. His dedication reads thus:

- To my country men:
- "Who gave unto themselves the Constitution but not the ability to keep it,
- Who inherited a resplendent heritage but not the wisdom to cherish it,
- Who suffer and endure in patience without the perception of their potential".
- I add,
- "Who could have built a splendid mansion
  but today live amidst ruins in
  hovels and zopadpattis."

When the British departed from this land there was one thing they could not take away— the institutions they had set up in this country to rule it effectively—a sound administration run by competent men. The administration could enforce law and order in the remotest villages. The British left behind an independent judiciary which was independent even during colonial days. After they left, we set up for ourselves what was lacking: their parliamentary system of government. We gave to ourselves a sound constitution tested on the anvil of experience— although in other lands. Yet we find today these sound institutions lying in ruins all around us. They have been touched by fingers which have turned them to dross—the fingers of an anti-Midas as it were, which turns everything to dust instead of gold. In anguish we ask ourselves why it is so. And the answer stares us in the face—the institutions have not failed us, we have failed institutions. Because we are notable to put in these institutions men and women with ideals and principles who can run them as they should be run. And without at least some such people, nothing can function. No country can function. The solitary institution which still stands amidst the ruins is the judiciary, which has used the mandate of our Constitution to protect human rights and our fundamental rights, though there may have been some lapses.

The Constitution has given value inputs into the system of governance it has set up. I like to call it our secular *Gita* or the secular holy book. The idealism of the makers of our Constitution is proclaimed in the Preamble which aims at creating a country where justice— social, economic and political—will prevail, where there will be liberty of thought, expression, belief, faith and worship; equality of status and of opportunity, and fraternity assuring the dignity of the individual. Part III gives a practical shape to this vision by safeguarding human rights and the civil and political values proclaimed in the Preamble through justiciable fundamental rights. Economic and social rights which require policy initiatives from the State for their realization are a part of the Directive Principles of State Policy. The entire human rights jurisprudence of this country is founded on these provisions. When we examine the functioning of the Constitution in the last fifty years in the area of human rights, we find that the human rights jurisprudence has also been deeply influenced in interpreting these two Parts of the Constitution by the international human rights norms first set out by the United Nations in the Universal Declaration of Human Rights in 1948 and other international covenants, treaties and conventions.

When the Constitution was framed in 1950, it is worth recalling that it was only the third written Constitution of a common law country which incorporated within it, a justiciable bill of rights—the other two Constitutions being those of the United States and of Ireland. In the same year European Convention on Human Rights was also framed. The subsequent developments in the international human rights jurisprudence include the International Covenant on Civil and the Political Rights and the International Covenant on Economic, Social and Cultural Rights framed in 1966, the Convention on the Elimination of all Forms of Discrimination

Against Women, the Right of the Child, the Convention against Torture and other Human Rights Conventions framed under auspices of the United Nations. Our courts have used these international covenants and other international norms for giving depth to the Fundamental Rights which have been laid down in the Constitution. It is important to remember that even the right to move the court for the enforcement of fundamental rights is itself a Fundamental Right. The courts have said that not only can international treaties be used for interpreting the content of these basic rights but they can also be applied to judge State actions unless there is any provision in our laws to the contrary.

Although social and economic rights have been put in the Directive Principles of State Policy requiring formulation of State policy for the protection and promotion of these rights, yet the courts have often read social and economic rights into fundamental rights and adjudicated upon a number of them, thus making many of them justiciable.

Article 21 has been widely interpreted to mean that every person is entitled to lead a life with dignity. Articles 21 and 22 have been used by the judiciary to lay down the human rights foundation of the criminal justice system and the working of the police. In *DK Basu,* the Supreme Court laid down the guidelines to be followed by the police while making an arrest. In *Ravi Kant Patil,* handcuffing and parading of an under trial was held violative of Article 21. In Hussainara Khatun, the right to a speedy trial was emphasised. The right to free legal aid was held to be fundamental in Madhav Hoskote. Deliberate inflicting of pain as in torture was held a violation of Article 21 and a breach of a justiciable fundamental right in Kharak Singh.

In order to provide an effective remedy for violations of human rights, the courts have promoted and supported public interest litigation on behalf of the downtrodden and the underprivileged, for enforcement of their fundamental rights. This has enabled the underprivileged groups in this country to bring their grievances before the courts and seek redress. A large number of human rights issues have been agitated before the courts with the help of the constitutional provisions through public interest litigation. When one hears complaints of misuse of public interest litigation, it is well to remember that maladministration in orphanages for destitute children, in protective homes for women, in jails, treatment of prisoners and undertrials in jails or in custody, have all been examined through public interest litigation. Bonded labour, child labour, workers' health in hazardous industries such as the asbestos, have all been adjudicated upon and relief granted through the medium of public interest litigation. Therefore, in effect, although economic and social rights are placed under Directive Principles of State Policy on the basis that these rights require for their enforcement, policy initiatives from the States, some of these basic rights have been judicially enforced through the medium of public interest litigation. It has been an important tool used in conjunction with constitutional rights and remedies for promoting human rights jurisprudence in the country in the last fifty years.

The Supreme Court had to face its first test within four months of its inauguration in the case of *A.K. Gopalan* who was detained under the Preventive Detention Act of 1950. This case was argued with great ability by the late Mr. Nambiar. The "procedure established by law" clause in the Constitution was sought to be widened to mean "due process of law" as under the American Constitution. Obviously the time was not ripe for this transformation then. In the light of the Constituent Assembly debates, the majority rejected the argument based on "due process" and refused to introduce it in the Indian constitutional law. Justice Fazal Ali, however, in his minority judgement said that there is nothing revolutionary in the view that procedure established by law must input the four principles of elementary justice which inhere in it and are at the root of all civilized systems of law. These are: (1) notice, (2) opportunity to be heard, (3) free impartial tribunal, and (4) orderly course of procedure. The wheel has now come full circle and the principles of natural justice are now deeply embedded in our constitutional jurisprudence, thanks to the subsequent judgements of the Supreme Court and the High Courts. Maneka Gandhi will be remembered, if not for anything else, for the contribution which she has made to the development of the rule of law in this country in the famous *Maneka Gandhi* case.

The challenge, however, to the personal laws under Article 14 of the constitution was turned down early. The court held that their amendment was a matter of social reform which the legislature alone could bring about by changes in the law.

In respect of the criminal justice system, Article 20(1) of the Constitution provides that no person shall be convicted of an offence except for the violation of a law in force when he committed the act. Article 20(2) provides that no person shall be prosecuted and punished for the same offence more than one; and Article 20(3) provides that no person convicted of an offence shall be compelled to be a witness against himself. With the use of these articles, the Supreme Court has held, as in *Union of India* v. *Sukumar and PV Mohammed* that higher penalties cannot be retrospectively imposed. In *JK Cotton*, the Court said that no one could be punished for an offence which was introduced by a retrospective amendment if the act was not an offence when it was committed.

Right to equality before the law and equal protection of laws within the territory of India is one of the basic tenets of the Constitution. For a society, which was for several centuries, hierarchical and rigidly structured with a pre-ordained place in the social pyramid for every group—whether based on caste, religion, vocation or sex, equality is a new value. It entails a total restructuring of our society on egalitarian principles. We must member that we have made this conscious choice to establish this egalitarian social order and it is our responsibility to create such an egalitarian polity. The doctrine of equality is one of the most difficult doctrines to apply to real life situations. The courts have been hard put to it, to devise suitable tests to see when the equality clause is violated. The fact remains that no two human beings are equal in all respects. People have unequal abilities, qualifications and equipment. That is why the courts have evolved early on, in *Dalmia's* case, certain tests on which equality and non-discrimination can be tested. It is permissible to classify individuals into different groups on the basis of criteria which are relevant to a set of facts requiring differentiation and it is only members who are similarly situated who can be treated similarly. Permissible classification, however, has to be founded on intelligible differentiation which should have a rational nexus with the object sought to be achieved by the statute in question. Even such a classification sometimes easy or free from difficulties. For example, In *Air India* v. *Nargesh Mirza*, different and discriminatory conditions service for air hostessses were held not to be discriminatory because they had been classified into one group on the basis of their sex which, the court said, was a relevant basis for differentiation. It was a sex-based differentiation and not discrimination on the ground of sex! It is difficult to understand this reasoning because it is precisely discrimination on the basis of sex, which is prohibited by Articles 14 and 15. Fortunately, most of the service conditions were held unreasonable and hence arbitrary and violative of Article 14.

The ambit of Article 14 has been expanded to strike down arbitrary actions. In *Royappa*, the Supreme Court looked upon Article 14 as a guarantee against arbitrary action. Since then, there have been many cases, Maneka Gandhi, Ajay Hasia and others where executive actions have been challenged under Article 14 as arbitrary. Many cases have also been fought on the doctrine of equal pay for equal work which is now considered a part of Article 14. The courts have had the difficult task of ascertaining what is to be considered as equal work. Discretionary powers have also come up for scrutiny before the courts and the exercise of this power has been tested on the basic principle whether it is an uncanalised power of choosing or whether it is a power which is to be exercised on the basis of certain relevant factors. While Articles 15 and 16 guarantee non-discrimination, there is also room for positive discrimination in favour of women and children and backward groups under Article 15. There is also an express provision for reservation for the backward groups, the Scheduled Castes and Scheduled Tribes in the area of employment under the State under Article 16.

While emphasising social and economic rights for a country where poverty and ignorance or lack of education are endemic, one must not also lose sight of the importance of civil and political rights which have been won by hard struggle and their importance for a proper functioning of the democratic form of Government. The judiciary has interpreted freedom of speech and expression widely as covering freedom of the Press. It would also cover free access to information. It is necessary to remember that such free access to information is inherent in freedom of speech and expression because unless one has free access to relevant information, one cannot form an informed opinion or participate in the democratic processes and express one's views, listen to the views of others and exercise one's choices in an informed manner. Leading cases like the *Sakal Newspaper, Bennet Colmen, Express Newspaper* have all upheld this fundamental right to free speech and expression so necessary for the democratic functioning of this country, and have given depth to its content.

No narration of the constitution in the last fifty years can be complete without reference to *Golaknath and Keshavanand Bharati* cases. The doctrine that the basic structure of the Constitution cannot be altered by amendment is a fundamental original doctrine evolved by the Indian judiciary. It is a singular contribution made by the court for the protection of human rights in this country. In the dark days of the Emergency, it was the High Courts in the country which upheld and wielded the writ of habeas corpus although unfortunately the Supreme Court took a different view.The court has since, however, made amends by giving a series of judgments upholding and enforcing human rights. One of the most important subsequent developments has been the evolution of Public Interest Litigation, giving the poor and the underprivileged an access to the courts and the judicial system for redressal of their grievances. This kind of litigation has also forced the courts to devise new kinds of reliefs. For example, in cases relating to harmful practices which violate human rights, such as bonded labour or child labour or sale of young girls for prostitution, the courts have had to resort to giving detailed administrative directions. Quite often these have to be given from time to time to ensure that the orders are complied with by the administration. Sometimes, the court appoints a monitoring committee or an organization to supervise the implementation of its directions. Of course, the task is easier when the administration cooperates as it should. That is why at times, this is described as non-adversarial jurisdiction. Obviously, there are possibilities of misuse of these procedures. But the court, if it is vigilant, can stop misuse of such a process which is essentially meant for the poor and the underprivileged. The National Human Rights Commission (NHRC) also monitors many of these orders and issues.

These Human Rights granted under the Constitution and the freedoms which we enjoy under the Constitution form the very essence of civilised life as we know it. Knowing how fragile and nascent this freedom is, we have to be constantly vigilant to see that our constitutional structure is not eroded and that we are ever vigilant to protect our freedoms and our basic human rights. The spirit of liberty is an eternal flame which we must keep burning with every means at our command, if we are going to create the kind of social, economic and political structure that was envisaged by our founding fathers.

2
The Promise, the Content and the Performance: The Human Rights Provisions in the Indian Constitution

V.S. Mani

On 22 January 1947, the Indian Constituent Assembly adopted the famous Objectives Resolution whereby the Assembly set the goals of a new constitution it was embarking upon. It proclaimed, *inter alia*, as follows:

> "THIS CONSTITUENT ASSEMBLY DECLARES ITS FIRM AND SOLEMN RESOLVE TO PROCLAIM INDIA AS AN INDEPENDENT SOVEREIGN REPUBLIC AND TO DRAW UP FOR HER FUTURE GOVERNANCE A CONSTITUTION:
>
> WHEREIN all power and authority of the SOVEREIGN INDEPENDENT INDIA, its constituent parts and organs of government, are derived from the people; and
>
> WHEREIN shall be guaranteed and secured to all the people of India justice, social, economic and political; equality of status; of opportunity and before the law; freedom of thought, expression, belief, faith, worship, vocation, association and action, subject to law and public morality; and
>
> WHEREIN adequate safeguards shall be provided for minorities, backward and tribal areas, and depressed and other backward classes;..."

Thus manifesting the intention of its makers, the PREAMBLE to the Constitution of India proclaims as follows:

"WE, THE PEOPLE OF INDIA, having solemnly resolved to constitute India into a SOVEREIGN SOCIALIST SECULAR DEMOCRATIC REPUBLIC and to secure to all its citizens:

JUSTICE, social, economic and political;

LIBERTY of thought, expression, belief, faith and worship; EQUALITY of status and of opportunity; and to promote among them all

FRATERNITY assuring the dignity of the individual and the unity and integrity of the Nation;

IN OUR CONSTITUENT ASSEMBLY this twenty-sixth day of November, 1949, DO HEREBY ADOPT, ENACT AND GIVE TO OURSELVES THIS CONSTITUTION."

In order to give effect to the above solemn resolve of the people of India, the Constitution makes elaborate provisions on human rights in Parts III and IV and establishes an equally elaborate institutional mechanism charged with the duty to pursue in right earnest this constitutional mandate.

These constitutional provisions reflect the aspirations of the people of free India as interpreted by the leaders of our independence movement. To Mahatma Gandhi, the ultimate test of freedom has always been what benefit it would accrue to the poorest of the land. "Whatever can be useful to starving millions is beautiful to my mind. Let us give today first the vital things of life and all the graces and ornaments of life will follow." His ambition, he said, was "to wipe every tear from every eye."[1] Gandhiji dreamt of an India "in which the poorest shall feel that it is their country, in whose making they have an effective voice, and India in which there shall be no high class and low class of people, an India in which all communities shall live in perfect harmony... there can be no room in such an India for the curse of untouchability or the curse of intoxicating drinks and drugs.... Women will enjoy the same rights as men."[2]

Addressing the nation on the threshold of independence, Jawaharlal Nehru declared in the same vein:

"We shall look to the common and forgotten man of India and seek to bring him relief and raise his standard of living. We shall continue our fight against the curse of untouchability and other forms of enforced inequality, and shall especially try to help those who are economically or otherwise backward. Today millions lack food and clothing and houses, and many are on the verge of starvation."[3]

II. The Performance

How have the provisions of the Constitution on human rights and on institutions mandated to translate them into action, fared in terms of ground realities, through half a century of travail? There is a charitable view that,"[t]he human rights record of India is, for all its deficiencies, comparable to that of many of the democracies in the world."[4] The leaders of India's freedom struggle turned at independence the builders of modern India. Most of them proved sincere and committed to the tasks ahead. Foundations were laid to facilitate modernisation and economic development of the country. At the hindsight of half a century of independence, views may, naturally, differ on the correctness or otherwise of the early policy decisions in respect of governance and development of the country, but the sense of commitment and integrity of purpose and endeavour shown by these leaders were exemplary and still stand out in sharp relief to those of the later leaders. Whatever degree of development and modernisation we have achieved so far—we have indeed experienced considerable development and modernisation—is attributable to them. Thanks to them we now have a vibrant democracy, even if with all its defects.

This general appreciation notwithstanding, it is generally agreed that we have not done enough and that there is a wide gap between the promise and performance, although views differ as to why it is so and what should be done about it.

The reasons for the performance gap are myriad and complex, and therefore no facile judgment on human rights performance record is possible. In the first place, there is always bound to be a gap between the ideal of human welfare or human rights that it seeks to ensure, and its attainment. This is because human rights and human welfare as a composite concept is of a constantly evolving character apace with the evolution of human civilisation in the context of a changing social, political, economic and cultural milieu. Newer and newer facets of human rights come up due to a wide variety of factors of day-to-day life, including the impact of the on-going revolution in science and technology. "Generations' of human rights get identified, and await implementation[5]. It is therefore a daunting task for anyone to assess the state of realisation of human welfare in a society. Secondly, judging performance levels in human rights is a highly subjective exercise, often tainted by a preferred perception and prioritisation of human rights *inter se* and at best an eclectic identification and impressionistic evaluation of human rights situations. Thirdly, the difficulties in performance assessment are compounded by the intrinsic correlationship of the development of the individual with the development of the society, and the issues of social and economic costs of conditioning this correlationship. Fourthly, the correlationship also points to the range of actors (not just state instrumentalities, but also individuals and groups who can be held responsible for performance or violation of specific human rights) and factors to be taken into account while formulating judgments on what order of performance gap there is, why it is so, who all must bear responsibility for failures, non-performance or underperformance, and what actions need to be taken to bridge the performance gap. Fifthly, one must also address the issues of shealisability of the specific human rights one aspires for, such as the possible creation of objective conditions conductive to their realisation and the optimum time-frame within which the realisation was anticipated. These issues must be examined in the context of a national society whose human rights performance is under review. Finally, are issues about levels of violations of human rights— What constitutes a human rights violation? Is there a threshold below which a human rights deprivation is "sufferable" or tolerable, and beyond which the depriver/violator should be held accountable? What are gross or serious violations of human rights and what are not so gross or serious? Does or should this threshold vary in time, space and context?

Additionally, there are some Western perspectives thrust upon the developing world in the label of "good governance," which has by now become part of the UN vocabulary. In UN Secretary-General Kofi Annan's view,

> "In practice, good governance involves promoting the rule of law, tolerance of minority and opposition groups, transparent political processes, an independent judiciary, an impartial police force, a military that is strictly subject to civilian control, a free press and vibrant civil society institutions, as well as meaningful elections. Above all, good governance means respect for human rights."[6]

While this formulation of good governance finds place in his *1999 Report on the Work of the Organization* (which also deals with several human rights-related issues such as eradication of poverty, social development and sustainable development), as formulated above it is indeed tilted in favour of the civil and political rights, almost to the exclusion of economic and other rights. In these days of high-handed "humanitarian" intervention selectively being engineered or resorted to by a big power, it is advisable to go 'native' in evolving and applying standards of evaluation of human rights performance of India, while recognising that's irreducible minimum of human rights emanating from the basic right to life and personal liberty.[7]

This paper does not, however, claim to engage in any "scientific" assessment of the performance gap. It assumes, as already indicated above, that since independence, the Indian society has progressed in diverse areas of human life. In terms of the current human rights challenges, however, there are miles to go, before one can lay the claim of substantial fulfillment of the constitutional promise. The prime challenges remain eradication of poverty, illiteracy, population control, and ensuring the right to work. This paper merely seeks to focus attention to some random issues of human rights violations in India.

A. Justice, Social, Economic and Political

Justice is a concept that compasses all aspects of human rights, as it reflects the ultimate condition of human welfare. It seeks to ensure the condition of liberty in the Laskian sense which includes equality as also fraternity, i.e., the feeling of oneness with the national society.

Social and Political Justice

After fifty-one years of the promise of justice, what kind of a national society have we evolved for ourselves? It is a violent society in which individuals are increasingly hypocritical (their regular *satsangs* and prayers notwithstanding), bereft of any commitment to the moral tenets of the ancient cultures they swear by, and ruthlessly self-centred, with little or no consideration for each other or even civic sense. Indeed, the entrenched state of inequality thrives on and is likely to beget violence, should the constitutional machinery mandated to eradicate it totally break down without even a feeble endeavour to fulfil its mission, or become, beyond redemption, an instrument for perpetuation of such inequality and coercion. Public institutions are increasingly hamstrung by corruption and unresponsive even to public outcries, let alone the general demands of the public. Public grievance redressal mechanisms, if exist, work at random, or in distortion. People are quickly losing faith in these institutions; there is a crisis of public authority, as a result of increasing erosion of legitimacy. Elections are quickly losing their meaning as a result of widespread malpractices and the criminal-politician nexus, despite the rare Seshans and Gills appearing on the stage and strenuously engaging in ad hoc fire-fighting exercises, but unable to cleanse the Aegean stable.

The physical, moral and spiritual deteriorations are all pervasive. It is no consolation to say that the phenomenon is evident all over the world to a lesser or a greater degree. Even religions have not been left untouched by the avalanche. They now produce at an alarming rate militants and terrorists, ignoring the truism that the fundamentals of all religions are similar if not identical—their aim is to build up good human beings and good societies, striving for all round self- development and the progress of humanity as a whole, in conditions of equality, peace and prosperity.

In many parts of the country, if immediate remedial action is not initiated, conditions exist with propensity to erupt with violence. The so-called people's war groups or other practitioners of violence with pretensions of Robin Hood must receive unqualified condemnation, but what about their fertile breeding grounds? The only way to prevent germination and growth of such violent movements is to make them unattractive to the common people by rendering public institutions more responsive to the urgent needs of the people, by creating effective public grievance redressal mechanisms from the grassroots level upwards, by ensuring transparency and public accountability in governmental functioning, and by actively encouraging peaceful (and genuine) non-governmental organisations (NGOS) to interface the 'official' developmental endeavours and the common people in the field. Even with the Panchayati Raj institutions, the real message of democracy has not percolated into many villages[8]. Democracy is often manipulated by the more powerful. Theoretically, all may be equal, but in reality some continue to be more equal than others.

Economic Justice

The level of economic justice achieved so far is revealed by the fact that nearly 40 per cent of the population is 'below the poverty line.'[9] This indeed is a dubious record, particularly because at independence, India's population was only 36 crores, whereas, it has now grown to 100 crores! Evidently, economic justice to the 400 crores below the poverty line is a far cry. Democracy, access to new technologies, and vast improvement in communications, have all catapulted the expectations of the people still higher. Economic policies change, and should change in response to the varying demands of time and context. There was a time when the government had to directly generate economic activity and produce goods and services, where private producers, traditionally shy of investing in 'uncharted' areas, were hard to come by. The winds of liberalisation and globalisation are now sweeping across the globe. Having been forced to open the door wide, we now seem to have suddenly realised that we have perhaps gone too far too soon, and now struggle to find a "Middle Path", or reorient the liberalisation process 'with a human face'. Has the sweep of globalisation and liberalisation shrunk further whatever modicum of human rights so far enjoyed by those hapless people below the poverty line? Are the Indian industrialists, who have benefited most by these winds of change and by government policies on subsidies, tax benefits, and easy bank/ public credit, willing and forthcoming to alleviate this social burden? These are among the issues of contemporary debates.

Experts, like Y.V. Reddy of the Reserve Bank of India, note that in terms of rate of economic growth, India has done "better in the latter half of the twentieth century than during the first half, and far better in the last two decades... Yet, we have pervading poverty, high illiteracy and poor condition of health and sanitation." "There are islands of excellence like information technology expert amidst a sea of deprivation and misery". While the liberalisation policy of 1990's has removed several constraints to growth, "there are lurking doubts on whether we are systematically building a system that would ensure continued high level of growth *and, achievement of minimum social objectives associated with such growth.*"[10] Reddy concludes:

> "Overall, we rank rather low in human development and high in human deprivation. In spite of this, one notices relatively low levels of public expenditures in health, and in primary education though mere expenditures may not reflect actual delivery services. The policymakers and more importantly opinion makers including academics perhaps need to consider issue of the mending of mindset in favour of the poor."[11]

The environmental issues apart, the public protests against the big dams such as the Sardar Sarovar Dam, have successfully highlighted the need for a national rehabilitation and resettlement policy for the thousands of people routinely displaced by the construction of big development projects.[12] Estimates of such displaced persons since independence vary—anywhere between 2.13 crores and 1.5 crores. Land was provided for only those who lost their land due to the projects. The multitude of landless received some monetary compensation, which they spent recklessly for lack of advice, and ended up in some urban slums. There has not been any 'rehabilitation' at all. The basis of the Land Acquisition Act of 1890, Usha Rai points out, has been the concept of eminent domain—i.e., the discretion of the governmemt to acquire private property, and this distortion needs to be changed in tune with our democracy by replacing it with the doctrine of trusteeship being applied by the American courts. Accordingly, "the Government is [the] trustee of the property and has a clear moral and legal responsibility to justify that the acquisition is for the welfare of the people"[13] (not merely for a public purpose,' by now a much maligned phrase in government acquisitions of private lands). The concept of rehabilitation, in the true sense of the word, must be built into the Land Acquisition Act.[14]

'Legal' Justice

The late V.K. Krishna Menon, the then President of the Indian Society of International Law, New Delhi, while introducing the then Law Minister H.R. Gokhale, at the annual conference of the Society in 1974, remarked with his characteristic sarcasm: "He is the Minister not only for Law, but also for Justice: as if the two are two different things." But the ground reality is that they remain separate. Law in action appears to keep an extremely tenuous link with justice, despite the best efforts of an independent higher judiciary. The maladies of the Indian society such as the deterioration in moral values and a progressive weakening of the commitment to social welfare, and gradual erosion of personal and professional integrity, appear to bite into many aspects of the law making, law enforcing and even adjudicatory mechanisms, which have for long been the repository of the people's faith and trust. The common people dread the prospect of going to courts now.

The whole system seems to be ready to burst at seams, unless urgent remedial action is taken by all concerned. Many eminent men of law underscored this at the Law Day, New Delhi on 26 November 2000. The backlog of cases continues to mount particularly before the lower judiciary. According to an official release reported in the Press, a total of 21,567 cases are pending disposal in the Supreme Court as on 1 November 2000. Of these, 8,472 cases have been pending for more than two years and 645 for more than 10 years. The backlog of cases before the various High Courts are reported to be around 18.86 lakhs pending for more than two years, and about five lakhs pending for more than ten years. Whereas, of a total of 2.01 crores of cases pending before the district and subordinate courts, 1.93 crore cases have been pending for less than ten years, and 8.19 lakh cases for more than ten years.[15] The reasons for this state of afairs are many—the population explosion, the increases awareness on the part of citizens of their rights, enormous multiplicity of laws, highly inadequate number of existing judges to deal with the increasing number of new cases, the frequent adjournments of cases, delays caused for various administrative and procedural reasons,[16] frequent strikes by lawyers, and the high propensity of the government bodies and public undertakings to prefer appeals and revisions up to the Supreme Court without adequate cost-benefit analysis (let alone issues of public justice), etc.

What are the remedies? A variety of measures have been proposed—increase in the number of judges[17], use of retired judges, shift system in law courts, crecations of special courts and tribunals, decentralisation, streamlining of procedural laws, tuning up of investigating bodies and other bodies which facilitate the court procedure, etc.[18] In the ultimate analysis, the Judiciary exists for the benefit of the people, not for the judges and lawyers. The touchstone of the 'Majesty of Law' is not the court system, but the capacity of the legal system to deliver justice to the common people.[19] Respect should be commanded, not demanded.

B. Liberty of Thought, Expression, Belief, Faith, and Worship

Liberty comprises the sum total of the bundle of human rights and duties. It is well known that the Constitution of India guarantees the right to equality, the right to freedom (including the right to life and personal liberty), the right against exploitation, the right to freedom of religion, cultural and educational rights, and the right to constitutional remedies,[20] besides a range of socio- economic-cultural rights[21] aimed at eventual establishment of "a social order in which justice, social, economic and political shall inform all the institutions of the national life."[22]

The reports prepared for the Institute for the World Congress of Human Rights in 1997 and 1998 have embodied a fair survey of the status of human rights implementation in India.[23] The situation has not changed to any discernible extent.

Right to Life and Personal Liberty

Instances of violations of the right to life and personal liberty at the instance of state agencies such as the security and police forces, continue to be reported in the media. Several cases of custodial torture and death have been brought to light by the media and NGO's.[24] The Commonwealth Human Rights Initiative (CHRI), an eminent NGO, has recently expressed serious concern over the media reports of police brutalities in India. Citing the data of the National Human Rights Commission (NHRC), it said that in 1999 alone there were 183 deaths in police custody, as against 193 in 1998. What is shocking, according to the CHRI report, is that "even women police personnel are involved in incidents of police brutality." In a recent meeting of the State police chiefs convened by NHRC, the Chairperson, Justice J.S. Varma, pointed out that on an average, the Commission received about 100 complaints a day alleging police excesses. He also highlighted "the erratic performance" of States in regard to the various guidelines issued by NHRC and remarked that this trend eroded the credibility of the police force and diminished the dignity of the nation.[25] The CHRI report also notes that among the reasons for the brutal behaviour of the police are the miserable service conditions, and the administrative decisions about their postings, transfers, rewards, suspensions, dismissals and punishments, all based on extraneous considerations.[26] The policemen, like any other functionary of government, belong to the lower rungs of the Indian society where violence and deprivations manifest themselves in diverse forms and to expect them to behave like 'saints' when their own human rights remain deprived and disregarded is indeed asking for the moon. Discussing "more lock-up deaths," *The Hindu* in an editorial noted the great normative contributions of the Indian judiciary for protection of the right to life of the detenues, but highlighted rather ominously the gulf between the salutary norms and the ground realities:

> "But putting aside for a moment all the outrage felt over police brutalities against those under detention, it seems rather naive

to suppose that the lofty proclamations of the apex court should have automatically translated into concrete reality. Such an expectation at best merely underestimates the magnitude of the problem. Doubtless, some of the recent judgements have set healthy precedents. But the essence of any of these must first be internalised before they can be emulated and this may be possible by uncovering the social conditions which occasion crime and the underlying purpose of punitive action... Clearly, the discourse on punishment has got entangled in legal jargon and consequently been severed from its ethical roots. Therefore, it is not surprising that it has not been made axiomatic that a humane police administration presupposes a humane society."[27]

The problems of humane administration of jails, despite the concerns frequently expressed by the judiciary and NHRC continue to remain largely unattended. Many jails all over the country are overcrowded. It is estimated that about 60 per cent of the jail population comprise undertrial prisoners. A number of reasons have been cited for such a large number of undertrials languishing in jails for several years— undue delays in investigation, shortage of police escorts, ropes and handcuffs(!), slow rate of disposal of cases, failure of a prisoner to furnish sureties or surety amount to avail of bail, arrest of persons charged with petty offences (such as ticketless travel), and so on.[28] NHRC's recent efforts in this area appear to have resulted in the release of some of these undertrial prisoners.

But none of these reasons explain why cases like that of *Ajoy Ghosh* surface with periodic regularity. Ajoy Ghosh has been a lunatic undertrial made to languish in a West Bengal jail for the last 38 years, and on the intervention of the Supreme Court he was moved to the Missionaries for Charity, Kolkata earlier this year. In a very recent judgment, the court is reported to have observed: "There has been a complete violation of the statutory provisions contained in the Prisons Act, the Code of Criminal Procedure and the Indian Lunacy Act in dealing with the case of Ajoy Ghosh." "The authorities are required to act according to law but the law has been unfortunately respected in its breach. There has been no fixing of accountability even after this court pointed out [the] existence of the sad state of affairs concerning Ajoy Ghosh," said the court. Ghosh had been held a prisoner since 1962. The court noted that between 1964 and 1995 the additional chief metropolitan magistrate, Howrah, made no effort to take any action. Even the medical treatment provided to him was at the intervention of the Calcutta High Court. "There may be many like Ajoy Ghosh languishing in other jails of the country," warned the Supreme Court, according to the media report.[30] Will privatisation of jail management, as suggested by the former Chairperson of NHRC[31], a panacea for all maladies of Indian jails? One wonders.

Regions continually disturbed by terrorism continue seriously to distort genuine efforts at human rights implementation. Actors responsible for this distortion are not merely the government agencies and security forces, but encompass terrorist/militant groups often aided and supported from across the borders. These terrorist groups, often manned by foreign mercenaries, with a *jihadi* agenda, act on their dogmatic conviction and use violence against all those who are not 'with them'. In the result, innocent people are being terrorised, forcibly displaced from their ancient lands, or butchered on ground of religion, language or culture, and the entire socio-politico- economic fabric of the region is torn asunder, holding the entire population to ransom and resulting in grave deprivation of all their basic human rights.[32] Terrorists give vent to their feelings of anger, frustration, and communal hatred, by heartless massacre of even innocent children,[33] or the entire families of the so-called 'outsiders.'[34] They muffle the freedom of speech, the freedom of the media, and in fact all freedoms flowing from liberty.

This however, does not justify mindless state action against individuals under extraordinary laws, justifying such action to counter terrorism. Any new law being contemplated to replace the now- expired Terrorists and Disturbed Areas (Prevention) Act, 1985-91 (TADA) must take into account the possibility for abuse of statutory power by the investigating agencies and the inability of the system to prevent such abuse or to bring the abuser to book. The Constitution guarantees to all citizens within the jurisdiction of the Republic (including terrorists) the right to life and the right to equality before law and equal protection of laws,[35] even when a situation of terrorism does not amount to an "armed conflict not of an international character" for application of the minimum standards of international humanitarian law.[36]

That notwithstanding, the heinous crimes committed by the terrorists have not yet been brought home. As one investigative journalist remarked: "After the administrative and military response to the problem of militancy in Jammu and Kashmir, legal rearguard action has been conspicuous by its absence".[37] She reported Chief Minister Farooq Abdullah as saying: "The problem is that no one comes forward to give evidence in courts. Besides, the Jamat-e-Islami has been active in the Bar and has hijacked the judiciary". Over 17,000 people have been killed in Kashmir since 1990. The government arrested 32,404 persons including 2,315 infiltrators across the LoC, between January 1990 and April 1997. Of these 16,900 persons were released at liberty, and only 15,233 remained detained under the now-expired Terrorist and Disruptive Activities (Prevention) Act or other laws like the Public Safety Act. 13,087 persons were further released from detention. But there has not been a single conviction against the several heinous crimes committed by the militancy.

Cases of fake encounters,[38] indiscriminate firings whether in dereliction of duty[39] or in excessive use of force,[40] and illegal detention[41] by the police continue to deprive citizens of their right to life or personal liberty.

The routine insensitivity of government agencies to accidental deaths that occur in 'normal' situations continues to be on display. The situations include issues of welfare of workers and industrial safety. The recent media report of the accidental death of two young labourers, aged 20 and 22, in an effluent treatment plant near Ahmedabad highlights this malady, indicted by the Gujarat High Court as unbecoming of a welfare state. The effluent plant is being operated jointly by the local private industries and a state government undertaking. The case uncovered the deficiencies in the protective equipment supplied to workers in hazardous zones, total lack of training of the workers, and undue delay in payment of compensation. The High Court has reportedly censored the government for allowing the various departments for disowning responsibility.[43] NHRC has had occasion to deal with situations of deprivation of workers' rights in workplace.[44] We—both the government and the private industry—are yet to develop a concern and respect for human life, and most of our industries manifest a disdain for industrial safety and occupational health of the workers. In the process workers keep dying sometimes years after even the closure of the industry.[45] The ghost of Bhopal Gas Tragedy, perhaps the biggest industrial tragedy ever to hit India, still haunts us, seventeen years since its eruption and it has not been finally laid to rest. Many questions and demands of justice still remain unanswered.[46]

Freedom from Bonded Labour

Despite the Constitutional interdiction of forced labour, poverty and illiteracy continue to be breeding grounds for sustenance of bonded labour, even after fifty years of proclamation of the Constitution. The Bonded Labour (Abolition) Act, 1976 has been an attempt to translate the Article 23 proscription into an operational framework. But the problems of poverty and hunger and a heartless, exploitative society, cannot be remedied by selective legislative feats alone. A humane Supreme Court, however, decided to do its bit towards resolution of this horrid social problem in the now famous *Bandhua Mukti Morcha* case.[45] The judgement was a trailblazer. It led to a 1985 amendment of the 1976 Act aimed to widen the ambit of the law. It also led to further court judgements declaring work exacted on payment of unreasonably low wages amounted to forced labour prohibited by law.[48] However, the problem of social and economic uplift of the common people remains too huge to be tackled by judiciary in a few random cases of bonded labour that come before it, its laudable normative contributions notwithstanding.

Right to Freedom

The right to freedom under Article 19 of the Constitution encompasses the right to freedom of speech, to peaceful assembly, to form associations or unions, to freedom of movement and to reside and settle in any part of India' all, however, subject to reasonable restrictions based on considerations of public interest, security of the nation, public order and morality. The Indian judiciary has had numerous occasions to rule on myriad aspects of these freedoms. It would appear now that not only law, but all claims of executive discretion[49] must be tested against the principle of reasonableness of restrictions underscored by the several judicial rulings since 1950.[50]

Lately there is much talk about the right to information, particularly in the context of the Official Secrets Act, 1923. It is axiomatic that the freedom of information forms the backbone of the democratic process, and gives a practical meaning to the lofty concepts of public accountability, public legitimacy, and public participation in the process.[51] Without it, the right to know can never be realised. One awaits the adoption of the Information Bill 2000, although one is aware that there are indeed ways of circumventing the implementation of any good law, including delaying tactics so well known even in developed countries where such a law on freedom of information is in force.

Freedom of Belief, Faith and Worship

In order to ensure the Indian polity remains committed to secularism, the Constitution was amended in 1976 and the adjective 'secular' was inserted in the Preamble to qualify the word 'Republic.'[52] Secularism seeks to ensure that the state has no religion, but that it must treat all religions equally and without discrimination. The Constitution guarantees to every individual his freedom of religion and conscience, it also guarantees freedom of belief to one who has no faith in any religion. Thus, Article 25(1) of the Constitution defines the right to freedom of religion as follows:

> "Subject to public order, morality and to the other provisions of this Part, all persons are equally entitled to freedom of conscience and the right freely to profess, practise and propagate religion."

Clearly, the right to freedom of religion is not an absolute right. It is subject to public order, morality and to other fundamental rights of every individual. The right includes a right freely to profess, practise and propagate religion. If the right to 'propagate' should include a right to 'convert' another person, evidently that right has to be exercised "subject to public order, morality and to the other provisions of this Part."[53] Conversion to be permissible must be with the free consent of the person to be converted, as it pre-eminently involves his right freely to change his faith and religion. The current, largely political, debate on 'forcible' conversions must be looked at from the perspective of this constitutional provision. Often the media blow out of proportion a situation that basically involves a claim of land rights or a right of property, into a religious divide, without any in-depth investigation. Also mass conversions are organised everby athiests to serve political ends.

C. Equality of Status and of Opportunity

The Constitution seeks to operationalise the ideal of equality principally in two ways: through a bundle of judicially enforceable fundamental rights and through the directive principles of state policy requiring the state to work towards an equitable social order in the long run. The justiciable fundamental rights relating to equality encompass the right to equality before the law and equal protection of laws; prohibition of discrimination on grounds of religion, race, caste, sex or birth place, equality of opportunity in matters of employment; abolition of untouchability and abolition of titles; as well as special provisions for special treatment of specially disadvantaged, deprived, or other vulnerable sections of the society (such as the Scheduled Castes and Scheduled Tribes, other backward classes, women and children), and for special protection of the rights of minorities. Laws have since been enacted to give effect to such special treatment or protection. The objective of these measures of special treatment and protection is to bring about economic and social equality, an objective still beckons us to hasten positive action.

Rights of the Scheduled Castes and Scheduled Tribes

For historically and socially wrong reasons, the Indian society perpetuated a system of exploitation and dehumanisation of some of the socially and economically most deprived classes. The founders of modern India, and particularly B.R. Ambedkar, spearheaded a movement to help uplift these classes of people. The provisions in the Constitution mandating affirmative discrimination in their favour have led to reservation of seats in legislatures, reservation of jobs, and seats in educational institutions, special scholarships, etc. The rationale behind the Scheduled Castes and the Scheduled Tribes (Prevention of Atrocities) Act, 1989 has been to stem the atrocities against them and to strengthen the constitutional interdiction. A National Commission for the Scheduled Castes and Scheduled Tribes has since been established to investigate and monitor all matters relating to the implementation of the various legal safeguards provided for the Scheduled Castes and Scheduled Tribes and to make recommendations to the governmemt to secure effective implementation of these safeguards. However, there are genuine complaints that the Commission's powers are rather feeble to play an effective role. Reports of atrocities on and other violations of the rights of the Scheduled Castes still keep coming up. Also, questions have been raised as to whether the benefits of the various legal provisions have in fact percolated to the most deprived of these deprived sections.

Although the official position of the Government of India is that we have no "indigenous' people in the country, it is submitted that the sweep of the concept of the Scheduled Tribes must cover all "indigenous' people as understood in the current UN vocabulary, and that, therefore, the rights of the indigenous peoples are subsumed in the rights of the Scheduled Castes and Scheduled Tribes.

Rights of the Backward Classes

Article 15(4) of the Constitution seeks to enable the state to make "special provision for the advancement of any socially and educationally backward classes of citizens or for the Scheduled Castes or the Scheduled Tribes." Two features of this provision are relevant here. One, the Constitution talks of backward classes and not backward castes. Two, it recognises two broad categories of backward classes—socially backward and educationally backward. This clarification is important, because the politicians have played haveoc with this constiutional provision and identified castes as classes, throwing to the winds the basic economic criterion to determine the backwardness of any group of people, as social and other kinds of backwardness follow economic backwardness. In other words, the totality of a backward caste may or may not be economically or socially backward in the real sense of the term. Further, what about the issues of social or economic status (including issues of vanity and claims of caste superiority) even as between various 'backward castes' *inter se*, or between 'forward castes' and 'backward castes.' Reports of caste conflicts often gloss over the social divide between some of the 'backward castes' themselves. The politicians' pronouncements on the uplift of the backward castes rather than the backward classes are generally "vote grabbing" exercises. There is much truth in the statement:-"Today backwardness is neither a social stigma nor a social handicap. It is the politician's chartered vehicle to power and pelf".[54]

Rights of Minorities

Categorisation or identification of a group of people or a section of a society as a minority is essentially a function of the applicable criteria.[55] Article 27 of the International Covenant on Civil and Political Rights, 1966 guarantees to 'ethnic, religious or linguistic minorities' of each state the rights to their own culture, religion and language. As the Sub-commission on Prevention of Discrimination and Protection of Minorities of the UN Commission on Human Rights elaborated, (much before the Covenant came into existence):

"(i) The term 'minority' includes only those non-dominant groups in a population which possess and wish to preserve stable ethnic, religious or linguistic traditions or characteristics markedly different from those of the rest of the population;

(ii) Such minorities should properly include a number of persons sufficient by themselves to preserve such traditions or characteristics; and

(iii) Such minorities must be loyal to the State of which they are nationals."[56]

It appears that neither the Motilal Nehru Report of 1928 nor the Tej Bahadur Sapru Report of 1945 (which had recommended establishment of a Minority Commission) defined a 'minority,'[57] probably because the leaders of the freedom struggle were most concerned at that time with the issue of welfare of the religious minorities.[58]

Two provisions of the Constitution are relevant in this regard, namely Articles 29 and 30. Although the marginal note to Article 29 is "Protection of interests of minorities," the contents of that provision seeks to guarantee the cultural and educational rights of "any section of the citizens residing in the territory of India or any part thereof having a distinct language, script or culture of its own." The Constitution makers used this phraseology instead of the term 'minority' because they thought that the latter term was liable to be construed rather narrowly, whereas they had intended to apply the benefits of the provision to all minorities in a wide sense.[59]

On the other hand, Article 30 recognises the right of all minorities, "whether based on religion or language" to establish and administer educational institutions of their choice. The qualification "whether based on religion or language" does not necessarily limit the constitutional perception of minorities to just religious and linguistic minorities, since it is only illustrative, not exhaustive.

The two-nation theory based on religion led to Partition resulting from false apprehensions that the majority community on the subcontinent would not ensure the rights of a minority community. Yet India has had a tradition of tolerance and social synthesis of diverse religions, a tadition lately marred by the rise of groups and political Parties advocating religious fanaticism. Luckily such groups are still unable to tear down the traditional social fabric of tolerance. The Babri Masjid tragedy of December 1992 and the Bombay riots of January 1993 must remain mere aberrations. Often some influential individuals show their religious partisanship by looking at issues deliberately through tinted glasses. Even the recent BCCI's decistion to penalise certain celebrated cricketers allegedly involved in the so-called match-fixing scam has been characterised as discriminatory on ground of religion.[60] If this allegation were true, the aggrieved are free to approach the judicial process.

The low level of economic development coupled with such religious-political fanaticism has been responsible for some of the minorities to feel insecure. Indeed, the situation has nurtured fanatical groups in minorities too.

The National Commission for Minorities came to be established in 1992 aimed at the protection of religious minorities. While its role further strengthening, the Commission in tandem with the NHRC can achieve much more than what it has been able to achieve so far. There is enough law to protect various religions, or to prevent misuse of religious institutions for purposes other religious. What is needed, however, is an enlightened leadership, celibacy from the politics of religious, promotion of the voices of moderation and accommodation, and spread of secular education. It is wrong to assume that minorities have been discriminated against as a matter of course. Everyone near or below the poverty line is bound to feel he is discriminated against. It is important, however, for the state to take overt action to demonstrate its commitment to the welfare of the minorities alongside the welfare of all deprived groups.

Rights of Women

Article 15(3) of the Constitution provides:

> "Nothing in this article or in clause (2) of Article 29 shall prevent the State from making any special provision for women and children."

The right of women to equality with men has traditionally been denied by most societies dominated by men who generally misinterpret[61] original religious texts to their advantage and keep the women subjugated and their role in society relegated to the background. Two principal facets of the rights of women may be highlighted, namely the problem of equality with men, and trafficking and other undesirable practices, crimes and atrocities against women. Underlying these are the age-old attitudes and customs of a male-dominated society. While violations of women's rights are not unknown in other societies, including the developed ones, what heighten their gravity in the context of the Indian society are poverty, illiteracy and some of the irrational and even immoral, and unjust social customs. Even while the existing legal regime for protection of women calls for a wholesome review, the laws that exist remain impotent to prevent grave violations of women's rights. The Equal Remuneration Act, 1961, the Dowry Prohibition Act, 1961, the Suppression of Immoral Traffic in Women and Girls Acts, 1956, Indecent Representation of Women (Prohibition) Act, 1986, the Commission of Sati (Prevention) Act, 1987, and a host of other laws, all legally in force, but remain confined to the pages of the proverbial statute book. Even the now celebrated ruling of the Supreme Court in the *Vishaka* case[62] on the protection of women in workplaces remains to be fully and widely implemented.[63] Law provides for a pittance as maintenance to separated women.[64]

Mrinal Pande[65] reports that malnutrition among young mothers and children remains rampant, as high as 48 per cent in Orissa and 44 per cent in West Bengal.[66] Citing a recent study, Second National Health Survey (1998-99), she says that 50 per cent of women are still married off illegally before the age of 18. Only four out of every 10 women surveyed (a total of about 90,000 women were surveyed) knew about AIDS. More than 75 per cent wanted only two children, but their menfolk did not agree. One out of every five women surveyed has been beaten or physically mistreated, since the age of 15, mostly by her husband. Yet, many women believe that the husband has a right to beat them. Women are still being sold and bought in some parts of the country.[67] While there are also a few of them resorting to abuse of the legal provisions meant for protection in genuine situations, [68] the alarming fact remains that there has lately been a significant increase in reported crimes against women at least in certain metropolitan cities like Delhi. The actual incidence of violence against women could indeed be greater, as the number of unreported cases may be equally alarming.

Recently the National Commission for Women (NCW) made two proposals to the Government of India to amend 12 existing laws and to enact six new laws for the protection of the rights of women. However, the NCW's enthusiasm does not appear to be shared by the Government.[69]

Commenting on a recent Calcutta High Court ruling in the *Shakila Parveen* case along with a recent Bombay High Court ruling in *Jaitunbi* vs. *Mubaarak Shaikh*, Syeda Saiyidain Hameed, a former member of NCW, remarks that while Islam has had a great tradition of protecting, women's rights, "Today, Muslim women, particularly in India, are among the most repressed and deprived sections in the world." She particularly highlights some of the problems which are being faced by Muslim women—"triple, verbal instantaneous 'talaq', multiple marriages, no 'mehr' and no maintenance."[70] In one sense, the Muslim society seems to share one of the traditional maladies of the Hindu society, namely, the gap between th spirit of the original religious scriptures and the priestly insistence on monopoly to decide what it means.

For much of the injustice being suffered by Indian women, be they Hindu, Muslim or of any other religion, the male-dominated society must take the blame. This is clear from the impediments the male members of Parliament place before the passing of the Women's Reservation Bill. It is also evident in the reported male proxy rule obtaining in many panchayats where women have been elected members or office bearers, following the 73rd Constitution (Amendment) Act, 1986 (whereby 30 per cent of seats in councils at village, block and district levels have been reserved for women).

Rights of the Child

India has become a party to the International Convention on the Rights of the Child of 1989. There is no doubt that all human rights (save perhaps the political rights) that apply to an adult human must apply to a child as well, as they are essential for the development of all human beings. The unique feature of the rights of the child is that a child, unlike an adult, may not necessarily comprehend the meaning, import and importance of his / her rights and that therefore he / she depends entirely on his family and society for the enjoyment of all the benefits of these rights. The realisation of the rights of the child is thus the special responsibility of the family, the society and the state as *parens patriae*.

There are principally four social issues that raise considerable concern in the context of implementation of the rights of the child, namely violence against children, children in crime and juvenile justice, child labour, and the rights of the girl child.[71] There is an urgent need to evolve a holistic view of child's right to development.

(i) Child Abuse

Violence against children occurs in a wide variety of situations, at home, at school, at workplace, on the street or in the fields, in jails and observation homes, and so on. Trafficking in children is prohibited by law but they are being heartlessly pushed into the 'business' of trafficking, and prostitution,[72] and the law is powerless and even 'clueless' to prevent it. NHRC launched a campaign to create awareness against child abuse on 12 August 1998. The Commission rightly recognised that child abuse was no longer an aberration, but had become a systemic scourge. As Justice M.N. Venkatachaliah, the then Chairperson of the Commission, pointed out on the occasion of the launch, child abuse in India was complex problem that did not have a simple answer, but it was the result of social bias and a history of neglect and exploitation. He also recognised that the existing legal structures to combat child abuse were seemingly inadequate, and that their effectiveness was far from satisfactory. The legal system was not preventive, but acted *post facto.* Child abuse, Justice Venkatachaliah remarked, was no longer restricted to the exploitation of a few, but had become a well-planned business for many. He rightly observed that child prostitution was a mark of degradation of our society, and it was important not to criminalise the victim. The children were victims, not criminals and their dignity must be maintained, he said.[73]

The corporal punishment meted out to children in schools was the focus of a recent Delhi High Court judgment. The court is reported to have held that corporal punishment is violative of children's fundamental right to equality before law and their life and personal liberty as well as the Directive Principles of State Policy. Striking down a provision of the Delhi School Education Rules, 1973 (which provided for corporal punishment of children in schools) a unconstitutional, the court underscored the importance of children receiving education in an environment of freedom and dignity, free from fear. The Court's ruling was based on Articles 14, 21 and 39 of the Constitution , interpreted in the light of the Convention on the Rights of Child, 1989 and the National Policy on Education. The court's warning on the effects of corporal punishment to enforce discipline and obedience was ominous:

> "Brutal treatment of children can never inculcate discipline in them and obedience exacted by striking fear of punishment can make them adopt the same tactics when they grow up for getting what they want."[74]

One hopes that this judicial intervention will have beneficent results on the ground, as corporal punishment is rampant in schools.

According to one estimate, there are nearly 30 million neglected children all over the country who are in desperate need of shelter and care, whereas there are about 600 government-run juvenile homes covering not more than 36,000 children. While the government has started encouraging NGO's to enter the field, no short or medium term solution is in sight.[75]

(ii) Child in Crime and Juvenile Justice

In one of her write ups on the slum children of Delhi, Kiran Bedi finds out the way 3-4 years old slum children pick up the drinking habit, and the parental neglect of children.[76] Children have now been introduced into serious crimes either under the influence of the entertainment television or by adult criminals. There have been house-breaking by four year olds.[77] In another incident that took place in March 1999 in a village near Kanpur three boys aged between three and four stoned a two-and-half year old girl to death and hid her body in a dry pond nearby because she had bit one of them while he tried to climb up a tamarind tree![78] There have been cases of a 15-years old boy robbing three shops and nearly killing a security guard, and a teenagers' gang raping girls in early teens, all imitating what they saw on the television.[79] There is an urgent need to attend to the problem of street children in urban areas.[80] If the society does not provide a humane atmosphere for a child to develop itself, there will be a considerable increase in the number of children born of inhumanity and violence and a significant segment of the coming generations will turn criminal and violent, with no regard for the feeling of humanity.

(iii) Child Labour

There is no reliable data on the exact number of children being exploited at work. The estimate range from 20 million (official) to 100 million (NGO).[81] They are engaged in a variety of industries or vocations—making of matches and fireworks, carpet making, glass bangle, making brasswares, plastics and rope weaving, salt extraction, incense stick production, tootball making, diamond cutting and polishing, biscuit-making, steel rolling and chips recycling, domestic work, prostitution, construction industry, tea shops and eateries, candy making, [82] etc. The law— the Employment of Children Act, 1938 (amended in 1985), the Child Labour (Prohibition and Regulation) Act, 1986 (which prohibits employment of children in hazardous occupations and regulates it in others) and other laws like the Factories Act, 1948—has done little to reduce, if not eliminate, this social evil. Child labour is more rampant in unorganisd sector than in organised. Children routinely meet with death or bodily injury at work. An NGO sent fact-finding teams comprising trade unionists, lawyers, journalists, medical practitioners and activists to different parts of the country to inquire into the deaths of five child labourers and concluded that "these deaths within quick succession only indicate a dramatic rise in the exploitation of children."[83]

Although the Prime Minister of India in his Independence Day address to the nation on 15 August 1994 pledged elimination of child labour from all hazardous industries by the year 2000, [84] and the judiciary did its bit to push for social reforms contributing to a possible solution of the problem,[85] the bane of child labour continues to be deeply entrenched in society. It will continue to defy all ad hocist solutions, and await realisation of wholesome measures for the social and economic welfare of the lower rungs of the society.

(iv) The Right of the Girl Child

The rights of the girl child have a special significance in a traditional male dominated society like the Indian society. The social prejudices have further dehumanised the deprivations of the Indian girl child (even an unborn female child[86]) much more than those of the male child.

(v) The Children's Right to Development

The Alternative Report on India submitted by the Butterflies, an Indian NGO, to the UN Rights of the Child Committee in 1998 (parallel to the official report submitted by the Government of India), examines the situation of children in education, health, enjoyment of civil liberties, children in conflict with law, child labour and street children. The report largely indicates the government for the failure of the political leadership and bureaucracy (both of whom continued, according to the report, to be titled in favour of the privileged classes) and for its eagerness to withdraw from the social sector under the structural adjustment programmes.

The report reveals an alarming fall in the enrolment of children in schools at primary levels, particularly in the case of children of lower rungs of society. There are also extreme inequities in the formal system of education in terms of access and also of quality. "This indirect subsidy should be withdrawn to make resources available for ploughing them into State-sponsored school," says the report.[87]

The UNICEF's *State of the Children 1999* Report attributes the disturbing trend of low education levels to the failure of governments to demonstrate the requisite political will or to mobilise necessary financial resources required for meaningful implementation of the UNESCO's "Education for All" initiative. The report notes that out of the estimated 130 million children world-wide aged six to eleven who are out of school (40 million of them in India), 73 million are girls.[88]

The Government of India announced in early 1999 its decision to set up a separate commission for children to deal with all aspects of children, like education, health, rights and abuse. However, some NGOs feel that child labour itself is a stupendous problem and a separate issue altogether and that it is desirable to entrust it to a separate commission.[89]

The Rights of the Disabled

Although the disabled are expected to be beneficiaries of Parts III and IV of the Constitution, social prejudices more than anything else stand in the way of the strife of the disabled to achieve equality of status and of opportunity. On the occasion of the International Day for Persons with Disabilities on 3 December 2000, the Union Ministry of Social Justice and Empowerment has rededicated itself to its commitment "to provide equal opportunities, protection of rights, full participation and all round development of persons with disabilities," and promised effective implementation of the Persons with Disabilities Act, 1995 in the new millennium.[90] In view of the lack of reliable of data on the disabled, the Census of India 2001 would also collect information on the disabled. The Government is also planning to issue a uniform identity card for the disabled to enable them to avail of various facilities under the Act.[91] The Act, which was passed with much fanfare, remains in the statute book without much implementation on the ground.

About 6 per cent of India's population is estimated to be disabled. They have attracted the government's attention only in the 1990's. Less than two per cent of them have had access to education. Most public places and transport systems are inaccessible to them, although the Disabilities Act assures them of a right to "barrier-free environment."[92]

According to a 1991 survey, there were about seven million employable disabled persons (and this figure could increase with the introduction of appropriate technologies), but the placement rate had been no more than 4,000 a year. The Chinese have tapped the potential of its disabled by finding productive employment for 70 per cent of them. In India, even the few who are lucky enough to find employment have rarely found it smooth sailing. Most of them are routinely superseded on ground apprehension of their disability hampering competence at work. With the help of new technologies, we should be able to utilise this undertapped workforce far better.[93]

It is gratifying to note, however, that the social awareness about the need for protection of the rights of the disabled and also the awareness on the part of the disabled themselves of their rights, have been growing lately.

III. Catalysis in Implementation of Constitutional Promises

The government has the ultimate responsibility to implement the constitutional promises. The Indian polity has by now, particularly in the post-Emergency era, thrown up four principal catalysts of human rights implementation, namely the judiciary, as NHRC, NGOs and the communication-information media.

A. The Judiciary

As one of the three organs of government, the judiciary must share the constitutional responsibility of translating the promises into realities. Luckily, it is this branch of government, much more than the other two—the executive and the legislature—that has shown acute awareness of its constitutional mandate and is now recognised as a vanguard of human rights in the country.

During the first two decades of the Constitution, the court did not assert itself as 'aggressively' as it does today, probably because the country was in the good hands of tall political leaders who had led the freedom struggle and held out a vision for a modern India and commitment to that vision. The court, therefore, confined itself, rather scrupulously, to the words of the Constitution, and left the task of legislation to the legislature, and governance to the executive. By late sixties, issues of social inequality came to occupy the forefront of the political agenda of the nation, and the court perhaps thought it wise to strengthen the hands of the executive to implement its social and economic programmes (like the New Deal Supreme Court in the US). However, this led to a feeling of 'subservience' to the executive—at least this is how academic commentators would view that period, albeit by hindsight—and the prestige of the judiciary hit its nadir, with its ruling in the *A.D.M. Jabalpur* vs. *Shivkant Shukla.*[94] Evidently, the Emergency taught the judiciary a lesson or two in the perennial significance of basic human rights. Since then it has come a long way by purposefully evolving an elaborate human rights jurisprudence.[95] Public interest litigation (PIL) is a procedural innovation, which the higher judiciary has by now given shape to for the benefit of the "weaker victims of injustices so that the court's door when they knock shall open.."[96] PIL, without much formalities of procedure, has facilitated judicial intervention in a variety of issues—solitary confinement in jails, jail administration, conditions of undertrial prisoners, sexual abuses, child abuse, child labour, detention of the mentally handicapped, minimum wages, bonded labour, illegal sale of children, juvenile homes and other care homes, environmental protection, ragging in colleges, developmental activities, conditions in hospitals, educational rights of children, rights of women, and so on. The judiciary has expanded the scope of PIL, even while being careful not "to allow it to degenerate to becoming Publicity Interest Litigation or Private Inquisitiveness Litigation."[97]

While the common man least worries as to where he should approach to get justice and is happy when he gets justice through the judicial process of PIL, there are apprehensions expressed on the judicial tendency to "usurp" the powers of the other organs of government, particularly discretionary powers of the executive.[98]

A second criticism of the functioning of judiciary could be its occasional failure in properly applying the doctrine of preferred freedom. Justice Krishna Iyer, commented on the 'demolition diktat' of the Bombay High Court, which sought to evict slum dwellers but in the process placed in jeopardy their rights to life and shelter, as no provision for rehabilitation was made. The situation evidently highlights a conflict of environmental concerns with the basis human rights to life and shelter. "Small people, may be, are on the judicial firing line, not within the hearing zone [of the court]," was the caustic remark of Justice Krishna Iyer.[99] The court was expected to apply the doctrine of preferred freedom and ensure rehabilitation first, before ordering forcible eviction of the slum-dwellers. A similar conflict of competing rights concerns can also be discerned in a judicial intervention resulting in closing down of a large number of small industries some of which have been polluting in Delhi, which involved uprooting of 15 to 20 lakh of working peoples, with relocation amounting to denial of livelihood to them and their families (a total of 60 lakh people including their families will be affected). Concerned over the pollution levels in the capital city, the judiciary at times orders relocation of polluting industries to the neighbouring places. Does this not conflict with the right to clean environment of the citizens in these neighbouring areas, besides of course uprooting the lives of the workers in those industries? These judicial decisions are handed down without even giving an opportunity to be heard to those people who are most directly affected by them. Judiciary must show in each case that comes before it greater sensitivity to the need to balance the competing rights and as far as possible ensuring the enjoyment of the right to food to livelihood.

Also, in appropriate cases, the judiciary should be solely guided by proper expert advice. In the *Delhi motor vehicles pollution* cases, the judiciary appears to have relied on affidavits/averments of parties to decide first in favour of CNG kits or catalytic converters to be fitted to motor vehicles, and then in favour of a ban on leaded petrol, causing in the process considerable inconvenience to people.[100] It is desirable that issues involving science and technology, engineering, medical sciences, complex economic and financial matters, etc. are adjudicated on the basis of expert advice given directly to the court, rather than through adversarial presentation of the case by two sets of legal counsel, however eminent they may be.

B. National Human Rights Institutions

The 1990's appear to have been a decade of national human rights institutions. In 1990 the Constitution was amended to establish a National Commission for the Scheduled Castes and Scheduled Tribes. Same year a National Commission for Women was set up. Since then a National Commission for Minorities was also established. All these commissions have varying powers. Besides the rights commissions mentioned above, one would also include institutions such as the Chief Vigilance Commissioner, the Grievance Redressal Forums under the Consumer Protection Act, 1986, and also the projected institutions like the Lok Pal, as part of the national institutional framework for implementation of human rights.

In 1993 the Protection of the Human Rights Act was enacted more in response to considerable international pressure than to domestic pressure, chiefly to ward off the criticism the government encountered on human rights violations in the terrorism or insurgency affected areas. Be that as it may, it established a National Human Rights Commission, which has since performed commendable work for protection of human rights in the country and has by now acquired considerable reputation in the field, starting with its very first case, the *Bijbehara* incident. NHRC's Annual Reports to Parliament and *Newsletter* regularly cover the various cases and other proceedings dealt with by the commission. Discriminate access to the media has probably been the major strength of the Commission. Publicity often embarrasses the perpetrators of human rights violations. The Commission has initiated court proceedings in appropriate cases—such as the second *Chakma Refugees* case.

The NHRC encourages States to establish State commissions. It has proposed a regional commission for the North-East. Uttar Pradesh, which recorded the maximum number of cases of human rights violations with NHRC, has since withdrawn its earlier order of setting up a state human rights commission.[101]

However, things can be still better with NHRC. The Commission itself has made a number of recommendations to government for enhancing and strengthening its powers and functions.[102]

Kuldip Nayar, for instance, raises a number of aspects of the Commission that need to be remedied.[103] First, the Commission "has an authority of sorts and cast itself in a mould which is appealing in form but lacking in substance."Second," [t]he Commission, however, lacks what a human rights agency demands. It is too legalistic, too bureaucratic [and the process] too mechanical. True, it sets in motion a process for redress. But it does not know what to do if it is stumped." Third, although " some grievances do get redressed and a few individuals do get justice and even compensation," the " activists' grièvance is that "they have been reduced to the status of defendants." Fourth, "In fact, it is dangerous to depend on the Commission for redress of human rights violations. It is essentially a status quo body. Its *obiter dicta* tally with the jargon of the establishment... What one misses in the Commission's decision is the criticism against the guardians of the system. When it does not want to hurt the establishment, it shies away from the real issue." Fifth, "strangely, the Commission keeps the problems of Dalits at a distance."The story of the backward classes is no different." Nayar cites the case of a woman belonging to a barber community having been gang-raped by Yadavs and set afire at Bhawanipur, near Kanpur, and all this because her son had eloped with a Yadav girl. The story was in the media. "Cannot the Human Rights Commission take notice of such cases on its own?" asks Nayar.

The Coordination Committee on Disappearances (during militancy in Punjab) is critical of NHRC's approach to compensation for human rights violations without bringing the violators to book. According to it, the Commission has side-tracked the basic issue of a thorough investigation to provide justice to the families of the victims and fix responsibility. "Rather than insulting the families of the victims by just providing compensation, the NHRC should go into the sufferings of such families," say the members of the committee. " These families are not begging. They are demanding justice. The compensation under the given situation was not acceptable to these families."[104]

There is a further criticism—that NHRC does not effectively support and strengthen the functioning of the other national commissions, whose chairpersons are in fact its *ex officio* members. On other hand, some critics of NHRC find fault with its lack proper perception of the concept of human rights as well. Raising the question whether the NHRC should look into police firings to disperse unlawful assemblies, P.K. Doraiswamy answers it himself by saying: "By its very nature, it has a specialised, partial orientation and cannot take a holistic view of a complex law and order situation." [105] Such a view, however, overlooks the composition and competence of the members of the Commission. It further ignores the fact that decisions on human rights violations must necessarily, and even routinely, involve balancing the rights and duties or the competing rights involved. NHRC must be aware that all rights are relative, and rights deprivations are contextual. Enforcing law and order, within the limits of the law, is the concern of the law enforcement authorities, human rights protection agencies come into picture if any failures or excesses committed by these authorities violate human rights.

There have been at least two aspects of NHRC, which must be discouraged by government, if it wants to instil confidence in the minds of the public about NHRC's impartiality and dependence from government. One, the government should discontinue the practice of 'lending' its officers to the Commission and transferring them back. Two, the government should also refrain from appointing members of the Commission to attractive and elevated positions like those of State Governors. Such practices do violence to the concept of institutional independence.

Finally, the parliamentarians should devote more time to issues relating to national human rights institutions. More often than not, the reports of these institutions are not even discussed, but relegated as "good archival material," in the words of Dr. Najma Heptullah, the Deputy Chairperson of the Rajya Sabha.[106]

Besides the rights commissions mentioned above, as mentioned already, one would also include institutions such as the Chief Vigilance Commissioner, the Grievance Redressal Forums under the Consumer Protection Act, 1986, and also the projected institutions like the Lok Pal, as part of the national institutional framework for implementation of human rights. The functional effectiveness of these institutions also calls for further strengthening to enable them to serve the cause of governance better.[107]

C. The Media

There have been uses and abuses of the freedom of the media. It is generally recognised that it is the duty of a true and responsible journalist to inform the people with accurate and impartial presentation of news and his views after dispassionate evaluation of the facts and information received by him to be published as a news item. The Indian media have by and large acquitted themselves well and contributed to sustaining the Indian democracy quite vibrant. They work in trying circumstances, and have even produced martyrs for the cause in the midst of terrorism. They continue to make significant contributions particularly in fields like human rights and environmental protection.

Lately, however, some of them have revealed a propensity for sensationalism, rather than for its traditional mandate for propagation of truth. Indeed, the standard of journalism has gone down the world over—we are no longer able to produce Walter Cipmanns, Max Lerners, and indeed our very own Inder Malhotras, Bhatias, Bhargavas and Nayars, who would do sincere home work including in-depth academic research, before they decided to publish their pieces. The recent 'trials' by the Indian media have claimed many hapless victims—and not all its victims are politicians.[108] The media must realise that they are in a position to promote or destroy the rights of individuals, and that everyone has a right to be heard before being condemned. There is a need for young journalists to undergo some special training in this regard before they are encouraged to engage in independent investigative journalism. Tendency to rush to publish unverified news has at times landed the media before the judiciary either for contempt of court or in suits for defamation. Journalism should not be equated with omniscience or a license to abuse the freedom of expression.

Emphasising the role of the press as "a social institution," Justice P.B. Savant, the Chairperson of the Press Council of India (PCI), has highlighted two major maladies afflicting the Indian Press, namely commercialisation and corruption. He warns ominously: "Unless timely steps are taken to check commercialisation and corruption, the Press which is already afflicted with a diseased limb of yellow jounalism, may as an institution, lose its credibility and respectability on account of the misdeeds of some."[109] Eminent journalists themselves recognize the need for self-regulation and introspection among the media persons for the healthy growth of the media.[110]

There is an on-going debate on the ownership structure of the Indian Media and the terms of journalists' employment.The Press Council appears to favour by journalists co-operative ownership of newspapers in addition to private ownership to ensure diverse sources of information which is necessary for debate and discussion in a democracy. On the other hand, the Newspaper Society of India (of publishers and editors of newspapers) seems to think that the PCI would exceed its jurisdiction if it were to dabble in issues of ownership structure.[111] One submits that the issue should be examined in terms of the benefits to be derived by the public. Monopolies whether in the field of media or elsewhere have produced large profits to the owners, but benefited the public far too little. Monopolistic ownership of news media has also tended to be partisan and eclectic in news gathering, analysis and dissemination. Pray, how much of development news or news from rural areas do we get through the media? Very little indeed, because they are not 'newsworthy', as they do not make profits for the media barons.

D. The NGOs

Non-governmental organizations (NGOs) have made a contribution to the long and strenuous processs of translation of the constitutional promises into realities on the ground. Their effectiveness is a function of their informal structures and procedures. They represent the interface between the government and the common people. They are ideally placed to promote the principles of self-government and self-reliance.

But then, the work of the NGOs in India suffers from a number of maladies. First , they generally work in small areas with little or no contact with other similarly placed NGOs. There is no co-ordination among them. Second, the financing of NGOs reveals serious problems. Many of the NGOs are hard up for funds, depending as they are on one or a few individuals. There are also NGOs that exist on paper, just to get funds from public funding agencies or government. Some receive funds from abroad, but criticise the government when they are asked to reveal the sources in terms of the law. Some receive funds from certain vested interests for whose benefit they function. Third, some NGOs cater to the interests of political parties, or to the political ambitions of particular individuals. Fourth, terrorism in different parts of the country has spawned and nurtured certain human rights NGOs which further the cause of the terrorist groups that patronise them.[112]

VI. Need for a Sense of Balance and Social Responsibility

Article 51-A of the Constitution, embodying Fundamental Duties of every citizen of India, underscores two basic principles, namely due regard for others' rights, and responsibility towards the community and the nation. Indeed, these two principles are also subsumed in the reasonable restrictions to which many of the fundamental rights are made subject. However, these reasonable restriction clauses most invariably empower the state to make law or to take other action on behalf of the community, with the judiciary placed as the arbiter in case of disputes. Claims of rights then often call for accommodation in due regard for the claims of others or of the community at large.

In discourses on human rights it is often assumed that the state is the perpetrator of violations of rights or that it is the sole responsibility of the state to ensure human welfare. It is usually an overlooked fact that human rights of an individual or a group are violated by fellow human beings themselves, whether behind the facade of the state or outside it. Abuse of rights often results in denial of the rights of others. When terrorists use violence against innocent human beings, they commit violence to the latter's human rights, which cannot be justified in terms of self-determination, autonomy, or expulsion of outsiders. When doctors, lawyers or teachers as a group frequently strike work for untenable reasons, they not only abuse their collective rights but also compromise the rights of thousands of innocent human beings, even if the ultimate responsibility of preventing such upheavls lies with the state. Each individual or group must feel responsible to the society, and indeed, to his own or each of its members' own conscience. The community violates human rights of individuals or groups such as girl children, women, and other vulnerable groups if it sticks to irrational age-old social or religious traditions. We as individuals carelittle about what happens to others on our actions or inactions. We are only concerned about our rights, but not our duties to others and to the community. Liberalisation and globalisation tend to make us more materialistic and less humanistic.

Realisation of human welfare is, in the ultimate analysis, a co-operative venture of all individuals constantly acting together and caring for one another as a humane society.

References

1. Quoted by Jawaharlal Nehru in his *The Discovery of India* (New Delhi, 1946, 12th impression, 1992), pp. 363-64.

2. Quoted in Nehru, *ibid*, p. 363.

3. First broadcast over the national radio as Vice-President of the Interim Government of India, 7 September 1946, reproduced in *The Hindustan Times* (New Delhi), 8 September 1946, and in *The Hindu* (Madras), 9 September 1946.

4. M.K. Nawaz, *The Changing Law of Nations: An Indian Focus* (Kolkata), 2000), p. 53. Nawaz's view takes into account the intense complexities of india as a nation— a vast country with a very large population, regional, religious, linguistic, cultural, class, caste and other economic diversities, coupled with the fact of colonial devastation ending with a debilitating Partition on the basis of religion. These indeed are the desiderata behind the Preamble, and Parts II and IV of the Constitution. Given these problems attenuated by the limited resources, Nawaz seems to argue, India's achievements in the field of human rights cannot be underrated.

5. Some Western scholars have so far identified three 'generations' of human rights. The principal flaw in this approach is that it reveals a failure to conceive human rights as a holistic and yet context-specific concept, a failure to comprehend it as part of "those conditions of social life without which no man can seek, in general, to be himself at his best." (The quoted words of Laski explain his concept of liberty—see Harold J. Laski, *A Grammar of Politics* (London, 4th edn., reprint), p. 91.)

6. Kofi A. Annan, *Preventing War and Disaster: A Growing Global Challenge* (1999 Annual Report on the Work of Organization, New York, 1999), pp. 16, para 53.

7. See the non-derogable rights under Article 4(2) of the International Covenant on Civil and Political Rights,1966.

8. There is a recent report from Jaipur according to which the demand

of the people of Janawada village of Ajmer district, Rajasthan, and its Sarpanch, Shrimati Bhuri Devi, for the details of development expenditure for the period 1995-2000 was frustrated by the former Sarpanch and other functionaries of the Panchayat, citing a non-existent resolution and formally refusing the information, despite the Rajasthan Freedom of Information Act, 1999. See " Panchayat 'apathy' irks villagers," *The Hindu* (New Delhi), 26 November 2000, p. 7.

9. Reports of starvation deaths and malnutrition keep coming in, and the heartless politicians use them to their political ends. See "Starvation deaths: Opp demands judicial probe," *The Indian Express*, 9 December 2000. p. 2, which reports on the political din made of a reported starvation death of a 30 year old woman in Bolangir District of Orissa.

10. Excerpts from a speech made by Y.V. Reddy, Deputy Governor of the Reserve Bank of India on 30 October 2000, at the Vivek Vardhini College, Hyderabad, A.P., second instalment reprinted in *The Hindu*, 30 November 2000, pp. BS-1 entitled "India in the global context." The first instalment appeared under the title "From colonial chaos to sustained growth-I," in *The Hindu*, 23 November 2000, pp. BS-I.

11. *Ibid.*

12. See Usha Rai, "Green Talk: Towards a fair exchange," *The Hindu*, Sunday, 26 November 2000, p.VIII. For the Supreme Court's judgment on the Sardar Sarovar Dam, see *Narmada Bachao Andolam* vs. *Union of India and Others*, 2000(7) SCALE, pp. 34-140.

13. Usha Rai, *ibid.*

14. The news item "Displaced face yet another ouster," in *The Hindu*, 6 March 1999, p. 6, speaks of people displaced some fourteen years ago to make way for a megadam for the Rihand super termal power project, now facing yet another ouster, this time to facilitate disposal of fly ash, stalling in the process the second stage of the project. These are some three lakh tribals and rural people from 162 villages of the Singrauli region (MP-UP).

15. "Pending cases in SC, HCs," *The Hindu*, 25, November 2000, p. 7. See also Bhadra Sinha, "Rs. 4.96 crore cheating case ends after 23 years, 6 convicted," *The Times of India*,12 December 2000, p. 2: pray, whatever happened to Rs. 4.96 crore of public money?

16. For a detailed treatment of these, see H. D. Shourie, "Clogged courts: Cases backlog can be cleared," *The Times of India* (New Delhi), 12 August 1998, p. 13. They include issues of full observance of court hours, administrative meetings, inspections, VIP related 'duties' deputation of judicial officers to government departments on non- judicial work, delays resulting from services of summons, issuance of interim orders, transfer of cases, proliferation of revisions and appeals on interim and interlocutory orders, piecemeal and truncated hearings, unduly long oral arguments, adjournments for various administrative and other reasons, delays in return of case files to original courts, delays resulting from supply of

documents or certified copies of the Supreme Court decisions, and so on. Shourie refers to two decisions of Allahabad High Court in *Ayodhya Sahai* vs. *District Judge, Jaunpur* (AIR 1998 All 285) and *Siddhartha Kumar* vs. *Upper Civil Judge* (Civil Writ Petition No. 25505 of 1997).

17. According to Shourie's estimate, while there are 51 judges per million population in England, 58 in Australia, 75 in Canada, and 107 in the USA, there are only 10.5 judges per million in India! See, *Ibid* The Law Commission of India has recommended a ratio of 50 judges per million in India.

18. See also "Reduce delay in justice delivery: Jaitley," *The Hindu*, 3 December 2000, p. 6, reporting the inaugural proceedings of a Chennai national seminar on judicial reforms. See further D.S. Mehta, "Justice at your Doorstep," *Express Newsline (Indian Express)*, 6 December 2000, pp. 5.

19. See also a recent perceptive piece on the backlog of cases and how the Supreme Court and some of the SDMs tried to tackle it, in Gurcharan Das, "Will Justice Prevail?," *The Times of India*, 2 December 2000, p. 14.

20. Part III of the Constitution of India.

21. Part IV of the Constitution of India.

22. Article 38 of the Constitution of India.

23. See V.S. Mani, "Human Rights in India: A Survey," in K.P. Saksena, ed., *Human Rights: Fifty Years of India's Independence* (New Delhi, 1999), pp. 170-193. This was an abridged but updated version of his *Human Rights in India: A Report* (IWOCHR Occasional Paper No. 5, New Delhi, 1997).

24. In a typical case of custodial death that took place last year, the media reported the death of Raziuddin who was arrested on a false complaint and tortured in custody. PUDR which investigated the case was reported to have expressed the view that the courts while refusing bail did not examine the evidence placed before them and that "this resulted in 100 days of wrongful detention of Raziuddin." The detenue died 'under mysterious circumstances' on the night between April 29 and 30, 1999. It was stated that he had commited suicide, and an electrical wire was found tied around his neck. According to PUDR, the body bore several injury marks. NHRC took *suo motu* cognizance of the incident. See "NHRC notice on death of undertrial," *The Hindu*, 3 June 1999, p. 3.

25. "NHRC reviews human rights situation in States: Meeting with all DGs & IGs," *Human Rights Newsletter* (New Delhi), Vol. 7, No. 9, September 2000, pp. 1-2. p.1.

26. J.Venkatesan, "NGO expresses concern over police brutality" *The Hindu*, 26 November 2000, p. 8.

27. Editorial, "More lockup Deaths," *The Hindu*, 14 July 1999, p. 10.

28. The adverse impact of delays on witness testimony and criminal justice was recently highlighted by an Additional Sessions Judge of Delhi, Judge B.S. Mathur, while convicting an accused in a murder case on the

basis of an eye-witness account of the deceased brother. He is reported to have observed: "If a prosecution witness in a criminal case is examined after four or five years or more, it would be absolutely unrealistic to expect him to reproduce each event of an occurrence graphically... Discrepancies in the testimonies of prosecution witnesses are bound to occur if the trial goes on endlessly." On the predicament of being a witness in criminal cases, the judge remarked: "Witnesses are a harassed lot and have to come to courts many times at their own costs. Not only is that, they are bribed, threatened, abducted, maimed, and in some cases, even done away with." "There is no protection for the witnesses. Neither the court nor the investigating agency treats them with respect. They have no place to sit in the courts nor are they provided any other facilities and have to undergo unchecked and prolong cross-examination, said judge Mathur. See the report entitled " Witnesses are a harassed lot. in *The Hindu*, 3 December 2000 p. 3.

29. See generally "NHRC comes to the aid of undertrials," *The Hindu*, 27 July 1999, p. 6.

30. See the PTI news item, "Compensate man wrongly jailed for 38 years: SC to WB," *The Indian Express* (New Delhi), 5 December 2000, p. 5.

31. "Privatise jail management: NHRC chief," *The Hindu*, 2 July 1999, pp. 20. Justice Venkatachalliah was delivering his keynote address at a seminar on "Human Rights and Prison Management" held in New Delhi on 1 July 1999 as part of an Indo-British project on prison reforms funded by the UK Foreign and Commonwealth Office.

32. The situation of terrorism in Kashmir has, among other things, resulted in creation of the problem of orphans. According to a 1998 report, the number of orphans has crossed 15,000 mark, with the border district of Kupwara topping the list. Most of these are victims of militancy. *The Hindu*, 2 December 1998, p. 8.

33. See "Four children gunned down," *The Hindu*, 3 December 2000, p. 1.

34. The Assam terrorists seem to target in planned way the non-Assamese people originally drawn from different parts of India who have adopted Assam as their permanent home for generations now. See "Extremists gun down 18 in Assam," *The Hindu*, 2 December 2000, p. 11. It seems that with the gunning down and killing of at least 30 people with 30 more critically injured (all Biharis and Nepalis) on 7 December 2000, the official figures of 'outsiders' killed by the ULFA extremists have reached 116, since October 2000. See *The Indian Express*, 8 December 2000. p. 1.

35. As the Supreme Court declared in one of the *Chakma Refugees* cases.

"We are a country governed by the Rule of Law. Our Constitution confers certain rights on every human being and certain other rights on citizens. Every person is entitled to equality before the law and equal protection of the laws. So also, no person can be deprived of his life or personal liberty except according to procedure established by law. Thus the State is bound to protect the life and liberty of every human being, be he a citizen or otherwise..."

See, *National Human Rights Commission* vs. *State of Arunachal Pradesh and another*, (1966) I SCC 742, para 20. The earlier *Chakma* case was *State of Arunachal Pradesh* vs. *Khudiram Chakma*, (1994) Supp. (1) endorsed by the Supreme Court in *Louis De Raedt* vs. *Union of India*, (1991) 3 SCC 554.

36. The common Article 3 of the 1949 Geneva Conventions on humanitarian law applicable in armed conflicts.

37. Ritu Sarin, " State of atrophy," *The Indian Express* (New Delhi), 6 July 1997, *The Express Magazine*, Section II, p.1.

38. In one case of fake encounter that occurred on 17 October 1998, four persons were killed by the UP police near Varanasi—even the state police chief later conceded that a fake encounter did indeed take place—NHRC asked the UP Government to pay compensation to the next of kin of the dead. It is recently reported that the NHRC direction is yet to be complied with. See news item, NHRC raps UP Govt. for not paying damages, *The Times of India* (New Delhi), 23 November 2000, p. 9.

39. See the report on "Pay compensation to police firing victim, " *The Hindu*, 30 June 1999, at p. 20. NHRC directed Manipur Government to pay interim compensation to an injured victim of an indiscriminate firing by two drunken policemen in a paddy field.

40. See "NHRC seeks report on alleged police atrocities in Sitamarhi," *The Times of India*, 4 September 1998, p. 8.

41. In many cases that came before NHRC, the complaint of illegal detention and torture has been *prima facie* found established. For a recent case of illegal detention of two workers on suspicion of being involved in illicit distillation of liquor, who were released by the Gujarat police perhaps after a visit to their colony by an *Indian Express* team of journalists inquiring about one of them, see Joydeep Ray, "Missing Workers return after two days in lock-up," *The Indian Express*, 10 December 2000, p. 3. The most shocking was the reported statement of Inspector R.K. Patel of the Sanand Police Station: "Sometimes, we detain people for investigation and that is a common practice." This was his reply to the question whether detaining a person in police lock up for recording witness testimony was not illegal!

42. See e.g., "Custodial death: NHRC asks report from Bihar ," *The Hindu*, 29 December 1998, p. 3.

43. See " govt. pulled up for passing the buck." *The Hindu*, 22 November 2000, at p.5.

44. See, e.g., the news item entitled, "NHRC directive to UP on factory explosion," *The Hindu*, 31 August 1998, at p. 2, on a major factory explosion in Kanpur as a result of the lapses on the part of the management, killing seven women and one man.

45. See the news item, "Another tribal dies of silicosis," *The Hindu*, 3

December 2000, p. 6, reporting the death of a total of 272 persons due to silicosis over a period of two decades, since the government-owned AP Mineral Development Corporation closed down its mines at Elkatta in Mahabubnagar district of Andhra Pradesh in 1974, with no provision for medical treatment or compensation for the victims of silicosis. NHRC is currently investigating the case, according to the media report.

46. See "Learn lessons from Bhopal gas tragedy," *The Hindu*, 4 December 2000, p. 8.

47. *Bandhua Mukti Morcha* vs. *Union of India*, AIR 1984 SC 802.

48. *People's Union of Democratic Rights* vs. *Union of India*, AIR 1985 SC 1473.

49. See, e.g., *DTC* vs. *Mazdoor Congress*, AIR 1991 SC 101.

50. For some of the rulings, see *Chintaman Rao* vs. *State of MP*, 1950 SCR 759; *Khare* vs. *State of Delhi*, 1950 SCR 519; *Qureshi* vs. *State of Bihar*, 1959 SCR 629; *Dwarka Prasad* vs. *State of UP*, 1954 SCR 803; *State of Maharashtra* vs. *Himmatbhai*, AIR 1970 SC 1157; *Laxmi* vs. *State of UP*, AIR 1981 SC 873.

51. For a news item on a proceeding before the Supreme Court, following the failure of the then Minister Ram Jethmalani's move to bring in transparency in the functioning of the department of Urban Development which was then in his charge, see "Apex court needs to lift the veil on Official Secrets Act," *The Times of India*, 4 January 1999, p.8.

52. Inserted by section 2 of the Constitution (Forty-second Amendment) Act, 1976, w.e.f. 3 January 1977.

53. In *Stainslaus* vs. *State of MP*, AIR 1977 SC 908, the Supreme Court of India has pointed out that propagation is concerned with the right to communicate beliefs to another person or to expound the tenets of one's religion, but does not include a right to forcible conversion.

54. Editorial, "Backward indeed," *The Hindustan Times*, 14 November 1996, p. 13.

55. For a sociological approach to defining/identifying a minority, see Imtiaz Ahmed, "Defining Minorities in India," *The Hindustan Times*, 17 October 1996, pp. 13, summarized in Mani (IWCOHR), note 23, footnote 106.

56. *Yearbook of Human Rights (1950)*, p. 490.

57. See P.M. Bakshi, *The Constitution of India* (Delhi, 3rd edn., reprint 1997), p. 53.

58. See, e.g., Nehru, note 1, p. 382-83.

59. See B. Shiva Rao, *Select Documents on the Constitution* (1957) Vol. 2, pp. 281, Vol. 3, pp. 525-26, cited in Bakshi, note 57, p. 51.

60. See "Ban on Azhar discriminatory, says Naib Imam," *The Times of India*, 7 December 2000, p. 17. On the other hand, for a more unbiased criticism of the BCCI's decision by Shivlal Yadav, a former Test player, see "Azhar's ban most unfortunate," *The Hindu*, 7 December 2000, p. 19.

61. There is a view that the ancient Hindu texts such as the *Manu*

Smrithi, are not necessarily chauvinistic and male-oriented, and that the criticism of these texts are "based on the misinterpretation of certain slokas which were intended for the benefit and protection of women [as *abalas*]." See "Equal, respected and legally protected," excerpts from Sri T. V. Muthukrishna Iyer Endowment Lecture by Vedantham Srinivasan, on 24 September 1998, published in *The Hindu*, 13 September 1999, p. 21. One may still demand a better explanation—as some of he protagonists of women's rights do—of why, according to *Ramayana*, Sita was asked to undergo *agnipareeksha* to prove her chastity during her captivity, merely on a wanton allegation of a washerman. Even the explanation that *Agnipareeksha* gave Rama an opportunity to do justice to Vedavati (another incarnation of Lakshmi, who in human form had intensely prayed for reunion with her consort), raises more questions than it seeks to answer. Indeed, one should always separate the original scriptures from the later *srutis, smritis, itihasas* and *puranas*.

62. *Vishaka and Others*, vs. *State of Rajasthan and Others*, 1997 (6) SCC 241. See also *Apparel Export Promotion Council* vs. *A.K. Chopra*, AIR 1999 SC 625.

63. Sanghamitra Chakraborty, "Sexual harassment at workplace: SC ruling falls on deaf ears, " *The Sunday Times of India*, 9 August 1998, p. 5.

64. See Rakesh Bhatnagar, "Separated women abandoned by law", *The Times of India*, 27 November 2000, pp. 9. Bhatnagar points out that initially section 125 of the Cr. P.C. had fixed the amount at Rs. 250, whereas in 1973 this was increased to Rs. 500. The Code does not also provide for urgent issuance of interim relief to the separated woman and her children.

65. See Mrinal Pande, "Decimation of a child's world," *The Hindu Magazine*, 10 December 2000, p. III.

66. The recent report of starvation death was of a 30 years old mother of three children. For more on this, see *The Indian Express*, 9 December 2000, p. 2.

67. See Mohammed Iqbal, "Women sold and bought in Rajasthan," *The Hindu*, 10 December 1998, p. 1.

68. See a report by Shardah Uniyal, "Women misusing dowry law to settle scores," *The Times of India*,1August 1998, p. 1.

69. The HRD Ministry's position is reported to be that in respect of most of the proposals, "there are likely to be wide-scale repercussions and the government feels that the move should come from the society, e.g., Uniform Civil Code." What a lovely way to shelve the issue to eternity! See more on this, Anita Katyal, "Centre rejects NCW's plea for amending laws concerning women," *The Times of India*, 2 January 1999, p. 9.

70. Syeda Saiyidain Hameed, "Shah Bano revalidated, "*The Hindu*, 9 June 2000.

71. For a presentation of the ground realities of the rights of the child in India, see R.M. Pal, "Wrongs and Rights of the Child," in K.P. Saksena ,

ed., note 23, pp. 47-58.

72. See a recent collection of true stories, in Lalit K. Jha, "Children's Day? What Children's Day?" *The Hindu,* 13 November 2000, p. 1. This is a stirring write up on child prostitutes and children of prostitutes. The writer discovers that there are about 3,500 prostitutes living in a hundred and odd brothels in G.B. Road, Delhi, of whom at least one-third are estimated to be children! According to the Butterflies, a Delhi based NGO, at least 400,000 sex workers in the country are estimated to be minors, of whom 20,000 are annually brought to India from Nepal. See "Govt. ignores child abuse issue, says report," *The Times of India,* 12 August 1998, p. 11.

73. See *Human Right Newsletter,* Vol. 5, No. 9, september 1998, pp. 1. See also "NHRC to launch campaign to curb child prostitution," *The Times of India,* 15 August 1998, p. 9.

74. For a report of the decision, see " Children to be spared the rod," *The Hindu,* 2 December 2000, at p. 4.

75. See the report on the possible involvement of NGOs such as the Prayas Institute for Juvenile Justice, "Spotlight on juvenile homes," *The Hindu,* 27 July 1999, pp. 18. For an earlier report on the entry of NGO's see, Sutirtho Patranobis,"Juvenile homes thrown open to NGO's" *The Hindu,* 4 March 1999, p. 20.

76. Kiran Bedi, "What Went Wrong : Toddler's toddy rocks the boat," *The Times of India (Delhi Times),* 30 November 2000, p. 4. She narrates the story of a four years old in a Delhi slum whose parents migrated to Delhi some 20 years ago, but now earning a comfortable sum nearly the whole of which they spend on liquor and drugs, and have a callous attitude towards proper upbringing of their eight children!

77. See, e.g., the report on " an innocence lost amidst crime," *The Indian Express,* 29 September 1996, p. 3. This news item was on an attempted burglary by three children aged four, seven and eight.

78. Raj Saran Varma, "The case of the four years old killers," *The Sunday Times of India,* 28 March 1999, p. 17.

79. Savitha G.L., "Stirring the seething cauldron, " *Ibid.*

80. For more on this, Mani, IWCOHR Occasional Paper, note 23, p. 118. For the report of a recent study of street children, see "Street kids most vulnerable to AIDS," *The Hindu,* 2 December 2000, p. 4.

81. For the latter estimate, see Kalpana Sharma,"Why should children work," *The Hindu,* 20 December 1996, p. 6 . For an estimate of 60 million, see *The Hindustan Times,* 2 January 1997, p. 3.

82. See " Their bitter experience in a sweet factory," *The Hindu,* 12 July 2000 reports of rescue of 33 bonded labourers including 15 children, all belonging to southern districts of Tamil Nadu, from a sugar candy factory at Valope near Chiplun in Maharashtra, by the Samarthan, a Mumbai-based NGO. Most of the children belonged to families living below the poverty line in backward and drought prone areas and their parents had

taken loans ranging from Rs. 700 to Rs. 7,000 from the owner of the factory. The children had been regularly tortured for not meeting conditions laid down by the factory owner, including the requirement of working long hours standing in front of huge ovens, and handling heavy steel pans.

83. One child worker, 14, was killed while working on Bhopal Hospital Trust building on 28 September 1997. A girl, also 14, was killed when she got caught in an overlocking machine at a hosiery units in Turuppur. She was one among the thousands of children between 6 and 14 years employed in the hosiery units. Three other child labourers died in separate incidents at work site in Gujarat. Two died at construction sites, while the third died of poisoning while cleaning pesticide bags. See "Child labourers die in dramatic succession," *The Hindu*, 5 August 1998, p. 2.

84. Swami Agnivesh, Chairman of Bandhua Mukti Morcha, called it a message of hope for all those sixty million children who are "languishing in conditions of servitude, being denied their fundamental right to childhood, to education, to play, to dream like any other normal child." See,"Abolish child labour, says Agnivesh", *The Hindustan Times*, 20 November 1994.

85. See *M.C. Mehta vs. Union of India*, commented, *inter alia*, in *The Times of India*, 11 December 1996, p. 1 under the heading, "Court orders welfare fund for child labour: Price of innocence," ibid., 12 December 1996, p.10; Editorial, "Another declaration," *The Indian Express*, 12 December 1996, p. 8.

86. It is reported that the Supreme Court is currently seized of the issue of tests for pre-natal sex selection and pre-implantation genetic diagnosis, mainly used for female foeticide. See PTI, "SC notice on plea to ban ways to pick babies' sex," *The Indian Express*, 4 December 2000, p. 4.

87. See "Indian child vulnerable in many ways," *The Hindu*, 3 August 1998, pp. 3.

88. "40 million children denied education in India: Report," *The Times of India*, 9 December 1998, p. 11.

89. Man Mohan, "NGO demands setting up of national commission on child labour," *The Times of India*, 27 January1999, p. 9.

90. See the public advertisement that appeared in all newspapers on 3 December 2000. For example, *The Hindu*, 3 December 2000, p. 9.

91. "Special identity cards for the disabled," *The Hindu*, 4 December 2000.

92. See an interview of Javed Abidi, "Only 2 per cent of disabled people are getting education at present," *The Indian Express (Express newsline)*, 6 December 2000, p. 5.

93. See the Editorial, "A Disabled Act," *The Times of India*, 20 October 1998, p. 10.

94. AIR 1976 SC 1207, in which the Supreme Court held that the right to life and personal liberty was a derogable right, during emergency.

95. Probably starting with *Maneka Gandhi* vs. *Union of India*, AIR 1978 SC 597. For an authentic expose on the Supreme Court's human rights jurisprudence, see *Justice Sujata* v. *Manohar*, " Judiciary and Human Rights," *Indian Journal of International Law*, Vol. 36 (1996), p. 39-54. For an appreciation of the judicial contribution to women's rights, see her "The Indian Judiciary and Women's Rights," *ibid.*, pp. 1-12.

96. Justice V.R. Krishna Iyer, " Judiciary: Law, Justice and Litigation," *The Hindustan Times*, 12 February 1995, p. 13. For a research study of PIL, see Rajeev Dhavan, "Law as Struggle: Public Interest Law in India," *Journal of the Indian Law Institute*, Vol. 36 (1994), pp. 302-338.

97. See *Narmada Bachao Andolan* vs. *Union of India and Others*, 2000 (7) SCALE 34, p. 120, para 226.

98. See Govind Narain Singh, "Judiciary is allowed to usurp executive powers," *The Hindu*, 1 January 1999, pp. 21. In the context of the various orders passed by the Supreme Court in the motor vehicle pollution cases in Delhi, Singh says: "Judiciary should have been well-confined to the issuance of direction—*quite strict, reprimanding and condemning to the Executive.* Fixation of a date usurps the Executive powers and it needs amending Motor Vehicles Act—powers of the Legislature too." See also the criticism of some parliamentarians, "MPs join issue with judiciary." *The Times of India*, 30 November 2000, p. 11.

99. Justice V.R. Krishna Iyer," Justices and justicing-II" *The Hindu*, 14 November 2000, at p. 10.

100. See *M.C. Mehta* vs. *Union of India*, Raj Panjwani (Compiler), *Environment Law Digest 1997* (WWF-India, June 1998), pp. 5, 7,13,119-123, 125-27.

101. *The Times of India*, 2 February 1999.

102. For a comment on these and the lackadaisical attitude of the government, see G.S. Bhargava, "Failure on human rights," *The Hindustan Times*, 18 February 1998, p. 12. See also, "Govt rejects NHRC plea on Army" *The Hindu*, 9 July 1998, p. 7.

103. Kuldip Nayar," A non- starter," *The Hindu*, 25 July 1999, at p. 10. See also Y.P.Chhibbar, "National Human Rights Commission: A View from People's Front," in K.P. Saksena , ed., note 23, at p. 119-28.

104. See, "Punjab panel rejects NHRC relief," *The Indian Express*, 11 December 2000, p. 4.

105. P.K. Doraiswamy, "Has NHRC a role? : Police firngs, " *The Hindu*, 19 September 2000, p. 21 (Open Page).

106. See the news item, "No provision for human rights courts: Minister," *The Hindu*, 30 November 2000. Reporting a patchy discussion that took place in the Rajya Sabha, while the House was considering a bill relating to salaries applicable to the employees of the NHRC.

107. See "CVC—quo vadis?," *The Hindu,* 28 November 2000, pp. OB-1; "Report reveals malfunctioning in Consumer Court," *The Hindu,* 4 January 1999, p. 7; "Will PM be brought under Lok Pal?" *The Hindu,* 24 November 2000, p. 11.

108. The negative role played by the media, particularly many of the newsmedia in Kerala, in the so- called ISRO Spying Case, leaves a bad taste in the mouth. Indeed, the media colluded with the State police and the Intelligence Bureau and perhaps 'encouraged' them to commit custodial torture and inhuman treatment not only on some hapless female foreigners, but also on some of the very eminent and highly respected space scientists of the country. One of the scientists has now approached the civil court for award of damages against the Kerala Government. For more on the case, see "ISRO scientist sues Keralas Govt.," *The Hindu,* 4 January 1999, p. 7. Also see, Buddhi Kota Subbarao, "ISRO case- what about public justice? *The Hindu,* 19 May 1998, at 21 .

109. Justice P.B. Savant, "the Press: The shadow and the guardian angel," *The Hindustan Times,* 1 December 1996. This was the keynote address delivered by Justice Savant on the occasion of the 30th Annivesary of the Press Council of India.

110. See " Self- regulation by media urged," *The Hindustan Times,* 2 November 1996, p. 3.

111. See " Press Council chief objects to IPI remarks," *The Hindu,* 29 October 1998, p.9.

112. See, e.g., the recent allegation made by Mrs. Jayanthi Natarajan of TMC, made in the Rajya Sabha that a certain NGO observed the birthday of the LTTE chief V. Prabhakaran. According to the media reports, she found the symbolism "sinister" and wanted the government to "ensure that the work of NGOs is not vitiated by bringing in other activities which pose a threat to national unity." *The Hindu,* 30 November 2000, p. 9.

3

Human Rights and Judicial Activism: Challenges and Opportunities

Prof. Mool Chand Sharma

Introduction

The notion of Human Rights is the most precious legacy of the classical and contemporary thought to culture and civilization. Few phenomena have made such a profound impact both in sweep and depth and few movements have acquired such a universal presence as the human rights movement. The concept of human rights is a dynamic one, which will find expanded expression and constantly cover new areas as human society continues to evolve to higher levels of development. The original content of philosophy of fundamental feedom was limited in the main to civil and political rights of the individual often referred to as 'First Generation' rights, which in large part called for negative obligations on the part of governments to desist from interfering with exercise of individual liberties. The realization that without guaranteeing economic, social and cultural rights, full enjoyment of civil and political rights was not possible led to inclusion of economic, social and cultural rights popularly described as 'Second Generation' rights. These rights impose more positive duty on governments to act for ensuring realization of these rights. The concept of human rights in its expanding comprehension, has now travelled to encompass what is calld 'Third Generation' or 'Solidarity' rights that include right to self-determination—a right regarded as belonging to people rather than individuals and right to development—right of considerable significance to peoples of developing countries. The 'third generation' rights extend to the right to international peace, the right to satisfactory environment favourable to sustainable development and the rights of the ethnic, religious and linguistic minorities. The journey, thus travelled by the human rights movement has really been long as well as significant, that acknowledges the brotherhood and sisterhood of the human race.

As of today most of the nations believing in rule of law have not only declared their commitment to but have also incorporated explicitly or implicitly the provisions of various international covenants on human rights in one way or the other. For example, India's concern and commitment to the cause of human rights is unambiguously stated in the text and scheme of its constitution. Representing the crystallization of values and concepts held dear in India's varied and rich cultural heritage and having its roots deep in motivational forces of the national struggle for independence, the formulation of bill of rights was among the first task to which the founding fathers addressed themselves. Coming closely on the heels the Universal Declaration of Human Rights (UDHR), inclusion of bill of rights in the constitution accorded with the contemporary democratic humanitarian temper and reflected in no simple measure, the anxiety of the founding fathers to incorporate and implement the basic principles enunciated the Universal Declaration. In fact, the Constituent Assembly incorporated in the constitution most of the rights enumerated in the Universal Declaration in two parts—the fundamental right (FRs) and the Directive Principles of the State Policy (DPs) and between them covered almost the entire field of the UDHR. The first set of rights enunciated in Articles 2 to 21 of the UDHR are incorporated under the Chapter on FRts—Articles 12 to 35 of the Constitution and the second set the rights enunciated in Articles 2 to 28 of the UDHR under the Chapter on DPs Articles 36 to 51 of the Constitution. While the first set guarantees the rights and liberties of the individual against coercive or arbitrary state action, the second seeks to lay down certain economic and social goals for attainment through a non-violent social evolution which would fulfil the basic needs of common man. In the Indian Constitutional Scheme the status of human rights is thus fairly high and inclusive of not only political and civil but also of social, cultural and economic rights. Bill of rights in the United States, European Convention on Human Rights and the Human Rights Act (1998) of U.K. are strong evidences of universal concern for and importance of human rights.

What is disturbing is that despite these numerous declarations of commitment and faith in human rights at global, regional and national levels violation of human rights is taking place at a massive scale all around day in and day out. increasing strives; heightened conflicts— ethnic, linguistic and others; glaring inequities within and amongst nations; poverty, diseases, deprivations and unfilled justified wants— all pose serious threat to protection and realization of human rights of vast section of human race. We doubt whether any country on the globe can look back to its record of human rights in the century we have just said good bye with any sense of pride. Estimates reveal that in the century just gone by some 100 million persons have been killed in armed conflict and 120 million more deaths have resulted from politically related violence. Talking of inequities 86 per cent of all wealth is enjoyed by just one fifth of the population and nearly 500 out of every 1000 persons eke out an existence on just $2 a day. Perhaps there is no need to recount the denial and violations of human rights, it is suffice to note that the basic theme of any discourse like the one we are holding today has to be and must be the conversion of rhetoric of human rights into reality.

Human Rights and Positivization

The rhetoric of human rights draws on the moral resources of our belief in the significance of an underlying common humanity and points in the direction of a type of society which ensures that the basic human dignity and reasonable aspirations of its members are effectively realised. Human rights movement can, therefore, both be a potential source for radical critique of actual social arrangements and also a powerful basis for working out alternative institutional practices. Thus the language of human rights carries with it a great forces of practical significance. However, what is necessary is that the highly general statements of these rights which ideally use the language of universality, inalienability and unfeasibility should be transferred into more particular formulations, if the rhetoric of human rights is to have any significant impact on the resolution of social, economic and other problems. The meaning and scope of each right has to be clarified, the content and location of any co-relative duties to which it give rise must be spelt out and the permissible range of exceptions and limitations specified. This work which is called positivization of human rights takes place at different levels that includes Constitution making, ordinary law making and judicial decision making.

The most obvious form in which human rights are positivized is through specific constitutional provisions which incorporate statement or bill of rights which are given the status of fundamental law as is the case in India (discussed earlier). These rights incorporated in bill of rights, are then regarded as superior to ordinary legislation and are used to render invalid any legislative action or administrative or governmental decisions which are held to run counter to the rights enumerated in the bill. Institutionally this invalidation is normally achieved through the medium of Courts whose task is to rule to the constitutionality of legislation as also executive action and to determine whether fundamental rights of the citizens have been infringed in particular cases.

Nature, Scope of Bill of Rights and Courts

The above mechanism allocates a crucial role and gives significant power in positivizing human rights to Courts, since the type of decisions to be made in applying highly general statements of rights to specific circumstances results in effect and substance in creating detailed formulations which are applicable in the particular circumstances of each case. The bill of rights can at best enumerate only the broad statements derived from human rights rhetoric but to spell out their contours and parameters, limitations and exceptions, reach and significance is the task that lies ultimately with the judiciary. Significance of the task assigned to the judiciary becomes further evident when one sees that there are certain human rights which operate as restraints on the power of the State, Judiciary is need and its role becomes crucial in enforcing these restraints when occasion demands as the possibility of the State abusing or misusing the massive power it possesses and violating these restraints is too high.

It is important to remember that the courts in many countries including the United States and India enjoy vast powers including the power to overturn actions both legislative as well as executive. In India now after the famous case of *Kesvananda Bharti* where the Apex Court invented the doctrine of 'basic features' of the

Constitution, even constitutional amendment could be struck down by the courts as violative of the 'basic features'. Thus the power of the judiciary to interpret laws including the provisions of the Constitution clubbed with power of judicial review and the growing acceptance of judicial law and sometimes judicial policy making puts judiciary in unequally important position for translating human rights rhetoric into reality. But as Justice Bhagwati has pointed out a judiciary which is, strong and independent; immune from pressures or influences; committed to the cause of human rights; alert to repel gross or subtle attacks against these rights; capable of rising above concealed political preferences, ambitions and other such weaknesses and fearless of executive reaction alone can discharge this heavy responsibility. As judiciary is the bulwark that stands between the state and its members protecting their human rights, judicial indifference and timidity is a greater threat to these rights than their violation by other branches of the state. Thus the task of a judge in human rights area is acute rather than deferential ; creative rather than mechanical; evolutionary rather than status-quoits; humanist rather than formalist. That judicial approach is crucial becomes evident when one sees how the same American Constitution in 1986 was read by the judges permitting social segregation in public sources and then in 1954 in *Brown* vs. *Board of Education* as forbidding it? On our own pitch, it is instructive to note as to how did the apex Court in 1950 reduced the constitutionally guaranteed fundamental right to liberty to a mere provision in the Code of Criminal Procedure in *A.K. Gopalan's* case showed firmness to stand on side of freedom and liberty in the case of *Menaka Gandhi* in the year 1978.

Human Rights and Judicial Activism

The proposition we would like to submit here is that the judicial activism and dynamic constitutional interpretation which some times include judicial law and policy-making is justified in the protection of human rights and individual liberties. It is stressed that the case made out here is for exercise of judicial activism in the field of fundamental human rights and not judicial activism, per se. In his famous work *Democracy and Distrust: A Theory of Judicial Review (1980)* justifies policy-making role (he and others described such role as non-interpreturist) of the U.S. Supreme Court in the limited areas of 'First Amendment' (freedom of expression, etc.) and 'equal protection' Reliance on judicial activism in these two areas, he thinks, is aimed at serving the norm of political participation— participation by common people in the political process—by "clearing the channels of political change on the one hand and by correcting certain kinds of discrimination against minorities". First amendment rights whether constitutionalised by framers or not, Ely asserts, "must none the less be protected (by the judiciary) strenuously so, because they are on heal to the functioning of an open and effective democratic process..." And since impediments to free speech, publication and political association hinder the democratic process, Ely argues that 'unblocking stoppages in the democratic process is what judicial review ought pre-eminently to be about'. He thinks that judiciary rather than an electoral accountable institutions is best suited to perform this task because have vested interest in presenting the status quo. Even in the area of equal protection, Ely's justification is the maintenance of the process of democratic government. Here the role of the judiciary becomes crucial in ensuring that the persons belonging to certain minorities are not denied, the opportunity to participate in the accommodation of the political processes and access to the bounty of representative government. However, Ely bound his support for judicial activism only to questions of participation in democratic processes which according to us is crucial and pre-condition for securing human rights.

The most unqualified justification for judicial activism and policy- making has come from Michael Perry. According to him, the greatest justification is the functional justification. He said the justification for non-interpretivism is in the fact that it serves a crucial governmental function, perhaps even an indispensable one, that no other practice can realistically be expected to serve—and serves in a manner that accommodates the principle of electorally accountable policy-making. And that crucial function, according to him, is the 'elaboration and enforcement by the Courts of values, pertaining to human rights, even if not constitutionalised...' it is the function of deciding what rights, beyond those specified by the framers, individuals should and shall have against government'. He points out that various political—moral issues which the U.S. Supreme Court has grappled for example, in the areas of freedom of expression, racial discrimination and due process the Court did not rely on tradition or established convention' but engaged in a moral revaluation of established conventions, redefinition of fundamental rights provisions to suit the modern context, thereby using such opportunities for moral development. Perry also points out that it is not as if in every case brought to the court on human rights issues that it grapples with a fundamental political moral problem. In many such cases the court is simply "elaborating" a principle working out what it understands to the details or implications of a principle that the court began to establish, but only began, more or less inchoately, in an earlier case or the court is devising procedures to enable it and other courts to enforce compliance with the principle.

When one considers comparative institutional competence to deal with issues such as distributive justice and the role of government, freedom of expression, sencism, rights of prisoners or bonded labourers, electorally accountable institutions seem unsuited to deal with such issues in a faithful way to the notion of moral re-evaluation and evolution as in opinion of many like Perry executive especially legislative officials tend to deal with fundamental political-moral problems, at least highly controversial ones, by reflexive reference to the established moral conventions of the greater part of their particular constituencies. A concern for popularity and for remaining in office is not particularly conducive to the notion of moral evolution. Legislators see their primary functions as registering the actual preferences of their constituents and generally excel at awarding highly controversial political-moral issues on which they do not like to gamble their political lives. This concern for remaining in office is not a particularly good way to keep faith with the notion of moral evolution, which according to the Perry and many others requires ongoing, vigorous re-evaluation of established moral conventions. Seen in this context, the courts taking active and creative approach at least on issues of human rights and human justice can remedy what would otherwise be a serious shortcoming in the political system—the absence if any policy-making institution that grapples with fundamental political moral questions on regular basis other than by mechanical reference to establish moral conventions. Thus a visionary and forward- looking judiciary is an essential ally in the march towards realizing human rights and human justice. Days for "Block Stonian" approach to judicial process are gone.

In India Courts particularly the apex Court in last about two decades has moved forward with speed in protecting human rights especially of marginalised, deprived and weak. It has revolutionalised the criminal justice system, evolved a new kind of prison jurisprudence and has come to protect interest of bonded, underpaid and exploited labourers. It has invented green jurisprudence and has created new rights such as right to education and also evolved a new kind of compensatory jurisprudence. Thus it has come to the aid of not only first generation rights but also social and economic rights. In order to do this judge liberalised various doctrines and technicalities, invented new methods and techniques; gave expansive interpretation to provisions in the Constitution such as Article 21; invented new means to make executive accountable. Of course this needed combination of conviction, courage and judicial craftsman skill on part of judges. The journey travelled is a unique blend of what Justice Bhagwati describes as 'technical', 'juristic' and 'social' activism.' Technical activism' consists of declaration by judges of freedom to have recourse to wide range of techniques and choices. Such activism is concerned merely with keeping juristic techniques open ended, it does not specify when and for what purpose a judge can have recourse to this kind of activism. In contrast 'juristic activism' is not concerned merely with the appropriation of increased power but is concerned as well with the creation of new concepts irrespective of the purpose they serve. The common law itself, which over the centuries has been fashioned and refashioned to deal with new claims and demands and thus develop new concepts and principles, is an example of 'juristic activism'. In this kind of activism judge is not so much concerned with the quality of social consequences generated. The new concepts may help to preserve the status quo. Thus what is necessary for human rights approach is blending of 'technical' and 'juristic' activism with the third kind, namely, 'social' activism. Judicial activism in any of its forms be it 'technical' or 'juristic' is always exercised for a purpose may be sometimes in a thin disguise. Thus what is important is not the form but the purpose for which activism is exercised. Thus, it is the instrumental or social use of the judicial activism that needs to be the *mantra* for human rights approach. It is this kind of activism that is 'social' activism that is the need of human rights approach. However, at the same time the note of caution administered by Lord Woolf Speaking for the Privy Council while construing the Hong Kong Bill of Rights in *Lee Kwongkut:s Case (1993)* and reiterated by India's Chief Justice while speaking on *'Human Rights and the Role of the Courts'* to Indo-British

Legal Forum (2000) should be borne in mind. Lord Woolf whilst Reaffirming the principles of construction of Bill of Rights adopted few earlier cases said that "while the Hong Kong judiciary should be zealous in upholding an individual's rights under the Hong Kong Bill, it is also necessary to ensure that disputes as to the effect of the Bill are not allowed to go out of hand. The issues involving the Hong Kong Bill should be approached with realism and good sense and kept in proportion." However, we think that care be taken that the wholesome prescription of good sense and realism is not misconstrued as a general prescription for undue judicial deference to the judgement of the legislature or the executive.

Judicial Approach

The judicial function in relation to human rights is thus to a significant extent a creative one. The creativity, however, is not absolutely unfettered. It is required to be informed and inspired by the social philosophy of the Constitution and Constitution alone. The social philosophy of the Indian Constitution resides in its Preamble and two chapters are one on Fundamental Rights and other on the Directive Principles of the State Policy. This philosophy is primarily aimed at ensuring social and economic justice to all with special focus on deprived, marginalised and exploited—another name for human rights for all.

It can be safely stated that the record of Indian Judiciary in performing its task in relation to human rights has by and large (except on few occasions) been laudatory. Due to the paucity of time and space neither we propose nor we consider it necessary to examine in detail various judicial developments and pronouncements but would only keep into few selected areas illustratively to understand the approach and techniques adopted by the courts.

Let us take criminal jurisprudence as illustration of how creative and human rights approach of the judiciary has brought structural as well as institutional reforms. An instance of literal and narrow interpretation of a vital fundamental right, namely Article 21 in the Indian Constitution is the early decision of the Indian Apex Court in the case of *A.K. Gopalan (1950)*. Article 21 of the Constitution reads: "No person shall be deprived of his life or personal liberty except according to procedure established by law". The court ruled that once there was a law, which prescribed a procedure, there was compliance with Article 21. The court refused to infuse the procedure with principles of natural justice and concentrated solely upon the existence of enacted law. Justice S.R. Das in his judgement gave an illustration that if a law provided that the cook of the Bishop of Rochester be boiled in oil, it would be valid under Article 21. This view stood for more than 27 years until it came to be overruled in *Maneka Gandhi's* Case. In this famous case the court held that the "procedure contemplated by Article 21 must answer the test of reasonableness. It must be 'right, just and fair', and not arbitrary, fanciful or oppressive; otherwise it would be no procedure at all and the requirements of Article 21 would not be satisfied." Thus, Article 21 assumed new dimension and the creative judicial approach led to introduction of procedural due process in the Indian constitutional jurisprudence with much positive impact on evolving human rights jurisprudence. It is significant to note that question of inclusion of requirement of due process in the provisions of Article 21 was discussed by the founding fathers, opinion was sought from Justice Falix Frankfurter and was ultimately decided not to include it in the provisions of Article 21. Thus, neither the text nor the history supported reading of 'due process' requirement in the provisions of Article 21. But aiming at providing greater protection of human rights of the citizens that court indulged into superb example of constitutional policy-making and read requirement of due process in the provisions of Article 21.

This new interpretation of Article 21 has laid the foundation of a new kind of criminal and prisons jurisprudence more sensitive and responsive to human rights approach. Based on the broad interpretation, Article 21 has been invoked in the case of numerous under trials languishing jails. The Supreme Court ruled that "speedy trial we mean reasonably expeditious trial. It is an integral and essential part of the fundamental right to life and liberty enshrined in Article 21 and a procedure whereby undertrials remained in jail for periods longer than the maximum term for which they could have been sentenced if considered was not a fair, just and reasonable procedure." It was held in *Hussainara Khatoon's Case (1979)* that in such cases Article 21 was violated and several undertrials were ordered to be released. Again in the case of *Madhav Hoskot* vs. *State of Maharashtra (1978)* the court by a liberal interpretation of Article 21 that a procedure that does not make legal services available to an accused who is poor and cannot afford a lawyer and would, therefore, go through the trial without legal assistance cannot be regarded as 'reasonable, fair and just'. Spelling out the right to legal aid in a criminal proceeding from the language of Article 21 the court ruled that 'this is a constitutional right of every accused unable to engage a lawyer ..... And the state is under a mandate to provide a lawyer to an accused if the circumstances and the needs of justice so require. This holding of the court is a major step in the direction of humanising criminal jurisprudence. In the same case the court gave further impetus to its human rights approach when it ordered the release of number of undertrial prisoners without insisting on monetary obligation. A great step towards humanizing bail system, which otherwise is heavily loaded in favour of rich and powerful.

The most significant instance of expansive interpretation of a fundamental right and powerful endorsement of social and economic rights is the decision in *Francis Coralie Mullan's Case (1981).* The court held that the expression"life" in Article 21 does not connote merely physical existence but embraces something more. It includes 'the right to live with human dignity and all that goes along with it, namely, the bare necessaries of life such as adequate nutrition, clothing and shelter over the head'. The court, however, realizing the complexities involved said that the magnitude of this right would depend upon the extent of economic development of the country, but in any case, the concept of 'life' must include the right to the basic necessities and the right to carry on such functions and activities as constitute the bare minimum expression of human life. The court in *Olga Tellis Case (1985)* held that the right to livelihood is included in the right to life, as no person can live without the means of living. Affirming its commitment to socio-economic rights and its abhorrence of human exploitation in the form of bonded labour the Court in *Bandhua Mukti Morcha's Case (1984)* stated that it is the fundamental right of everyone in this country to live with human dignity and that it is the plainest requirement of Articles 21 and 23 and that bonded labourers must be identified and on release be rehabilitated. The court not only issued various directions regarding rehabilitation but also required the progress in the matter to be periodically reported to the court. Thus it evolved a monitoring approach as well.

In *Paschim Bangal Khet Mazdoor Sabha* vs. *State of West Bengal (1996)* the court carried forward its human rights approach to include various social and economic aspects and held that providing medical facilities for the people is an essential obligation of the State.

The court recognized the importance of financial resources but ruled that the state cannot avoid its constitutional obligation in this regard on account of financial constraints.

Expansive interpretation to Article 21 has been relied for environmental protection, to guarantee pollution free air and water on the reasoning that the expression 'life' connotes not merely physical existence but also the quality of life. In *M.C. Mehta* vs. *Union of India (1987)* the court ordered the closure of some tanneries which were discharging industrial effluents into the river Ganga. The court justified the closure by invoking the expanded meaning of the expression 'life' in Article 21. The court was conscious that closure of tanneries may bring unemployment and loss of revenue but in its view, life, health and ecology have greater importance for the people. adopting a similar approach the court in *Rural Litigation and Entitlement Kendra* vs. *State of U.P.* (1997) pointed out harmful effects of reckless exploitation of natural resource by deforestation and mining operation in the Doon Valley. The court directed the stoppage of further mining operations in certain areas.

Recently the court has issued several directions to combat pollution. In *M.C. Mehta* vs. *Union of India (1998)* the court in a Writ Petition filed in public interest raising various issues concerning proper management and control of traffic and vehicular pollution noticed that control of vehicular pollution and protection of environment is primarily the function of the executive and its obligation to devise suitable measures and provide machinery for rigid enforcement of statutory rules, etc., but that the executive had failed to discharge its obligations. The court taking recourse to Article 142 therefore issued various directions.

Another area in which the court has given strong evidences of using its power creatively is its concern for women's rights. Taking aid of international covenants in an imaginative fashion the court in a recent judgement in the case of *Vishakha* vs. *State of Rajasthan* dealing with a case of sexual harassment referred to the rule of judicial construction that regard must be paid to international conventions and norms for construing domestic law when there is no inconsistency between them and there is a void in domestic law. The court in this case protected the rights of working women against sexual harassment in workplaces relying on provisions of the convention on the *Elimination of all Forms of Discrimination against Women (CEDAW).* The court issued detailed guidelines including for constituting committee and its composition for looking into complaints of harassment in each department and organization. The court also held that unless a detailed law is enacted there guidelines are bending. In its subsequent judgement in *Apparel Export Promotion Council* vs. *A.K. Chopra (1999)* the court went a step forward and defined 'sexual harassment' as there existed no other specific legislation dealing with the subject.

Apart from giving expensive interpretation to fundamental rights such as to right to life and liberty enshrined in Article 21, the judiciary in India like its counterpart in the United States has also deduced fundamental rights which are not specifically mentioned in the chapter on Fundamental Rights on the principle that certain unarticulated rights are implicit in the enumerated guarantees. For example, in several decisions of the Supreme Court freedom of the press has been held to be implicit in the guarantee of freedom of speech and expression. In India there is no legislation securing freedom of information. The Supreme Court deduced the right to know and the right of access to information on the reasoning that "the concept of an open government is the direct emanation from the right to know which seems implicit in the right of free speech and expression guaranteed under Article 19(1) (a)".

Another significant aspect of judicial approach has been the evolution of compensatory jurisprudence. It has rightly been said that rights without remedies are useless. As the present Chief Justice of India has said, a mere declaration of invalidity of a detention order or finding of a custodial violence would not provide meaningful remedy to a person whose human rights have been violated." Although the Indian Constitution contains no provision for awarding compensation for infringement of a person's fundamental right, the Supreme Court has, in some cases, ordered compensation by the State. Finally it is in the case of *Nilabati Behra* vs. *State of Orissa (1993)* the court created an obligation on the part of the state to compensate to the victim and relatives of the one whose death occurs in the custody of the police. It said: "where the infringement of fundamental rights is established, the court cannot stop by giving a mere declaration. It must proceed further and give compensatory relief, not by way of damages as in civil action but by way of compensation under the public law jurisdiction for the wrong done, due to breach of public duty by the State of not protecting the fundamental right to life of the citizen. To repair the wrong done and given judicial redress for legal injury is a compulsion of judicial conscience." This approach represents the finest example not only of judicialy craftsmanship but also of responsiveness and sensitivity to the cause of human rights. Carrying forward this approach the court in the case of *D.K. Basu* vs. *State of West Bengal (1997)* went to the extent of holding that since compensation was directed by the courts to be paid by the State, was vicariously liable for the illegal acts of its officials and the reservation entered by the Government of India to Article 9(5) of the International Covenant on Civil and Political Rights which confers on the victim of unlawful arrest or detention an enforceable right to compensation, had lost its relevance. Supreme example of policy-making in the hands of the judiciary in the service of cause of human rights.

Conclusion

Looking into above discussed developments one can easily state that the judiciary in India except on certain occasions such as emergency period (1975-77) has performed its role in relation to human rights with fair degree of sensitivity and responsiveness. However, that does not mean that everything is all right. There are those who and with some justification disapprove the growing judicial indulgence into the domain of other branches and consider it undemocratic. Also there are those who think that in certain key areas of human rights violations the courts have not shown the responsiveness it ought to have. Recently the judgement of the Supreme Court in the matter of Sardar Sarover Dam has come under a lot of criticisms in the hands of various human rights groups. They considered this judgement as in sensitive to the cause of human rights particularly of those who are going to be displaced as a result of this project. These groups believe that this judgement would not only deprive displaced of their rights to livelihood but would also violate their cultural rights and rights to heritage.

In conclusion we would say that there can be no two opinions that the judiciary is under an obligation more than any other branches of governance to protect and promote human rights. The courts must ensure that these rights are easily accessible particularly to the poor and marginalised and should not remains the preserve of only rich and mighty. If the last decades of gone by century witnessed the ever expanding role of the state, the next few decades of the new millennium in our view are going to experience increasing role of

Multinational Corporations (MNCs).These MNCs in certain respects are going to exercise power and influence greater than and even on States and thus the challenge including before the judiciary would be how to make them accountable and responsive to the needs of human rights jurisprudence. Again new millennium is going to be led by science and technology revolution more than the gone by. We have already witnessed the emergence of gene-technology, biologically manipulated products and many other such wonders.Thus another challenge before human rights jurisprudence is to ensure that modern developments in science and technology do not acquire the arrogance and be the carrier of new kinds of human exploitation. The need is to ensure that new science and technology become responsive and gets dedicated to the course of humanity and human development.

4
Public Interest Litigation

J.C. Batra

It is imperative to examine the term 'Public Interest' before we embark upon the sphere of Public Interest Litigation (PIL). The 'Public Interest' signifies the interest of all citizens. A judicial pronouncement which serves the ends of whole public rather than some individuals. In other words, the results of a litigation which serves the members of the whole community is a PIL. A procedural public interest would consist of an assurance, in the decision process, that widest interest possible range of interests will be consulted.

The struggle to solve socio-economic problems is never ending. There is no single institution or mechanism which can solve the problems facing the society. It is difficult to imagine that we can succeed here in defining the "Public Interest" in a manner that will resolve the matter and end the debate.

The Supreme Court of India and certain High Courts have assumed the role of creator of laws, law reformers and as well as administrators of justice. They have entered into the hereto forbidden grounds as saviors of the teeming millions have -nots, naked, starved, people through judicial activism and by the aid of dispensing justice summarily in PIL. It has its own disadvantage. No expert evidence is available. No thorough examination of the adverse interests of the parties involved is conducted. Short-term solutions of the long-term problems are handed over without looking into the economic, social and legal compatibility.

The Supreme Court has earned laurels by pronouncing the judgments in the field of preventing pollution and environment degradation. But if one examines closely, he finds that things at the ground level have remained unchanged. The holy Ganges is still polluted. The river Yamuna which has been turned into a sewage drain continues to flow near the Supreme Court of India. The pollution due to motor vehicles, buses, trucks, three wheelers is on the increase in each big city.

The administrative machinery has become totally corrupt and lacking in its will to implement the legislation to prevent pollution and environmental degradation. No order of the Supreme Court can be implemented, where there is unwilling bureaucracy.

The judicial activism through PIL may seem to give a ray of hope but infinite resources economic as well as technical are required to solve the socio-economic and environmental problems faced by the country. No judgement of any court, unless it is implemented can change the ground level realities in the fields of environment pollution.

The latest controversy over the CNG buses... vs... Diesel buses has in fact brought more suffering for the general public and the commuters in Delhi. The Supreme Court of India could not force the State or the Central Government to provide sufficient supply of CNG Gas and replace the diesel buses. The lawful permit holders of diesel buses have been grounded, without being given any prior show cause notice or reason and without cancellation of their road permits. They have also suffered huge losses which neither the State nor the Centre is likely to compensate. Even imposition of penalty for Rs. 500 and or Rs. 1000 per day on the diesel bus operators does not solve the pollution problem. In *M.C. Mehta's Case* (1987) I SSC P 898 the Supreme Court has mentioned that all the letters addressed to the judges should be processed through PIL cell in the Supreme Court of India and after scrutiny be placed before the Chief Justice. Similar cells have been established in the High Courts also to save precious time of the Supreme Court and High Courts.

The predominant concern of the social activists like H.D. Shourie and M.C. Mehta have been to bring to the notice of the Apex Court. Some of the acute socio-economic and environmental problems facing the country through PIL do not provide any permanent solution. The PIL provides the very prestigious forum to them to get good publicity rather than punish the guilty and / or set the administrative machinery in action.

The PIL is not a panacea to cure all ills for it partakes the limitation of law, resources and of authority of the court in getting its order implemented.

The perpetual problems like environmental pollution and ecological imbalances call for greater, in-depth study and solution with the cooperation of the State and the authorities concerned. The vigilant public can also cooperate. There is no shortcut solution.

PIL has mainly been encouraged by judicial activism, where government fails or its functionaries or the instrumentality show apathy and indifference towards their obligations. To illustrate, the damage which was being caused to the Taj Mahal due to Mathura Refinery was prevented on Supreme Court's intervention. Recently the security aspect of the said monument has been taken care of by the Supreme Court of India again due to threat by terrorist organizations.

Polluting leather tanneries of Kanpur have been stopped.

The Common Cause Society even filed a petition against the striking lawyers and the Supreme Court intervened and set forth the guidelines in this regard.

But all this is at the cost of common consumers of justice, whose cases are undecided. As PIL, and these by lanes of dispensing justice like a by-pass surgery and not curing the disease. The arrears of cases pending in the subordinate courts and High Courts are a slur on the judicial system which is collapsing. PIL is no remedy for providing speedy justice to the millions of litigants who are waiting their cases to be decided for years.

PIL has no doubt served as a warning to the slow and sluggish government machinery. It has yet not provided the common man any remedy or relief against poverty, illiteracy, unemployment, disease and deprivation nor has it made justice which could accessible to him at his door step which could make his life more meaningful and dignified.

5

Constitutional Governance and Economic-Social Rights

N.R. Madhava Menon

One of the greatest accomplishments of civilization in the twentieth century is the acceptance of human rights as an integral part of governance for which the state, whatever its form, has accepted obligations and accountability. Today the United Nations may be characterized as a human rights maintenance organization, clarifying, promoting and monitoring the human rights related activities of governments the world over. There is hardly a constitution which does not speak of the rights of the individual vis-a-vis the state and the mechanisms whereby they are to be made accessible to the citizens. There is a strong NGO movement supported by an increasingly activist judiciary and an independent media to monitor human rights violations and to seek accountability of the powers that be at different levels of government. Admittedly, there is a human rights ideology emerging everywhere informing and illuminating public policy and governance with varying degrees of success against strong currents of authoritarianism and abuse of power.

In India, the story of this progress towards democratic governance based on human rights is indeed impressive during the last fifty one years though the picture is not as rosy as one would expect. Communal politics and violence are still real threats to peace and fraternity. Corruption in government and public life is eating up whatever progress made so far and is constantly making the life of the ordinary citizen miserable. Increasing criminalisation and decreasing efficiency of the law enforcement apparatus pose a real and imminent danger to the fragile human rights situation in the country. Militancy and terrorism in some parts of the country complicate the situation tending to brutalise the security forces and in the process, expose the hollowness of the human rights record of an otherwise peace-loving nation with rich cultural traditions. While a lot still remains to be done both in policies and programmes, no one can deny that the "right consciousness" acquired during the last few decades in the country is capable of sustaining itself hopefully with increasing efficiency in the future. Given the democratic nature of the policy, given the commitment to rule of law and independence of the judiciary, one can argue that at least in the area of civil and political rights, the future holds out promises which can put India in the forefront of nations honouring human rights.

Poverty: A Threat to Human Rights

However, the picture is not so reassuring when one looks at the state of socio-economic rights. Poverty is indeed the greatest threat to humn dignity and a nation which cannot provide for the basic needs of all human beings has no prospects for good governance. Statistics in this regard is shocking and the reality is shameful for every self-respecting citizen. Some take satisfaction by arguing that socio-economic rights are not rights in the strict sense of the term. Others point out that the situation is same or even worse in most parts of the developing world and therefore the Indian State cannot be particularly accused of rights violation. Yet another group even go to the extent of saying that individuals themselves are the cause to their poverty and the State cannot be blamed for their condition! Unfortunately, the rights in liberal societies. During the days of the cold war, the Communist Bloc countries and others following a middle path were giving equal, if not greater, attention to poverty eradication justifying it in terms of the right to equality. In capitalist societies, the emphasis was more on freedom, liberty and equality was considered a natural result of a free society. The role of the State in building and egalitaring social order has been rather minimal in western capitalist societies where individual choice was taken to be the key for rights and good governance. Of course, the condition of western societies, many of them being former colonial powers, was much different because of historical reasons. Poverty in absolute terms was a negligible phenomenon in the developed world. Till the breaking up of the former Soviet Union and the disintegration of communism in Eastern Europe, poverty jurisprudence gave a different ideological thrust to the "Rights Debate" in nearly half the world. The rights discourse was more friendly in socio-economic rights and state organs took the responsibilities in this regard very seriously.

With the advent of competitive free market economy and globalization in trade relations, a situation is fast emerging which does not augur well for marginalised and underprivileged sections of society. The name of the game is survival of the fittest and there is no level playing field for the late starters. The State is expected to withdraw from economic operations and the market, dominated by the economic of developed countries, will dictate policies for production and distribution of wealth. Individualism and consumerism will be the dominant ideology and equality which cannot support it may not find acceptance in the rights discourse. While the middle and upper classes may reap the benefits, the lower classes may suffer increasing deprivation because of labour displacement as a result of changes in the agrarian economy.This is already evident in places where agriculture is changed to cash crops or when fishing is mechanised to suit an export market. With rising level of consumption on the part of the urban middle class and the inability of the state to adequately support the social welfare sector, there is every likelihood of social tensions resulting in terrorism and violence which again impacts adversely on the poorer classes. The pressure on the state for reduction of subsidies and for limiting the public distribution system is indicative of the trends which a weakend state will find increasingly difficult to resist. The inevitable consequence of such a development is starvation for those living below the poverty line. It is in this context, human rights discourse will have to exmine the prospects of better implementation of right to live, right to education, right to health care and clean environment, right to work, right to food, right to housing, etc.

It seems difficult to reverse the march of globalisation and marketisation absorbing the Third World economies. The only option seems to be to take advantage of emerging opportunities while ensuring the basic needs of those who are outside the competitive market. Human rights language is what state entities and world bodies understand. However, human rights technology does not at present provide adequate techniques and tools to realize basic human needs ever though the Universal Declaration and Bill or Rights contain guarantees in this regard. There is indeed a poverty in the laws and legal institutions when it comes to the protection of socio-economic rights to the same level of civil and political rights. This is where the legal community will have to work with the economists and other social scientists for evolving acceptable norms and procedures in the introduction of human rights discipline in the municipal and global markets. The next few years are crucial for India and its human rights commitment, we cannot afford to fail lest posterity should blame us for lip service to human aspirations and the right to be human.

SOCIO-ECONOMIC RIGHTS AND THE UNIVERSAL DECLARATION OF HUMAN RIGHTS

In 1976, the International Covenant on Economic, Social and Cultural Rights came into force with 35 State Parties ratifying it. India ratified it later. Today more than 125 State Parties have ratified it. The different rights recognized in the Covenant are described in Articles 6 to 15.

Economic Rights

Article 6 - Right to Work, Vocational Guidance and Training.
Article 7 - Right to Just and Favourable Condition of Work.
Article 8 - Right to form and join Trade Unions, Right to Strike.
Article 11 - Right the adequate standard of living including Food and Shelter.

Social Rights

Article 9 - Right to Social Security.
Article 10 - Rights of the Family, Mothers and Children.
Article 12 - Right to Physical and Mental Health.

Cultural Rights

Article 13 - Right to Education.
Article 14 - Right to Compulsory Primary Education.
Article 15 - Right to participate in cultural activities and to enjoy Scientific Progress.

There is no International Court for Human Rights, nor is there at the current stage of international law, a possibility to address individual complaints or State complaints about alleged violations of the rights enshrined in the Covenant on Economic, Social and Cultural Rights. The Covenant does include a system of obliging

State Parties to report on the "measures which they have adopted and the progress made in achieving the observance of the rights recognized herein" (Article 16).

The reporting procedure to the Covenant on Economic, Social and Cultural Rights had a slow start as the UN was more concerned with Civil and Political Rights. In 1985 the UN established a Committee on Economic, Social and Cultural Rights of 18 independent experts which meets annually for three weeks to review the States reports. The Committee started its work in 1987. It revised its procedures and gave comments on the contents of specific rights and in 1990 issued revised guidelines for the submission of reports by States. The reports are to be submitted every five years. The reporting guidelines have no legal force and are merely recommendations concerning the reporting procedures. However, they do contribute to standard setting and in this sense, is a landmark in the process of strengthening these rights.

The Committee on Economic, Social and Cultural Rights entertains additional information from non-governmental organizations (NGOs) and encourages participation of NGOs in the preparation of the reports and in their publication in the respective countries after submission.

While thousands of reports on violations of civil and political rights are submitted to the UN Centre on Human Rights every year, reports on violations of economic, social or cultural rights have practically been negligible. If socio-economic rights have to assume a better status in the Human Rights agenda of the United Nations, States as well as NGOs should start taking them seriously, monitor and report its violations to the UN Human Rights Centre and evolve techniques and tools to direct international efforts for better protection of basic needs. The parallel reporting procedure for NGOs now evolved by the Economic Rights Committee in Geneva provides an opportunity to get the system of work for the advancement of socio-economic rights.

It is now acknowledged that Human Rights are indivisible, and as such, there cannot be sufficient protection for civil and political rights without equal protection for socio-economic rights. In fact, claims of equality and non-discrimination have often revolved around social security benefits. The reason offered for the grouping of human rights into two distinct categories was that socio-economic rights, unlike civil and political rights, were not immediately realisable and could only be achieved over a period of time as resources become available. The nature of state obligations differed in the two sets of rights.

Whatever the reasons for the prioritisation of human rights and the relative neglect of soci-economic rights in the past, today experience has revealed the indivisibility of rights and the importance of enriching individual capabilities rather than overdependence on restructuring political and economic systems. Education and health care are needed to find employment and to lead free and fulfilling lives. It is perhaps the realisation of this obvious connection which compelled the United Nations to call the Social Summit of 1995 at Copenhagen. The proceedings of this World Summit constitute a reiteration of the States Parties commitment to work towards the early eradication of poverty and to provide a favourable climate for enjoyment of socio-economic rights.

Socio-Economic Rights and the Indian Constitution

The bifurcation of human rights in the International Bill of Rights seem to have influenced the treatment of human rights in the constitutions throughout the world. Civil and political rights are given greater importance and put in a higher pedestal in terms of enforceability and respect. Social and economic rights are treated as judicially not enforceable directives or policy guidelines for the governments. Thus socio-economic rights came to be regarded as the exclusive domain of the executive and legislative branches of the government with the judiciary having to do very little in terms of their enforcement. The Indian Constitution reflects this dual approach to human rights. While Part III dealing with Fundamental Rights deals largely with what are called civil and political rights, Part IV titled the Directive Principles of State Policy in corporate what the International Human Rights Instruments designate as socio-economic rights. Concerned with the importance of the latter for realising the goals of the Preamble, the constitution makers while excluding the courts from enforcement of socio-economic rights, declared that "they are nevertheless fundamental in the governance of the country and it shall be the duty of the State to apply these principles in making laws (Article 37)."

The broad scheme of Part IV on Directive Principles of State Policy reflect the range of socio-economic Rights (or entitlements recognized by the Indian Constitution.)

Article 38	:	State to secure a social order for the promotion of welfare of people.
Article 39	:	State to direct its polity towards securing equality in the matter of access to resources.
Article 39A	:	State to secure equal justice and free legal aid to the poor.
Article 41	:	Right to work, to education and public assistance in cases of unemployment, old age, sickness, disablement and of undeserved want.
Article 42	:	State to make provision for just and maternity relief.
Article 43	:	State to secure a living wage and decent standard of life as well as full enjoyment of leisure.
Article 43A	:	State to secure participation of workers in management of industries.
Article 44	:	State to secure a uniform civil code.
Article 45	:	State to provide for free and compulsory education for all children until the age of 14 years within a period of ten years from the commencement of the constitution.
Article 46	:	State to promote the educational and economic interests of the Scheduled Castes, Scheduled Tribes and other weaker sections.
Article 47	:	Duty of the State to raise the level of nutrition, standard of living and public health.
Article 48A	:	State to protect and improve the environment, to safeguard the forests and wildlife.

It is often pointed out that the civil and political rights in Part III are couched in negative language injuncting the State from doing certain things. Of course, there are exceptions where affirmative action is expected of State for fulfilling some of the obligations in the Part [Articles 15 (4), 16 (4)]. For a long time, the judiciary adopted an approach of helplessness and treated socio-economic rights as subservient to fundamental rights (civil and political rights). This philosophy permeated the civil society as well. It was taken for granted that no viable legal claims against the government can arise for non-fulfilment of obligations under Part IV which contained the socio-economic rights. The dominant view is the courts are ill- equipped to adjudicate socio-economic rights, because:

(a) these rights are not precise and well articulated (b) they involve complex question of competing social policies (c) they require substantial resources the disposition of which only elected bodies can decide and (d) the adversary system is ill-suited for organizing public goods in the best public interest.

There is an impression in society that governments are expected to provide socio-economic services free of charge to all citizens which tend to support the separation of these rights from the civil and political rights. Primarily betterment of standard of living is the responsibility of individuals. State obligations are intended to supplement these individual efforts whenever and wherever needed and to enhance the capacity of individuals to achieve such conditions on all equal opportunity basis. Those who cannot meet basic needs and have no opportunities should be the responsibility of the State.

The Indian Supreme Court had to abandon its earlier approach of all ofness and detachment with Part IV. Invoking the mandate of Article 37 that the obligations of Part IV are "fundamental in the governance of the country and therefore binding on all three wings of government, the Court evolved a strategy of seeking support from Directive Principles of State Policy for interpreting the scope of State obligations in respecting Fundamental Rights. In this exercise the judiciary also sought assistance of international treaties and agreements obligating States parties to enforce socio-economic rights.What emerged from an activist court is a new human rights jurisprudence obliterating the division and prioritisation of rights and giving a fresh lease of life in honouring socio-economic rights. Through this process of judicial activism during the last two decades in India, the following socio-economic rights are judicially declared as enforceable fundamental rights as they form integral part of: (a) right to life and personal liberty (Article 21) and (b) right to equality (Article 14).

(1) Right to education, especially primary education
(2) Right to health
(3) Right to livelihood/Right to work
(4) Right to a clean environment
(5) Right to development.

The story of this transition of socio-economic benefits (entitlements) into fundamental rights is still unfinished. What is means in real terms to the citizens is unclear. It did focus of public attention on the obligations of government in the realisation of these rights and have put some pressure on legislatures and governments to adopt policies and programmes directed towards early realisation of these rights. Beyond this, the judicial initiatives remained unfulfilled in delivery of social justice to the poverty-sticken masses of the country. The judiciary has also been cautious about directing the government to undertake expensive socio-economic programmes even if they are fundamental for the fulfilment of basic needs of people. Only when governments have shown marked recalcitrance in meeting its own legislative mandates or fulfillng constitutional obligations thereby putting the lives of citizens in jeopardy, that courts directed for governmental action involving budgetary resources. Public interest litigation, judicial activism and human rights consciousness among the general public have contributed to the emergence of a new era in the enjoyment of socio-economic rights. If it is sustained for some time, there is bound to be some difference in the prevailing climate of frustration and despondency. Political and social actions are bound to pick up momentum with judiciary showing the directions and monitoring the implementation. Other institutions outside the judiciary now available for human rights protection will also support the initiatives which may tend to generate the necessary momentum for better realisation of socio-economic rights.

6

State Accountability for Torture and Custodial Crimes

Abhishek M. Singhvi

Whenever subjects as significant as the issue of human rights violations are discussed, a debate on the accountability of the custodians of those rights in event of violation by those very custodians is customary and, perhaps, inevitable. The proposition of state human rights, is so axiomatic as to be almost superfluous. protection of Human Rights, therefore, occupies slots of pristine glory everywhere—it is there in the United Nations Universal Declaration, in the International Covenant, the European Convention, the American Convention, the SAARC Declarations, the Cairo Declaration and in a diverse array of domestic and international law generating documents. Most significantly, it is the subject as aspecific limited National Convertion.[1] And yet, in a strange inversion of Rousseau's warning- "*Man is free, but is everywhere in chains,* one finds political and authoritative pronouncements from rooftops of protection of human rights everywhere, mandatory commandments in religious scriptures of all faiths, legislative and judicial instructions in all countries and yet their violation pathologically pervasive. In the unforgetful words of Deshbandhu Chittaranjan Das- *The Lord of humanity was not crucified only once. Every outrage on humanity is a fresh nail driven through his sacred flesh.*

"Torture" has not been defined in the constitution or in other penal laws. "Torture" of a human being by another human being is essentially an instrument to impose the will of "strong" over the "weak" by suffering. This word today has become synonymous with the darker side to human civilisation. To quote Andriana Bartow:

"Torture is a wound in the soul so painful that sometimes you can almost touch it, but it is also so intangible that there is no way to heal it. Torture is anguish squeezing in your chest, cold as ice and heavy as a stone, paralyzing as sleep and dark as the abyss. Torture is despair and fear ane range and hate. It is a desire to kill and destroy including yourself."

Comparative Global Trends

Crimes of torture and custodial violence are, indeed heinous violations of human rights of the most reprehensible order, at the same time, compounded if the state turns a blind eye to them for the reason that most of these crimes are committed by instruments of State itself. Lawyers and political scientists would shake their heads and say that the fact that the State wields such wide ranging powers is the very reason to exercise such powers judiciously and with an utmost sense of judicial discretion. The reality, however, was put very well by Lord Acton in his famous dictum- *"Power corrupts, absoulute power corrupts and absolutely."*

While some states have blatantly refused to join the international community in their struggle against human rights violations, may have time and again, inexorably failed to implement their international human rights obligations concerning prevention of torture and custodial crimes, and still some, though having formally translated these commitments into their domestic law, remain affected by the disease as much as their brethren who have refused to recognise the need to do so.

In England, torture was once regarded as a normal practice to get information regarding the crime, the accomplices, the case property and to extract confessions, but with the development of common law and more radical ideas imbibing human thought and approach, such inhuman practices were initially discouraged and eventually almost done away with certain aberrations here and there notwithstanding. The police powers of arrest detention and interrogation in England were examined in depth by Sir Cyril Philips Committee. The report of the Royal Commission is instructive . In regard to the power of arrest, the Report recommended that the power to arrest without a warrant must be related to and limited by the object to be served by the arrest, namely, to prevent the suspect from destroying evidence or interfering with witnesses or warning accomplices who have not yet been arrested or where there is a good reason to suspct the repetition of the offence and not to every case irrespective of the object sought to be achieved. The Royal Commission suggested certain restrictions on the power of arrest on the basis of the "necessity principle". The Royal Commission said [2]:

"... We recommend that detention upon arrest for an offence should continue only on one or more of the following criteria"

(a) *the person's unwillingness to identify himself so that a summon may be served upon him;*
(b) *the need to prevent the continuation or repetition of that offence;*
(c) *the need to protect the arrested person himself or other persons or property:*
(d) *the need to secure or preserve evidence of or relating to that offence or to obtain such evidence from suspect by questioning him ; and*
(e) *the likelihood of the person failing to appear at court to answer any charge made against him."*

The Royal Commission also Suggested

"To help to reduce the use of arrest we would also propose the introduction here of a scheme that is used on Ontario enabling a police officer to issue what is called an appearance notice. The procedure can be used to obtain attendance at the police station without resorting to arrest provided a power to arrest exists, for example, to be fingerprinted or to participate in an identification parade. It could also be extended to attendance for interview at a time convenient both to the suspect and to the police officer investigating the case...." The power of arrest, interrogation and detention has now been streamlined in England on the basis of the suggestions made by the Royal Commission and incorporated in Police and Criminal Evidence Act, 1984 and the incidence of custodial violence has been minimised there to a very great extent.

United Nations International Day in Support of Victims of Torture, 26 June, was officially proclaimed on December 12, 1997 when the General Assembly resolved "total eradication of torture and the effective functioning of the 'Convention against Torture and Other Cruel, Inhuman or Degrading Treatment or Punishment' which entered into force on 26 June 1987." [3]

The International Rehabilitation Council for Torture Victims subsequently launched an international campaign urging a faithful adherence to the Convention and commemoration of this international day in each country.[4] In pursuance of this forceful call, some countries—notably the United States-commenced the process of improvements in investigation procedures and monitoring of the police and other law enforcement agencies.

Some examples from the United States illustate how official torture has been eliminated during the last 25 years in the US. Though there area still cases of illtreatment especially of vulnerable groups such as common criminals and ethnic minorities, but many improvements have been made.

The use of torture to extract confessions was not uncommon in the United States some 60 years ago. This was especially true for black criminal suspects in the south . In one death sentence case[5] the Supreme Court found that the confession had been obtained under torture and stated forcefully that such methods violated the fundamental guarantees of Due Process in the US Constitution. However, this official condemnation, abuses of custodial interrogation by the police officers, often referred to as the third degree" was a common feature in American criminal justice practices well into the 1960s. The Supreme Court developed a jurisprudence in which confessions that were not "voluntary" were not admitted as evidence, but abusive interrogation practices continued to be commonplace throughout the United States.

The Supreme Court's landmark was the 1996 decision in the case of "*Miranda* v *Arzona*" [6]. In this decision, the Court candidly acknowledged the continued existence of the "third degree" on American police stations and detentions facilities, and came up with certain basic requirements to ensure that the police officers did not engage in coercive interrogation practices associated with torture and ill-treatment . The requirements, often referred to as the *Miranda Warnings*, required the police officers to inform criminal suspects of their rights in detention such as that he/she has the right to remain silent and has the right to the presence of an attorney at the interrogation. Failure to give these warnings and to abide by the substance of these rights led to the exclusion of any confession obtained from the suspect.

Although there has been public and political controversy regarding this decision and its implementation and interpretation, it has had a great impact. Law enforcement officials have changed their practices to conform to these basic requirements and the judiciary in the US continues to enforce these requirements. The result has been to almost eliminate an enormous amount of abusive police interrogation and to protect criminal suspects from torture and ill-treatment during the crucial early stages of detention.

The development of special safeguards to ensure that any statement used in a criminal proceeding is voluntary, is necessary to reduce the incentives for police officers to engage in abusive tactics in order to obtain confessions. These safeguards need not be judicially created. They may come out of the legislative process or by executive decision. The existence of these safeguards has led police officials to videotape interrogations and to engage in various steps to ensure that their interrogation practices cannot be questioned. This does not mean that violations do not occur, but it has certainly greatly reduced the existence of torture and ill-treatment.

An important tool against torture in the United States is the federal courts authorisation to bring a lawsuit whenever a person, a prisoner's rights have been violated. A person who suffers torture or other forms of ill-treatment by any governmental official may sue for compensatory and punitive damages of the official has acted with international or reckless disregard for his or her rights. One advantage of civil rights lawsuits in the United States is that they are undertaken by the person whose rights have been violated by their attorneys. If the victim prevails in the case the government will pay the attorney's fees. This system has played an enormous role in eliminating and redressing civil violations, including physical abuse by police and prison officials.

There has also been a development in the United States of laws allowing tortures who enter the United States tobe sued by their victims for damages. [7] Additionally there are laws in nearly every state in the United States which enable prosecution of government officials involved in torture or ill-treatment. The use of criminal sanctions against law enforcement officials have, however, been a rare phenomenon in the United States. The jurisdiction has been reluctant to convict police officers accused of human rights violations during their duties. The threat of criminal penalties for abuses remains, however, as an important deterrent factor.

One major hindrance is the "Code of Silence" which has a blocking effect in all disciplinary proceedings against law enforcement officials. This unofficial code operated to prevent law enforcement officials from reporting on abusive actions by their colleagues in the course of their duties. There is an uneasy answer how to get rid of this phenomenon but there should be criminal and civil sanctions for most forms that the "Code of Silence" takes and these sanctions must be enforced vigorously.

The above examples of the United States is a case in point to show that it is important that the fight against torture not be limited to its judicial aspects, and that various methods are used in an over all strategy to combat torture.

On the agenda should be the development of practical steps which the authorities should take to prevent torture and ill-treatment. Such steps include introducing safeguards during detention, allowing access to prisoners from family members, lawyers and doctors carrying out investigations of torture and ending the impunity of law enforcement personnel who commit human rights violations.

An important step towards stopping torture in a society is that the government officially condemns the use of torture in all cases. If the authorities do not give this clear message, the risk is that both torture and ill-treatment will continue to take place. Remaining silent in the face of torture would amount to condone it as an acceptable practice.

At Home: Constitutional and Statutory Mandates

At home, in India, Article 21 of our Constitution provides that "no person shall be deprived of his life or personal liberty except according *to procedure established by law*". Personal liberty, thus, is a sacred and cherished right under the Constitution. The expression "life or personal liberty" has been held to include the right to live with human dignity and thus it would also include within itself a guarantee against torture and assault by the State or its functionaries. Article 22 guarantees protection against arrest and detention in certain cases and declares that no person who is arrested shall be detained in police custody without being informed of the grounds of such arrest and he shall not be denied the right to consult and defend himself by a legal practitioner of his choice. Clause (2) of Article 22 directs that the person arrested and detained in custody shall be produced before the nearest magistrate within a period of 24 hours of such arrest, excluding the time necessary for the journey from the place of arrest to the Court of Magistrate. On the lines of the fifth amendment to the US Constitution, Article 20 (3) of our Constitution lays down that a person accused of an offence shall not be compelled to be a witness against himself. These are some of the constitutional safeguards provided to a person with a view to protect his personal liberty against any unjustified assault by the State. In keeping with the constitutional guarantees a number of statutory provisions also seek to protect personal liberty, dignity and basic human rights of the citizens . Chapter V of the Criminal Procedure Code 1973 deals with the powers or arrest of a person and the safeguards which are required to be followed by the police to protect the interest of the arrested person. Section 41 Cr PC confers powers on any police officer to arrest a person under the circumstances specified therein without any order or a warrant of arrest from a magistrate. Section 46 provides the method and manner of arrest. Under this section no formality is necessary while arresting a peson . Under Section 49, the police is not permitted to use more restraint than is necessary to prevent the escape of the person. Section 50 enjoins every police officer arresting any persons without warrant to communicate to him the full particulars of the offence for which he is arrested and the grounds for such arrest. The police officer is further enjoined to inform the person arrested that he is entitled to be released on bail and he may arrange for sureties in the event of his arrest for a non-bailable offence . Section 56 contains a mandatory provision requiring the police officer making an arrest without warrant to produce the arrested person before a magistrate without unnecessary delay and Section 57 echoes clause (2) of Article 22 of the Constitution of India. There are some other provisions also like Sections 53, 54 and 167 which are aimed at affording procedural safeguards to a person arrested by the police. Whenever a person dies in police custody of the Section 176 requires the magistrate to hold an inquiry into the cause of death. Further, while section 25 of the Evidence Act declares a confession made to a police officer to be futile, Section 26 makes such a confession, unless made in the presence of a magistrate, inadmissible against the confessor.

Alas, in spite of the constitutional and statutory provisions aimed at safeguarding the personal liberty and life of a citizen, growing incidents of torture and deaths in police custody have been a disturbing factor. Experience shows that worst violations of human rights take place during the course of investigation, when the police with a view of secure evidence or confession often resorts to third-degree methods including torture and adopts techniques of screening arrest by either not recording the arrest or describing the deprivation of liberty merely as a prolonged interrogation.

Politico-Legal Developments

The Third Report of the National Police Commission in India expressed its deep concern with custodial violence and lock-up deaths.[8] It appreciated the demoralising effect which custodial torture was creating on the society as a whole . It made some very useful suggestions.

"...an arrest during the investigation of a cognizable case may be considered justified in one or other of the following circumstances:

(i) The case involves a grave offence like murder, dacoity, robbery, rape, etc., and it necessary to arrest the accused and bring his movements under restraint to infuse confidence among the terror-stricken victims.

(ii) The accused is likely to abscond and evade the process of law.

(iii) The accused is given to violent behaviour and is likely to commit further offences unless his movements are brought under restraint.

(iv) The accused is a habitual and unless kept in police custody he is likely to commit similar ofences again. It would be desirable to insist through departmental instructions that a police officer making an arrest should also record in the case diary the reasons for making the arrest, thereby clarifying his conformity to the specified guidelines."

The recommendations of the Police Commission reflect the constitutional concomitants of the fundamental right to personal liberty and freedom. These recommendations, however, have not acquired any statutory status so far.

The issue of police reform has become a matter of public debate and is being vigorously pursued by non-governmental organisations (NGOs) committed to the cause of good governance. The establishment of the NHRC a statutory body of an eminent status has given a boost to the human rights movement all over India. By giving a special attention to complaints of torture and harassment by the police, NHRC has produced a significant, albeit slow, impact on the working of law enforcement agencies. Its efforts are steadily building a favourable climate for the observance of human rights in the country.

The failure of the criminal justice system in India to prevent or deal with both custodial and domestic violence is unfortunate but real. While the Supreme Court of India has said all that is possible on the subject of custodial violence, incidents of torture and death in police stations across the country continue to mount.

The main reason why torture is continued to be practised on such a wide scale throughout India was that the police felt themselves to be immune from any consequence. Since human rights enforcement and judicial monitoring of compliance have hung over the heads of the police and paramilitary forces like the sword of Damocles, there has been a change for the better.

Law enforcement agencies in India routinely resort to torture, euphemistically called "third degree'. The fact that law specifically prohibits torture does not alter the situation on the ground. If the use of torture were only an aberration, the problem could have been solved quite easily through stricter disciplinary procedures against the police officers involved. But it is an open secret that many police officers with outstanding professional reputations see noting wrong in the use of third degree methods. Some so-called supercops are openly accused of resorting to custodial torture against criminals and terrorists. This practice enjoys sanction at influential levels of the administration and society at large. As long as the end result is socially acceptable, few questions are asked. The general belief is that it is impossible to control crime and criminals without resorting to "third degree " methods.

Loss of faith in the efficiency of the criminal justice system is one of the major reasons for the police use of torture against criminals. Others include impractical laws and legal procedures, lack of police resources and skills, and the attitude among police that the use of torture is legitimate. Mere preaching and lecturing will not achieve a change. The police officers have to be convinced by practical example that they can perform their task effectively without resort of torture. Other components of the criminal justice system will also have to share the responsibility for controlling crime and punishing offenders.

Crucially, society at large, especially the administrators, the political class, the judiciary, the media and the opinion-makers, will have to renounce their ambivalence towards the use of toture. It should not be justified on any ground whatsoever, not even "public order" but because public order is obviously critical. There is a need for review of our laws and reform of the entire criminal justice system. The police are not the only problem.

Over the last two decades, several developments combined to foster in India a keener sense of accountability for any infliction of torture. In 1978, Justice M.M. Ismail, (later Chief Justice of the Madras High Court) submitted a report on outrage in the Central Prison in Madras during the emergency[9]. It caught national attention for it reflected similar happenings elsewhere in the country. The report contains detailed recommendations for preventing torture in prisons which remain relevant today.

In 1979, the Government of India ratified the International Covenant on Economic, Social and Cultural Rights and the International Covenant on Civil and Political Rights. No reservation was made in respect of Article 7 of the latter which outlaws torture and other cruel, inhuman or degrading treatment or punishment. As required by Article 40, India has periodically submitted reports to the UN Human Rights Committee on its observance of the covenant. Three Attorney Generals have appeared before the UN. to explain India's reports in the last decade and a half. Sadly, however, we are not amongst the123 countries which have ratified the covenant against torture and other cruel, inhuman and degrading treatment or punishment.

Apex Court's Concerns

In the early 1980s, two other developments occurred and interacted with each other. One was investigative journalism which exposed the practice of torture. The other was public interest litigation based at times on press reports.

Though, the Supreme Court had from the very beginning been concerned about the tortuous liability of the State in event of violation of fundamental rights by its functionaries[10], the real breakthrough came in the 1980s when the Apex Court inaugurated the philosophy of public interest litigation by deciding to entertain press reports, letters and petitions from persons lacking a formal *locus standi*, as writ petitions in public interest. The court took the view that the words "appropriate proceedings" in Article 32 (by way of which one could move the Supreme Court for enforcement of fundamental right) included proceedings made by any public spirited citizen on behalf of an affected person who is unable, for various reasons, to approach the court himself[11].

While in Sunil Batra[12], *Francis Coralie Mullin*[13] and *Rudul Sah*[14] the Supreme Court took a stern view of custodial torture and crimes, in Saheli vs. Commissioner of Police[15], while holding that "in the matter of liability of the State for the torts committed by its employees, it is now the settled law that the State is liable for tortious acts committed by its employees in the course of their employment", the court ordered a payment of Rs. 75,000 as compensation to the mother of a 9 years old boy who died in police custody. And, in a recent ruling[16], the Supreme Court has confirmed a Calcutta High Court order directing payment of Rs. 1 lakh by the Railway Board as compensation to a Bangladeshi woman who was gang-raped by railway employees at Howrah Railway Station.

In 1993, in a classic case of progressively expanding the public law doctrine of compensatory jurisprudence, in *Nilabati Behera* vs *State of Orissa*[17] a three-judge Bench of the Supreme Court pointed out that prisoners and detenus are not denuded of their fundamental rights under Article 21 and it is only such restrictions as are permitted by law, which can be imposed on the enjoyment of the fundamental rights of the arrests and detenus. It was observed:

"It is axiomatic that convicts, prisoners or undertrials are not denuded of their fundamental rights under Article 21 and it is only such restrictions, as are permitted by law, which can be imposed on the enjoyment of he fundamental right by such persons. It is an obligation of the State to ensure that there is no infringement of the indefeasible rights of a citizen to life, except in accordance with law, while the citizen is in its custody. The precious right guaranteed by Article 21 of the Constitution of India cannot be denied to convicts, undertrials or other prisoners in custody, except according to procedure established by law. There is a great responsibility on the police or prison authorities to ensure that the citizen in its custody is not deprived of his right to life. His liberty is in the very nature of things circumscribed by the very fact of his confinement and therefore his interest in the limited liberty left to and admits of no exceptions. The wrongdoer is accountable and the State is responsible if the person in custody of the police is deprived of his life except according to the established by law."[18]

Ink was not yet dry on the apex court ruling in *Nilabati Behera*[19] when the same court was again called upon to decide yet another case relating to illegal detention—*Joginder Kumar*[20] wherein the court ruled that:

"No arrest can be made because it is lawful for the police officer to do so. The existence of the power to arrest is one thing. The justification for the exercise of it is quite another... No arrest should be made without a reasonable satisfaction reached after some investigation as to the genuineness and bona fides of a complaint and a reasonable belief both as the person's complicity and even so as to the need to effect arrest. Denying a person of his liberty is a serious matter."

While Lamenting that

"The horizon of human rights is expanding. At the same time, the crime rate is also increasing. Of late, this Court has been receiving complaints about violations of human rights because of indiscriminate arrests. How are we to strike a balance between the two?" the court further held that:

"A realistic approach should be made in this direction. The law of arrest is one of balancing individual rights, liberties and privileges, on the one hand and individual duties, obligations and responsibilities on the other; of weighing and balancing the right, liberties and privileges of the single individual and those of individuals collectively; of simply deciding what is wanted and where to put the weight and the emphasis; of deciding which comes first—the criminal or society, the law violator or the law abider. And then set down certain procedural "requirements" in cases of arrest.

For the citizen the most tangible gain is in the ruling of the Supreme Court in the case of *D.K. Basu* vs *State of West Bengal*[21]. The Supreme Court ruled that it could award monetary compensation to the petitioner in the exercise of its jurisdiction to enforce fundamental rights (Article 32) and so can the high courts:

"Public law proceedings serve a different purpose than the private law proceedings. Award of compensation for established infringement of the rights guaranteed under Article 21 of the Constitution is a remedy available in Public law since the purpose of public law is not only to civilise public power but also to assure the citizens that they live under a legal system wherein their rights and interest shall be protected and preserved. Grant of compensation in proceedings under Article 32 or Article 226 of the Constitution of India for the established violation of the fundamental rights guaranteed under Article 21 is an exercise of the courts under the public law jurisdiction for penalising the wrongdoer and fixing the liability for the public wrong on the state which failed in the discharge of its public duty to protect the fundamental rights of the citizen." [22]

But it is the court's 11 pathbreaking and inimitable directives, called 'requirements' which are the tour de force of the judgement:

"(1) The police personnel carrying out the arrest and handling the interrogation of the arrested should bear accurate, visible and clear identification and name tags with their designations. The particulars of all such police personnel who handle interrogation of the arrestee must be recorded in a register.

(2) The police officer carrying out the arrest of the arrestee shall prepare a memo of arrest at the time of arrest and such memo shall be attested by at least one witness who may be either a member of the family of the arrestee or a respectable person of the locality from where the arrest is made. It shall also be countersigned by the arrestee and shall contain the time and date of arrest.

(3) A person who has been arrrested or detained and is being held in custody in a police station or interrogation centre or other lock-up shall be entitled to have one friend or relative or other person known to him or having interest in his welfare being informed, as soon as practicable, that he has been arrested and is being detained at the particular place, unless the attesting witness of the memo of arrest is himself such a friend or a relative of the arrestee.

(4) The time, place of arrest and venue of custody of an arrestee must be notified by the police where the next friend or relative of the arrestee lives outside the district or town through the legal aid organisation in the district and the police station of the area concerned telegraphically within a period of 8 to 12 hours after the arrest.

(5) The person arrested must be made aware of this right to have someone informed to his arrest or detention as soon as he is put under arrest or is detained.

(6) An entry must be made in the diary at the place of detention regarding the arrest of the person which shall also disclose the name of the next friend of the person who has been informed of the arrest and the names and particulars of the police officials in whose custody the arrestee is.

(7) The arrestee should, where he so requests, be also examined at the time of his arrest, and major and minor injuries, if any present on his /her body, must be recorded at that time. The inspection memo must be signed both by the arrestee and the police officer effecting the arrest and is copy provided to the arrestee.

(8) The arrestee should be subjected to medical examination by a trained doctor every 48 hours during his detention in custody by a doctor on the panel of approved doctors appointed by Director, Health Services of the concerned state or union territory. Director, Health Services should prepare such panel for all tehsils and districts as well.

(9) Copies of all the documents including the memo of arrest referred to above should be sent to the Illaqa Magistrate for his record.

(10) The arrestee may be permitted to meet his lawyer during interrogation though not throughout the interrogation.

(11) A police control room should be provided at all district and state headquarters, where information regarding the arrest and the place of custody of the arrestee shall be communicated by the officer causing the arrest. Within 12 hours of effecting the arrest and at the police controlroom it should be displayed on a conspicuous noticeboard.

Failure to comply with the requirements herein above mentioned shall apart from rendering the concerned officer liable to departmental action, also render him liable to be punished for contempt of court and the proceedings for contempt of court of may be instituted in any high court the country having territorial jurisdiction over the matter. The requirements referred to above, flow from Articles 21 and 22 (1) of the Constitution and need to be strictly followed."[23]

The court directed that these guidelines be forwarded to Directors General of Police and Home secretaries of each State / Union Territory who shall be obliged to circulate the same to all the police stations in their respective jurisdictions. It was further directed that said requirements be broadcast on All India Radio, l telecast on the National Television channel and published and distributed in venaculars all over the country.

And now, even four years after the judgement, the apex court has not let its ink dry over the case and, in an unparalleled shining example of continuing mandamus, is monitoring and foreseeing the enforcement of its directions. In the second round, therefore, the Court issued notices to all 35 States and Union Territories directing them to file specific affidavits and the same have been examined by the courts. Regrettably, it has been seen during the course of these proceedings that the functionaries in the higher echelon of State bureaucracy and police, instead of truthfully and honestly serving the cause of justice, invariably try to defend violations committed by their departments . The issue with which we really have to grapple is torture committed in the period between *de facto* arrest and dejure arrest. The D.K. Basu guidelines come in only on formal de jure arrest by when the enforcement agencies have already extracted, out of the arrestee, what they want to.

Discussions regarding the next step towards a faithful implementation of the apex court directives are not being made with experts. It is the next phase of D.K. Basu—the phase of grassroots implementation that would be an exciting phase and on which suggestions are invited from this august house for development of a remedial framework.

A Remedial Framework

Here follows a list of some suggestions in this regard (apart from general human rights sensitization of police officials) that have found general acceptance.[24]

A. Preventive Measures

1. Since persons usually run a higher risk of being ill-treated while they are detained, opening up and accessing places of detention is of crucial importance in order to reduce the risks of torture/ ill-treatment in custody.
2. A Handbook of Police Code of Conduct, with particular emphasis on the imperatives of total abjuration of custodial abuses merits to be made available to every policemen irrespective of rank or position.
3. Greater and closer supervision of all the works that go on in the police stations must be ensured. Systematic and effective inspections and other form of periodical visits must be backed up by a substantial number of surprise visits by the senior officers.
4 As a part of improved Police Community understanding, it would be worthwhile for the police leaders to venture in enabling periodical/surprise visits to police lock-ups by apolitical Citizens Committees in at least all the urban and semiurbn areas where such a scheme can be made workable.
5. Police interrogation is a professional need and it has to be done by skilled and competent personnel who can elicit information from an accused or a suspect within the prescribed limits of law and police ethics. This clearly focuses the need for higher

training, in the art of interrogation and the need to restrict the power of such probes in the well trained as well as capable amongst the staff. Further, all such professional activities must be closely monitored.

6. Suggestions had been made that at least in urban and semi-urban areas, the administration can establish "Arrest Centres", which should have hygienic and scientifically updated facilities to further police enquiries and also have the benefit of the presence of a medical officer and a Magistrate. Such an arrangement can on the one hand ensure lawful humane and justified penal procedural actions like, arrest, search, seizure and interrogations of the accused / suspect and at the same time guarantee all legally provided rights like bail, release and so on. Further, it can enable the police to keep in mind the essential fact that the public interest in bringing the offenders to book is fully ensured within the bounds of law. In the lights of the fact that majority of arrests are made in urban or semi-urban areas, the proposal to establish such centres merits a close consideration.[25]

B. Statutory Measures

1. *Prescribing mandatory judicial enquiry into all cases of custodial deaths;* Section 176 of the Code of Criminal Procedure, 1973 provides for a magisterial enquiry into the circumstances leading to an unnatural death. But, such an enquiry can be conducted by an Executive Magistrate. It appears necessary that such a provision in relation to all custodial deaths must be amended to provide for a mandatory enquiry by a Judicial Magistrate.
2. *Fixing the time limit for finalising such enquiries:* Further, a maximum time frame to commence, hold and finalise such a judicial enquiry must be made explicit under the appropriate law. (Till such time the appropriate legal provisions are made to cover the suggestion as above, a time limit for all the executive magisterial enquiry must be prescribed by the State Governments).
3. *Publication of such proceedings in the gazettes:* All proceedings under section 176 of the Code of Criminal Procedures,1973 must be published in the official gazettes by the respective State Governments soon after the receipt of the report.
4. *Presumption in cases of custodial violence:* The Law Commission

had recommended that a rebuttable presumption should be enacted in the Indian Evidence Act to the effect that every death/violence in custody is presumed to be result of custodial torture.

5. *Adding a sub-section to Section 302 of the Indian Penal Code:* An amendment to section 302 of the I.P.C. is necessary by adding a Sub- section 302 (A) of the Indian Penal Code to make the penal consequences grave and stringent against perpetrators of such custodial crimes. Similar to a specific provision made under the Indian Penal Code to deal with cases of custodial rapes).
6. *No arrests in bailable offences:* The Law Commission of India has reported that large percentage of arrest ranging between 80-90 per cent in most states are in respect of in bailable offences. The following amendments have been suggested in this respect.[26]
   (i) In respect of bailable offences categorised as bailable and non-cognizable, no arrest should be made by the police and no arrest warrant issued by court but only summons to be issued and served otherwise than through a constable.
   (ii) In respect of offences which are categorized as bailable and cognizable, (barring a few) there should be no arrest. Only an 'appearance notice' (like in Australia and New Zealand) should be served up on the accused to present himself before the police or court.
   (iii) In respect of offences which are non-bailable and cognizable, a distinction should be made between offences punishable with imprisonment of more than seven years and ones up to seven years.

C. Administrative Measures

1. As stated earlier, the cases of custodial deaths must be enquired judicially and the legal representatives of the victim must have the full opportunity to get a copy of the enquiry report, free of cost, from the office of the concerned District Magistrate.
2. All cases of custodial deaths must perforce be investigated by an officer of a rank not less than of a Deputy Superintendent of Police.
3. Post mortem in such cases provides the most important evidence. Therefore, all the steps taken by the medical authorities must be very systematic and comprehensive. Post mortem must invariable be done by a team of doctors of not less than two and not more than three. Further, findings by each member of the team must be independently recorded and it should not be a

joint report. In case of difference as to the final findings, the seniormost doctor of the District/City must record his finding. Post mortem, in all such cases of custodial deaths must be done within a period of 24 hours of the report of the incident and in-event of non compliance with this requirement reasons must be recorded in-writing. Further, Post mortem must be videographed, according to standardized rules, and preserved as a document.

4. The state police must establish a nodal officer for the entire state at the level of a DIG who will ensure follow up of such cases.
5. Payment of compensation to the relatives of the deceased who suffered a custodial death owing to a wanton physical abuse by torture or other forms of criminal action or due to negligence on the part of the police must be made from out of the police funds, as is being done in U.K. Recovery of the payments so made towards the compensation must be made from the erring personnel after a quick and prompt departmental proceedings. The current experience is that departmental proceedings cannot get started so long as the criminal proceedings do not get over, though technically there is no bar on holding the D.E.
6. A police fund must be made to meet cost of compensations in cases where negligence or complicity on the part of the police is *prima facie* established.
7. Strong penal action must be taken against any police officer who found guilty of any legal or administrative violations or failures. Personal liability of the erring policeman is necessary and such a step would go a long way in bringing some attitudinal change in a large mass of the average policeman. The compensation in all deserving cases must be first meet by the Government and later by the due process the responsibility must be fixed to enable recovery of damage imposed on the guilty policeman.

Where do we go from here?

So far India has presented three reports under Article 40 of the International Covenant on Civil and Political Rights for examination by the Human Rights Committee constituted under the Covenant. They were on July, 4 1983, on July 12, 1989 and on November 29, 1995. They were examined by the committee on March 28 and 30, 1984, March 26 and 27, 1991 and July 24 and 25, 1997, respectively.

On each of the three occasions, the issue of practice of torture was raised in the proceedings. At the last meeting on July 25, 1997, the committee expressed its "concern about the incidence of custodial deaths, rape and torture, and at the failure of the Indian government to receive the United Nations Special Rapporteur on Torture and Other Cruel, Inhuman or Degrading Treatment of Punishment". Permission has been refused, though requested repeatedly. The Rapporteur's Annual Report for 1997 recorded that the "continues to be concerned at the persistence of allegations of torture, followed often by custodial death and to regreat the reluctance of the government to invite him to visit the country." Such criticism detracts from India's international accountability. Periodic Reports to the Human Rights Committee are no substitute for lack of co-operation with a Rapporteur of acknowledged expertise.

Domestically, despite the improvements in the last two decades, there has been no attempt at systematic reforms. The eight-volume of report of the National Police Commission has been ignored. Not have there been any worth while efforts at prison reform and reforms in the police services.

Unless access to prisons in freely given to the media and concerned citizens belonging to the medical and legal professions, transparency will remain a distant goal. Two of the most powerful deterrent to the practice or torture are transparency and award of swift punishment to the wrongdoer.

The Supreme Court touched the core of the problem when it said in D.K. Basu "How do we check the abuse of police power? Transparency of action and accountability perhaps are two possible safeguards, which this courts must insist upon. Attention is also required to be paid to properly develop the culture, training and orientation of the police force consistent with the human values. Training methodology of the police needs restructuring, the force needs to be infused with basic human values and made sensitive to the constitutional ethos. Efforts must be made to change the attitude and approach of the police personnel handling investigations so that they do not sacrifice basis human values during interrogation and do not resort to questionable forms of interrogation."[27]

Respect for human rights is inherent in professional policing. Education should be integrated into training programmes on police ethics and professional conduct. Training programmes should emphasize the ability of a professional police force to investigate crime and maintain law and order without resorting to torture.

An international code of practice for the professional conduct of interrogation should be developed, recognizing that no police or other law enforcement official may inflict, investigate or tolerate torture or other cruel, inhuman or degrading treatment. As a first step towards our International Human Rights commitments, let us hope that India ratifies if not wholly, with just exceptions, the Convention against Torture and other Cruel, Inhuman or Degrading Treatment or Punishments. This will, indeed, be in consonance both with the constitutional mandate and with India's authoritative pronouncements made over the years on the global stage. Complete non-ratification, in-fact is a constitutional sacrilege which the apex court in *D.K. Basu* has abhorred.

References

1. Convention against Torture and Other Cruel, Inhuman or Degrading Treatment or Punishments, entered into force on 26 June 1987.

2. "Report of a Royal Commission on Criminal Procedure" (Command Papers 8092 of 1981).

3. General Assembly's Adoption of Resolution No. 52/149.

4. See Generally. "Torture: Never More" Newsletter of the International Rehabilitation Council for Torture Victims, June 1999.

5. *Chambers* v *Florida* 309 US 227: 84 LEd 716 (1940).

6. 384 US 436: 16 Led 2d 694 (1966).

7. See theAlient Tort Stature. The law was used in1980 by the father of a torture victim who had been tortured in Paraguay to see the torturer who was then living in New York.

8. See report of the Third National Police Commission, chaired by Dharam Vira.

9. See report of the Ismail Commission of Inquiry 1978, Madras.

10. See Kasturi Lal Ralia Ram Jain (AIR 1965 SC 1039).

11. See Bandhua Mukti Morcha (AIR 1984 SC 802).

12. (19080) 3 SCC 488.

13. AIR 1981 SC 746.

14. AIR 1983 SC 1086.

15. AIR 1990 SC 513.

16. Chairman, Railway Board (2000) 2 SCC-465.

17. (1993) 2 SCC 746, His judgement has been relied upon by the Newzealand Supreme Court in a recent ruling.

18. *Ibid*, para 31.

19. Supra note 12.

20. 1994 (4) SCC 260.

21. AIR 1997 SC 610, the author was appointed by the Supreme Court and continues to be amicus Curiae in this case.

22. *Ibid*, para 44.

23. *Ibid*, para 35.

24. See, "A review of cases of police custodial deaths in Karnataka" by Dr. S. Krishnamurthy. BPRD, New Delhi, 1997.

25. See generally "Human Rights" by Dr. S. Subramaniam. AF AP & SF . Hyderabad, 1992.

26. Custodial Crimes: An affront against humanity, Address by Justice B.P. Jeevan Reddy at IIHR 10th December 2000. (unpublished).

27. Supra note para 29.

7

Protection of Right to Life and Personal Liberty (Article 21) and Law Enforcement

Chaman Lal

The Universal Declaration of Human Rights (1948) says that 'everyone has the Right to Life, Liberty and Security of Person' (Article 3) and no one shall be subjected to arbitrary arrest, detention or exile' (Article 9). India has incorporated these provisions in Article 21 of the Constitution which guarantees that 'no person shall be deprived of his life or personal liberty except according to procedure established by law'. While fundamental rights enshrined in Article 19 of the Constitution are meant only for the citizens of the country, the right to life and liberty is available to every person within the territory of India whether Indian, foreigner or stateless. The Supreme Court has held that the 'procedure' contemplated by Article 21 has to be just, fair and reasonable and not 'arbitrary, fanciful or oppressive'.

The expression 'life' in Article 21 has been interpreted by the Supreme Court to mean not merely animal existence or survival but a life with full human dignity. Some landmark judgements of the Apex Court have expanded the scope of Article 21 to bring in its fold the right to basic necessities of life such as food and shelter (reasonable accommodation), right to pollution-free water and air, right to primary health, right to education, right to livelihood and right to just and humane conditions of work. In essence it would include all those aspects of life which go to make a man's life meaningful.

Declaring the assault on human dignity in any form as

unconstitutional even in respect of persons lawfully deprived of their personal liberty, the Supreme Court has, through its rulings, extended the amplitude of the expression 'personal liberty' in Article 21 to include the right to privacy, right against solitary confinement, right against barfetters, right against hand-cuffing, right to confer with legal adviser, right to meet family members and friends, right to legal aid to poor or indigent accused, right to speedy trial, and right to commutation of death sentence on the grounds of delay in execution of sentence.

Article 21 includes within itself a guarantee against torture and other cruely, inhuman or degrading form of treatment or punishment to persons in police or judicial custody. Prisoners are thus entitled to all fundamental rights except those affected by their incarceration and any punishment or humilation not sanctioned by Prison Regulations, would constitute violation of their fundamental rights under Article 21.

Article 21 together with Article 20 of the Constitution occupies an exalted place among the fundamental rights by virtue of their being emergency proof. When Emergency is proclaimed on grounds of war or external aggression or armed rebellion, all the fundamental rights except those guaranteed by Article 20 (protections against ex-post facto culpability, self-incrimination and double jeopardy) and Article 21 cease to be enforceable by the courts during the period of Emergency.

Article 22 of the Constitution gives the arrested persons the right to be informed of the grounds of arrest and the right to be produced before the nearest magistrate within a period of 24 hours of arrest. Article 20 (3) lays down that a person accused of an offence shall not be compelled to be a witness against himself. These are important safeguards provided in the Constitution for protecting life and personal liberty against unjustified assaults by the State.

Chapter V (Sections 41 to 60) of the Code of Criminal Procedure 1973 deals with the powers and procedure of arrest of a person involved in a criminal offence and includes the safeguards which are required to be observed to protect the constitutional rights of the accused persons. Section 50 (Communication of grounds of arrest and the right to bail), Sections 56 and 57 (production of the arrested persons before magistrate within a period of 24 hours) echo the provisions of Article 22 of the Constitution.

The statutory and constitutional provisions for effective

enforcement of the fundamental rights to life and liberty have been reinforced by the following instructions issued by the Supreme Court in *Joginder Kumar* vs *State of UP* (JT 1994 (3) SC 243) and *D.K. Basu* vs *State of West Bengal* (AIR 1997 SC 610) with a view to providing an appropriate machinery for "contemporaneous recording and notification of all cases of arrest and detention and bring in transparency and accountability."

(i) Police personnel carrying out arrest and handling the interrogation of an arrestee must wear accurate, visible and clear identification and name tags giving their designations. The particulars of all such personnel who handle interrogation must be recorded in a register.

(ii) The police officer carrying out the arrest must prepare a memo of arrest at the time of arrest; this memo must be attested by a witness who may be either a family member of the arrestee or a responsible person of the locality from where the arrest has been made.

(iii) The person arrested or detained shall be entitled to have a friend, relative or other person known to him or having an interest in his welfare informed as soon as practicable.

(iv) The arrestee should be medically examined at the time of arrest and major injuries, if any, present on his or her body must recorded in a memo. The inspection memo should be signed both by the arrestee and by the concerned police officer and a copy should be given to the arrestee.

(v) The arrestee should undergo a medical examination by a trained doctor every 48 hours of his detention in custody.

(vi) The arrestee should be permitted to meet his lawyer during interrogation.

Failure to comply with these requirements shall, apart from, rendering the concerned police officer liable for departmental action, invite action for contempt of court, proceedings for which can be instituted in any high court of the country having territorial jurisdiction over the matter.

Rule of Law is the bedrock of civilized existence. It is an integral constituent of democratic governance which derives it authority from the sanction of the people. The Rule of Law is established by enactment of just laws in tune with the needs and aspirations of the people and their firm and impartial enforcement with support and cooperation of the community. The law enforcement agencies are armed with necessary powers for ensuring the observance of laws and dealing with cases of their infringement. Appropriate institutional mechanisms have to be provided to prevent abuse and misuse of the special powers and to protect innocent people against unjustified and arbitrary interference with their rights by the authorities.

Constitutional guarantees reinforced by specific provisions made in the substantive laws can protect people's Right to Life and Liberty only if the criminal justice system functions effectively. It is sad but true that all the wings of the system—police, prosecution, judiciary and prison administration have over the years registered an alarming fall in the standards of their performance and integrity.This has brought the system on the verge of collapse and made the common man lose his faith in the ability of law and its courts to punish the criminals.

Police as the main law enforcing agency is responsible for maintaining law and order which alone can ensure that people enjoy their basic rights and fundamental rights guaranteed by the Constitution. The police in India organized and run on an archaic model of the colonial period is ill-equipped to cope with the process of socio-economic transformation of society and the strains of democratic governance. It also suffers from the handicap of poor image and low credibility and is generally perceived to be inefficient, arrogant and corrupt. Its track record even in the field of normal law and order is not very impressive. It has miserably failed to meet the challenges of terrorism, insurgency and separatists' militant movements which have been taking a heavy toll of citizens lives. It's limited successes achieved in some parts of the country notably Punjab are tainted with accusation of questionable methods. While its professional competence has fallen alarmingly over the years since independence, the graph of its excesses and abuse of power has been rising steadily. Instead of respecting and protecting the human rights of the people, the police has become notorious as the single largest violator of human rights. Policing the police has thus become an urgent national task.

Third degree the popular name for the police practice of using force and violence during interrogation to extract confession by torture or bullying is widely prevalent all over India despite specific legal provisions such as Sections 220, 330 and 331 of IPC and the constitutional guarantee against self-incrimination given in

Article 20(3). The largest chunk of the complaints received by the NHRC concern police with most to these complaints relating to custodial violence. The following data on death in police custody and complaints of illegal detention given in the annual reports of the NHRC clearly indicate that despite a growing human rights movement in the country, the police brutality is continuing unabated:

	1996-97	*97-98*	*98-99*	*99-2000*
Death in police custody	136	193	183	185
Illegal detention	282	330	436	1157

Poor investigation by the police, indifferent handling of cases by the prosecution and the slow and cumbersome court procedure are largely responsible for the alarming fall in the conviction rate (averaging around 25 per cent) which has virtually rendered the criminal unpunishable by law.

The directions of the Apex Court regarding the right to human dignity of prisoners are routinely flouted because the jails are unmanageably overcrowded with undertrials whose crimes are yet to be proved constituting over 80 per cent of the prison population. The jail administration is unable to protect the prisons' rights to basic needs such as food, accommodation and health care. The police cannot ensure proper security arrangements for timely production of the undertrials before the court. Realisation of speedy trial declared a fundamental right under Article 21 remains a distant dream. These victims of unfortunate circumstances suffer untold harassment and indignities despite repeated assertions of their entitlement to all human rights except those taken a way by their imprisonment. They are confused and over awed by the mystified court procedure and mysterious conduct of the lawyers. Their cases do not start for long and when they do, they do not end. As pointed out Justice Bhagwati Committee on Juridicare the poor and disadvantaged after being priced out of the legal system by reasons of it's 'expensiveness and dilatoriness', get alienated from the judicial process.

Policing in disturbed areas affected by terrorism, insurgency and extremist violence offers a real test of the effective enforcement of fundamental rights to life and liberty. One of the major reasons of continued prevalence of custodial violence in the country is the apathy of the civil society particularly the dominant middle class to arbitrary exercise and abuse of authority by the functionaries of the Government. No one comes forward to protest against police high-handedness, though it is resented and condemned by all and sundry unless they are personally affected by it. Vast sections of population still associate police effectiveness with aggressive behaviour and imperious manner of the men in uniform. Patently illegal methods adopted by the police in dealing with criminals (Bhagalpur blindings) receive ready sanction from the majority of the people who feel disgusted with increasing criminality and violence on the one hand and proven inability of the criminal justice system to combat them effectively on the other. Most of them will be found to endorse the majority opinion in police circles that terrorists and insurgents have forfeited their human rights by virtue of their inhuman acts of murder, kidnapping and extortion. I have come across a good number of senior politicians and top bureaucrats who question the propriety of observance of 'constitutional niceties' in respect of the avowed enemies of public order. In their overriding concern for unity and integrity of the nation, they end to overlook the constitutionl guarantee to assure the dignity of the individuals who constitute the nation and for whom the State exists. It is the growth of this mind set in general public that facilitates abrasive policing and accords sanction to police practices like fake encounters and unexplained disappearances. Fake encounters have come to be accepted as a routine answer and matching reply to perpetrators of terrorist violence and organised crime. The police officers willing to undertake these illegal tasks are considered brave and rated highly not only by their bosses and colleagues but also by influential sections of public. By according some kinds of social sanctions to these unlawful police practices on the ground that extra-ordinary situations demand radical responses, society is simply assisting in the growth of brutalisation in the rank and file of police.

Additional powers given to the police and security forces under special laws enacted for meeting serious threats to internal security are seen to have become a major obstacle in effective enforcement of right to life and liberty. Special acts such as TADA, the Armed Force Act, the Unlawful Assembly Act, the Disturbed Area Act, etc. are meant to be temporary deviations from the normal jurisprudence founded on the norm of natural justice. They deal with discernible threats to peace and order and provide for adequate checks and balances and safeguards to protect the rights of innocent citizens. They are required to be reviewed periodically to decide the need and justification of their continuation and not allowed to become permanent pieces of legislation. Our experience of the special laws can be summed up in one sentence; special laws have not served the intended purpose of effectively dealing with threats to internal security but have been abused extensively.

Though I am not in a position to comment on the need of the police and security forces for additional powers to deal with serious situations like terrorism and insurgency, I agree with the stand taken by the NHRC against the enactment of the Criminal Law Amendment Act aimed at resurrecting the TADA with some modifications. However, I have slightly different reasons to oppose the proposed move. I cannot say with certainty that the police and security forces do not need additional powers to deal with complex situations of public order. In fact, I am inclined to endorse their demands considering the enormity of the challenges facing them and the sacrifices they are making. But I firmly believe they do not deserve the powers they are seeking. I have no hesitation in stating that whatever powers are available with them under the normal and existing special laws are mostly being abused for personal gain or extraneous purposes because of decline in professionalism, almost non- existent ethical standards and poor leadership at various levels. The nation cannot feel safe in arming them with more powers, however justified their demands may be.

Addressing the problems of custodial violence by the police and security forces even in areas afflicted by terrorism and insurgencies has been a major concern of the NHRC ever since its creation in September 1993. One of the functions of the Commission spelt out in Section 12 of the Protection of Human Rights Act 1993 is to 'review the factors including acts of terrorism that inhibit the enjoyment of human rights and recommend appropriate remedial measures'. The Commission has, despite its limited powers vis-a-vis the armed forces, been viewing with seriousness the complaints of violation of human rights relating to anti-terrorist operations involving the police and security forces.

The Commission has taken a clear position on the vexed question of terrorism and human rights. It has reiterated more than once that terrorism cannot be justified as it has now been recognized by the international community as an enemy of Human Rights Rule of Law and Democracy that aims at the destruction of civil society and unravelling of the state. It has been very emphatic in articulating it's conviction that it is the duty of the police and armed forces of the country backed by all elements of civil society to fight and defeat terrorism. It has, however, been emphasizing from time to time that fight against terrorism has to be won in a manner that respects the Constitution of the Rupublic, the laws of the land and the treaty obligations of the nation.

The NHRC has taken a number of initiatives to remove the infrastructural and procedural inadequacies in the existing machinery provided for enforcement of the Right to Life and Liberty. Important points are listed below:

1. The Commission had in September 93 directed the SPs and DMs of districts all over the country to report to it directly every incident of death and rape in police custody within a period of 24 hours of its occurrence. Failure to send such reports, it was made clear that it would lead to a presumption that an effort was being made to suppress the facts. The instructions were subsequently extended to cover death in judicial custody as well.
2. The Commission has issued directions for the video filming of post mortem in cases of death in police custody and introduced a model autopsy form.
3. The Commission has endorsed the recommendations of the Indian Law Commission to the effect that Section 114 (b) should be inserted in the Indian Evidence Act, 1872 to introduce a rebuttable presumption that injuries sustained by a person in police custody, may be presumed to have been caused by a police officer.
4. The Commission has supported the recommendations of ILC to amend section 197 Cr. PC in order to obviate the necessity for Government sanction for the prosecution of police officers when a prima facie case of custodial violence has been established in an inquiry conducted by a Session Judge.
5. The Commission has endorsed the recommendations of the National Police Commission for mandatory judicial inquiry in every case of custodial death or rape.
6. The Commission has endorsed the observations of the NPC that the power of arrest vested in the police is one of the chief sources of corruption in the police and is being widely abused to harass and humiliate persons in several situations for malafide considerations.The Commission has endorsed the guidelines recommended by the NPC on exercise of powers of arrest by the

police which severely restrict these powers to the cases of heinous offences only. The NPC had found that 60 per cent of the arrests made by the police which accounted for 43.2 per cent of expenditure on jails are either unnecessary or unjustified. It has recently helped the Law Commission in an exercise to analyse the issue in depth and come out with a consultation paper on the law of arrests. The Law Commission has broadly reiterated the recommendations of the NPC in this paper.

7. The Commission's support to the demand of human rights proponents for withdrawal of TADA was instrumental in government decision not to extend it beyond May 1997. The Commission impleaded itself in the proceedings before the Supreme Court in respect of the Armed Forces (Special Powers) Act, 1958. The Apex Court,while confirming it's constitutional validity on 27.11.97, held that:
   (i) The Declaration designating an area as disturbed u/s 3 of the Act should be reviewed periodically;
   (ii) Powers to be exercised u/s 4 (a) would minimum necessary for effective control of the situation;
   (iii) Persons arrested by armed forces should be handed over to the nearest police station with least possible delay;
   (iv) Provisions of Cr. PC shall be observed in matters of search and seizure; and
   (v) The instructions contained in the list of do's and don't's issued by the army authorities shall be strictly followed.

9. The Commission strongly feels that the growing lawlessness of the police causing large scale violation of human rights of the citizens, can be checked not merely by punishing the delinquent officers but with systematic police reforms to change the character and functioning of the police in accordance with the imperatives of policing a democratic society. The NHRC endorses the NPC recommendations regarding insulation of the police from extraneous pressures, accountability of the police to law, creation of a State Security Commission to exercise people's control over the police and a fixed tenure after proper selection of the Chief of the Police in every State. The Commission has impleaded itself as a party in a writ petition filed by Prakash Singh and N.K. Singh, retired IPS officers in the Supreme Court which relates to implementation of the crucial recommendations of the NPC.

10. The Commission has taken the issue of 'fake encounter' head-on in its orders on a petition submitted by the Andhra Pradesh Civil Liberty Committee (APCLC) which alleged that the Andhra Pradesh police has been, instead of following the due process of law, resorting to 'executive elimination ' and killed a number of PWG members and their supporters and sympathisers in fake encounters. In its order passed on 5.11.96, the Commission held that the police do not possess unchartered right to kill any person with impunity. The Commission explained that the death of any person caused by the police in an operation against militants can be justified only by the right of private defence (Section 96 IPC) or the provisions of Section 46(3) Cr. PC regarding the arrest of a person wanted for an offence punishable with death or life imprisonment. However, the matter whether the death was caused by the police officer in exercising the legitimate right of private defence or proper exercise of the Powers of Arrest u/s 46 (3) Cr. PC can be decided by proper investigation and not otherwise. The Commission, therefore, recommended that in every case of death in encounter, a case u/s 304 IPC (Culpable Homicide not amounting to murder) will be registered at the police station concerned but investigated by the State CID. The Commission has condemned the current practice of registering a case under Section 307 IPC against the deceased militants in such cases. These cases registered for the purpose of justifying the exercise of Right of Private Defence by the police party involved in the encounter are closed as abated with no further investigation. These instructions were reiterated by the Chairman in a DO letter addressed to the Chief Ministers of all the States / UTs expressing the resolve of the commission that it will not allow the Right of Private Defence to be manipulated to justify fake encounters or the provisions of Section 46 (3) to be subverted to serve such an end.

The Commission has been making full use of it's powers under Section 18(3) of the Human Rights Act to arrange immediate interim relief for the victims of violation of human rights particularly in cases of custodial violence and illegal detention following the principal of compensation in public law settled by the Supreme Court in the case of *Nilabati Behera* vs. *the State of Orissa*. It has awarded compensations amounting to over Rs. 4.5 crore in 360 cases till now.

It is now firmly established that the plea of sovereign immunity is inadmissible in proceedings under Articles 32 and 226 of the Constitution for deciding liability of the public servants for violation of human rights of the citizens and awarding relief including monetary compensation to the victims. Earlier the courts were ordering in such cases the Governments concerned to make payment of 'amends' to the victims or their family members in cases of violation of their right to life and liberty. Of late, a new and welcome trend has emerged which makes the guilty public servant pay the compensation from his pocket. Though the fear of monetary punishment is deterring the police to some extent from wantonly violating the right to life and liberty of the citizens, full realization of this most fundamental human right will become a reality only if the respect for human rights is in-built into professional ethics of the police service.

8
Right to Equality

K.P. Saksena

History has it that from time immemorial, equal respect for human being and of human dignity have been disregarded with impunity; except for a comparatively very small so-called elite, which enjoyed all the privileges and luxuries in society, vast majority of mankind lived in conditions of economic, social and political inequality. A person's descent, colour, ethnicity, gender, race, religion, etc, determines the status in a hierarchical society. Indeed, the vast majority was regarded as ordained by the so-called 'divine theory' to subserve the needs of the elite or the so-called 'noble class', who by virtue of their birth- descent, were 'divinely' ordained to carry the burden of promoting art, science and philosophy and to help advance civilization. For this purpose, they needed 'leisure' - unencumbered by any kind of physical work which should be provided by the services of the remaining class (vast majority) of people.

In modern times (i.e., the western world), the dictum of 'equality' first came in vogue in the wake of the American Declaration of Independence (1776) and the French Declaration of the Rights of Men (1789). The American Declaration asserted that 'all men are created equal', that they are "endowed by their Creator with certain unalienable rights that include Life, Liberty and pursuit of happiness..." However, in reality 'equality' of 'men' in the American Declaration (of course, excluded women) was confined to what is commonly referred to as WASP, i.e., White, Anglo- Saxona and Protestant, Such a parochial approach is not surprising since the framers of the American Declaration were White Protestant Christians and were largely influenced, among others, by the writings of the British political philosopher, John Locke[1] who has confined equal rights to the white propertied male only; to him, wage-earners, peasants and other working-class people, both male and female (white and, of course, non-white) were not entitled to equal rights and liberty.

The French Declaration, on the other hand, emphasising "Liberty, Equality and 'Fraternity" is more comprehensive in its content and universal in its application, Equality, in the French Declaration-included all men (but not women), irrespective of one's birth, colour, descent, ethnicity, religion and vocation, etc. The French Declaration was revolutionary in character since a widely prevalent practice in France, at that time, as in whole Europe and North America was discrimination on the basis of birth colour, descent, religion, vocation, wealth etc. Whether the French Declaration on equality included the non- Europeans remains a moot point because until then colonial prejudices has not yet surfaced.

Nonetheless, the American Declaration and, more so, the French Declaration became a source of inspiration for the peoples all over the world, in their struggle to seek equality and dignity as human beings. Lord Aeton, the British historian is reported to have said that 'the single confused page of the French Declaration outweighs libraries and is stronger than all the armies of Napolean."[2]

However, the American and French Declarations, racial and religious discrimination remained widely prevalent in the western world. Other parts of the world have had their own respective prejudices and discriminatory social practices, for instance, caste system and the so-called 'untouchability' in India.

We have to traverse a long way before the concept of equality gained world-wide acceptance at least in theory.

Indeed, one of the most revolutionary development that occurred in the mid-twentieth century is the idea that all human beings, irrespective of one's birth, religion, gender, nationality, etc. are bestowed with equal rights as *human beings*.

Such an idea is not a new one. Many social religious leaders and philosophers of both the East and the West have advocated, time and again, respect for all human beings without distinction of any kind. Swami Vivekanand, more than a century ago (to be precise, 23 September, 1893) in his address to the World Congress on Religion, held at Chicago, called for universal brotherhood and respect for all human beings irrespective of one's race, religion, birth, caste, colour, creed, gender, etc., and respect for all religions, cultures and ways of life.

What is new is that, such a revolutionary assertion, as first made in the United Nation's Charter followed by Universal Declaration of Human Rights and other international instruments, emanated from a congregation, not of individual idealists or religious leaders, but of representatives of governments from all over the world, including those of the erstwhile colonial powers. Various international conventions, both global and regional, having legally binding obligations have, reemphasised the concept of equality and respect of human rights of all human beings.

It has been the most revolutionary development because until recently, so it seems, western colonial powers,[3] who practised racial and colour discrimination in its most brutal, inhuman form in the name of so-called 'White Man's Burden' and three-fourths human beings of the world under colonial rule, were referred to as 'sullen people, half devil, half child.'[4]

II

Right to equality is one of the most important human rights. It is linked with the concept of liberty and justice and is manifested through the two fundamental and complimentary principles. The first is affirmed in Article 1 of the UN Charter, which asserts observance of and respect for human rights and fundamental freedoms for **all** without distincton as to race, sex, language or religion. The other principles that all human beings are born free and equal in dignity and in rights, are reaffirmed in the Universal Declaration of Human Rights. It is upon these two principles that all international instruments on human rights are based.

Equality and non-discrimination constitute the dominant single theme of the two International Covenants on Human Rights. Equality, of course, implied that the rights recognized by the Covenants are rights of all human beings equally and the various provisions apply to 'all persons','everyone', 'every human being' and that 'no-one' shall be deprived of those rights.

It has been noted that such words as 'every one' and 'no-one' etc. are the hardest for most people to accept, especially in Asia, where hierarchical social relations loaded with distinction of caste, creed, religion, sex and birth still prevail.

What is meant by equality? It does not mean that all human

beings are similar or identical in terms of their talent and capability. There are certainly differences in physical and intellectual capacity, in shape, colour and size, likes and dislikes, cultural background, etc. Indeed, human beings are deeply diverse in internal charactaristics (such as gender, general abilities, particular talents, age, proneness to illness, etc.) as well as in external circumstances such as ownership of financial assets, social backgrounds, environmental predicaments and so on. [5] Hence, the term equality takes into account all these differences.

What is emphasized is that there are certain inherent and inalienable rights of every person, not because he belongs to a particular religion, race, gender or nationality but because he is a human being. Equality means that the good of one person is of as much intrinsic value as the good of the other, that no person should be treated as a means to the good of the other.

It means that all are equal before law, that there is not one set of laws for some persons and another set of laws for others; and that everyone is entitled to participate in public affairs and seek a public office on the basis of one's merit, experience and training.

Again, equality does not mean identical opportunities, since opportunities in life, as noted, by Harold Laski, are very much determined by one's place of birth. A child born in a rich, well-educated family, in a metropolitan town, is likely to have advantage of much more and better opportunities than a child born in a poor, illiterate family in rural area or in some small town. Hence, the emphasis is on 'adequate' opportunities, which would allow everyone to develop one's potentiality which nature has bestowed him/her with, as a human being.

This need of adequate opportunity has led to a legal-political system what is often referred to as 'affirmative actions' or 'protective measures' taken in favour of certain classes of people which are likely to be denied adequate or equal opportunities. For instance, in India, under the traditional caste system, a large number of people was referred to as untouchables who were assigned menial work in society. For centuries, education facilities and opportunities for social uplift were denied to them. They were born a destitute and died as such. Hence, the Indian Constitution in its schedule has listed such people and they are known as the Scheduled Castes and Scheduled Tribes. There are free educational facilities for them and a certain percentage of posts in various government services are reserved for them. However, such protective measures which deviate from the principle of equality before law are for specific duration—until these 'disadvantaged groups' reach certain level of development to enable them to compete with others on merit.

In Asia, a few countries have opted for protective measures of a different kind. On gaining independence, these countries found that migrant citizens have obtained certain advantages over the indigenous people who are often referred to as 'bhumi putra' or sons of the soil, as for instance, in Malaysia. In some countries, such as Fiji, migrant citizens outnumber the natives. Hence, their constitution provides safeguard to protect the special interest of the indigenous population and also in terms of 'weightage' of seats in legislature, educational institutions and government services.

Are these protective measures violation of the principle of equality? The principle of equality is violated if the protective measures or distinction applied has no objective and reasonable justification. Prohibition of discrimination does not preclude positive measure, in favour of disadvantaged sections of society. One should hope, however, that such measures are of a temporary nature and that they will soon be removed, once the disadvantaged groups have reached adequate advancement, socially and educationally; and that non-discrimination both in law and practice shall be adhered to.

Equality before Law

The principle of equality as a human right does not exclude distinctions based on differences of two kind, which are generally considered admissible and justified: (a) differentiation based on character imputable to the individual for which he may properly be held responsible (examples are: industriousness or idleness, merit/ demerit, carefulness/ carelessness, delinquency/lawfulness etc.); (b) differentiation based on individual qualifications which inspire of not being qualities for which the individual can be held responsible, are relevant to social values and may be taken into account (for example, in matters of appointment to a particular position, physical and mental capacities, talent, professional training of respective candidates need to be given due consideration).

Judicial equality excludes any differentiation based on grounds which have no relevance to merit or social value and should not be considered as having any social or legal meaning, whether they are innate such as colour, race or sex or social generic category such as language, political or other opinions, national or social origin, property, birth or other status. Article 7 of the Universal Declaration and Article 26 of the Covenant reiterate this principle when they respectively state that all human beings are equal before the law and are entitled without any discrimination, as noted above, to the equal protection of the law.

Equality before the law or equal protection of the law has wider egalitarian meaning, which prohibits all kinds of discriminations. The law must prohibit discrimination and prevent discrimination by officials, and perhaps by private individuals, who interfere with equality before the law, with the equal protection of the laws including equal access to public accommodation. The concept of equality implies both de jure and de facto equality.

It should be noted that a distinction obtainable in some countries in terms of affirmative or protective measures oradvancement of socially and educationally disadvantaged segment of society (which we have discussed earlier) is not applicable in the context of equality before law. In other words, no discrimination is permissible in regard to equal access to judiciary and application of rule of law.

Equality in the Administration of Justice

This right entails that no one should be imprisoned or movement restricted unless proved guilty through a due process of law by competent court in an open trial. This right is emphasized as against arbitary arrest, summary trial and detention without any trial. Article 10 of the Universal Declaration lays down that everyone accused of a crime is entitled to a fair and public trial by an independent and impartial court or tribunal. The principle is elaborated in some legal details in Articles 14 and 15 of the Covenant.

What does fair trial or competent court mean?

The basic idea is that the person should be tried in courts, duly established by law and not by functionaries specifically appointed to try a particular individual or a set of alleged criminals; that the judiciary should be independent of the law-making and law-enforcing authorities. In other words, the same authority should not act as the legislator (laying down the law), the prosecutor (deciding that the law has been violated) and the judge as well as the jury. This right also entails that a person shall not be punished for those actions, which were legal, when they were carried out. It also means that if an act was punishable in one way when committed, no later change in the law may effect the punishment given.

The individual accused should have a right to be informed about the charge against him. He should be entitled to have a lawyer of his own choice and that trial should be completed within a reasonable time. In many countries accused individuals entitled to be released on bail. This means that an accused may retain his or her liberty pending trial. In most of the countries in Asia as in other parts of the world this right is well recognized in the legal system but the practice is different. One common flaw relates to unusual delay in the process to trial. The principle that justice delayed is justice denied is honoured more in its breach than observance. There are instances when individuals stayed in jail for as long as twenty years and more without ever being charged of any offence. In some cases trial dragged on for years. On the other hand, instances abound when people were put to summary trial, sometime leading to prompt execution.

Illiteracy, ignorance and poverty are largely responsible for the grim situation that prevails in Asian countries, as in other parts of the Third World. More conspicuous violators of these rights are the law enforcement officials, who are, indeed, supposed to protect uphold human rights of the community. In 1979, the General Assembly adopted a "Code of Conduct for Law Enforcement Officials" and recommended it to the Governments for national legislation and adherence in practice as a body of principles for observance by law enforcement officials.

Responsibility for respecting and protecting this most commonly violated right of the individual, of course, rests with the government concerned , but people themselves have to share the responsibility. They have to assert themselves and obtain wholly and demonstrably the benefit of these rights recognized by the international community. Those who are fortunate enough to have education and better means of living should organize legal aid societies and vigilant groups to aid and safeguard the rights of the more unfortunate (illiterate and poor), innocent people.

It should be noted that wrongful arrest or confinement entitles the victim under Article 9(5) of the Covenant, to have an enforceable right to compensation for moral as well as actual damage done to him. Unfortunately, barring one or two Asian countries, the legal system of most of the Asian countries, does not have provisions for compensation. People should seek such a provision.

Let us turn another aspect; right to life and liberty necessarily entails the right to live with dignity, privacy and enjoyment of family life. However, institution of modern society with ever expanding authority of the state, the growing network of socio-economic relations and the criss-crossing of the communication systems have increasingly reduced the individual's autonomy, leaving him victim of forces beyond his control. The Universal Declaration of Human Rights in Articles 6, 12 and 16 and the Covenant , in Article 16, 17, 23 and 24 provides protection to the individual from these forces.

Right to Legal Personality

In identical language, the Universal Declaration (Article 6) and the Covenant (Article 16) provides that "everyone shall have the right to recognition as a person before the law". It should be noted that term 'everyone' is used here to include men and women and the children of both sexes, citizens as well as non-citizens and foreigners. Each of these is a person with legal status; each has rights and assumed obligations. A child acquires certain rights from the moment of its birth; and, in some legal system, these rights are retroactive from the time of its conception.

Legal personality is a crucial aspect of freedom. It distinguishes one from others and permits an individual to assert his essential dignity as a human being, endows him with power to make legal dispositions and to claim an area of privacy.

In brief, the Covenant requires state parties to treat every human being every where, male or female, young or old, alien or citizen, as a person before the law enjoying the protection of law, and with legal status to have rights and assumed obligations: to own, acquire, and dispose of property; to use and be used; and to invoke other legal remedies.

III

Let us turn to the situation in terms of right to equality in India. Here, from time immemorial, religious teachers and philosophers have preached equality of all human beings, but history has it that social inequality and discrimination of the worst kind, consequential to caste system, remained the hallmark of Indian way of life.

In its inception, the caste system emerged from the social structure based on three concepts: the autonomous village community, the caste or vocational system and the joint family system. In all the three, it was the group that counted; individual had a secondary place. The aim was social security, avoidance of conflicting interest and continuance of the group, i.e., society. Within each group, whether village community or the large joint family or within the caste, there was a communal life shared together essence of equality and democratic method. Live and let live was the motto. Conflict of interest and competitiveness was to be avoided.

Economic and social progress was not the aim and, therefore, progress suffered and stagnation crept in, what was worse was that caste system initially based on each one doing what was one capable of doing one's part towards the welfare of the community, became a highly rigid system. Those who took to religious teachings or priesthood, established their superiority and those who took to menial work were destined to live a life of humiliation and became known as 'untouchables'. Although through the ages, social reformers appeared on the scene and preached equality of all human beings, but in the actual life things continue the same way.

In the ninteenth century, with the advent of religious renaissance, teachings of such thinkers as Raja Rammohan Roy, Ramakrishna Paramhansa, Swami Dayanand Saraswati, Swami Vivekananda and others, movement against caste system and untouchability, and for equality of human being and human dignity got a new lease

An added re-emphasis on equality came from the Indian national movement demanding that Indians should be extended the same treatment under the law as British nationals in India. Intelligentsia in India felt highly humiliated when British rulers asserted their superiority and British nationals were not subjected to the laws meant for Indian 'subjects'. There were exclusive clubs and residential areas for British nationals where Indians were not allowed.

This demand and assertion for equality was reflected in the draft Constitution prepared by a committee with Motilal Nehru as Chairman (1928), which laid emphasis on right to equality and with the provisions that all persons without distinction of gender, race or religion were to have equal rights to the use of public places, courts of justice and equality before law.

Again, the Karachi Declaration (1931) of the Indian National Congress reiterated *inter alia* this right of equality in the resolution of fundamental rights and economic and social change. Thus, the National Movement look forward to a constitutional framework, which would ensure equality between one section of the community and another in the matter of religion, worship and the pursuit or ordinary obligation of life.

It was, therefore, inevitable that the Indian Constitution, linked up with the history of the freedom movement, the right to equality is reflected primarily in its preamble.

There are five Articles (14-18) dealing with the Right to Equality. Article 14, in a negative language asserts that State shall not deny to any person equality before law then goes on to assert in positive language: 'equal protection of the laws within the territory of India.'

Article 15 prohibits discrimination on grounds of religion, race, caste, sex or in place of birth. It explicitly declares that no citizen shall on grounds only of religion, race, caste, sex or place birth be subjected to any disability or restriction with regard to acccess to public places like shops , restaurants, places of worship or the use of public facilities like wells, tanks, etc. However, the State is empowered to make special provisions for women and children.

Equality of opportunity is guaranteed under Article 16. The commitment of the Constitution eradicating untouchability find emphasis in Article 17 which abolishes untouchability. To emphasise equality Article 18 lays down that no title, other than being a military or academic distinction, shall be conferred by the State.

Over the period, judicial decisions interpreting Article 14 while recognising the nature of the fundamental right of equlity recognised the need of reconsideration of certain limitations. For instance, the Constitution itself gives certain privileges to the President and the Governors (and also to members of Parliament and State Legislators). As such the incumbent of these offices cannot be sued in the courts of law.

There is more to the situation; some of the provisions, as interpreted by the judiciary have resulted in a certain element of discrimination. For example, the liability of the State in tort is even today not (necessarily) the same as the liability of a private employer. No suit lies against government for an injury in the course of exercises of the sovereign functions of the government. Similarly, in the statutory framework of India, there are provisions which introduce or maintain certain amount of inequality between government officials and the ordinary citizens. For example, for a legal suit against the government or against a government employee, for an act purporting to be done by the latter in his official capacity, a two month notice is ordinarily required under Section 80 of the

Code of Civil Procedure similarly, a public servant who is not removable from his office except by or with the sanction of the government, if accused of an offence committed by him while acting or purporting to act in the discharge of his official duties, Criminal Courts are barred from taking cognizance of such an offence without sanction of the Central Goverment or the State Government (as the case may be) under Section 197 of the Code of Criminal Procedure.

Another aspect, and a very significant one, to be noted is that the framers of the Indian Constitution recognised the hard reality of how a large section of the society, as a result of caste system, was discriminated against and destined to lead a life of deprivation and humiliation. As such, the Constitution embraces equality as a cardinal value against a back ground of elaborate value and clearly perceived inequalities. The result has been an array of provisions which could collectively be referred to as compensatory or protective discrimination.

Thus, while clause 1 and 2 of Article 15 prevent discrimination on grounds of religion, race, caste, sex etc., subsequent clauses (3 and 4) provide exceptions for a protective discrimination in favour of women and children and for the advancement of any socially or educationally backward classes of citizens and for the so-called Scheduled Castes and Scheduled Tribes (SCs and STs).

Similarly, Article 16 which guarantees equality of opportunity in matters of public employment and non-discrimination also provides for the following exceptions: Parliament is empowered to make prior residence in a State as a requirement for appointments; further, the State can make any provision in the reservation of appointments of posts in-favour of any backward class of citizens, which in opinion of the State, is not adequately represented in the services; and thirdly that the law can provide the incumbent of an office relating to the affairs of a religious or denominational institution to belong to that particular religion or denomination.

Similar to that, Article 16(4) empowers the State to make reservation in educational institutions. The first amendement to the Constitution in 1951 contained Article 15.4. Article 335 emphasises that the claims of the members of the SCs and STs shall be taken into consideration consistently with the maintenance of efficiency, in the making of appointments to services and posts in connection with the affairs of the Union, or of a State.

In sum, the Constitution permits discrimination by reserving seats for admission in educational institutions and jobs for women and children and socially and educationlly backward class of citizens for the SCs and STs. It should, however, be noted that the Constitution does not define what constitutes "a socially and educationally backward class of citizens." It just leaves wide scope of legislators to take decision about defining or identifying them. Some suggest backwardness in terms of caste while others point out that poverty, occupation and place of habitation are more related factors for determining backwardness. This led to disputes and tensions over reservation issues.

Indeed, the question on reservations has become an important aspect of party-politics for election purposes. For instance, initially reservations were made for employment only, for a period of ten years, with the exception that those who were deprived would come up and could compete with others, on merit. But today after fifty-five years, no political party dares to say that merit and not reservation on the basis of caste, be the criteria for employment and education - again, only a very low percentage of SCs and STs have benefitted from the reservation clause. This is so, simply because the few families took advantage at the initial stage continue to monopolise the 'benefits'. For instance, a Scheduled Caste (Jagjeevan Ram), who first gained ministership at cabinet level way back in1946, his family members continue to take advantages by obtaining positions, under reservation clause, in IAS and in technical education, till this day. Again, first generation SCs/ STs, who became IAS officers, say in (1950s), and got the full advantage of providing education and bringing up their children in much better social environments, still continue (after some 55 years) to benefit from reservation clause.

Again, there are instances where laws have been enacted for the purposes of providing additional protective discriminations; but, executive apathy, administrative indifference and the conflicts between social, political and bureaucratic power structures have kept them as merely pious wishes. For example, after the Constitution came into force, to give effect to the declaration contained in Article 17 that practice of untouchability would be an offence punishable under criminal law; that was not considered adequate enough and the Parliament to further strengthen the provision, enacted the Untouchability (Offence) Act in 1955 providing for stringent punitive measures. However, despite the fact that the Act has been in force for more than four decades and was amended in 1976 to make its enforcement and consequent punishment more stringent, the SCs and the so-called untouchables continue to suffer from social disabilities and discriminations in most parts of the country.

Further, despite the Constitutional guarantee of equality before law, there remains gross inequality based on gender. This gender inequality continue in law among women belonging to different religions and communities. Indeed, courts have upheld this legal inequality among women on the ground of so-called reasonable classification. For instance, in April 1985, the Supreme Court in the case of *Md. Ahmed Khan* vs. *Shah Bano* declared that a Muslim husband of sufficient means must provide maintenance to his divorced wife, who is without any source of income of her own. The Court in the same judgement also asked the Government to implement Article 45A of the Directive Principles of the Constitution to secure a uniform civil code for all the citizens throughout territory of India. However, the then political party in power (Congress) succumbed to the political pressure of Muslim fundamentalists who described the Supreme Court's judgement as an attack on Muslim Personal Law and the Muslim Community. The then Government introduced before Parliament an Act and got it adopted in May 1986, what is known as Muslim Women (Protection Rights on Divorce) Act, 1986, to negate the Supreme Court decision.

It is not only with Muslim women alone; in fact, the law, in general, does not provide equality for women in such matters. In recent times Government and various political parties have been talking for removal of inequalities and discrimination against women and for their development in making reservations in jobs for them. Recently, proposals have been made to make reservation of 33 per cent in all elective bodies, but till this day, no steps have taken in that regard. The proposal is held up because some parties want that 33 per cent reservation should be distributed to SCs/ STs and also among so-called other Backward Classes.

The reality is that throughout history, women have been discriminated against. For instance, in countries like the United States of America, France and England, though claiming democratic system of Government, did not initially grant right to vote to women until 1921 in Britain and USA, and much later in France and there are still countries where equality of law and political rights have not been extended to women. As regards services, there are on an average 27.4 per cent of women administrators in industrially advanced nations and 10 per cent in developing countries. In India, it is only 2.3 per cent.

The provisions relating to equality in the Indian Constitution are more elaborate than found in any other constitution. They guarantee equality of law and equal protection of the law, but this guarantee is of equal treatment of persons in equal circumstances. In other words equality does not mean every law must have universal application for all persons, who are not by nature attainment and, most significantly, by circumstances in the same provision as the varying needs of different classes of persons require separate treatment. Hence, the need of protective discrimination. As such, the Constitution does not take away from the State the power of classifying persons of legitimate purposes. This classification must not be arbitrary but must be rationale. Articles 14-16 taken together enshrine the principle of equality and absence of discrimination.

While the Constitution provisions do emphasise right to equality, but to cover various aspects, it has been loaded with plethora of 'exceptions', provisions, reservations, by amendments and counter amendments, judicial interpretations and counter-interpretations as to create such a maze as to leave the common people confused and confounded. Indeed, leave aside the common people even highly educated persons would need a legal expert to explain what is indeed meant by right to equality in the Indian constitutional system.

Further, despite constitutional guarantee of equality before law and equal protection of laws, the practice remains very different because of wide disparities in terms of social status,wealth and political contacts. There are instances galore where wealthy and socially, politically well-connected individuals get legal protection and release on bail by hiring the services of top lawyers and knocking door of the highest court, even if one is accused of murder. On the other hand, more than 150,000 persons are in prison as undertrials, some of them for more than 20 years, largely because they do not have financial sources to seek equal protection of law and even to arrange for bail.

In sum, while right to equality of all human beings, irrespective of race, religion, ethnicity, birth, descent, etc. is being universally accepted, still right to equality remains a mirage. There is no country in the world, where discrimination of one kind or the other does not exist. However, while the right to equality has not been attained in any part of the world, but it is significant to note that it has not been repudiated either. The concept of equality continues to set the norms and standards for judging the extent to which human rights are available in a country.

References

1. It is intriguing to note that despite such views, which are highly discriminatory and amounts to the very negation of the concept of human rights, John Locke is regarded in the western world as to quote an eminent American scholar 'the father of human rights''. Louis Henkin, et.al. eds., *Human Rights* (New York: Foundation Press, 1999), p. 22.

Also see, ''Inequality and the [U.S.] Constitution'', in J.R Pole, *The Pursuit of Equality in American History* (Los Angeles; University of California Press, 1978), pp. 148-77.

2. Cited in Hersch Lauterpacht, ''The International Protection of Human Rights'', *Recuerl des Cours*, Vol. 70, 1947, p. 126.

3. The term is used in the civilisational sense and includes all colonial powers including the USA, Russia and Japan.

4. This phrase is excerpted from Rudyard Kiplings's (famous/ infamous) poem: ''The White Man's Burden'' (1901). Its full text is reproduced in Martin Gilbert, *The European Powers 1900-45* (New York: the New American Library, 1965), pp.18-19.

5. In this context, see, in particular, Amartya Sen, *Inequality Re-examined* (Oxford: Clarendon Press, 1992). In this inclusive and thought provoking analysis, the eminent social scientist raises the question; 'Equality of What? and turn on the pervasive diversity of human beings. He argues that often-repeated rhetoric of equality such as all men are created equal can deflect attention from diversities that are crucial in understanding claims of equality. He concentrates on the capability of different persons to achieve valuable functioning, and more generally on the human freedom to pursue their respective objectives.

9

Women's Right to Equality—From Theory to Practice

Jayashree Gupta

"All human beings are born free and equal in dignity and rights" said the Universal Declaration of Human Rights which was adopted by the General Assembly of the United Nations on 10th December 1948. This date is celebrated as Human Rights Day all over the world, year after year.

Equality has been a focal point for discussion in several international conventions since then. The convention on the Elimination of all forms of Discrimination Against Women, which was adopted by the General Assembly of the United Nations on 18th December 1979 had reiterated the determination of the nations to adopt the measures required for the elimination of discrimination in all its forms and manifestations. 165 countries of the world, including India have ratified this Convention (as on 16th February, 2000) and are legally bound to implement it.

The Fourth World Conference on Women, held at Beijing in September, 1995, further glorified the concept of 'Equality' and obtained commitment from nations not only to reduce gender inequalities and inadequacies in all spheres, but also to ensure that gender perspective is reflected in all policies and programmes. The Indian delegation not only played a leading role in drafting the Declaration and Platform for Action, but also earned the distinction of being the first to endorse them without reservation.

Besides being signatory to most of the international treaties and conventions on the subject, India has also adopted a progressive Constitution and equally progressive laws. "Right to Equality" finds its place of pride amongst fundamental rights and can be enforced through the Supreme Court of India, under Article 32 of the Constitution. The Supreme Court has also laid down elaborate norms for protecting the 'equality' and 'dignity' of working women in its judgment of August 1997 in the case of *Visakha* vs *State of Rajasthan*. With the back up support of international treaties and conventions on the one hand and constitutional provisions and institutions like National Human Rights Commission and National Commission for Women on the other hand, let us see how equal women are in actual practice in India.

The discrimination between the male and the female becomes visible well before their birth. The son-preference syndrome is so strong that many parents do not even hesitate to kill this girls well before their birth. The desire to have a son, coupled with the desire to have a small family, compels women to resort to sex determination tests followed by termination of female foetus. This fact is borne out by diminishing number of females in successive census reports. We landed into the twentieth century with a sex ratio (males per 100 females) of 102.9 in1901. By the middle of the century (1951) the number of males for every 100 females rose to 105.7, and by 1991 we have increased the sex ratio further to 107.9. Haryana has the highest sex ratio of 115.6.

It is a common saying in India that bringing up a daughter is like watering a plant in another's courtyard. So not only is she underfed, she is also made to work, at the cost of her education and is not even provided proper medical care when she is ill.

According to a study conducted in villages of Rajasthan, a female child in the age group of 5-9 years works for 5.50 hours per day, against 1.83 hours of work by the male child in the same age group. Their working hours are increased further to 7.66 hours in the age group of 6-14 years, whereas boys in this age group work for only 2.98 hours. Female literacy is only 20.8 per cent in Rajasthan (1991 census) against male literacy of 55.1 per cent. At the national level also the position is not at all encouraging with female literacy rate of 39.4 per cent only against male literacy of 63.9 per cent.

The International Conference on Population and Development (ICPD), held at Cairo in 1994, stressed the need to promote reproductive health with a view to promote women's empowerment. Seen in the context of reproductive health indicators India lags behind many countries in developed as well as developing world. The findings of National Family Health Survey 1998-99, indicate that only 42.8 per cent of the currently married women in the age -group of 15-49 are protected by modern methods of contraception. And men, who consider themselves to be head of the family, the decision-takers, the bread-winners, contribute only 5 per cent of this.

Coming to the quality of health care, even the basic antenatal care is unavailable to approximately 50 per cent women. About two-thirds deliveries take place at home, mostly attended by quack nurses. No wonder, maternal mortality rates are unacceptably high in India. According to recent estimates, maternal mortality rate (number of maternal deaths per one lakh live births) in India is 407. In most of the developed countries of the world this ratio is less than 25.

According to Survey of Causes of Death (Rural), 1995, 9.8 per cent of the total female deaths in reproductive age-group (15-44) are due to child-birth and pregnancy. Despite abortion being legalised, 17.6 per cent of maternal deaths occur due to abortion. Obviously people still prefer going to quacks.

Due to malnutrition since infancy, anaemia is prevalent amongst more that 50 per cent women in India. This is a grave risk during pregnancy and 17 per cent of the total maternal deaths are directly attributed to anaemia.

Even amongst children, boys are more likely to receive health care from qualified doctors as compared to girls. Studies of hospital admissions show that more men are admitted than women in almost all parts of the country. Northern India has 2.1 male admissions to every female admission. It is because of this neglect of women that their death rate is higher that men upto 34 years of age. In children aged 0-4 years female death rate is 24.8 against 22.7 for male for India as a whole. The disparity is highest in Uttar Pradesh with female mortality rate of 36.7 against 29.7 for male.

Our social customs also perpetuate these inequalities. Despite the law against dowry, dowry is gaining higher social acceptance day by day. It has become an accepted means of vulgar display of wealth for the rich and a source of perpetual indebtedness for the poor. Dowry related crimes, suicides and deaths have become a common place news item today, so much so that it is easily shrugged aside as a routine matter. Statistical details brought out by National Crime Records Bureau also indicate a rising trend in dowry related crimes. The total number of dowry deaths has increased from 5092 in 1995 to 6006 in 1997. Similarly cases of torture (violence by husband and relatives) have also increased from 31127 in 1995 to 36592 in 1997. Overall crimes against women have increased from 1.09 lakh in 1995 to 1.21 lakh in 1997. Whether it is rape or molestation, crimes against women are increasing day by day.

It is felt that increased participation of women in income earning activities would reduce gender inequalities. But, unfortunately, their participation in economic activities outside home is very limited. According to 1991 census, female work participation rate is only 22.27 against male work participation rate of 51.61. Percentage of women in organised sector further comes down to 14.8 with the share of public sector at 12.8 per cent and of the private sector at 19.7 per cent. Central Government had 2.83 lakh female employees in 1990, but in terms of percentage it dwindles to 7.50 per cent of the total work force of the Government of India. According to Human Development Report, 1998, only 2.3 per cent of administrators and managers are women in India as compared to 42.7 per cent in the USA and 53.8 per cent in Italy. A recent study carried out by Lal Bahadur Shastri National Academy of Administration, Mussoorie brings out interesting details regarding gender-bias in the Civil Services. About 30 per cent women and 25 per cent male officers belonging to various civil services have accepted that there is gender-stereotyping in postings and assignments. Sexual harassment is another problem accepted by about 7 per cent male and 22 per cent female officers in various civil services. It was also felt that the redressal mechanism is inadequate and is unable to repond to such issues when raised. Obviously, the landmark judgement delivered by the Supreme Court in 1997 regarding sexual harassment of working women has not changed the ground realities.

It is clear from the preceding details , that "Right to Equality" cannot be achieved merely by signing of Treaties and Declarations by the Nations. It will become a reality only when women come out openly and unitedly in their fight against injustice. They will have to refuse not only being mute victims of inequalities but also of being active perpetuators of injustice and inequalities on fellow women, be they daughters (born or unborn), daughters-in-law or colleagues. There is no easy way to achieving equality of status and opportunity.

10
Right to Equality for Women and Ground Realities

Smt. Pritam Arora

The words "We, the people of India" in the constitution encompasses in itself a common gender perception which includes all men and women for equal rights and put them on equal footing.

When the UN was founded in 1945 it resolved that respect for human rights and the dignity is the foundation of freedom, justice and peace in the world.

The word "Human" means the total segment of humanity but women empowerment, welfare and women rights/ reservation are a few fashionable words used to protect women considered to be a weaker section and labelled as a case of charity. By whom? By the other half, coming forward to lift it up from the morass of neglect, suffered throughout the ages just because it has learnt to be docile and has been programmed to be guided and controlled. This attitude has subdued her will power.

What is this weakness? Which has destined her to a limitless state of tolerance why woman is being compartmentalized; why she is put aside for quotas, fitted into formulas for discriminatory protectionism?

It is true she is in capacitated during certain stages of life in her physical dispensation during child birth and needs to be looked after and those short periods in her life have changed the entire structural set up of the human mind which labels her to be weak, actually she is brave enough to conceive, to rear, to breed but sparks of love make her vulnerable to tolerance, she sacrifices her comforts to look after the human race and to perpetuate the norms of civilization. Her physical capacity to smile during hardships is the rare blessing, which the Mother Nature has bestowed on her. The pain is entirely her own, the part of an experience to create humanity to bring into this world a set up of human beings, who do not have the capacity to share it, feel it and come to the same wave length so when they grow up, they forget her travails and become the saviours.

Does religion? Whose moral teaching they have nurtured together. Does earth? Whose grains they have consumed together. Does the quality of blood which they have inherited, changes the thought patterns of communities and the togetherness part is cast aside and norms are prepared for her to accept with complete humility when and how to get married, divorced, whether to limit/control families, whether to stay inside four walls, whether to have freedom to move about in a civilized dress of her choice, to get education or even not dare to come into this world. Her right to utter even a first cry into this world is stifled.

Women is more prone to religion and its rituals, because from her very birth she is fed on this opium, to always remain in stupor, lazy to ask for rights and stay in a state of blissful ignorance. She considers these divine feelings as her spiritual food, though she may be starved of actual food, needed for her physical well-being and healthy existence. She can tolerate hunger in diverse conditions and channel of release of all frustrations finds a way into religion and spirit of sacrifice take precedence over all other emotions.

Yashoda brought up Krishna as her own son and sacrificed her daughter for his sake. Panna Dai a nurse replaced her son and got him killed by Banbir and saved Prince Udai, who became King of Mewar and father of Maharana Pratap. Mata Sundari sacrificed her husband and sons to save the *Dharma*.

14000 queens died at the alter and performed Jauhar instead of fighting with the enemies. Women in Rajasthan had learnt the use of arms and the art of self-defence but they preferred to die for the sake of honour, which could be defiled by the touch of invaders.

Thousands of women came out of their homes to fight for independence of their motherland and sacrificed their comforts and burnt the foreign goods.

Woman has always proved to be a *shakti* (power) for man, a power always saving him from evils and plays the Devi part to her last breath.

Behavioural norms and laws for women in India have come

from men. It was Manu whose injunctions saw to the deterioration of the status of women and it were men like, Raja Rammohan Roy, Ishwar Chandra Vidyasagar and Pt. Madan Mohan Malviya who fought against child marrige, and favoured abolition of Sati, widow remarriage and education for girls.

Even Hindu Code Bill was opposed by conservative lobby in Parliament and maintenance decision was opposed by fundamentalists.

Struggles by women have mostly failed because there were social pressures and muscle power to restrain them from opposing the rules that are uncomfortable and inconvenient for the male lobby.

33 per cent reservation bill in Parliament and Assemblies is opposed by men because it is natural for men to cry foul when their territory is being invaded and inclusion of women is impossible unless some men are deprived but some women also support them because they have been motivated to speak in their language. She has become a programmed specimen and ready to do anything, which pleases them. They do not belong to themselves; they are not their own self because they have acquired their present position and status through favours and back door entries. They have been launched into the system, not because they have fought for the women's rights and struggled for their upliftment and empowerment, but only worked for themselves and earned the position; such leaders are manufactured in political workshops and just remain as symbols. Men provoke them to speak on their behalf and maintain their liberal image through proxy discussion and protests.

In such circumstances the protective legislation just to fill the democratic deficit becomes a farce when only manufactured specimens occupy the position of power and strugglers are ignored.

Education and economic independence are only answers to fight discriminations and the will to survive the only strength. Even after struggling hard the political power will be available to very few so there is need to improve social status, to fight against social evils, exploitation and atrocities against female foetus destruction, evils of dowry and bride burning. Against rape which is raising its hydra head in society. Where minors are raped and killed by their own fathers and close relatives. To fight for property rights, security at workplaces and develop sharing and caring attitude into men by bringing up girls and boys on equal footings since childhood.

It is necessary to struggle to achieve easy accessibility into the judicial system. To try to make it cheaper and faster because it is an uphill task to reach the courts of laws and get justice; for lack of resources and awareness to fight against vultures in society. To make our daughters brave and bold to fight repression and injustice and develop a sense of self-sufficiency and work for the welfare of those who suffer from social and economic handicaps by the accident of birth, caste, region and religion.

If half of the population of the country is deprived of equal status and powers to acquire education, earn livelihood, enjoy political status and protection and security of their life and liberty democracy is not real.

There is need of a movement to the awareness to encourage girls to enter into the profession to prove the strength as equal partner in life.

In view of the equality of women and men in eyes of the Constitution nobody should expect women in India in be motivated to play subordinate role and remain in somebody's power and to prove this, strength lies in the women itself and it is she who has to assert herself by improving her capabilities and strength to survive in adverse circumstances and create a better tomorrow for the whole humanity.

Passage for Women Empowerment

In the Vedic era woman was treated as a partner, in fact in certain situations she had superior status. She used to take part in decision making and played a more assertive role and female members had the moral obligation to obey her to learnt the use of arms, and excelled in fine arts and studied Vedas. Many known Maharishis and have appreciated her as a creator of Srishti, i.e. the entire human kind and declared, "Where women worshipped there live the gods". There were many women like Lopamudra, Vidyotama, Maiteryi, Sita, Ansuya, Savitri, and Draupadi played an assertive role. Razia Sultana was a great ruler and Chand Bibi was a great warrior.

During Independence struggle we had Jija Bai, Jhansi Ki Rani, and Mata Sundari who played an exemplary role for Indian womanhood.

Kasturba Gandhi was a silent but loyal partner and Aruna Asaf Ali was a firebrand companion. Indiraji was an example of daring statesmanship and nine women C.M.'s in India are reflective of the emerging strength of womanpower. In other fields Indian women are not behind anybody. Arti Saha crossed the English Channel, Bachendri Pal conquered Himalayas and scaled the Everest, P.T. Usha and Malleshwari reached in Olympics. Lata Mangeshkar has stunned the world with her melodious songs and M.S. Subbalakshmi with her classical music, Dr. Indira Ahuja produced the first test-tube baby in India. Kiran Bedi, the first women IPS officer, Kalpana Chawla our space woman is an example of endurance to complete with men, Fatima Bibi was the first woman judge of the Supreme Court of India and Chokila Iyer the first foreign secretary of India.

Women are in IPS, IAS and allied services. They are in banks, education, medical profession, science and technology. In government services, media art, culture, sports fashion, beauty, acting, culture, modelling. In NGOs movement and in co-operative sectors they have also kept on the dual role by keeping balance in family life and do not like to come out by breaking homes.

But it is feared that with a view to capture 1/3 seats in Lok Sabha and assemblies women who are now happy in the kitchen and insufficiently educated are being groomed by male leaders to take their seats if and when they have to vacate and trying to do marketing through back door politics, preparing them to smoothly take control over majority of about 1550 seats which they themselves will ontrol. For others they are not ready to leave the field because they cannot expect from strong and capable women to play the proxy role.

In such a case the crutches of reservation help the women from creamy layer only and the women who can assert themselves will have to come up on their own.

Quotas can empower only when the democratic process is genuine otherwise it is a political dacoity. If dummy candidates get elected, their role will be limited to obeying their promoters. The times have changed now; she is not just the rib of man, created by God as a play-mate for him when even just a rib she was more ambitious and could prompt the man to eat the forbiden fruit she was reckless to accept expulsion from the heaven and bold enough to seek fortunes outside where they could grow anything and eat what they pleased.

Nehruji said "the women of India will not attain their full rights by the mere generosity of men, they will have to fight and force their will on the men folk if they want to succeed". He was in favour of women taking to self-defence to cross the danger-zones.

In early 1960 U.N. asked member nations to prepare report on women's status and declared 1975-85 as women's decade.

In India in 1971 Smt. Phulrenu Guha was appointed to head the committee to prepare a report on women's status. Smt. Veena Mazumdar was appointed as Member Secretary (On deputation from U.G.C.). The 480-page report of great academic merit was tabled in Parliament in 1975.

The report was forgotten till Rajiv Gandhi raised this issue at a conference of CM's on 5 May 1989 and laid stress on the importance of reservation for women in Panchayats, Assemblies and Parliament. He said, "We cannot strenghten the roots of democracy if we do not take co-operation from women, he felt that status of women in society is a yardstick of nation's advancement". K.R. Narayanan, our Hon'ble former President once said, "Participation in political process is necessary for empowerment of women".

In election manifesto for 1991 Lok Sabha elections Rajiv Gandhi promised to pass the bill within 100 days of coming to power but due to his tragic assassination, the onus fell on P.V. Narasimha Rao to present the bill, which was passed on 22 December 1991 in Lok Sabha and on 23 December 1991 in Rajya Sabha , after consent from States the President approved it on 20 April 1993 and 73rd Constitution Amendment Act 1992 came into effect from 24 April 1993.

Thus the transfer of power to the grass root democracy empowered 30 lakh representatives with 10 lakh women, sharing the power in local self-government. Bill for reservation of seats in Parliament and assemblies was tabled on 12/9/96 but it was blocked on the point of reservation for OBC women and religious minorities. Some responsible leaders passed derogatory remarks. The bill was twice stalled and a select committee was appointed under Smt Geeta Mukherjee.

Congress party reserved 1/3rd seats for women in its party constitution on 18th December 1998 to prepare them to pay a greater role in political process. On 22nd December 1999. Sonia Gandhi as leader of opposition stood up in Parliament and demanded that the bill be passed in this session itself. N.D.A. Government introduced it once again on 23/12/1999 amidst shouts and tearing of papers by the opposition. Again on 21th, 22nd Dec. 2000, the bill suffered the same fate.

We wait for the day when process of justice to women begins in a true democratic spirit and they get representation not just in Parliament and assemblies but in every field and can work in safe and secure environment as equal partners with self-confidence. We expect the things to improve in the year 2001, the year of women empowerment.

11

Minorities and the Right to Equality

Imtiaz Ahmad

Why has the right to equality become such an important and contentious part of our politics? It appears that, in order to understand the contentiousness and depth of feeling about the right to equality, we must understand the nature of the polity established by our Constitution. Human beings have shown an almost amazing ability to deal with and accept diverse political and legal systems when the general rules of these systems are known in advance. 'Known in advance' means that the social, political, economic and civil rules by which people live are established and known well before they are applied to concrete situations. This 'advance knowledge' may occur through tradition, through acceptance overtime, through a recognised historical event, or through common agreement at a time certain in history. It may be contrasted with the arbitrary exercise of power that responds only to the will of the person or official exercising that power. The Indian Constitution, and the polity it created, represents the historical creation of a system of rules of the game.

The preamble to the Constitution resolved to secure to all Indians social, economic and political justice and provide equality of status and opportunity. Towards this end, Article 15 prohibits discrimination on grounds of religion, race, caste or any other such grounds, and Article 16(2) lays down that no person can be discriminated against in the matter of public employment on grounds of race, religion and caste. Nonetheless, the framers of our Constitution were aware that the greatest dilemma of human society is that government has necessary functions because human are not angels. Yet, it is precisely those non-angelic human beings who are the only way that governments can be staffed. Thus, while government was placed under the obligation to ensure equality of all citizens, it could be presumed that certain cultural and linguistic minorities might have a different experience of political practices.

Specific protections were provided by way of fundamental rights to ensure that the right to equality was not denied to such communities. Article 29(1) laid down that any section of citizens having a distinct language, script or culture of its own shall have the fundamental right to conserve the same. This means that if there is a cultural minority which wishes to preserve its own language or culture the state shall not by law impose upon it any culture or language belonging to the majority in that region. Again, the promotion of Hindi as the national language or introduction of compulsory primary education cannot be used as a device to take away the linguistic safeguard of a minority community as guaranteed under Articles 29 and 30. Thus, while Article 29(2) rules out discrimination in state educational institutions and ensures that there is no discrimination against any citizen on grounds of religion, language, race or caste, Article 30 (1) provides that all minorities, whether based on religion or language, shall have the fundamental right to establish educational institutions of their choice and Article 30 (2) guarantees that the state shall not in granting aid to educational institutions discriminate against any educational institution on the ground that it is under the management of a minority, whether based on religion or language.

Clearly, the discourse on minorities was overshadowed by the historical experience of partition. It did not view minorities from the perspective of human rights, but defined them within the parameters of the discourse of communalism versus secularism and nationalism versus separatism. When the preamble to the Constitution was discussed in the Constituent Assembly, all the members agreed on the necessity of establishing a secular state. Most shared an understanding of history in which the 'movement for the separation of religion and state was irrevocably a part of the project for the democratisation of the latter'. How could a democratic state represent a religious majority at the expense of the rights and liberties of a minority? In Europe, 'the idea of democratic dissent was posed initially as the idea of religious difference. It became the premise gradually for the liberation of the individual in general in raising the question of equality and equal rights for all, the idea of secularism became the chief force behind the subsequent idea of political democracy'. Since Independent India was seen to be a democracy, secularism was accepted as a fait accompli. Shiva Rao notes, 'it is essential to for the proper functioning of democracy that communalism should be eliminated from Indian life'.

But what kind of secularism was to be established in India faced with the problem of creating a secular state in a religious society? Was the state to be secular only if stayed strictly away from religion? Or, was the state to be secular in the sense that it was to respect all religions equally? On this issue, a number of distinctive positions developed during the controversy around the Preamble. The first advocated a clear line of separation between religion and state. Given the diverse nature of Indian society, it was argued that religion should be relegated to the private sphere. Many members declared that the need of the hour was to strengthen the identity of Indians as citizens of the state as opposed to being members of some community or religious group. A variant of this position was that no links between the state and religion should be permitted, not because this would weaken the state but because it would demean religion. Religion as a system of absolute truths could not be made subject to the whims of changing majorities by allowing the democratic state to have a say in religious matters. Finally, the third position held that in a society like India where religion was such an important part of most of the people's lives, secularism warranted not that the state stay away from all religions but respect all religions. In this view, instead of distancing itself from all religions of tolerating them equivalently as sets of superstitions that could be indulged in as long as they remained a private affair, a secular state should base its dealings with religion on equal respect of all religions.

Simultaneously with discussing the kind of religious rights permitted under secularism. The Constituent Assembly also debated the political rights of minorities. The Sub-Commitee on Minorities based itself on the response of members to a questionnaire on safeguards for minorities prepared by K.M. Munshi and on Ambedkar's suggested safeguards for the Scheduled Castes. Although Ambedkar had named only the Scheduled Castes as a minority, he did assume the inclusion of other minorities when he wrote that the share of the Scheduled Castes in the reserved seats in the legislatures and services could not be at the cost of the other minorities. In this document Ambedkar stated categorically that social discrimination constituted the real test for determining whether a social group is or is not a minority. Thus, both the Scheduled Castes and certain religious communities were in his view minorities in India 'since administration in India is completely in the hands of the Hindus, and under Swaraj (Independance) the Legislature and Executive will also be in the hands of Hindus. Even though the Sub-Committee initially began with the proposal to establish religious communities and for the Scheduled Castes and Scheduled Tribes separate electorates, and reservation in legislative bodies, ministries, and the civil, military and judicial services of the government. Separate electorates and reservation in the ministries and the government services were given up in the name of an unalloyed, pure nationalism. On 8 August 1947, the Advisory Committee of the Constituent Assembly categorically stated in its report that separate electorates sharpened communal differences to a dangerous extent and have proved to be the main stumbling block to the development of a healthy national life. This was done despite the Sub-Committee on Fundamental Rights admitting with much candour that 'it is difficult to expect that a country like India where most of the persons are communally minded those in authority will give equal treatment to those who do not belong to their communit'.

The disadvantaged position of the minorities and the deprivations to which they could be exposed in independent India can be traced back to the knowledge produced by European scholars and the European representations of the Orient. One of the dominant paradigms of knowledge generated was the Aryan theory. It can be argued that the mythical search for Hindu Arya had has very wide ramifications for the discourse on religion, caste and community. The defining of India as Hindu India and the centralisation of caste as the most important marker of that India concomitant with the marginalisation of other 'communities', whether Islamic or Christian, may be traced through paths direct or winding to this paradigmatic, overarching myth. It has its reverberations also in contemporary politics, the politics of identity, religion and on the discourse on the right to equality. For the high castes, the idea that they are the linear, biological descendants of the Aryans makes good sense. It enables them to appropriate Indian civilisation and then India.

Some of the not so nice variations on this theme even got

articulated in the Constitution and formal law. For example, the Hindu Code Bill of 1955-56 divided the nation by categorically stating that the meaning of Hindu was: (1) a person who is Hindu by religion in any of its forms or developments; (2) any person who is Buddhist, Jain or Sikh by religion; and (3) any person domiciled in territories to which this Act extends who is not a Muslim, Christian, Parsi or Jew by religion unless it I proved that any such person would not have been governed by Hindu law or custom. In other words, all are 'Hindu' *other than those belonging to religions originating outside India.* The definition of Hindu therefore embodies the well-established principle that application of the term 'Hindu' is not confined to persons actually professing Hinduism in any form but extends to all persons except those belonging to religions coming from outside Indian shores.

The Hindu Marriage Act introduced a uniform marriage system for all castes and classes of Hindus, namely monogamy with a possibility of divorce. Accordingly, a Hindu may marry a Buddhist, Jain or Sikh but cannot marry a Christian or Muslim under the Act. A later conversion by one of the Hindu spouses to another religion within the range of Hinduism would have no effect on the status of the marriage. However, *Conversion to any 'alien' religion would constitute a ground for divorce.*

Other provisions show more clearly the character of there being a sanction against anyone leaving the Hindu community. For example, all claims to maintenance under the Hindu Adoption and Maintenance Act 195 by spoose, children, parents, etc., are lost upon conversion to any non-Hindu religion. A wife may have grounds for separate residence and maintenance but loses both if she is unchaste or ceases to be a Hindu by conversion to another 'alien' religion. The discrimination becomes all the more glaring and unreasonable. Even children of former Hindus born after conversion 'to another religion' are disqualified from in heriting property from Hindu relatives. Legal disabilities do not arise in case conversion between Hinduism 'proper' and Jainism, Buddhism and Sikhism.

Likewise, the Scheduled Castes can avail of the benefits of reservation only if they continued to remain within the Hindu fold. An 'untouchable' who converts to Islam or Christianity has to forgo the benefits of reservation. Until recently, even religions like Sikhism or Buddhism were treated likewise. However, a strong movement on the part of the Dalits led to Sikh and Buddhist Dalits gaining the benefits of reservation. But Dalit Christians have not yet been able to make a dent. Even on the question of personal laws the bias in obvious. Equity considerations are raised regarding the personal laws of minority groups while similar considerations are glossed over in the case of the personal laws of Hindus, as, for example, in the case of Hindu undivided family.

The concern of the law is exclusively directed to conversion from one of the 'native' religions to 'alien' religions like Christianity, Islam, Judaism or Zoroastrianism. This demonstrates to some extent at least the complex inter-linkages that occur across a variety of discourses and articulate as well as express the idea of India as a Hindu nation, a civilisation synthesised by Hinduism, and critically by caste. Hinduism emerges full-blown and complete transcending time capturing space, suppressing differences and variation.

This tendency has recently begun to overshadow the discourse on the right to equality. One the one hand, there has emerged a strong political voice against the constitutional scheme of providing the right to absolute equality to all citizens and guaranteeing certain protections to cultural religious minorities. It is argued that such a scheme violates the principle of equality in a democracy and should be abandoned in favour of a unified right to equality. In other words, the thrust of this argument is that the protections guaranteed to cultural, religious and linguistic minorities should be done away with in the pursuit of equality of all citizens in a democracy. On the other hand, the organs of government are beginning to interpret the right to equality in ways in clear violation of the intentions of the framers of the Constitution. In particularly, Judges dressed in black robes, similar to what some magicians wear, with audiences often in no less a we/than those who witness magic, have begun to perform slight of- hand feats by interpreting the right to equality. Most have been to the delight of audience that are demanding withdrawal of constitutional guarantees to minorities. Unlike the magician, who, most of the audience feel is creating an illusion, the judge is understood to deal with reality. This belief has been seriously challenged, in the last several decades, by the public debate over judicial activism.

Let me refer to a few of the straws in the wind. In the context of the two-way cross border movement between India and Bangladesh, certain political groups are trying to brand millions of Indian Muslims as foreigners. The security forces and the Election

Commission have interpreted laws in continuation of this onslaught. In one incident in 1992, the BSF rounded up scores of Muslims, adults and children, from the slums of Delhi on the supposed ground that they were foreigners. They were tortured severely in police custody, paraded before the public with shaven heads and pushed forcibly into Bangladesh without judicial proceedings to determine nationality. Even the high constitutional authority such as the Chief Election Commission had been issuing circulars regarding disenfranchisement of Muslims. In Assam he asked for striking out of the names of foreigners from precisely those constituencies where Muslims are concentrated. In Maharashtra, the CEC demanded that 'suspected Bangladeshis and Pakistanis' would be struck off the voters' list unless they could produce a whole host of documents most of the Indians would find difficult to produce.

On the judicial side of the unprincipled decision-making has been frequent. In the Shahbano case the point before the court was whether a Muslim woman who was a Indian citizen was entitled to maintenance under the criminal code. Even they decided the case correctly, it used it to issue an *obita dicta* on the state to enact a Uniform Civil Code to do away with the system of personal laws. In the case of *Faruqi* vs. *Union Government*, the Supreme Court dealt with the validity of the Acquisition of Certain Areas Act 1993, two significant questions were involved: could places of worship be acquired by the state without violating the freedom of religion and did the Act not give a preferred treatment to Hindus as against Muslims? The majority judgement (Verma, Venketachalliah and Ray) gave positive response to the first question and negative to the second question. On this issue, Justice Suresh observes, 'the majority judgement of the Supreme Court while returning the Presidential reference on Ayodhya... is blatantly perverse. The whole world knows who were responsible for the demolition of the mosque, yet the Supreme Court says that the demolition was the act of unidentified persons.'

The Bombay High Court absolved Shiv Sena chief for his editorial in *Saamna* for inciting violence against Muslims and the Supreme Court refused to entertain a special leave petition against the Bombay High Court judgement. Again, Justice Suresh found the Supreme Court's ruling shocking and subversive of the rule of law. Finally, the 1995 judgement of the Supreme Court on Hindutva sought to give a benign interpretation to the term Hindutva, describing it merely as a way of life. This wider meaning of Hindutva is an imposition of the majority's way of life on all Indians and denies the diversity and pluralistic character of Indian. A Constitutional Court, with secularism as part of its basic structure, ought not to praise one religion as being more tolerant and generous than other religions. Therefore, it was amazing that the Supreme Court found nothing objectionable in Manohar Joshi's statement that if his party comes to power, Maharashtra would be the first Hindu state.

The individuals who drafted the Constitution and ratified it were practical people. They knew that life and history are dynamic. The needs of government change over time. But they also knew that the rule of law, embodied in the process of a written Constitution, must be the vehicle for change or the Constitution would mean nothing. The degree to which a country has recognised rights and a minimum of arbitrary decision-making is the degree to which we call the government of that country legitimate or illegitimate. The conceptual framework of 'legitimacy' is generally not one of the degree, average citizens view governments as either legitimate or illegitimate, not somewhere on a continuum. For this reason, once any significant minority of the population considers the government illegitimate, a serious line has been crossed, and the government risks destruction. Legitimacy is, thus, a fragile thing.

Much of the controversy involving the recent legal interpretations involving the right to equality is generated because significant numbers of people think that judges and state functionaries, in a number of cases, involving ideologically contentious issues have changed the rules without any authority to do so. This is seen as cheating by one faction. Those opposing that faction's views feel that this violates the fundamental principle of democracy that the will of the majority shall prevail. To the extent this controversy involves a fundamental critique of the legitimacy of the executive and judicial branches of the government, it is very important to society. Thus, lack of fidelity to the Constitution, is an issue of great importance and political interest because it involves a challenge to the rule of law.

This brings to the fore the question, after all what is a Constitution? It is only a method by which powers may be used within limits. If the executive, legislature or judiciary can ignore a Constitution's rules, then the Constitution is no more than a relatively old piece of paper. And, without a constitution one has a very different political system. Here one is not referring to the written constitution, but to the real one. This is the one carved into the hearts of citizens. This real Constitution is a set of deeply held values and principles enjoying willing acceptance of all citizens. It function restrain and control what government does. Without constitutional values, principles and rules, the system becomes arbitrary, the tool of faction and personality, and a threat to every citizen within its power. Such were the Nazi and Soviet states.

Unprincipled decision-making, whether by executive, legislature or judiciary, if accepted, spells the end of any real Constitution. This is so because, if a Constitution does not mean what the framers who wrote and ratified it meant by it, then it means nothing at all. It then becomes a tool rather than a barrier to tyranny. Policy then becomes the province of power, not law or reason. Here we come to the fundamental question: what are our rights? They are integral to the existence of a Constitution. Without them it cannot operate. They are much like antibodies that circulate through the bloodstream. They protect the integrity of the rules that make up the Constitution, giving to citizens a tool to challenge actions that violate the rules of the Constitution. They provide guidelines for executive action; they set limits to legislation and offer the judiciary a devise for overturning decisions made by the political or democratic branches of the government. However, when distortions, whose origins we are only beginning to understand, affect biological antibodies, those antibodies can turn on the human body wreaking all manner of harm from allergies to death. Likewise, when rights are created to achieve political goals, they can become carriers of tyranny and arbitrary power, rather than the primary defence of equality or liberty.

Not only is such possible, but also that it is a very real problem in the current rights oriented jurisprudence and public discourse. Empirically, rights are claims that someone else must recognise. If one has a right to a piece of land, then another person cannot do anything with that land in consistent with rights to it. If one has a right to vote, the government may not prevent that person from voting. Constitutional rights make perfect sense when they are understood as claims against the government. Historically, and one could argue logically, this leads to all rights being negative. Rights are negative claims. But if constitutional rights are positively interpreted, all manner of illogic occurs, as well as potential threats to equality and liberty. For then we will end up arguing that rights, like the rabbit in the magician's hat, things that can be materialised by mere will. We will argue that rights are just a manifestation of the will of the legislature or the democratic majority as adopted in a written document.

If rights are nothing but expressions of political will, then they may be created or destroyed by the political actions of society. Thus, the long-term security for rights is the political process. Further, if there is nothing to a right but positive law, that is, the will of society as expressed through the law-making process, any deep attachment to rights, or even descriptions of rights as fundamental, should be replaced with a candid recognition that rights are nothing but one era's fancy. However, this is not the view the vast majority of our citizens hold. They value, honour and almost idolise rights. This implies that rights, or some of what we call rights, are not just statements of political will. Right, real rights, the fundamental rights found in our Constitution, come not from political compromise, but from the core of human nature. They express the fundamental integrity of the human being. When life, equality and liberty are at the whim of arbitrary power, then the subject is not only the victim of tyranny, but the subject's basic dignity is denied. This is the fundamental evil of slavery. It is the fundamental threat that all free societies have to be ever vigilant against.

Since fundamental rights are an aspect of what it means to be human, a society that does not embody them in its system of government and law or takes them away after providing for them is not a good society. Rights are not simply a creation of the human will. They exist independent of whether governments or current majorities recognise or honour them. Whether based in purely secular philosophies or in deeply held religious views, a belief in the objective reality of certain fundamental rights has significant consequences for the way in which we think about law and government. If rights are real, and independent of a particular regime's recognition of them, then they, by their very existence, impose significant restrictions on what government and law may permissibly do. When the executive fails to recognise the real rights to life, liberty and equality, the harm to the rule of law and the liberty of society is clear and understandable. It is less clear, but no less true, that when courts create rights out of their own ideological predispositions or out of their own feelings of what is correct or just trendy, serious harm is done.

Our Constitution and the law have provided our nation with unique freedom. At times vast carnage and harm have been visited on human beings. But out of this history, with its abiding faith in law and constitutional rights, a free, egalitarian, prosperous and tolerant open society has been in the process of emergence. Buttressed by the institutions of federalism and the common law traditions, India's best hope for a good society has grown. In order to preserve this opportunity, and it is only each generation's opportunity, we must like our constitutional ancestors be ever vigilant. This is the eternal price of liberty and equality.

12

Right to Education

R.M. Pal

May I seek your indulgence to quote from my own writing— editorial in the *PUCL Bulletin*, September 1990. (Since then I have written extensively on the subject of right to education and free compulsory basic education maintaining that non-implementation of the provision of Article 45 of our Constitution is one of the worst form of human rights violations, that child labour can never be eliminated without implementing provision of this article, and that India cannot make any progress in any field without achieving the goal of universal compulsory basic education.): "There is one field... which does not appear to be in the priority list of human rights organisations--education and schooling of children... It was stipulated by our Constitution makers that children upto the age of fourteen years will be given free and compulsory education... The attempts made by Union and State Governments since the time India attained independence indicate that education is not a subject which deserves top priority. The Government has, however, spent huge amount by way of setting up commissions and committees which in turn have produced voluminous reports. Some of these commissions started with the assumption that anything that was recommended by any Commission during the British regime must be scrapped—for example, the Sargent Commission Report...The fact remains that an increasing number of children are growing as illiterates..."

"It is said that parents do not send their children to schools because of economic reasons--they want their children to add to the family income and therefore they either do not send their children to school or children drop out after a year or two. This is at best only half-truth, and half-truth is more dangerous than falsehood... Even where schools function, the physical condition is deplorable-- there are no desks, no drinking water facilities, no lavatories. You visit any Corporation and Goverment schools in Delhi and you find that children in primary sections are not provided with desks; they are required to squat. Children from poor families do deserve better physical environment than in their places of residence where they have no amenities of life, let them have some amenities at least in their school where they can feel happiness, and if they are happy may not drop out" (September 1990). Amartya Sen's thesis was propounded five years later.

What does the concept, "Right to Education " mean? And who is to enforce this right of the child?[1] Let me say at once that this right can become a reality in India, as also in other developing countries, if the State implements the programme of universal free compulsory education. It is the duty and primary responsibility of the State to enforce this right, but the State has failed to perform its duty-- its duty to introduce universal free compulsory education. I maintain that there is no shortcut—the State must become guardian of all citizens upto the age of fourteen. It is important, therefore, that we concentrate on the rights of the child in the perspective of the education challenge.

When the United Front came to power at the centre, an attempt was made to enforce this right—it introduced a Bill (83rd Constitutional Amendment) in the Rajya Sabha on 28 July, 1997 with a view to recognising elementary education as a fundamental right of all citizens, that is, to make Article 45 of the Constitution a fundamental right. (The present BJP-led Government has revived the Bill -- reluctantly through, but there is no indication that the matter will be pursued. In fact, the proposal to make this a fundamental right is gathering dust.)

The United Front Government in its "Statement of objects and reasons" declared that "this historical amendment of the Constitution in the 50th year of our independence should inspire the nation to meet the daunting challenge of achieving the goal of education for all by 2000 AD".[2] It is hardly necessary for me to make any comments about "pious and fond" hopes and wishes. While the United Front HRD minister made this statement, the bureaucrats in this Ministry said in no uncertain terms that it is not a viable proposition since it will cost forty thousand crore rupees over a period of five years to implement the obligation. The fact remains that none seriously takes the concept of the right to education.

II

In pre-independent India, a couple of significant efforts were made to introduce universal free compulsory basic education. Gokhale– one of the very few freedom fighters who gave importance to universal compulsory free basic education--made an effort to make primary education compulsory. He moved a resolution (19 March, 1910) in the Imperial Legislative Council: "a beginning should be made in the direction of making elementary education free and compulsory throughout the country." The Bill was, however, rejected. Another effort was made by Gandhiji and Dr. Zakir Hussain—what is popularly known as Wardha Scheme of Education.

Another important landmark during the British period was the plan of Post -War Educational Development in India prepared by the Central Advisory Board of Education (1944) popularly known as the Sargent Plan (after the name of the then Educational Advisor to the Government of India, Sir John Sargent). The plan recommended a system of universal, compulsory and free education for all children 6-14 age group. It was a highly realistic plan; in view of the non-availability of teachers, the Plan suggested that the Plan would be implemented (i.e., all children 6-14 age group would receive education) within forty years. (At this point, I seek your permission to digress a little. In 1966, when the Kothari Commission Report was published, a seminar was organised to discuss the Report. The Secretary of the Commission, the well known Gandhian scholar, Dr. J.P. Naik referred to a number of reports and recommendations made during the British period and in independent India, but he did not refer to the Sargent Plan. When I drew his attention to the plan, Dr. Naik dismissed the Plan, rather contemptuously. His main objection was to the long period of forty years, and that it was made by a British imperialist ! Well, do we have to make any comments about such patriotic zeal and the fact that we are nowhere the goal even after 54 years!)

I may now add that our founding fathers—the Constitution makers played politics with the Right to Education and free compulsory basic education. They did not give any importance to the right to education, and did not accept it as a social welfare programme. It may be recalled that originally, the Sub-Committee on Fundamental Rights of the Constituent Assembly proposed that basic education be included in the list of fundamental rights, but subsequently it was rejected by the Constitution makers. One member said, "Is this a justiciable right? Suppose the Government has no money?" Pandit Govind Ballabh Pant quipped, "It cannot be justiciable. No court can possibly adjudicate", so "this clause be transferred to Part 11 (Directive Principles of State Policy)."

Although this committee had distinguished and self proclaimed liberals and Gandhians like, M.R. Masani, only one member, K.T. Shah had the courage of conviction and gave a dissenting note. He said that if a right to education becomes non-justiciable, it "would remain as no more than so many pious wishes." He added that if it does not become "imperative obligations of the State towards the citizen, we would be perpetuating a needless fraud." Furthermore, he wrote in the dissenting note, "once an unambiguous declaration of such a right is made (justiciable), those responsible for it would have to find ways and means to give effect to it. If they had no such responsibility placed upon them, they might be inclined to avail themselves of every excuse to justify their own inactivity in the matter, indifference, or worse". Prophetic words, indeed! No surprise, therefore, that the operative part of Pandit Nehru's famous tryst with destiny speech was not meant to be implemented.

What is worse is that even NGO's, "progressive" intellectuals and activists like the Sarvodayists, Radical Humanists and other activist groups do not place compulsory education at the top of their agenda . V.M. Tarkunde once prepared a document on behalf of the Radical Humanist Association, "People's Minimum Programme for Prompt Action by the New Government", the last BJP Government, demanding that "resources should be made available to provide free primary education, but not compulsory. (See *The Radical Humanist*, June 1998, p. 11) . Tarkunde told me in a meeting of radical humanists and a few trustees of the Indian Renaissance Institute including its chairperson— all of them agreed with Tarkunde. I expressed my disagreement; indeed, I was amazed.

Tarkunde does not consider "compulsory education" to be a feasible proposition for legal and other reasons, reminiscent of what our Constitution makers said, Madhu Dandavate, when he was Vice-Chairman of the Planning Commission— this subject is supposed to be on the agenda of the commission— did not find time even to have an in-depth discussion on the subject, with experts, not to speak of implementing it. His Secretary did not consider it necessary to acknowledge receipt of a letter from this writer on this subject, not to speak of having any discussion! I.K. Gujral, the former Prime Minister, dispensed with the subject by making an announcement from the Red Fort that the provisions of Article 45 would be implemented. His Government's performance in this regard was limited to the production of a totally unreadable report to make elementary education a fundamental right, and more importantly, a fundamental duty without spelling out the responsibilities of the State for non-compliance.

Another argument advanced by economists and even Gandhians is that poverty of resources stands in the way of introducing compulsory education. No less a person that J.P. Naik maintained this in a report prepared for the Citizens for Democracy of which Jayaprakash Narayan was President and Tarkunde, General Secretary. (Obviously he forgot what he had said in 1966 apropos of the Sargent Plan! The main argument of the report, education for our people is: "one of the principal reasons which has hindered the progress of universal elementary education in the paucity of financial resources. If this is to be overcome the unit cost of educating a child at the elementary stage should be kept within reasonable limits... that, in poor nations, money will always be in short supply...[and] that we have given education a high priority as indicated by the high level of total educational expenditures already reached, [so] that the possibilities of further growth in educational expenditures is limited... The formal system of education is wasteful and inefficient. In this 77-page document right to education and non-implementation of the provision of Article 44 of the Constitution are hardly ever referred to.

We may give a quick look at the West Bengal Government's performance. I refer to West Bengal since the communists claim to be the only "progressive" force in the country (the State has now been ruled by a CPM-led front for 24 years). The literacy rate of the Scheduled Castes in West Bengal is 42.21 per cent of the total population in the state, again, way behind that in most SC population of the state—this ranks way behind that of most other States in India. The literacy rate of the Scheduled Tribes is worse, 27.78 per cent of the total ST population in the State, again, way behind that in most other States in the country. With regard to SC/ST female literacy, the percentage is much lower. This state does not come anywhere near states like Kerala and Tamil Nadu, or even Himachal Pradesh in respect of overall literacy and education— it is in the company of Bihar and U.P. The communists did not seem to regard education as child's right, if it did would have implemented the provision of Article 45 of the Constitution. Twenty-four years is a long time. Communist China did not take such a long time to eradicate illiteracy. According to the latest statistical profile in respect of women's development programmes brought out by the Planning Commission, the ranking of West Bengal (status of women) is "low" as against "very good", "good", and "medium" ranking of the States (except the BIMARU States whose ranking is "very low"). The fact is that the middle class in our country including the communists, as also their leader, Mr. Jyoti Basu are bereft of sensitivity.

III

At this point, we may take note of the approach of some of our influential activists and their organisations. For a long time now they have concentrated on eradicating child labour without giving any importance to the right to education and our constitutional provision of free and compulsory education to all children 6-14 age group. It is only very recently that some of the internationally known activists have started talking about "quality education, education to children below the age of six, free meal", and so on in the context of the 83rd Amendment Bill. I do not remember having heard from these NGO quarters about the importance of the right to education. They don't refer to the middle-class mindset which stands in the way of the education challenge.

We as a nation are known for shibboleths. The latest one relates to presentation of chalks and slates to MPs! One should have thought the education challenge, and the right to education is a very serious matter.

I may refer to a revealing controversy between two activists, who have made themselves known to VIPs, NHRC, Governments, both Indian and foreign, and organisations abroad. I quote from both without any comment (see, *Against Child Labour* edited by Klaus Voll).

Swamy Agnivesh apropos of child labour in India. He says in his contribution to the book: "I accuse the western powers of hoodwinking the poorer countries, politically as well as economically, and their in sincerity is writ large. They don't want to grip the problem and solve it once and for all. They are playing truant with the problem. They are trying to run with the hare and hunt with the hounds. It's a double standard game and therefore I don't trust even the Western media, which initially, I thought, were doing a great service by highlighting the plight of child labour and bonded labour in my country. With regard to the much talked about 'Rugmark Lebel' and the 'Global March' in 1998, widely reported in the West, organised by Kailash Sathyarthi, among others, the Swami says: ''After the initial enthusiasm died down, we found that there were certain other motives.. [with regard to] the problem of child labour in India... We got to know that it was the German government which has largely funded the Indo-German Export Promotion Project (IGEP), to bring about the 'Rugmark' Foundation... We grew a little suspicious.. when my own colleague, Kailash Sathyarthi drifted away from the mainstream of Bandhua Mukti Morcha... Surprisingly, the vested interests started projecting him as the champion of the cause of the child labour in India and there after honours were poured on him... Our suspicions and our worst fears came true when we saw a huge march against child labour... The western countries helped him to raise the money, around US $2 million or more.. may be doubled it subsequently. The ILO decided to promote it because the International Confederation of Free Trade Unions (ICFTU) was supporting it... We have seen the game plan through and we think that the western powers are out to sabotage the real onslaught against child labour exploitation. They are going to cash in on this whole situation. They are propping up leaders, they are propping up NGOs .... The American celebrities who participated, and some of them were here in Delhi, were not shown child labour in agriculture or in brick-kilns or in the stone quarries, things which are not exported. They were straight away taken to Jaipur... This made it very clear that the intention of 'Global March' was not to fight the child labour in its entirety, but just to highlight child labour in export oriented industries... Nearly half of child labour is in agriculture, the other half's predominant share is in industries or activities which are not at all exported.''

With regard to the 'Global March' Kailash Sathyarthi says (Chapter 8): ''We have been able to initiate discussion, debate and some sort of movement in many countries [other than India and Pakistan].. That was another important achievement.. [Another] aim was to sensitize, galvanize and influence the whole ILO process of the new convention of the worst forms of child labour.. One could observe an unprecedented harmony on the issue... The March was officially welcomed by the whole ILO-convention.. The most important part is the implementation of the upcoming convention". In Chapter 22, Sathyarthi says: "People should feel that it [child labour] is a serious problem . If there is a culture shock, so much the better. I believe that we have been able to hammer this into the heads of the politicians, the bureaucracy, the common people and the parents themselves... We could not do more because of our own constraints. I would like to say that the part of a huge rehabilitative basic education is still lacking. It is a part of the government programmes and policies. In India we have not been able to build up a national movement for basic education. Education is the most important alternative to child labour and unless the former is made available, the later will not be eliminated...Regarding the foreign funds we personally were never influenced by their agendas. Rather, in most of the cases, we have influenced their agendas. [However] I personally know several NGOs where the people believe that if someone is a donor, then that someone is a great person. When any donor comes, they virtually lie at their feet, touch their feet, surrender everything..."

It is hardly necessary to add any comments for an enlightened and intelligent audience.

IV

Let us be clear. There are not many takers for the implementation of Article 45, and the right to education. (We must not confuse the provisions of Article 45— free compulsory basic education to children upto the age of fourteen— with literacy programme, and campaign, adult education, non-formal education package, and so on).

I may add that those who maintain this social welfare programme cannot be implemented for various reasons and yet, at the same time, bring out plans for eradicating child labour, indulge in unalloyed hypocrisy. Child labour is, of course, a human rights violation. What I have been stressing over the years is that deprivation of the right to basic education is also a human rights violation— equally obnoxious and atrocious, if not more. This second aspect has been almost totally neglected, both by Indian NGOs, NHRC, as I have indicated above, and those from abroad. They have been concerned, rightly, with child labour; but they have hardly been agitated over the non-introduction of universal basic education. Why? This must be investigated by both NHRC and the civil society who are engaged in human rights education. They might find that one of the reasons is the middle class mindset which would have taken this violation seriously if the victims belonged to their class— the NGOs too belong to this class; the fact is that the victims, almost all, belong to SCs/STs, OBCs, Muslim minority, and the girl children.

Politicians and bureaucrats averse to or unable to implement a social welfare programme for the deprived sections of our people, know how to get away with it through the inbuilt escape route in the system. Over the years, they have perfected and legitimised the art of doublespeak and the language of deceit and arrogance, like George Orwell's four-legged dictator who quietly changed the original thesis of the revolution, "four legs are good, two legs are bad" to "four legs are good, two legs are better", and from "all animals are equal" to "all animals are equal but some animals are more equal than others". Our political rulers and bureaucrats justify and rationalise non-implementation of Article 45 and non-recognition of the right to education in the kind of language referred to above. Language of reason has been totally lost on them. I am giving below a couple of examples of such language as also of quibbling backtracking which is insulting to millions of our illiterates.

The first announcement made by Dr. Murli Manohar Joshi, an eminent RSS ideologue and present Human Resource Development Minister, during the last BJP government, even before the Prime Minister sought the vote of confidence in the Lok Sabha (during the second term of Atal Behari Vajpayee's government), that all efforts will be made to provide education to children up to class 'V' — indeed, a "fresh" interpretation of the Constitutional provisions!

On another occasion, sharply reacting to India being called the "illiteracy Capital of the world", Dr. Joshi retorted, "India has a very large number of literates also. Why don't you talk about them? The literacy rate is 50 per cent, so we have about 50 crore literates in India, which is double the population of the U.S.A. "Victims of human rights violation—deprivation of the right to basic education—know why Dr. Joshi and his likes get annoyed when reminded that are illiterate population exceeds the total population of the USA, Canada and Japan.

The mindset behind this kind of quibbling and false pride cannot be expected to implement faithfully this social welfare programme and to recognise the right to education. So that a vast number of our people will continue to be deprived of this basic human right; and our country will remain deprived of all the benefits including economic development, social progress, population control, reduction in infant and child mortality rate, and so on.

Dr. Joshi and his ministry seem to have evolved a new scheme (reminiscent of former Prime Minister I.K. Gujral's scheme of making it mandatory for all fresh graduates to teach at least five children for receiving the Bachelor's degree). It is called the National Reconstruction Corps (NRC) which is to launch the literacy drive because, Dr. Joshi said, "the ministry doesn't have enough money" to impart basic education to our children. Under this scheme, boys and girls in the age group of 18-21 who have passed their 10+2 examination will be employed to teach children and paid Rs. 1, 500 per month. (*Source: Outlook* magazine, 6 July 1998.)

Two short points in this regard are: First, since the minimum qualification for teaching primary classes is 10+2 pass certificate, why not appoint them as regular teachers and pay them the prescribed pay and allowances? (The obvious answer; the government doesn't have the money! The government has not been short of funds for anything except the programme of basic education). Second, boys and girls having +2 certificates are not equipped to teach students of class VII and VIII— children up to the age of 14 years. So that the NRC cannot be a substitute for compulsory basic education as a fundamental right. NRC can be introduced in addition to regular schooling with full-time teachers, proper classrooms, and other educational equipment. Or, is it that Dr. Joshi has now finally decided to stick to his earlier announcement namely, that primary education will be provided up to Class V and not up to the age of fourteen years? (Here again, we are reminded of Orwell's Animal Farm and the sheep chanting regularly the revised lessons and the animals in the farm begin to believe that these are the true lessons! They forget the original lessons, "all animals are equal", and "four legs are good"!

Dr Joshi, at one stage, decided not to revive the constitutional amendment bill, making free and compulsory elementary education a fundamental right (which had been moved by the United Front Government). He and his ministry feel that it is unnecessary to make it a fundamental right. As mentioned above, now, under the compulsion of electoral politics, the present BJP-led government has revived the bill. It is known, however, that Dr. Joshi is very unhappy over the development! When it will go through is anybody's guess!

This is further reinforced by another exercise undertaken by a

Government of India Research Institute , the V.V. Giri National Labour Institute in Noida. Some time back it prepared a draft bill, the title of which is "The Child Labour Rehabilitation Bill 1998—an Act to Prohibit and Regulate Employment of Children". Note, it is to regulate child labour! Furthermore, may one ask, what has happened to the number of constitutional provisions and the 21 legislative enactments on the subject? Nobody, certainly not those in the Government, need be told and reminded that these provisions as well as the 1993 and 1996 Supreme Court Judgements have not made any dent in the Government's immunity from action. Such negative and futile exercise is undertaken because it is an unwritten and unstated fact that illiteracy, which is limited largely to the marginalised section of our society, does not find a place on the agenda of Government's priority.

V

It is in the above context that we must take serious note of the report, *Human Development in South Asia 1998: The Education Challenge* (written by the late Mahbub -ul-Haq, one of the best known economists of our time and Khadija Haq for Human Development Centre, Islamabad and published by O. U. P.).

The report presents a dismal picture. I am giving below a very brief summary of the report as also a few statistics given in the report relating to India, which should make all thoughtful people sit up and work for a movement to compel the Government to implement the programme without diluting the provision of Article 45. Once this is done, all other problems like family planning, health care, economic development, successful management of local self-government, and so on will become tractable.

Summary of the report; South Asia has emerged by now as the most illiterate region in the world, and that low income and poverty are no barriers to the spread of basic education. If Sri Lanka and the Maldives could achieve over 90 per cent adult literacy rate, and if Bangladesh could make rapid strides in this regard, why can't India make progress?

Political commitment to basic education in India remains both faint and fragile. With the result that India has the largest illiterate population in the world. Many countries which are poorer than India have managed a much higher rate of literacy. (1) Tazakistan—real GDP per capita income $1117, and literacy rate 98 per cent; (2) Kenya -$1404 and literacy rate 94 per cent; (3) Vietnam - $1208 and literacy rate 78 per cent. In1994, India's real per capita income was $1348 but its literacy rate was 52 per cent. So that poverty of resources [the reason for not achieving literacy not only given by government agencies but also by intellectuals and activists like the late J.P. Naik, as mentioned above] is not the real reason for India's dismal performance in the field of basic education.

Even in India, there are some States which have made rapid progress in this field, which in turn has ushered in improvements in other spheres like population control, health care, quality of life, etc. Kerala whose per capita income is less than the All-India figures, has a literacy rate of about 90 per cent. The other extreme is that about three-quarters of out-of-school children live in six states— Andhra Pradesh, Bihar, Madhya Pradesh, Rajasthan and West Bengal.

In short, India, the report points out, is still first in the world in terms of the number of total illiterates. According to official sources, female literacy is 26 percentage points below the male literacy, that is, there are 91 million more adult illiterate females than males in India. About 35 million children in the 6-10 age group do not attend primary school; 37 per cent of all primary school children drop out before reaching grade 5.

According to statistics collected by the authors of the report, from official sources, vulnerable groups in India are often deprived of educational opportunities. The literacy rate varies from 90 per cent for rich urban males to a mere 17 per cent for poor rural Scheduled Caste women. SCs/STs have a literacy rate of 40 per cent compared to nearly 60 per cent for higher caste Hindus. The enrollment rate of 6 to 14 years old Muslim children is 62 per cent compared to 77 per cent for non-SC Hindus.

The main thesis of the report is; education leads to many social benefits, including "improvement in standards of hygiene, reduction in infant and child mortality rates, decline in population growth rates, increase in labour production and an improved sense of national unity... It is certain that South Asian economies cannot hope to engineer a decisive breakthrough in development or to become the industrialisation tigers of the future without a generous investment in basic education and technical skills".

This thesis was also propounded by Prof. Jean Dreze and Prof. Amartya Sen in 1995 in their book, *India: Economic Development and Social Opportunities*. What they wrote regarding the wilful neglect of this programme deserves to be quoted: "In India, both ancient and modern biases shape our policies reflecting prejudices of class division as well as of traditional cultures. The difficulty in getting even left wing parties interested in combating inequalities in education relates to the general social atmosphere in India, including the nature of the leadership of the different parties which takes some major disparities as simply 'given' and not particularly worth battling against in view of other—perceived to be more pressing—challenges."

VI

Some economists hold the view that basic education does not necessarily lead to economic development. They give the instances of Sri Lanka, Jamaica and Costa Rica where the literacy rate is very high but the economy has not grown very fast. These economists maintain, therefore, that economic growth leads to widespread education, and not other way. Which means, in plain and simple language, that eradication of poverty is the precondition for implementing this welfare programme of basic education. This amounts to putting the cart before the horse, for poverty can be eliminated only when the people are literate. Even if we accept their thesis, for the sake of argument, does it mean that the right to education is not a human right?

These economists also maintain that government should not be involved in education, both with regard to finance and provision of education. They do not take into account the fact that implementation of social welfare programmes is one of the primary duties of a democratic government. How can a country like India where the vast majority of the people are poor achieve the goal of universal basic education without the active involvement of government? The governments of Japan and Great Britain in the nineteenth century carried out this welfare programme and took care of the total financial obligation in this regard. The results are there for all to see. Today, there is no western country which is not wholly and solely responsible for school education. The private sector and NGOs cannot implement this programme; they can and should supplement as they have done in Kerala.

It might interest the participants to know that Professor Andre Betille of Delhi University— I sometime wonder if most social anthropologists are not reactionaries— maintains that the right to education is useless because it is not enforceable. He has, therefore, argued that elementary education must not be made a fundamental right.

I appeal to you to start a movement with a view to compelling the government to perform its duty— to implement the provision of Article 45. Let me repeat, India cannot take its place in the community of civilised nations without achieving this goal.

Notes and References

1. Professor Jean Dreze's (one of the team members of Probe— Public Report on Basic Education in India 1999 observations about right to education are apt; "Education itself is the most important form of human rights education. Indeed, education has a major role to play in empowering marginalised sections of the population to participate in the democratic system and to defend their human rights in education in general can be seen as a form of human rights education. From that perspective (among others) the ongoing campaign for official recognition of elementary education as a fundamental right assumes great importance.

"First of all, what is the right to education? One reason why this point calls for clarification is that the right to education is often confused with compulsory education. The two are not the same thing at all. As per my opinion the right to education, points is a right of the child vis-a- vis society. It states that every child is entitled, say, to eight years of schooling. Who is responsible for translating that right into reality? According to one school of thought, anyone's right has to be someone else's responsibility. However, I do not think that the right to education is of this kind. One child's right to education is not the responsibility of one particular person or institution. It is a shared responsibility. First and foremost, it is a responsibility of the state, which has to provide the necessary, facilities, outline the curriculum, make sure that teachers are qualified and accountable, and so on. But parents also have a responsibility to send their children to school, teachers to impart learning, and employers not to employ children in ways that conflict with their education. Thus, the overall responsibility of guaranteeing the right to education is shared between different persons and institutions, though not in equal parts.

"This feature has led my esteemed colleague Andre Beteille

[Professor of Sociology in Delhi University] to argue that the right to education is useless because it is not enforceable. Since the right to education is nobody's specific responsibility, says he, it cannot be enforced in court and therefore has no teeth. Following on this, he has argued against elementary education being made a fundamental constitutional right, on the grounds this would devalue the nation of fundamental right. With due respect, I disagree. It is true that, in so far as the responsibility for implementing the right to education is a shared responsibility, not all aspects of it can be enforced in court. For instance, if a teacher sleeps in the classroom, I don't think that taking him or her to court would be the best course of action. Other aspects, however, are enforceable. For instance, if elementary education is made a fundamental right, those who live in a village where there is no school will be able to demand one as a matter of right (instead of depending on the good will of the administration). This would be an important step forward.

"With this background, let me come back to the relation between the right to education and compulsory education. As I said, the two point are not the same, and conflating these distinct notions (as is often done in official circles) would be a dangerous dilution of the right to education. However, compulsory education is one of the means that may be used (in some circumstances at least) to make the right to education a reality. Compulsory education sends an important message to parents, to the effect that it is not up to them to decide whether to send their children to school or to keep them at home. They have a duty to send their children to school. This message is very important, even if reluctance to send children to school is confined to a minority of parents.

"One striking finding of the PROBE survey is that an overwhelming majority of parents are in favour of compulsory education. One reason for this is that people understand very well that when other parents in the village send their children to school, it also makes it easier for them to send their children. This applies especially in the case of girls. Those who take the first step in sending their daughters to school often find it difficult to go against the current norm. If school participation itself is the norm, things are much easier for hesitant parents. Compulsory education has an important role to play in shaping these norms and perceptions.

"Having said this, it is easy to trivialise compulsory education and even to make it counter-productive. For example, if compulsory education involves authoritarian sanctions against recalcitrant parents (even those who face real difficulties in sending their children to school), it may undermine the perception that education is important for its own sake and foster resentment against the schooling system.

"The fact that compulsory education can be trivialised was brought home to me in a striking manner a few months ago, in a conversation with a Block Education Officer in Rajsamand district, Rajasthan. This was on Ist April, 1998—a most appropriate date. As we were talking about recent education-related initiatives, BEO suddenly remembered (just "by the way") that compulsory education was about to be introduced in the district. I asked him to tell me more, upon which he summoned his peon and instructed him to fish out the relevant papers. After a brief perusal of the documents, 'he said', as it happens, it starts from today !' That was the end of the matter as far as he was concerned" (*Human Rights Education*, ed R.M. Pal and Somen Chakraborty, 2000, published by Indian Social Institute, New Delhi).

2. Statement by S.R. Bommai, HRD Minister in United Front Government: "The founding fathers of our Constitution made a privision imposing an obligation, under Article 45 in Part IV relating to the Directive Principles of State Policy, upon the State to endeavour to provide within a period of one decade from the commencement of the Constitution, for free and compulsory education for children up to fourteen years of age. However, this goal has proved elusive so far. Our inability to achieve this goal 37 years after the target period has been a cause for serious concern. Reiterating the constitutional directive, the National Policy on Education (NPE), 1985, as modified in 1992, states that free and compulsory elementary education of satisfactory quality shall be provided to all children up to the age of fourteen years before we enter the twenty-first century. The Supreme Court in its judgement in *Unni Krishnan J.P.* vs. *State of Andhra Pradesh*, AIR 1993 SC 2178, has held that children of this country have a fundamental right to free education until they complete the age of fourteen years. The Common Minimum Programme of the United Front government, resolves to make a right to free and compulsory elementary education a fundamental right and to enforce it through suitable statutory measures.

"The Committee of Education Ministers which was set up to

examine the implications of the aforesaid resolution have recommended that the Costitution be amended to make the Right to Free and Compulsory Education from six to fourteen years of age as a fundamental right and to make a fundamental duty of parents to provide opportunities for education to their children of this age group. Consequent thereupon, provision in the nature of compulsory and free education as a Directive Principle of State Policy under Article 45 is no more required. States and Union Territories would be required to enact laws for the enforcement of free and compulsory education within one year from the commencement of the Constitution (Eighty- third Amendment) Act, 1997.

"The amendment of the Constitution to provide for compulsory education of children as a fundamental right would demonstrate the necessary political will and administrative resolve of the country to achieve universalisation of elementary education and to eradicate illiteracy. This historical amendment of the Constitution in the 50th year of our independence should inspire the nation to meet the daunting challenge of achieving the goal of education for all by 2000 AD."

13
Constitution and Human Rights Culture

G.S. Bhargava

On the face of it, linking the Constitution of India or for that matter a similar document, written or otherwise, of any country with human rights culture might sound far-fetched. By human rights culture is meant the historical, psychological and traditional factors contributing to the milieu in which the Constitution operates. If it is conducive to the achievement of liberal and egalitarian objectives and purposes, like those enshrined in the Indian Constitution it can be said to foster a human rights culture. This paper tries to examine how far and with what assurance the Indian Constitution in its working in the last fifty-one years has lived up to the promise of ushering in a humane and human rights-prone society in the country. In other words, the approach is broad and more journalistic than scholarly.

Of course, caveats are in order. For countries, which go by the nomenclature of Islamic or for that matter any theocratic qualification, to claim to be republics or democracies can be a mixture of contradictions. Islam in theory is a highly egalitarian faith free of the curse of caste system marring Hindu society. The practice, however, is different. They are rarely democratic in the sense of endowing every citizen, man and woman, with the right to vote and to be entitled to equality before law. Gender discrimination is the rule, rather than the exception. Persons belonging to non-Islamic faiths are denied equal opportunities, especially in the political sphere. No non-Muslim can be elected President or Prime Minister in an Islamic State.

In India, the situation is further complicated by both Islam and Christianity in practice being contaminated by the caste system. Followers of these faiths cannot shed their pre- conversion caste label. I have seen in Pakistan that *bhangi* (sweeper) Christians cannot go in for inter-marriages with their fellow Christians. The only saving grace is that during Id and other religious community feasts they are not excluded even if they do not mix with better-off or upper caste guests. I was told that it was due to class differences, rampant in the semi-feudal social system.

It is so to an extent in Anglican and other non-Catholic theocracies. But when they are Constitutional monarchies like the United Kingdom or countries of Scandinavia and northern Europe (Norway, Sweden, Denmark, the Netherlands, Belgium, etc.) the problem is simplified due to the practice of dynastic succession of the Constitutional Head of State. Since the custodian of executive authority, the prime ministership is a political office open to all citizens they are democracies. In the democratic republic of the United States of America, as Dr. Henry Kissinger ruefully noted, birth as US citizens is necessary for seeking the Presidentship. Naturalized Americans like the celebrated former Secretary of State are barred. Still, eyebrows are raised when a Roman Catholic or a Jew is on the slate of nominees for the posts of President and Vice-President. Blacks, once victims of racism and slavery, have graduated to top military and other positions. So might Hispanics and Asian Americans in the not too distant future, thanks to the vibrant dynamism of the system and the social mobility engined by a free enterprise economy.

In India, on the other hand, form outshines facts of life as the determinant. We have had two Muslims (and the present one is also Muslim) and one Sikh of Heads of State. Non-Hindus have held top positions in the defence services. Only the prime ministership has so far escaped such pluralism. The view that only persons of Indian birth should be eligible for the top elective posts of President, Vice-President and Prime Minister has been under intense discussion in the recent years. If it is motivated by a desire to exclude non- Hindus, by making it virtually communal, it will be obnoxious. But if the purpose to stall dynastic succession to political positions in a republican democracy it is to be welcomed. In the name of keeping open the top positions in the polity to all faiths and persuasions, a backdoor cannot be opened to perpetuate feudalistic dynastic in the polity, thus vitiating the basic republican structure of our polity.

Part 3 (Fundamental Rights) of our Constitution, covering equality before law (Article 14), prohibition discrimination on grounds of religion, race, caste, sex or birth place (Article 15), equality of opportunity in matters of public employment (Article 16), abolition of untouchability (Article 17), protection of certain rights regarding freedom of speech (Article 19), protection in respect of conviction for offences (Article 20), protection of life and personal liberty (Article 21) and freedom of conscience and free profession, practice and propagation of religion (Article 25), to cite the vital privileges of Indian citizens are veritable Magna Carta of human rights culture. According to Subhash Kashyap[1] "Coming closely on the heels of the Universal Declaration of Human Rights, inclusion of a bill of rights in the Constitution of India accorded with the contemporary democratic and humanitarian temper and Constitutional practice in other nations of the world. It reflected in no small measure the anxiety of the founding fathers to incorporate and implement the basic principles enunciated in the Universal Declaration of Human Rights. Also incorporation of a charter on fundamental rights in the Constitution became necessary in view of the special problem of minorities and the need to assure them of the fullest protection of their rights" (Emphasis added).

In retrospect, however, some of the guaranteed rights like that to propagate religion have in practice vitiated into licence for proselitisation. It is incorporated with a view to ensuring India's continuance as a secular State. The idea as elaborated by Pandit Nehru and other founding fathers of the Constitution was to keep India non-denominational, not "secular" in the western sense, which requires religion "not to interfere in State affairs"[2] It will mean equality for all religions, incumbent and new, named and unnamed, to be practised without let or hindrance. It also implies that no religion should interfere with the practice of other religions through pressure and other tactics by its practitioners.

Such secularism could have better ensured by making it rooted in Hindu spiritualist approach, as Dr. S. Radhakrishnan had said, "An ample expression of all sides of human nature in their highest forms, economic organization animated by community feeling, a democratic system supported by education and striving for the least inequality of opportunity and the fostering of oneness of outlook and feeling as the basis of international relations, these were the goals of a truly religious person, whatever his denomination...."[3]

The question of relevance of secularism and its operation in India to human rights culture will naturally arise. The answer is simple and straightforward. Inter-religious disharmony and strife flowing from it are least conducive to human rights culture. It is evident in India for the last few years. First, the right to propagate religion enshrined in the Constitution of secular India has become grist to persons claiming to be followers of the incumbent Pope, his Holiness Pope Paul. His theme of the twenty-first century being the millennium of Christianisation is being sought to be achieved through religious conversion by all means. Its backlash among intolerant Hindus is on expected lines of fanaticism and fantasy. They even want us to believe that Christians who now constitute less than two per cent of India's will one day overwhelm the Hindus accounting for about eight per cent of the populations ! Egged by anti-Christian propaganda there have been incidents of violence against Christian institutions and personnel. The resultant tension and turmoil have vitiated the prospects of human rights culture being promoted.

Meanwhile, the state policy of secularism has been professionalised and debased into a tool of power politics. The Ram Janmabhoomi movement and the subsequent outrage of the demolition of Babri mosque at Ayodhya would not have been possible but for the widespread feeling among even educated Hindus that Muslims were being 'appeased' for their block votes as a community. This will be evident from the aversion for temple politics in recent years- since the Bhartiya Janata Party (BJP) formed coalition government at the Centre—as distinct from its endorsement by the silent majority in the late 1980s and the early 1990s. The BJP would not have dropped it from its governmental programme if it enjoyed the salience of the 1980s responsible for its elevation to the party with the largest voter support in the country. In fact, the Vishwa Hindu Parishad (VHP) as an irredentist offshoot of the Rashtriya Swayamsevak Sangh (RSS) owes itself to the conversion to Islam of sizable Dalits in Tamil Nadu. Launched ostensibly to facilitate a memorial for Swami Vivekananda at the southern most Kanniya-kumari tip of the country, the VHP has grown into a veritable Frankenstein. The spread of separatist Muslim politics also has the stamp of 'secularist' approval. In other words, an atmosphere of inter-religious antagonism reminiscent of the Middle Ages cannot go hand in hand with human right culture.

Maybe, the Constitution *per se* is not responsible for the state of affairs. It is more the handiwork of persons working the Constitution. In the ordinary course, considering the use being made of the letter of Article 25 of the Constitution—in gross violation of its spirit—it should have been possible to make its purpose and scope explicit. But being a part of the basic structure of the Constitution, the fundamental rights chapter is beyond amendment according to the Keshavanand Bharati judgment of the Supreme Court. In the prevailing surcharged atmosphere it is not also possible to touch any statutory provision or law concerning Christians or Muslims. If the reigning Pope had been a liberal like his Predecessor, His Holiness Pope Pus who had spoken of the greatness of Hinduism and put all faiths on par in his address at the Eucharistic Congress in Bombay in 1965. His help could have been forthcoming in redeeming the situation. But Pope Paul, presumably on account of his role in shaping the minds of the majority Roman Catholics in Poland during the last phase of the East-West cold war, has a different attitude to co-existence with non-Christian faiths.

As for professionalising the policy of secularism and using it as a vote catching device at the expense of the Muslim community as well as the health of the polity that is a sign of degeneration of politics after the Nehru-Shastry period. If the Constitution, after fifty-one years of operation, is found wanting in fosterng a climate of human rights culture the blame should be laid at the door of politicians who are tragically revered as martyrs because of their violent death. As stated at the outset, in judging the Constitution as a means of promoting human rights culture in the country naturally the focus is on the document and its provisions but the way the leadership of the country worked it. The founding fathers of the Constitution could be faulted, if at all, for no anticipating the caliber of men and women in to whose hands the baton might fall. Dr. B. R. Ambedkar and his colleagues treated it as an intellectual exercise, examining the suitability of American, Irish and other republican systems to India. It has in retrospect proved to be—at least in parts—as an ivory tower exercise because they did not seem to have paid enough attention to our society and its social, economic and moral failings.[4]

Dr. Ambedkar, especially, had first hand experience of the havoc wrought by the caste system among Hindus and its oppressive effect on the Dalits, or the untouchables as he called to counter Gandhiji's term of reverence, Harijans. He had suffered personally as well as at the community level and had even been thinking of puting out of the faith. Still, he was content with a fundamental right abolishing untouchability in all forms and provision of reservation in the legislatures and in respect of employment opportunities in Government service for the Scheduled Castes and Scheduld Tribes. He had rightly realised that empowerment of the socially oppressed was the surest, even if somewhat slow, way of their emancipation. In retrospect, he is right. Several million Dalits have benefited out of the reservation even if it has not always been faithfully implemented in Government service.They have found their voice, which, unfortunately, does no longer speak Dr. Ambedkar's language. Like Mahatma Jotibhau Phule, Dr. Ambedkar was a man of peace and law abiding. He did not lay store by extra-Constitutional methods of political action. Above all, he was an intellectual who preferred debate and discussion although, like Gandhiji, he was a Constitutional and non-violent agitator.

It might also be true that Indian society was not so disfigured and ugly three decades ago as it has been lately with the scum of sectarianism showing up. The prevailing situation of division and sub-division of Hindu society is the harvest of leaders like Vishwanath Pratap Singh and his political progeny, Mulayam Singh Yadav, Laloo Prasad Yadav, etc. balanced by the likes of Kashi Ram and Mrs. Mayawati. The objection is not so much to their language and behaviour as to the mindset. V.P. Singh had so distorted the idea of affirmative action that instead of promoting egalitarianism in thought and action it fostered sectarianism and strife. One does not know whether Chaudhri Charan Singh, by no means a champion of the Dalits had like V.P. Singh, ten years later, looked upon the caste card as an easy vehicle to durable political power, when he set up the Mandal Commission as Union Home Minister. Its mandate of ensuring empowerment and employment opportunities for the so- called Other Backward Castes (OBCs) has in effect brought out the fragmentation of Hindu society as it moved out of its feudal moorings. By no stretch of imagination has the Mandal Commission unified the OBC ranks. Above all, it exposed the vulnerability of such reform to cynical exploitation for narrow political ends. The upshot has been a setback to promotion of human rights culture in the country. You cannot foster culture through civil war. The assertion of Dalit rights has evoked from the OBCs an extremely unhealthy reaction of violence and counter-violence and competition for reservation of legislative seats. In the process, the Dalit movement also has shed the positive visage of Ambedkar and Phule. In parts of Tamil Nadu, for instance, the Dalits and Thevars (OBCs) are prone to fight pitched battles on the streets. They resemble rival war camps. Instead of the accursed caste system melting or being diluted, it has become more rigid than ever before. Ironically, some of the contemporary Dalit scholars swear by the caste system to the delight of the spirit of its originator, Manu. Ambedkar, Gandhiji and Phule have become back numbers.

Could the caste system have evaporated or withered away if the Constitution had formally abolished as it did untouchability. The experience with the proscription by law of the practice of untouchability speaks for itself. It is mostly a paper reform because the community has no reformers to prepare the ground for the law to operate smoothly and effectively. Making the offence under the provision a cognisable offence will not also help. Even a police state cannot enforce it faithfully. A sustained effort over the years to educate the upper castes in the inhumanity and counter productiveness of practising untouchability might have helped but once the British rulers were replaced and Indian leaders came to occupy positions of power the tendency has been to depend solely on the administration for accomplishing even social reform.[5] A more unwholesome rider is the easy way out of blaming every evil on the ubiquitous bureaucracy. In short, the socio-political milieu is hardly conducive to promotion of human rights culture. It shows the magnitude of the task of reforming Hindu society and bringing it in tune with human rights culture.

References

1. *Our Constitution*, National Book Trust, New Delhi, 1994.

2. Dr. R.N. Pal in a conversation.

3. *Dr. Radhakrishnan, A Biography* by Sarvepalli Gopal, Oxford, Delhi, 1989.

4. "Part 3 dealing with Fundamental Rights was discussed for as many as 38 days—11 in the sub-committee, 2 in the advisory Committee and 25 in the Constituent Assembly" Kashyap *op. cit*.

5. Even Tulsidas was said to have written in his immortal *Shri Ram Charitramanas* that "the Lord done well to teach me this *lesston*, but still it was you who first set my bounds drum, a rustic, a Shudra and a woman—all these are fit subjects for beating" (*Sundarkanda*).

14
International Human Rights Covenants and Treaties: Their Applicability in Domestic Jurisdiction

Rajindar Sachar

In his foreword to the U.N. publication (September 2000) entitled "Millennium Summit-Multilateral Treaty Framework", Kofi A. Annan, U.N. Secretary General had noted that:

> "Since the founding of the United Nations in 1945, over 500 multilateral treaties have been deposited with the Secretary General. Without exception, all of these treaties have been the result of meticulous negotiations and reflect a careful balance of national, regional, economic and other interests. The aspirations of nations and of individuals for a better world governed by clear and predictable rules agreed upon at the international level are reflected in these instruments. They constitute a comprehensive international legal frame work covering the whole spectrum of human activity, including human rights, humanitarian affairs, the environment, disarmament, international criminal matters, narcotics, outer space, trade, commodities and transportation. The norms of international behaviour expressed through these treaties make the modern world a far better place to live in than before".

He further notes:

> "Some of these multilateral treaties, though negotiated many years ago, are still to receive the minimum number of ratifications

and accessions required for their entry into force. Others are still far from achieving universal participation. It is my hope that Heads of different States and Governments will make use of the unique opportunity provided by the Millennium Summit, which will take place in New York in September 2000 to rededicate themselves to the multilateral treaty framework and thereby contribute to advancing the international rule of law and the cause of peace by signing and ratifying and, where appropriate, acceding to those treaties to which they are not already party".

In similar vein a large number of people continue to pose queries as to applicability of these conventions within the frontiers of a country. Are these coventions, covenants mere high sounding phrases, pious wishes or something more. In very few countries the international treaties are deemed to be absorbed automatically in national legislation. But by far most of nations consider these treaties as mere pleasant sermons and nothing more.

It is taken for granted by many countries that unless the relevant provisions of these treaties are made a part of domestic legislation, they remain empty rhetorics without placing any obligation on countries to implement them. Is this perception correct, is what I wish to examine here.

It may be more informative to study this aspect in the context of the "Right to adequate housing", which as a distinct and unique component of international human rights law, finds recognition within a broad and diverse range of treaties, declarations, agreements, recommendations, resolutions and other legal texts.

Within the system of international human rights law, an analysis of the legal recognition and formulation of housing rights must begin with Article 25(1) of the Universal Declaration of Human Rights which reads:

"Everyone has the right to a standard of living adequate for the health and well-being of himself and of his family, including food, clothing and housing".

The said Article 25, formed the basis for Article 11.1 or the International Covenant on Economic, Social and Cultural Rights (ICESR) (1966) states:

"The States Parties to the present covenant recognize the right of everyone to an adequate standard of living for himself and his family, including adequate food, clothing and housing and to the continuous improvement of living conditions. The

States parties will take appropriate steps to ensure the realization of this right, recognizing to this effect the essential importance of international cooperation based on free consent."

Now admittedly the various treaties, conventions and covenants have been accepted and ratified by most of the countries of the world, e.g., ICESR has been ratified by 108 countries since last year.

In my view, jurisprudentially speaking, all these conventions and treaties fulfill the test of being called international law.

I say this because "historically", treaties are the second source of international law; they developed as the means whereby States could give to rules for their mutual conduct a greater particularity than was provided by custom".

The moral element as foundation for international owes a great deal to the writings of Prof. Brierly. As pointed out by Sir Hersch Lanterpacht, Judge, International Court of Justice, that Brierly emphasised the beneficient potentialities of a revived law of nature as one of the main elements of moral foundation of international law.[2]

Of particular importance is the Charter of the United Nations which, in addition to being a treaty embodying the Constitution of that organisation, has become the basic legal instrument for the international community.

The adoption of the UN Charter and the subsequent enactment of such Fundamental international instruments as the Universal Declaration of 1948 and the two covenants of Human Rights of 1966 had such an impact on the international community that no state currently challenges the concept that human rights must be cherished and respected everywhere in the world. As a result, on the one hand, those general texts and a host of specific conventions and international resolutions, and, on the other hand, the consistent practice of international bodies- especially the multifarious activities carried out by various UN organs—a general principle has gradually emerged prohibiting gross and large scale violation of basic human rights and fundamental freedoms.[3]

This hightening of the consciousness of human right necessity calls for an instrument of protection.

If as pointed out above a claim by citizen for adequate housing is not only a right but a human right certain inevitable conclusions must flow, the top most being as to what is the implementation machinery to effectuate this human right.

In the search for principle to make international law enforceable big boost was given by what Sir Lauterpacht called Brierly's beneficial doctrine of incorporation according to which "courts apply international law; per se, as being part of the law of the land. It is, in his view, beneficial not only as showing that municipal courts apply international law as authoritative in its own right, but also because by asserting that it is a part of the law of the land we deny that it has any specific quality which distinguishes it from that law. The doctrine of incorporation has constituted one of the main contributions of the common law to international legal tradition." It is in this light that "Brierly arrived at the affirmation of the essential unity and identity of international and municipal law and the rejection of the then still predominant dualistic view. He deprecated the customary exaggerations of the absence of sanctions of international law and the laxity of its observance."

A survey of the varied practices of states show that, except possibly in terms of dialectics, it is impossible to accept the view that rules of international law cannot, without express municipal adoption, operate as part of municipal law or the opposite view that they always so operate. On the contrary, states show considerable flexibility in the procedures whereby they give effect within their territories to the rules of international law, although many states adopt the doctrine that international law is part of the law of the land. But while the procedures vary, the result that effect is given within states to the requirements of international law is by and large achieved by all states. This result may be called for in relation to almost any held of activity which is regulated by international law, although in certain fields, such as the observance of human rights, it has assumed special importance.[4]

And for the protection of human rights generally, have testified to the intimate connection between the interests of the individual and international law. The Charter of the United Nations with its repeated recognition of human rights and fundamental freedoms, inaugurated a new and decisive departure with regard to this abiding problem of law and government. In some instances as, for example, in the European convention on Human Rights, and the two United Nations Covenants on Economic, Social and Cultural Rights and on Civil and Political Rights-that development has assumed the complexion of explicit rules legally binding upon States.

As Prof. Van Dijk and Van Hoof noted: "Nevertheless, it would appear to us that in view of its character the European convention contains the germs for a gradual development into a common legal system for the contracting States, to which their national law must be subordinate."[5]

The two International covenants namely civil and economic marked a notable step forward in the protection of human rights within the framework of the United Nations, and largely constitute the basic provisions of an International Bill of Rights.

The two covenants also demonstrated the way in which the United Nations is overcoming its earlier hesitations about the enforcement of human rights obligations.

Ratification is defined in the Vienna convention on the Law of Treaties 1969 as the international act so named whereby a state establishes on the international plane its consent to be bound by a treaty.

Georg Schwarzenberger maintains that a state which has contracted international obligations is bound to make in its municipal law such alterations as may be necessary to ensure the fulfilment of its international obligations.

Despite, the inclination of a few observers who continue to suggest the non-justiciability of social and economic human rights, including housing rights, a deeper examination of the normative content of housing rights, decisions and approaches taken by national judiciaries and the jurisprudence of the regional and international human rights bodies especially committee on ESCR reveals that the vast majority of the constituent elements of housing rights as recognized under international and national laws are in fact, justiciable.

I am inclined to agree with the following:

> "Denying an individual or group the ability to make Constitutional claims against the state with respect to nutrition, housing, health and education excludes those interest from a process of reasoned interchange and discussion, and forecloses a useful forum for the recognition and redressing of injustices."[6]

The application of international law as part of the law of the land means that, subject to the overriding effect of statute law, rights and duties flowing, from rules of customary international law will be recognised and given effect by courts without the need for any specific act adopting those rules into domestic law.

It is self evident that unless the right to adequate housing is legally enforceable by an individual, it will only remain a moral imperative, but of no practical benefit. What then is the position in law.

Now as Salmond on Jurisprudence says "All rights whatever correspond to duties". The right of a citizen, therefore, corresponds to a duty on the part of a State. Thus as Salmond again puts it "when the law recognises an act as a duty it commonly enforces the performance of it, or punishes the disregard of it".

Now, it admits of no doubt that covenants fully qualify to be called international law. Courts have evolved a harmonious role of interpretation, namely that an international convention is binding in international law on all countries which have ratified it, and it is the duty of the court to construe legislation so as to be in conformity with international law and not in conflict with it.

The comity of nations further requires that rules of international law may be accommodated in municipal law even without express legislative sanction provided they do not run into conflict with Acts of Parliament. The doctrine of incorporation popularised by Brierley also recognises that rules of international law are incorporated into national law and considered to be a part of national law, unless they are in direct conflict with domestic law.

As a matter of fact jurisprudence under the compulsion of universality of human rights is developing into own Human Rights Jurisprudence.

As a result of this development, and the compulsion and obligation to comply with international treaties, even when the former seem to be conflict with domestic legislation, it is being accepted even in the United Kingdom, which has had its fundamental basis in the complete sovereignty of its Parliament that conventions should prevail. This welcome trend has been noted (Wade and Forsyth in *The Administrative Law*, (7th Edition) as follows:[7]

"Unlike other States who are parties to the European Convention on Human Rights and Fundamental Freedoms of 1950. Britain has failed to incorporate the convention into domestic law, so that its status is that of a treaty only and complainants must undertake long and expensive litigation in Strasbourg. But the courts, though unable to enforce the convention directly, have made some progress towards giving effect to it indirectly. They will take it into account in construing statutes or regulations in cases of ambiguity. In one case

Lord Reid said that it was hardly credible that Parliament or any government department would act contrary to it. Several times it has been held that regard ought to be had to the Convention as an aid to interpretation, and in one case under the common law, where arguments were evenly balanced, they treated the convention as decisive. Distinguished judges, speaking extrajudicially, have suggested how this House of Lords, Lord Griffiths acknowledges the responsibility of the juridicary to refuse to countenance behaviour that threatens either basic human rights or the rule of the law."

The principle of English Courts has been also aptly put by (Maxwell on Interpretation of Statutes) thus[8] "Under the general presumption that the legislature does not intend to exceed its jurisdiction, every statute is interpreted, so far as its language permits so as not to be inconsistent with the committee of nations or the established rules of international law and the court will avoid a construction which would give rise to such inconsistency unless compelled to adopt it by plain, and unambiguous language."

A similar view was expressed in an English case[9]. It was observed "the Warsaw Convention is an International Convention which is binding in International Law and all the countries who have ratified it and it is the duty of our courts to so construe our Legislation, so as to be in conformity with the International Law and not conflict with it". *Concocraft Ltd.* vs. *American Airways*; (1969) I AER 80).

In India, there is no domestic law casting obligation on the State to house the homeless. The Supreme Court has however in an innovative way sought to incorporate this right to housing by so interpreting Article 21 of the Constitution which provides that no citizen shall be deprived of his life or personal liberty except according to procedure established by law, and interpreting in the context of various International covenants.

The Supreme Court in (8) (*Jolly George Varghese* vs. *Bank of Cochin*: (1980) 2 SCC 360), posed the question from the international law as to whether it is right to enforce a contractual liability by imprisoning a debtor in the teeth of Article 11 of the International Covenant on Civil and Political Rights. The Article reads:

"No one shall be imprisoned merely on the ground of inability to fulfil a contractual obligation.

At the earlier stage though the Supreme Court accepted the principle of law that from the national point of view the national rules alone count, but it emphasised that "India is now a signatory to this Covenant and Article 51(c) of the Constitution obligates the State to "foster respect for international law and treaty obligations in the dealings of organised people with another" and invoking the well recognised rule of interpretation, viz, "it is a principle generally recognised in national legal systems that, in the event of doubt, the national rule is to be interpreted in accordance with the State's international obligations" it set aside the detention of the debtor.

In the most publicised case Indian Supreme Court said[9]:

"Eviction of the petitioners from their dwellings would result in the deprivation of their livelihood. There is thus a close nexus between life and means of livelihood. And as such that which alone makes it possible to live, leave aside what makes life liveable, must be deemed to be an integral component of the right to life."

In another case it was held the right to life "would take within its sweep the right to ... a reasonable accommodation to live in .."[10]

Indian Supreme Court has been consistently upholding the view that the right to life guaranteed under Article 21 of the Indian Constitution includes the right to a shelter. In this view it invoked to its aid Article 25(1) of the U.D.R. and Article 11(1) of ICESR. [11]

In another case[12] the Supreme Court reads the right of privacy in Indian law though there is no specific rights in domestic law by invoking International Covenants, by observing:

"India is a signatory to the International Covenant on Civil and Political Rights, 1966. Article 17 of the said covenant is as under:

"Article 17

1. No one shall be subject to arbitrary or unlawful interference with his privacy, family, human or correspondence, nor to unlawful attacks on his honour and reputation.
2. Everyone has the right to the protection of the law against such interference or attacks."

Article 12 of the Universal Declaration of Human Rights, 1948 is almost in similar terms.

21. International law today is not confined to regulating the relations between the States. Scope continues to extend. Today matters of social concern, such as health, education and economics apart from human rights fall within the ambit of International Regulations. International law is more than ever aimed at individuals.

22. It is almost an accepted proposition of law that the rules of

customary international law which are not contrary to the municipal law shall be deemed to be incorporated in the domestic law."

Many jurisdictions in Anglo-Saxon Law, including India accept that if there is any ambiguity in a statute, and particularly (but not necessarily only) where it is expressly enacted to give effect to a treaty, it will be interpreted in the light of and, if possible, in such a way as to be consistent with the country's international obligations.

One of the helpful and progressive development recently in giving support to the binding effect of right to adequate housing has been the role of United Nations Committee on Economic, Social and Cultural Rights. The committee has specifically addressed rights issues and has urged the State party to recall General Comment No. 4 91991) in which it noted that "the committee considers that instances of forced eviction are prima facie incompatible with the requirements of the covenant and can only be justified in the most exceptional circumstances, and in accordance with the relevant principles of international law" (Mexico, ninth session).

The plea of enforceability of housing rights should not now be a matter of debate after Habitat II at Istanbul (1996).

Istanbul Declaration commits the Heads of States/Governments to the objective principle and recommendations contained in Habitat Agenda and they have pledged their mutual support for its implementation.

Now Habitat Agenda accepts that everyone has the right to an adequate standard of living for themselves and their families including adequate food, clothing, housing shelter.... (emphasis supplied).

Further, there is a promise to implement and promote this objective in a manner fully consistent with human rights standard.

There is a further promise of protecting all people from and providing legal protection and redress for forced evictions that are contrary to law, taking human rights into consideration.

These declarations and promises by the Heads of States create legitimate expectations in the minds of citizens that the State will implement its promise to provide adequate housing. Now, law is well settled that in such situation jurisprudentially a citizen can invoke the jurisdiction of the courts and pray for mandomus to carry out their obligations. In this eventuality the State will be further stopped from pleading any defence against the claim put forth by the citizens.

This further strengthened my conclusions that right to adequate housing can be legally enforced in a court of law.

However, some irritant hesitations by some courts, I am, therefore, more than convinced that the right to adequate housing can be legally enforced against the States which are not fulfilling their obligations as mentioned above. I also believe that State must ensure the provision of domestic remedies for each of these fundamental aspects and core contents of the human right to adequate housing.

This course flows from the indisputable proposition about the indivisibility and interdependence of all human beings and the inherent, indispensable and permeable relationship between the full enjoyment of the right to adequate housing and certain civil and political rights. I am convinced that a wide range of civil and political rights like the right to privacy, the right to family law, the right to equal protection and benefit of the law, the right to gender equality, the right to be free from discrimination, the right to property will be seriously compromised in the absence of measures geared towards respecting, protecting and ensuring the right to adequate housing.

Although governmental accountability for the respect, protection, promotion and fulfilment of housing rights is now well established under international law, measures of implementation and, in particular, judicial enforcement have remained somewhat hesitant. Despite major progress regarding the definition of housing right and the concomitant State obligations, the much enhanced stature of this norm at both the international level will only be possible through an optional protocol to the International Covenant on Economic, Social and Cultural Rights like the one in covenant on civil and political rights.

References

1. Oppenhein's International Law (19th Edn.) Vol. I, p. 31.

2. Brierly's Contribution to International Law-by Sir Hersch Lauterpacht. Q.C. LL.D. F.B.A. p. XV at XXI.

3. International Law in a Divided World - Antonio Cassese-Clarendonpress, Oxford, p. 148.

4. *Ibid* (1), p. 54.

5. Theory and Practices of European Convention on Human Rights by Professors Van Dink and Van Hoof.

6. Craig Scott and Patrick Macklem in University of Pennsylvania Law Review, Vol. 141, No. 1. 1992, p. 28.

7. Wade and Forsyth in The Administrative Law (7th Edn.).

8. Jolly George Varghese V. Bank of Cochin : (1980) 2 Supreme Court Cases 360.

9. Olaga Tellis vs. Bombay Municipal Corpn .: (1985) 3 SCC 545.

10. Chameli Singh, vs. State of U.P.: (1996) 2 SCC 549.

11. Shantistar Builders vs. Narayan Khimalal Totane : (1990) 1 SCC 520.

12. People's Union for Civil Liberties vs. UOI.: (1997) 1 SCC 301.

15

Domestic Application of the International Covenant on Civil and Political Rights—With Special Reference to Rights of Minorities in India

Abdulrahim P. Vijapur

Introduction

The International Covenant on Civil and Political Rights (ICCPR), which was adopted by the UN General Assembly on 16 December 1966 (and entered into force on 23 March 1976) was acceded to by India on 10 April 1979 (and became operational on 10 July 1976, i.e., three months after the date of depositing its instrument of ratification or accession). It is the only international human rights treaty which includes a provision (under Article 27) on the rights of persons belonging to various minority groups. The purpose of this Article is to analyse the domestic application of the provisions of the ICCPR specially with regard to Article 27 which provides for the rights of persons belonging to minorities. What are the rights of minorities under ICCPR? How these rights have been further elaborated in the 1992 UN Declaration on the Rights of Persons belonging to National or Ethnic, Religious and Linguistic Minorities? What is the domestic status of international covenants in India? What special measures have been undertaken by the Indian Government to give effect to minority rights guaranteed in the covenants and the Constitution? What provisions on minority rights exist in the Constitutional and other statutory laws? To what extent these and the covenant provisions are complied with by the Indian State? Whether gross violations of the rights of minorities is reflected in India's periodic reports? Answers to these and other related questions are explored in this paper.

I

Domestic Implementation of International Covenants on Human Rights

One of the greatest, in fact revolutionary, developments in the annals of history is that for the first time in international relations a comprehensive list of human rights has been evolved (under the aegis of the United Nations) which every individual, irrespective of his/her origin, religion, race, colour, sex, nationality, etc., can claim as a member of human society. During the last five decades the United Nations has adopted around 100 human rights instruments (such as declarations, conventions, covenants, etc.) on various facets of human rights, covering the entire gamut of human relationship.[1] However, it must be noted that the most important among all these instruments are the Universal Declaration of Human Rights (UDHR) (1948), the International Covenant on Economic, Social and Cultural Rights (ICESCR) (1966), the International Covenant on Civil and Political Rights (ICCPR) and two Optional Protocols thereto, providing for the right of individual petition (1966), and aiming at the abolition of death penalty (1989), which together form the five constituent parts of the International Bill of Rights. This Bill, the first ever adopted in the history of the world, has brought the matter of human rights on the agenda of international relations. Now human rights have truly become matters of international jurisdiction/action. It is no longer possible for States Parties to various LLN conventions to argue that protection of human rights is simply a matter within their domestic jurisdiction.[2] It is gratifying to note that these two International Covenants on human rights— ICESCR and ICCPR— create legally binding obligations for the States, which have ratified them. By 3 December 1999 the former was ratified by 143 States and the latter by 145 States (by 28 July 2000).

Notwithstanding the internationalization of human rights, it is pertinent to note that, as recognized in Part II of the Covenants, the "State" remains the guarantor and protector of human rights of their individuals (including non-citizens) residing in the State. It is not just the question of domestic jurisdiction or state sovereignty —of course it is still there in legal terms, but States differ from one another in their socio-economic, political, historical and cultural conditions and traditions. Since human rights are intrinsically related to the socio-economic systems, and their realization depends to a greater extent on the political, economic, and central development of a particular State, they are, therefore, in reality to be enjoyed by individuals in their own States and implemented under their domestic laws and institutions. Indeed, all the instruments of human rights recognize this fact. Moreover, these instruments are evolved on the principle that State is the guarantor and protector of human rights. Thus, at this stage of the development of international law and relations, no global authority has been envisaged for implementation of human rights. The human rights obligations of the covenants do not operate directly upon the individuals, but work on the States and are designed to induce them to adhere to the minimum norms agreed upon and spelled out in them. They serve only as an international process to encourage States to carry out their international obligations in respect of human rights and to desist from their violations.[3]

The principle of domestic application of international human rights has been explicitly recognized in Part II of both the covenants in identical Articles. Article 2(1) of ICESCR provides that each State party "undertakes to take steps ... to the maximum of its available resources, with a view to achieving progressively the full realization of the rights recognized in ... the covenant by all appropriate means, including particularly the adoption of legislative measures". The ICCPR, under Article 2(1), provides that the State party "undertake to respect and to ensure to all individuals within its territory and subject to its jurisdiction the rights recognize in the ... Covenant" without any discrimination. This provision is further supplemented by para 2 of the Article which requires the State parties "to adopt such legislative or other measures as may be necessary to give effect to the rights" guaranteed in the covenant whenever such provisions do not already exist in its domestic law. This provision specifically States that such measures have to be in accordance with their "Constitutional processes".

II

Rights of Minorities under ICCPR

At the outset it must be said that like all human rights instruments, the two international covenants contain a general principle of non-discrimination concerning the enjoyment of rights and freedoms.[4] This principle states that each State party to the covenants undertakes to respect and to ensure to all individuals the rights recognized in these covenants, without discrimination of any kind such as race, colour, sex, language, religion, political or other opinion, national or social origin, property, birth or other status. This provision indirectly protects the rights of persons belonging to minorities. Since such a general principle is insufficient, the ICCPR contains an Article on the rights of individuals belonging to minorities (Article 27). Though the rights of minorities Article is not very detailed one, it is nevertheless a significant provision, as the ICCPR is the only international human rights treaty, which binds States parties to guarantee rights of minorities.[5] Article 27 states:

> In those States in which ethnic, religious or linguistic minorities exist, persons belonging to such minorities shall not be denied the right, in community with the other members of their group, to enjoy their own culture, to profess and practice their own religion, or to use their own language.

Besides this Article there are certain other UN instruments concerning one or the other minorities. These are: the Genocide Convention (1948), the Convention on the Elimination of All Forms of Racial Discrimination (1965), Declaration on the Elimination of All Forms of Discrimination Based on Religion or Belief (1981) and the Declaration on the Rights of Persons Belonging to National or Ethnic, Religious and Linguistic Minorities (1992).

Article 27 of the ICCPR grants rights to individuals but not to groups or minorities, though they may enjoy these rights in community with the other members of their group. During its drafting the phrase "persons belonging to minorities" was deliberately added with a view to avoid giving to the minorities an international personality. Such international personality, it was feared, might have given a minority the capacity to vindicate its rights before the Human Rights Committee, the 18-member expert body created under ICCPR to monitor compliance of its provisions by the States Parties. The First Optional Protocol to the ICCPR gives the right to submit petitions/communications only to individuals. Groups and organizations cannot submit petitions as collective entities, but individual members may do so, alleging violations of their individual and collective rights.[6]

Some questions arise in a minority rights discourse, such as:

Are minority rights individual or collective? Or both? Are minority rights also human rights?[7] A reading of Article 27 reveals that minority rights are also human rights. Francesco Capotorti confirms that this Article grants individual rights. However, he adds that the rights in question will be exercised by their holders in community with the other members of their group and this is "understandable when it is considered that the rights provided are based on the interests of a collectivity, and consequently, it is the individual as a member of all minority group and not just any individual, who is destined to benefit from the protection by Article 27".[8]

Whether persons belonging to minorities are entitled to enjoy only those rights mentioned in Article 27 (namely to enjoy one's own culture, profess and practice one's own religion and use one's own language)? The answer is no, as this Article establishes and recognizes a right which is conferred on individuals belonging to minority groups and which is distinct from, and additional to, all the other rights which, as individuals in common with everyone else, they are already entitled to enjoy under the ICCPR. In other words, persons belonging to minorities are entitled to enjoy, as individuals, all the other rights mentioned in the covenant, i.e., the rights mentioned in Articles 6 to 26.

Let us briefly elaborate the rights mentioned in Articles 6 to 26. The list is quite comprehensive. These rights are: right to life (Article 6); freedom from torture or cruelty, inhuman or degrading treatment (Article 7); freedom from slavery (Article 8); freedom from arbitrary arrest or detention (Article 9); right to be treated with humanity when deprived of one's liberty (Article 10); freedom from imprisonment merely on the ground of inability to fulfil a contractual obligation (Article 11); freedom of movement and freedom to choose a residence (Article 12); freedom from arbitrary explusion of aliens (Article 13); equality before the courts and tribunals and guarantees in criminal and civil procedure (including the right to be presumed innocent until proved guilty by law) (Article 14); freedom from the application of retroactive criminal legislation (Article 15); the right of everyone to recognition everywhere as a person before the law (Article 16); freedom from arbitrary or unlawful interference with an individual's privacy, family, home or correspondence (Article 17); freedom of thought, conscience and religion (Article 18); freedom of opinion and expression (Article 19); prohibition by law of any propaganda for war and of any advocacy of national, racial or religious hatred that constitutes an incitement to discrimination, hostility or violence (Article 20); right of peaceful assembly (Article 21); right to freedom of association (Article 22); right to marry and to found a family based on the principle of equality of rights and responsibilities of spouses at the time of marriage, during marriage and at its dissolution (Article 23); a child's right not to be discriminated, to be registered after birth and to have a name subsequently and right to acquire a nationality (Article 24); the right to take part (as citizens) in the conduct of public affairs, to vote and to be elected, and to have access to public service (Article 25); and equality before law and the equal protection of the law (Article 26).

Article 27 of the ICCPR, which is the most widely accepted legally binding provision, grants persons belonging to minorities the right to national, ethnic, religious or linguistic identity, or a combination thereof, and to preserve the characteristics which they wish to maintain and develop. Although this Article refers to the rights of minorities in those States in which they exist, its applicability is not subject to official recognition of a minority by State.

It is also worth recalling here, briefly however, the provisions of the 1992 UN Declaration on the Rights of Minorities, as it further elaborates and enriches the concept of the rights of minorities.[9] Its preamble rightly proclaims that the promotion and protection of the rights of persons belonging to minorities contributes to the political and social stability of States in which they live. The preamble and its nine Articles mostly restate the general contents of existing rights. Articles 1 to 6 are its substantive provisions. Article 1 addresses their existence and identity. Article 2 sets forth a series of rights and freedoms such as their right to enjoy their own culture, to profess and practice their own religion and to use their own language in private and public places; the right to participate in cultural, religious, social, economic and public life; the right to participate in decisions which affect them on the national and regional levels; the right to establish and maintain their own associations and the right to establish and maintain peaceful contacts with other members of their group and with persons belonging to other minorities, both within their own country and across State borders. Article 3 repeats the language employed by Article 27 of the ICCPR concerning the exercise of these rights individually and "in community with other members of their group". Article 4 obligates States to take special measures. These measures include, among others, creating favourable conditions to enable minorities to express their characteristics and to develop their culture, language, religion, traditions and customs; allowing them adequate opportunities to learn their mother tongue or to have instruction in their mother tongue and allowing their participation in economic progress and development. Article 5 requires States to take measures in developing national policies and programmes for minorities. Article 6 deals with having cooperation with other States on questions relating to minorities, including the exchange of information and experiences, in order to promote mutual understanding and confidence.

Though the Declaration on Minorities is a non-binding document, it is of great significance it is the first international instrument solely devoted to rights of the minorities. Under Article 9, the Declaration states clearly that the organizations of the UN system have a role to play in "the full realization of the rights and principles set forth in the Declaration".

Article 27 of the covenant does not call for special measures to be adopted by States, but States that have ratified the covenant are obliged to ensure that all individuals under their jurisdiction enjoy their rights; this may require specific action, like affirmative action, to correct inequalities to which minorities are subjected. It is instructive to note here the general comment of Human Rights Committee on Article 26 of the ICCPR.[10] The committee points out that the principle of equality sometimes requires States parties to take and affirmative action in order to diminish or eliminate conditions which cause or help to perpetuate discrimination. For example, in a State where the general conditions of a certain part of the population prevent or impair their enjoyment of human rights, the State should take a specific action to correct these conditions. Such action may involve granting for a specified time certain preferential treatment in specific matters. Since such action can lead to group conflict it should not be continued beyond the time when equality has been achieved. Such differentiation will not constitute discrimination, if the criteria for such differentiation are reasonable and objective and if the aim is to achieve a purpose, which is legitimate under the ICCPR.

The doctrine of affirmative action has been supported by many scholars. Prominent among them are Asbjorn Eide,[11] Will Kymlicka[12] and Warwick McKean. McKean argues[13] that positive discrimination measures are temporary and compensatory for past discrimination, while protective measures providing for "special rights for minority groups" (such as to maintain their own languages, cultures and traditions, and religious practices and to establish schools, libraries, churches and similar institutions), produce "an equilibrium" between different situations and "should be maintained as long as the groups concerned wish". Thus, the protective measures have to be permanent, whereas compensatory measures like reservation of jobs, etc. (as it prevails in India) have to be temporary.

Implementing the Covenant : Reporting and Complaint Procedures

To monitor the compliance of international obligations to promote, protect and guarantee human rights of its individuals, including the rights of minorities, the ICCPR provides for a mandatory reporting procedure. Under this procedure all States parties are required to submit periodic reports to the Human Rights Committee on the measures they have adopted which give effect to the rights contained in the covenant and on the progress made in the enjoyment of those rights. These reports are supposed to indicate also the factors and difficulties, if any, affecting the implementation of the covenant rights. When a State report comes before the Human Rights Committee, a representative of the country concerned introduces it, questions and answers from the expert members of the Committee, and comments on the observations made. In this way the Committee engages into a dialogue with the State representative. The discussion and perusal of State reports by the Committee reveals the degree of compliance of the Covenant provisions.[14]

The Committee has provided States with a set of reporting guidelines specifying the type of information required. For reporting under Article 27 of the ICCPR information contained in the report must be provided about minorities in a State, their respective numbers as compared to the majority and the concrete measures adopted by the reporting State to preserve minorities' ethnic, religious, cultural and linguistic identity as well as other measures to provide minorities with equal economic and political opportunities. Particular reference should be made to their representation in central and local government bodies.[15]

Besides the reporting procedure, the ICCPR provides two optional complaint procedures. They may be submitted by an individual or a State. One, the first Optional Protocol to the ICCPR provides for individual communications by a State party of any of the Covenant articles, including Article 27. Unfortunately, the Indian Government has not acceded to this protocol. Second, under Article 41, the ICCPR provides State to State complaints, if the State party has recognized to competence of the Human Rights Committee to receive and consider such complaints. In this case, the Committee may consider communications to the effect that a State party claims that another State party (which has also accepted this optional procedure) is not respecting the rights set out in the Covenant, including Article 27. It is regretting to note that India has not accepted this procedure also.

III

Domestic Human Rights and Minority Rights Law

India is a mosaic of different religious, cultural and linguistic minorities. It is a home of all major religions of the world. There are eight major religious communities. According to 1991 census, Hindus constitute 82.7 per cent of the population, (of which 15 per cent belong to the Scheduled Castes and 7.8 per cent to the Scheduled Tribes), form the majority. The rest are minorities. Muslims constitute the largest minority; having 120 million population (i.e., 11.8 per cent which is the second largest Muslim population in any country in the world. Christians (2.6 per cent) Sikhs (2 per cent, Buddhists (0.7 per cent) Jains (0.5 per cent, and Jews (0.1 per cent, are other religious minorities. Its linguistic diversity is reflected in 18 major languages which are recognized in VIII Schedule of the Constitution (which are spoken in one or more of the 28 States and 7 Union Teritories of India). Ninety per cent of our population speaks one of these 18 languages. Regarding the total number of languages and dialects spoken in India different estimates are available. According to 1981 Census over 1,500 dialects are spoken in the country,[16] whereas in the third periodic report under ICCPR the government discloses that 844 different dialects are spoken in India.[17] Besides the religious and linguistic minorities, there are different cultural, tribal and untouchable groups in the country. The Indian government has been denying that the term "ethnic minority" applies to Indian society.[18]

To ensure peaceful coexistence of divergent groups, the Indian Constitution provides a comprehensive framework to safeguard the group rights of religious, cultural and linguistic minorities against majority encroachments. However, for reasons of space, this Article deals mostly with the religious minorities. It studies the rights of minorities and their violations in a comparative perspective of international and national laws.

Many of the human rights and freedoms contained in the International Bill of Rights are guaranteed under the Indian Constitution, in Articles 12-35. Any law inconsistent with or in derogation of these rights is void to the extent of its inconsistency (Article 13). Also, some sections of Indian Penal Code, personal laws applicable to different communities, and many legislative acts, deal with the matters concerning human rights and freedoms.

What is of great significance is that the individuals, including those belonging to minorities,[19] who feel that their rights are violated, can directly move the Supreme Court (Article 32 of the Constitution) and the High Courts (Article 226). These Articles empower the Courts to issue directions or orders or writs including writs in the nature of: (a) Habeas Corpus, (b) Mandamus (c) Prohibition, (d) Quo warranto and (e) Certiorari.

In recent years, the Supreme Court has been taking up the cases of human rights violation under its newly developed "Public Interest Litigation" (PIL) system.[20] Under this novel system, issues of locus standi, burden of proof, time constraints, and legal aid have all been construed in a way that benefits the victims of human rights violations. This judicial activism represents an outstanding development in Indian legal system, and can be considered as a "Constitutional revolution", unparalleled anywhere in the world.

The right to freedom of thought, conscience and religion, as contained in Article 18 of the UDHR and ICCPR and further elaborated in Article 6 of the 1981 Declaration on the Elimination of Religious Discrimination is included in Articles 25-29 of the Constitution and other legal codes. Article 25 guarantees not only freedom of conscience, free profession, and practice of religion, but also the right to propagate religion. Article 25(2b) provides that the State can make law for social welfare and reform or the throwing open of Hindu religious institutions of a public character to all classes and sections of Hindus. Every religious community is guaranteed the right to establish and maintain institutions for religious and charitable purposes; to manage its own affairs in matters of religion; to own and acquire movable and immovable property; and to administer such property in accordance with law

(Article 26). Under Article 27, individuals are guaranteed that State shall not compel them to pay any taxes, the proceeds of which are specially used for the promotion or maintenance of any particular religion or religions. This Article implies that State can give financial aid to the promotion of every religion with only one reservation. This aid should be non-discriminatory. These rights are subject to considerations of public order, morality and health, which are necessary in the interests of general public.

The customary and codified personal laws of different communities also provide for the liberty of children to develop their own religious convictions. In addition (under Article 28), the Constitution prohibits imposition of religious beliefs on the persons attending any educational institutions receiving State aid. The Article further adds that no student can be required to take part in any religious instructions that may be imparted in such an institution recognized by State or to attend to any worship that may be conducted in such institutions without the individual's consent or without the consent of the guardian in case the student is a minor.

Articles 29 and 30 of the Constitution deal with cultural and educational rights. The former guarantees any section of the citizens having a distinct language, script or culture of its own the right to conserve the same. No one can be denied admission into any educational institution maintained by the State or receiving aid/funds from it on the grounds of religion, race, caste, language, etc. The latter guarantees the minorities, both linguistic and religious, the right to establish and administer educational institutions. It further adds that the State cannot discriminate such institutions either in granting recognition or providing aid. To safeguard the interests of linguistic minorities a special officer is appointed to investigate all matters relating to the Constitutional rights of the minorities (Article 350B).

The Indian Penal Code treats the offences relating to religion such as injuring or defiling places of worship with an intention to insult the religion of any class, acts against any religion, disturb religious assemblies and utterances to wound the religious feelings of others as "crimes" inviting specified punishments.

Indian religious organizations are allowed to maintain communications with co-religionists abroad. Financial contributions from abroad are subject to scrutiny and licensing by the Ministry of Home Affairs of the Federal/Union Government.

The Religious Institutions (Prevention of Misuse) Act, 1988, makes it an offence to use any religious site for political purposes or to use places of worship for harbouring persons accused or convicted of any crime. While especially designed to deal with Gurudwaras in Punjab, the Act technically applies to all religious sites. However, the government has been careful to avoid placing restrictions on Sikh religious practices or on the management of their Gurudwaras.

What emerges from the overview of the Indian law concerning the freedom of religion is that the State has no official religion. It treats all religions equal. It keeps a safe distance with each one of them. It does not discriminate between them. Indian State is truly secular, at least in law.

However, it needs to be pointed out that the definition of a "Hindu" emerging from Article 25 of the Constitution, the Hindu Code Bill, the Untouchability Abolition Act and the temple entry legislations is a source of great concern as they do not accord Buddhism, Jainism and Sikhism any autonomous or independent identity. These documents define Hindus in such a way as to include Buddhists, Jains and Sikhs.[21] Many scholars and legal authorities have examined the problem of definition.[22]

With a view to ensuring effective enforcement of the Constitutional provisions relating to minorities, a National Commission for Minorities (NCM) was created in 1978, which was, (i) given statutory status in 1992. Its functions included, inter alia monitoring of Constitutional and legislative safeguards and making recommendations for their effective implementation; (ii) evaluating the progress of minorities and (iii) investigation of specific complaints regarding violations of the rights of minorities. The Commission has been given powers comparable to a civil court, particularly in investigating allegations of violations of the rights of minorities. In 1993, the Government also established the National Human Rights Commission (NHRC). It has been quite active in promoting human rights of all citizens, including those of minorities. Both the NCM and NHRC are required to submit annual reports on their activities, which must be tabled in Parliament along with the Action Taken Report of Government, allowing for discussion, dissemination and transparency at the highest level.

IV

Domestic Status of International Covenants

Unlike the USA and Germany, treaties are not self-executing in India and their provisions do not automatically form part of the domestic law. In this regard to a large extent India follows the Anglo-Saxon tradition. The Commonwealth countries while interpreting their Constitutions drew inspiration from the international charter and instruments.[23] According to the Anglo-Saxon tradition, customary international law is considered as a part of the law of the land as long as they are not inconsistent with national statutes. In its reply to the UN rapporteur the Government of India stated that "the treaty or convention has to be given effect through national legislation." [24] The Parliament, the executive and judiciary have the power to interpret a treaty or international instruments, whenever called upon do so during the course of their business.[25] The Parliament has exclusive powers to enact on matters concerning treaties. In certain cases a treaty might be implemented by the exercise of the executive power of the President in accordance with Article 53 of the Constitution.

Under Article 51(c), the Constitution further provides that the State shall "foster respect for international law and treaty obligations in the dealings of organized people with one another". This provision, however, is non-enforceable by a court of law.

V

A Critique of Rights of Minorities in India

This section essays a critique of Indian laws, government policies and State practices besides analysing the policies and practices of certain religious communities to discern the level of rights of minorities protection available. At the outset it must be admitted that there is a wide disparity between Constitutional precepts on rights of minority or the Covenant rights and the State practices.

As noted earlier, India has an obligation to submit periodic reports to the UN on the state of compliance of human rights norms of the covenant. Since the ratification of the ICCPR on 10 July 1979, India has submitted three periodic reports to the Human Rights Committee. The first report[26], which was due in 1980, was submitted on July 1983; the second report,[27] which was due in 1985, was submitted on 12 July 1989; the third report, [28] which was due by 31 March 1992, was submitted on 29 November 1995 and the fourth report are due on 31 December 2001 and it is not yet submitted.

In most of the cases the periodic reports of the States Parties under ICCPR enumerate the existing Constitutional and statutory provisions concerning minorities rather than providing supportive data to demonstrate their compliance of covenant provisions in by practice. All the three Indian reports follow this pattern of reporting. Also the State reports generally provide a splendid picture of human rights situation. For instance, India's third report pronounces that "India is ... a ... mosaic of different religions and cultures. It has a tolerant eclectic society .... ." (p. 4) The discussion in the following pages concerning inter-religious riots and atrocities on religious minorities contradicts this pronouncement.

The first report provides just one page information on minorities. It reproduces Articles 29 and 30 of the Constitution and briefly mentions about the setting up of a Minorities Commission. It does not provide data about the population of minorities. During its consideration and discussion by the Human Rights Committee, some members stated that India's report was brief and too vague and that it did not sufficiently indicate the factors and difficulties affecting the implementation of the covenant. One member lamented that it did not reflect the actual human rights situation. Referring to inter-religious confrontations and violence a member noted that the report made no mention of that fact and asked whether efforts were made by government to prevent such confrontations and whether religious tolerance was taught to school children. Regarding Article 27 of the covenant, the statement of India that the concept of minorities did not apply to it as far as ethnic groups such as Scheduled Tribes are concerned. This statement evoked surprise at the committee. Commenting on the reference made by members to minorities, the Indian representative insisted that ethnic minorities did not exist in India, since the country had no ethnic majority either, all the different tribes in India were not racial categories but had different religious, linguistic and cultural background.[29]

The second periodic report too contained one and a half pages information on Article 27. This information was concerning Articles 29-30 and 350B of the Constitution and the functions of the Minorities Commission. The committee's concluding observation on India's report is worth noting here. It noted that the report failed to refer to practice and the specific implementation of legislative provisions and, in that respect, it was deficient. [30] Its information pertained to the period 1984-1988, but the human rights situation in the country during the period and subsequently bore a dismal picture. The

International NGO reports, specially the one by Amnesty International, fully contradicted the official presentation of the situation.[31] The Terrorist and Disruptive Activities (Prevention) Act (TADA) was misused. According to India's then Minister of State for Home Affairs, M.M. Jacob, a total of 26,915 had been detained under TADA between 1988-1991. Surprisingly the highest figures were recorded in Gujarat (9569) where the menace of terrorism was very low compared to Punjab, Jammu and Kashmir and Assam. According to Amnesty's report TADA was disproportionately used against tribals and Muslims. In Gujarat three quarters of those held under TADA at the end of 1989 were Muslims.[32]

The third report also reproduced, in one page, the information given in earlier two reports on minorities and the National Commission on Minorities (NCM). It stated that the NCM submits annual reports to the Government which must be tabled in Parliament along with the Action Taken Report of the Government, allowing for discussion, dissemination and transparency at the highest level. But the Government has not tabled NCM reports in Parliament for more than a decade. In fact, according to a former Chairman of NCM, Tahir Mahmood, it has been made to play a minor role.[33]

After considering the third report, the committee made many concluding observations. First, the report failed to refer to practice and the specific implementation of legislative provisions and, in that respect, was deficient. The committee expressed concern about a number of subjects. It recommended that steps be taken to incorporate fully the provisions of the covenant into domestic law, so that individuals may invoke them directly before the courts. It also recommended that consideration be given by the authorities to ratifying the first Optional Protocol to the covenant, enabling the committee to receive individual communications. The committee, noting India's reservations and declarations to seven Articles of the covenant (Articles 1, 9, 12, 13, 19 paras 3, 21 and 22), invited the government to review them with a view to withdrawing them, so as to ensure progress in the implementation of the rights contained in those Articles.[34]

Some gaps can be seen in Indian reports. Firstly, these reports do not provide, as required in the reporting guidelines devised by the Human Rights Committee, information about the percent of each minority group in comparison to the population of majority community. Secondly, no data has been included about the representation of minorities in central and local government offices. Thirdly, information concerning the representation of minorities in the Parliament and State Assemblies is absent. Also, the members of Human Rights Committee (HRC) did not seek additional information on these issues or posed questions on them to the government representative. This is because of the conspicuous absence of effective NGOs from minorities, which can provide information on these matters by publishing alternative reports, to members of HRC before India report is taken up for discussion. Moreover, such NGOs can exert influence on government to take measures for increasing their participation in political decision-making and government offices. They may even pressurise government to introduce "affirmative action" in this regard.

Many studies have been conducted on the plight of minorities[35] especially dealing with the questions of their security, educational backwardness, religious and cultural rights, representation in political bodies, opportunities for employment and economic development.

Let us elaborate some aspects of these issues. Among the various minorities the plight of Muslims is very deplorable as far as their representation in Parliament/State Assemblies and Government jobs is concerned. Their members in Lok Sabha were around 5 per cent (average). For instance, in 1952 they constituted 4.4 per cent; in 1962, 4.7 per cent; in 1967, 5.5 per cent; in 1977, 6.2 per cent; 1980, 9.2 per cent (it was the highest number so far); in 1984, 8.7 per cent; in 1989, 5.4 per cent and in 1996, 4.9 per cent. In some State Assemblies there was not a single member from their community. For instance, under this category were following states: Madhya Pradesh (1993), Orissa (1961), Pondicherry (1977), Goa, Daman & Diu (1972 and 1974) and Nagaland (1974 and 1987).[36]

The problem of Muslim representation in civil services is far more deplorable than their representation in legislative bodies. There is more to it. Their share in government jobs is far less compared to other minorities like Christians and Sikhs. The Gopal Singh Panel report provides many tables on minorities' representation in Indian Administrative Service (IAS), Indian Police Service (IPS), and other central and state government services, etc. These tables disclose startling facts. Between 1971 and 1980 the representation of Muslims in IAS was 2.86 per cent which was extremely low compared to their population proportion of 11.20 per cent. The share of Christians was 2.64 per cent (their population proportion was 2.60 per cent) and of Sikhs was 4.71 per cent (their population proportion was 1.89 per cent). In IPS the representation of Muslims, Christians and Sikhs was 2 per cent, 2.27 per cent and 5.34 per cent respectively.[37] Many Muslim scholars and politicians are demanding preferential/ affirmative action for Muslims to improve their participation in central and state civil services.

Discrimination Based on Religion

Discrimination based on religion is perpetrated or religious hatred is practised not only by various religious communities against each other but also by the State itself through its executive agencies like the police or sometimes in subtle way through legislative Acts. The report of the Special Rapporteur of the UN on the Elimination of Religious Discrimination[38] provides a broad overview of the pattern of incidents revealing communal tensions/riots following the demolition of Babri Mosque on 6 December 1992.

The Rapporteur had sought comments by the Indian Government on some of these incidents: that more than 1200 people died or were killed by the police in Hindu-Muslim riots after the mosque demolition, that in Bombay at least 200 people died in inter-community clashes, where police sided with the Hindus and fired upon the Muslims; more than 2,50,000 Kashmiri Hindus have left their homes and sought refugee status in their own country; that between 40,000 and 50,000 Sikhs—men, women and children—have fallen victim to the Indian forces in Punjab (many have just disappeared); that in November 1992, 2000 Christians demonstrated in Ahmadnagar to protest against the Shiva Sena's attempt to convert hundreds of Christians to Hinduism, etc. With a few exceptions, many of these incidents were confirmed by the Government.

Almost all religious communities have experienced discrimination, in various manifestations, from certain sections of Hindu majority. The report of the Special Rapporteur only provides a sample of these cases. Though communal riots have occurred sporadically since independence, what is of grave concern is the alarming increase in their number and intensity in the 1980s and 1990s.

Legal Provisions Concerning Religion/ Belief - Subtle Bias Towards Minorities

There are many striking inconsistencies in the Constitutional law and the ICCPR. While Article 4(2) of the ICCPR makes as many as seven rights and freedoms, (including freedom of thought, conscience and religion) valueless during a state of emergency, Article 359(1) of the Constitution confers that status only on two rights— protection in respect of conviction for offences (Article 20) and protection of life and personal liberty (Article 21). The Indian Government has neither submitted any reservation to Article 4(2) nor it has incorporated its contents into the Constitution. Moreover, due to Indian reservation to Article 9(5) of the ICCPR, there is no right to compensation for unlawful arrest and detention. Detention is permissible under many statutes, such as Preventive Detention Act, (1950) (lapsed in 1969), National Security Act (1980); Terrorist and Disruptive Activities Act, (1987) (lapsed on 24 May 1995). Thousands of people have been detained under these Acts, but the minority communities have felt their severity more than others. Thus, these inconsistencies between domestic law and the international norms create impediments in the implementation of rights of persons belonging to minorities.

One of the important causes of tension between Hindus and other religious communities comes from the projected definition of Hinduism, as noted earlier (in section III), in Article 25 of the Constitution and the Hindu Code Bill. These and other documents provide an expansionist definition, and treat Buddhists, Sikhs and Jains as "Hindus" for legal purposes (in effect treating their religions as offshoots of Hinduism). Though Jains have not objected to this definition, Buddhists, especially neo-Buddhists (converted from low caste Hindus) have expressed disagreement and Sikhs have strongly protested against it. The Akali Dal members had publicly burnt the copies of the Constitution in New Delhi in the 1980s.

The Ayodhya episode in 1990s had created apprehensions amongst Buddhists. They launched an agitation to secure the Buddhist majority in the trust controlling the holy Buddhist shrine, the Bodh Gaya temple (a place where the Buddha experienced enlightenment). At present, the temple is managed, under the Bodh Gaya Temple Management Act, 1949, by an eight-member committee appointed by the Bihar Governor. Half of these members are Hindus, the district magistrate of Gaya being its ex-officio chairman. Buddhists are demanding that all members on the management committee should belong to their community. Out of the four Buddhist members of the committee, two resigned in protest in 1993.

Another member, Lawang, is a BJP supporter. The agitating leaders lament that for the last 16 years, Vishwa Hindu Parishad (VHP) Chief adviser, Gayan Jagat Bhikku, remained the chief superintendent of the temple committee. He resigned in 1993 under pressure from Buddhists. This agitation gained international prominence when Buddhist monks from many parts of the world assembled in 1993 to demand change in law. Though the non-Congress Bihar Government of Rashtriya Janta Dal supported their demand, it failed to amend the Act till its term ended in March 1995 and did not commit to amend the law even after getting re-elected to a second term in1995.

The recent report of the National Minorities Commission points out that despite the take over of the management by the Union Government of the world famous Buddhist Centre, Nalanda Mahavihara at Patna, the centre and its buildings are in a state of neglect. There has been a mismanagement of large funds by the Central Institute of Buddhist Studies at Leh made available by the Japanese Government for the development of the places of Buddhist interest. The commission finds that the educational institutions set up by the minorities do not get recognition easily and permission for opening technical institution is generally denied. The Tamil Nadu Government has amended certain acts governing schools and colleges, which affect the policies of the minority-run institutions. These changes go against the spirit of Article 30 of the Constitution.[39]

As regards reforming religious practices and dogmas, one scholar opines that, Indian government follows a policy of double standard. It has consciously intervened, although not effectively, as a reformer in the case of Hinduism, by adopting Hindu Code Bills and outlawing Sati, devadasi system, human sacrifice and the practice of untouchability, etc. In contrast, no effort is made to reform the personal laws of Muslims and Christians, though several oppressive/unjust practices against women prevail in them.[40] In the name of secularism or rights of minorities the State shows its "political expediency" by adopting a non-intervention policy in reforming them. However, it needs to be mentioned that the reason why this has happened is because opinion within the communities is divided and the majority opinion does not come out strongly in favour of such reform. In fact, these communities prefer reforms from within rather than with State initiative, which will be perceived as imposition from outside.

Law Affecting Conversions

From time to time unsuccessful attempts were made to introduce in the Parliament restricting conversions of untouchable and tribal Hindus to other religions especially Christianity and Islam. In 1954 the Indian Converts (Regulation and Registration) Bill was introduced and was rejected, as it proposed to give power to the Deputy Commissioner to issue a license for converting people. In 1960, the Lok Sabha rejected the Backward Communities (Religious Protection) Bill. Again in 1978, the Freedom of Religion Bill was introduced in the Lok Sabha and was withdrawn subsequently. However, in some States such bills have been passed. For example, Orissa State Assembly passed the Freedom of Religion Act in 1969. Similarly, in 1978, Arunachal Pradesh passed the Freedom of Religion Act. The Arunachal Act was perceived by Christians and Muslims as directed specifically against them, as it ruled against converting but not against "reconversion" (to Hinduism). An ominous feature of the time was the absence of public opposition to such erosion of tolerance. Moreover, these Bills are not intended to prevent conversion per se but are geared to prevent the use of force, inducement or fraud means in conversion. It is paradoxical to note that intentionally or unintentionally, the government policy of protective discrimination law (reservation of jobs and seats in educational institutions and legislatures) for ex-untouchables and tribals has tended to perpetuate the solidarity of Hindu community and to prevent their conversion to other religions.

Thus such Acts, Bills and policies are aimed at putting restrictions on the Constitutionally guaranteed right to propagate religion. Most of these acts treated conversions merely as law and order problem by the State. The selective approach of these restrictions was only for Islam and Christianity as these religions are projected by Hindus as products of conquest and colonization. The acceptance of Islam by 200 ex-untouchables in 1981 in Meenakshipuram village (Tamil Nadu) sent shock waves among Hindu religious organizations, which raised slogans of "Hinduism in danger". In contrast, one does not come across such a response/concern when a large number of people embrace one of the religions of Indian origin—Buddhism, Jainism and Sikhism. For instance, between February and August 1981, soon after stopping the Meenakshipuram conversions, the VHP 'reconverted' 50,000 Christians and 4,000 Muslims into Hinduism and in October under the leadership of R.S.

Gavai, some 1,50,000 to 3,00,000 untouchables embraced Buddhism to celebrate the 25th anniversary of B.R. Ambedkar's conversion from Hinduism. These two events of mass conversion did not move the conscience of the Indian State to intervene, partly because no organized pressure was put on it and presumably because the public order was intact. Thus, the freedom of religion operates only in one direction. While widespread public remorse was expressed on Meenakshipuram episode in the Indian Press, the VHP reconversions to Hinduism and the conversions to Buddhism evoked no strong reactions. Therefore, it is clear that State intervention is selective. Such a response erodes the meaning of secularism. A major shock came to these religious minorities of non-Indian origin when the Supreme Court decided in 1977 that there can be no such thing as a fundamental right to convert any person to one's own religion (*Rev. Stainislaus* vs. *State of Madhya Pradesh*).[41]

There is more to it. Three acts concerning Hindu Code Bill (governing personal law), as our analysis reveals, have also touched the question of conversion indirectly.

1. The Hindu Marriage Act of 1955 lists as one of the nine grounds for divorce the other party's ceasing to be a Hindu by conversion to another religion. S. Natarajan commented that this provision is understandable from the viewpoint of Hindu marriage as a religious sacrament, but added: "It is strange that a secular State should not insist on further proof to establish that the conversion interferes with the religious life and practice of other party."[42]
2. Under the Hindu Adoptions and Maintenance Act of 1956, a Hindu wife is entitled to live separately from her husband with maintenance if he is converted to other religion. Further, the Act includes a discriminatory clause which reads: "A Hindu wife shall not be entitled to separate residence from her husband if she is unchaste or ceases to be Hindu by conversion to another religion" In other words, unchastity and conversion must be penalized! Thus, even if her husband treated her with cruelty, were a leper, or kept a concubine in the same house in which the wife was living (all grounds for separate maintenance under the Act), she would still not be entitled to separate maintenance if she ceased to be a Hindu. The principle is broadened further; the Act gives an elaborate definition of the relatives deemed to

be dependents but then states that no person shall be entitled to claim maintenance under these provisions upon conversion to another religion.

3. The Hindu Succession Act of 1956 also follows the same spirit. It made sure that none of the converts' children or their descendants would be entitled to inherit the property of any of their Hindu relatives, unless such children or descendants are Hindus at the time when the succession opens. An American scholar commented that intentionally or unintentionally, this act could in some cases constitute a powerful financial inducement for the children or descendants to be converted to Hinduism. He further adds that the net effect of these provisions in the Hindu Code Bill is to discourage conversion from Hinduism and to reinforce the religious status quo. However, progressive, even radical, these laws are in terms of Hindu social system (the introduction of divorce, etc.), they actively discourage change in religious affiliation. There are definite penalties to be borne if the exercise of freedom of conscience leads Hindu outside the fold.[43] Thus, the Shuddhi (purification) movement, which started in the 1930s, and is quite active even now, can be seen in this perspective. Through Shuddhi people from Islam or Christianity are reconverted to Hinduism.

These legal, social and cultural barriers to the freedom to change or choose one's belief by professing another belief goes against the provision of Article 18 of the ICCPR as interpreted by the Human Rights Committee in its general comment on the Article.[44]

Communal Killings/Riots—Role of the Police and Politicians

India gave the philosophy of non-violence to the world, but the people of religious minorities have been made targets of violence. India has witnessed the unprecedented scale of inter-community violence, especially between Hindus and Muslims (Christians, Buddhists and Sikhs have also suffered). Since independence thousands of Hindu-Muslim riots have taken place. The most heinous among them were Biharsharif riots (1981), Meerut and Baroda (1982), Nelli in Assam (in 1983, where over 1800 Muslims were butchered according to *India Today*, October 6, 1997), the Bhagalpur riots in 1989 (1000 dead), Aligarh in December 1990 (120 died), Meerut in 1987 (150 died) and post-Babri demolition riots all over India leaving 1,200 dead, and 4,000 seriously injured. Following table sketches communal scenario that prevails in India.

Number of Communal Incidents and Persons Killed between 1954 and 1991

Year	*Number of Incidents*	*Persons Killed*
1954-63	630	344
1964	1070	1919
1965-75	3157	1798
1976	169	39
1977	188	36
1978	230	110
1979	304	261
1980	421	372
1981	319	196
1982	470	238
1983	500	1143
1984	476	445
1985	525	328
1986	NA	492
1987	689	341
1988	238	NA
1989	19	1178
1990	28	693
1991	16	158

Source: Rakhahari Chatterji (ed.) *Religion, Politics and Communalism - The South Asian Experience* (New Delhi: South Asian Publishers, 1994), pp. 32-33. Table in this book gives a year-wise break up, but for reasons of space data for the years 1954-63 and 1965-75 have been put together.

However, one report says that in the 1980s, more than 7000 people were killed in some 4,500 communal incidents, almost a four-fold increase in the toll for the 1970s.[45]

In many instances, the police and the other executive authorities deliberately discriminate the minority religious groups, as the following select incidents corroborate.

(i) In the anti-Sikh riots in November 1984 that followed the assassination of the then Prime Minister Indira Gandhi by two of her Sikh bodyguards, the death toll of the Sikhs killed in Delhi was 2,733 or one every 30 seconds. This was one of the most well-organized communal riots in connivance with the ruling party (Indian National Congress) in power. Despite the submission of reports by three commissions of enquiry - Justice

Ranganath Misra Commission report (1987), Jain-Agarwal Committee report (1990) and Justice R.S. Narula panel report (1994), all of which had indicted 72 police officers, two Union Ministers and a Congress MP, no prosecution has been initiated against any one of them so far. The Union Home Ministry is not granting permission to the Central Bureau of Investigation (CBI) to file charge sheet against politicians named in these reports. The former BJP Government of Delhi State had stated that it had no legal power to bring action against the accused because the subjects of law and order and Police of Delhi are still with the Union Government.[46] It is well known that the Delhi carnage was instigated by local Congress party MPs, and even with the passive complicity of the security forces.[47] (Mr. P.V. Narasimha Rao, who was Prime Minister, during 1991-96 was the then Home Minister).The present Congress Government headed by Sheila Dikshit of Delhi State has shown no interest in the matter.

(ii) After Hindu-Muslim Communal rioting in Meerut in May 1987, in which 91 people were killed, over 600 were arrested on 22 May in the Hashimpura area of Meerut by the Provincial Armed Constabulary (PAC)—a predominantly Hindu force. According to press reports, 32 of them "disappeared: and were presumed killed. Aged between 13 and 65, they were reportedly taken by truck to the banks of the Upper Ganga Canal near Muradnagar by the PAC. Here they are believed to have been shot in secret and their bodies thrown into canal. Two survivors have testified that they were taken to the Canal by PAC men. However, the PAC denied the killings. Official enquiries, not made public so far, confirmed the gruesome killings and blamed the PAC for it. Nonetheless, the government has said that ex-gratia payments were made to relatives of 13 people whose bodies were found and identified, and to 17 of the other 19 people killed whose bodies had been found. In making these payments, the government did not accept official responsibility for the killings.[48] On 23 May, some PAC men were alleged to have gone on a rampage in Maliana, a village near Meerut, shooting unarmed men, women and children of Muslim community indiscriminately. Some 80 bodies were later found, Sixteen other Muslims died in police custody.[49]

(iii) On 13 August 1980, on the day of Id (Ramdhan), ten PAC men fired upon a congregation of 50,000 people in Moradabad city who had come to Idgah (the name means where Id prayers are held) for offering namaz (prayers) killing 50 persons. The exact death toll was unknown because the PAC removed some of the bodies. According to eyewitnesses, Dr. Nassem Ahmed recounted and picked up 24 bodies from the mosque's compound including 13 children[50].

Hundreds of such incidents have been taking place in other parts of the country (e.g., in Bombay riots of January 1993) which reveal direct involvement of law enforcing agencies in the killings of the people of religious minorities. The occurrence of such incidents prompted an Allahabad High Court Judge to remark that *the police represent the most organised group of criminals in India.*[51]

The fact of communal bias on the part of the police is worse than the role of Hindu communal outfits in inciting violence against minorities. This is a fact on which not only the officially appointed commissions of enquiry have adversely commented upon, even the sixth report of the National Police Commission, dated March 1981, was constrained to say: "[In] several instances police officers and policemen have shown an unmistakable bias against a particular community while dealing with communal riots."[52]

Policies and Practices of Religious and other Communities

Due to widespread illiteracy and ignorance about one's own religion, the masses at large are not religiously motivated or bigoted. Another factor contributing towards this is centuries of traditions of intermingling of the people of different religions and their harmonious co-existence in everyday life. However, some politico-religious organizations have vitiated against this harmonious living by using /misusing religious sentiments of the masses for their political gains. The programmes and policies of these groups, like the RSS (Rashtriya Swayamsevak Sangh), VHP (Vishva Hindu Parishad), Bajrang Dal, Jamat-e-Islami, and ISS (Islamic Sevak Sangh) disrupt the social fabric and infuse communal hatred in an otherwise cohesive Indian society. (Though a ban was imposed on these groups soon after the demolition of Babri Mosque, most of them publicly hold their meetings defiantly and are quite active politically). They popularize their own version of religious dogmas and stress on religious cleavages to achieve their political ends. Such policies have given rise to inter-community and intra-community clashes during which common people and uncommitted persons belonging to all religions suffer. Following examples may be noted:

1. After the demolition of Babri Mosque, which (according to some protagonists of secularism) amounts to the demolition of the Constitutional values of secular State and civil society, some militant Hindu groups openly demanded a new Constitution. The leaders of VHP denounced the Indian Constitution and talked of restoring the *Manusmriti* or a Constitution based on it.
2. It is regretting to note that on 6 December 1992, a large number of IAS probationary officers belonging to a particular community at the National Academy of Administration, Mussoorie, celebrated the demolition of the Babri Mosque. The press did not publicize this event. A senior journalist, Praful Bidwai, had referred to this disgraceful event in his column in *The Time of India* on 8 September 1994.
3. In their annual meeting in January 1988, the Bishops of Tamil Nadu noted that the Untouchable Christians, even after conversion, continue to suffer from caste distinctions, segregation and violence. The Indian church now realizes that 60 per cent of Indian Christians are subjected to discriminatory practices and are treated as second class Christians or worse. They are segregated both in their settlements and in the church. In church services they are asked to sit separately and are forbidden to read scriptural pieces during the service or to assist the priest. They are the last to receive the holy sacraments during baptism, confirmation, and marriage. Their marriage and funeral processions are forbidden to pass through the streets of the main settlement. They have separate cemeteries. The church bells do not toll for their dead, nor does the priest visit the home of the dead to pray. The dead body cannot be taken into the church for the funeral service. There is no inter-marriage or inter-dining among the "high caste" and the "low caste" Christians. Clashes between them also occur.[53]
4. The Hindu Munnani Community in Pondicherry, launched an agitation in March 1994 to construct a Shiva temple at the site of the Immaculate Conception Cathedral. This church was constructed in 1748 by French authorities. The Munnani people believe that this church was built by destroying a temple. However, historical facts as recorded in a published diary maintained by a Hindu official who served the French Governor

of the time gives a different story. These people's claim was based on a private diary maintained by Anand Ranga Pillai, who was interpreter to the Governor. His diary has been published in 12 volumes. Its editor, H. Dodwell, however described Pillai as "a prejudiced witness". However, no official documents of that period are available to corroborate Pillai's version of events, as all of them have disappeared.[54]

The following examples of intolerance may also be noted: (1) In 1991 elections to Parliament and State Assemblies, the BJP election manifesto stated "if it comes to power it is committed to the construction of Ram temple by relocating Babri Mosque". (2) The Election slogans of BJP - Shiv Sena combine were anti-communal. Their favourite slogan was: 'Musalmanon ka do hi sthan — Pakistan ya Kabrastan' (Muslims have only two abodes — Pakistan or graveyard). (3) In 1980s, a "Dharam Sansad"(religious parliament) was established by Hindu rightist organizations, which was attended by saints, politicians and others. (4) In response, the Muslim fundamentalists established "Milli Parliament" (Parliament of the Community) in 1993.

Communication Media and Minorities

Radio and television are State-controlled (although many private news channels of T.V. have come up during the last one decade which present a balanced news coverage), whereas press is not. English press is generally (not always) objective/balanced towards all religious minorities. However, sometimes this objectivity is tainted during communal riots. The vernacular press is more biased towards religions minorities and publishes provocative accounts of communal violence. Their reportage of such events sometimes is based on conjectures having no veracity and reflect their prejudice. Following select examples confirm this.

1. *The Times of India* published an Article (during Moradabad riot) on 23 August 1980 by a former Inspector General of Police titled "Moradabad has more Arms than the U.K.". The title is provocative and its contents belie the title. On 16 October 1990, this paper described Advani's rath yatra as a "harmless expression of religious *bhakti* (devotion) and not of communal *Shakti* (force). The paper expressed that as long as a "sober and respectable" politician like Mr. Advani was in command, nothing untoward was likely to happen. This newspaper found it possible to said this, when 7000 lives had already been lost in

various parts of the country since 1987. Between 1990 and 1992, majority of the newspapers sought to legitimize the communal politics of the BJP. There was sudden shift in their attitude following the demolition of Babri Mosque. Almost all of them declared in their editorials that 6 December 1992 was the blackest day in India's post-independence history and characterized the event as a national shame because the whole world was watching India through the CNN and the BBC TV networks.

2. During the Bhiwandi-Bombay riots of 1984, a reporter of a major English daily in Bombay published an "investigative" report, which asserted that Muslims stabbed more than 18 Hindus in a day. The report was false, and even the police authorities declared it invalid. The vernacular press astonishingly published different reports from the English counterparts of the same group of newspapers. For example, *Loksatta* and the *Maharashtra Times of the Indian Express* and the *Times of India* group carried entirely different versions of the same events. It is important to note that vernacular papers are read by the lower-middle classes and poor masses who are generally victims of communalism.[55]
3. During January 1993 Bombay riots, Bombay Doordarshan (TV) telecast a Marathi programme on Shivaji's weapons.
4. In 1986, a junior judicial officer issued an order, violating all norms of law, on the question of Babri Mosque, which allowed the opening of locks of the dispute site, though the main case was pending before the High Court. There was connivance if not abatement by the state government as proved by alacrity of the district magistrate in opening the building and handing it over to the opposite party, instead of going in appeal against the lawless order. Indian TV (Doordarshan) gleefully announced this "great" event. This made the secular minded persons in the majority community aghast and angry. This is proved by an Article in *Patriot* (New Delhi), a daily of leftist leaning. Immediately after the order was issued the paper published an Article sharply criticizing the government of allowing this miscarriage of justice.
5. During December 1990 Aligarh riots, a local Hindi newspaper, i.e., *Amar Ujala*, published a report that in the Medical College of Aligarh Muslim University, 50 Hindu patients were killed by doctors. The report was absolutely baseless as the investigations

by Indian Council of Medical Research, New Delhi and the Press Council of India revealed.

Biased Textbooks and Denial of Education in Mother Tongue

The BJP Government has been continuously engaged in revising history books to project distorted view of minorities' role in the past. After making attempts at the State level, now it is revising school texts at the national level and already many NCERT(National Council of Educational Research and Training) books have been changed.[56] Let us elaborate this aspect further.

Former BJP government in north Indian State of Uttar Pradesh has made a concerted attempt to change the contents of the school textbooks of history to give a communal projection/interpretation of certain historical developments in medieval India. Among many changes that are incorporated in these books, two are most striking. First, the revised text inserts a three-page narration on Keshavarao Hedgewar, the founder of RSS, while making no mention of other leaders of freedom struggle. What is more objectionable is that the one-page narrative which the older text had on Mahatma Gandhi has been deleted in the new edition. Second addition pertains to the controversy of Ayodhya mosque/temple. The revised text says: "Babur's local official Mirwaqui (sic) got a mosque built in place of the temple demolished at Ayodhya. Although this building is controversial, nevertheless the Hindu public believes it to be a temple."[57]

A noted historian, R. Nath, discovered in 1993 that the original will of Emperor Babur, to his son, which was preserved in the Madhya Pradesh State Library, is missing. In this will he had laid down the policy for the governance of the country. He warned his son not to meddle in the religious affairs of the people and leave them free to practice their religion in accordance with their own faiths and beliefs. He warned against the demolition of temples. He advised that religious bigotry should be shed and the King should live with his subjects in the spirit of peaceful coexistence, tolerance and non-interference in their religious matters. However, a photographed copy of the will (taken on 11 December 1921) and duly certified by the curator of the library is available with H.K. Sherwani of Hyderabad. The mystery of the lost testament casts doubt about the communal role of the then BJP government in the State.[58]

Another form of prejudice experienced by Muslims is the denial of an opportunity by the State-run schools to provide education to their children in mother tongue, in most cases it is Urdu. In most of north India, Muslim children are compelled to study in Hindi medium, which of late is becoming, due to State patronage, highly Sanskritized. However, it is encouraging to note that in other linguistic States (especially in South India) the government does not discriminate the Muslims in this regard and has established Urdu-medium schools. The attitude of North Indian States violates Article 5 of the 1981 UN Declaration on the Elimination of Discrimination based on Religion/Belief.

Sometimes, the spirit of tolerance towards minorities is being enforced by the Supreme Court, when in one of its judgements it struck down the expulsion from schools of three students belonging to Jehovah's Witnesses faith who refused to sing the national anthem though they respectfully stood up in silence when it was sung.[59]

There is more to it. The Government bias towards minorities is also manifested in its treatment of languages, of minorities especially while allocating funds for their development. The Government of India allocates funds annually for the development of all Indian languages, including classical, modern and tribal. A careful perusal of the expenditure incurred on this scheme reveals bias towards Urdu (though it is not entirely a language of Muslims). For instance, the Lok Sabha was informed on 25 February 1992 that in the year 1990-91 the Government spent Rs. 966.91 lakh on Hindi, Rs. 829.73 lakh on Sanskrit and Rs. 79.48 lakh on Urdu. The allocation of Urdu was made to Tarraqi-e-Urdu Board which spent most of this amount on I.K. Gujral Committee. The fact that the Government is spending a meager sum on Urdu, although 5.7 per cent of total population speaks Urdu, whereas it spends huge amount on Sanskrit, which is spoken by less than 1 per cent people and is almost a dead language reveals its step motherly treatment towards the minority language, i.e., Urdu.

Conclusion

India's record of domestic application of human rights and minority rights standards, contained in the ICCPR, is far from satisfactory. The same is true of its implementation of Constitutional and other legal provisions on minority rights. As far as the Constitutional law and the record of judiciary in upholding minorities' rights is concerned, it represents the best secular values/traditions in the world. Only some statutory laws, as our analysis in this paper revealed, advertently or inadvertently deviate from the spirit of these secular traditions. Also, some of the policies and practices of the Federal and State governments and certain religious and other groups (including those of minorities) are not only a source of dissatisfaction but also violative of many national and international norms and standards promoting and protecting the rights of minorities and its people. Much can be achieved hopefully with their efforts and cooperation.

By way of conclusion it can be said that India needs to take many legislative, administrative measures and political decisions with a view to improving its compliance of international human rights/minority rights obligations. First, the Indian government should amend Article 359(1) of the Constitution, which grants non-derogatory status to only two rights--protection in respect of conviction for offences (Article 20) and protection of life and personal liberty (Article 21). This amendment is needed in view of our ratification of ICCPR, which under Article 4 (2) grants non-derogatory status on as many as seven rights and freedoms (contained in Articles 6, 7, 8 (1 and 2), 11, 15, 16 and 18). Second, the Constitution should be suitably amended to introduce affirmative action programme for those minorities, which are educationally backward and under represented in legislative bodies and civil services. Third, Article 350A of the Constitution, which obligates State to provide primary education to children in their mother tongue, should be shifted to Part III of the Constitution (dealing with Fundamental Rights). This part of the Constitution is enforceable by court of law. This step will go a long way to protect linguistic minorities. Fourth, India should ratify the first Optional Protocol to the ICCPR so that individuals, including those belonging to minorities, can send their petitions/communications to the Human Rights Committee. Fifth, the government should review India's reservations and declarations to the seven Articles of the covenant with a view to withdrawing them, so as to ensure progress in the implementation of the rights contained in those Articles. Sixth, India should submit its reports timely and before getting reminders from the Human Rights Committee. Presently, the government is behind schedule by more than four years. Moreover, the reports should contain more information on minorities. The reporting guidelines should be strictly adhered to by officials who are preparing the report. Seventh, these periodic reports should be publicized in the media . These reports and the comments of the HRC should be brought to the notice of top officers of legislative, executive and judicial organs of the government. Finally, the government should consult and interact with our NGOs on minorities while preparing these reports. NGOs can also bring out alternative reports on the state of human rights.

It is worth recalling here the words of Mahatma Gandhi, who once said, "a civilization can be judged by the way it treats its minorities."[60] If the Indian Government acts on the policy recommendations suggested above, it would be strengthening the foundations of our civilization which has accommodated diverse religious, cultural and linguistic minorities during the last five millennia.

References

1. For the text of these documents, See *Human Rights — A Compilation of International Instruments*, Vol. 1, Parts First and Second, Universal Instruments (New York : United Nations, 1993). [Sales No. E. 93, XIX, 1 (Vol. 1, Parts 1 and 2).]

2. David P. Forsythe, *Human Rights in International Relations*, (Cambridge: Cambridge University Press, 2000), p. 4. Also see Abdulrahim P. Vijapur, "Promotion of Human Rights and the Problem of Domestic Jurisdiction in the United Nations" (Ph.D.Thesis, Jawaharlal Nehru University, New Delhi, 1986).

3. Vijapur, *ibid.*, pp. 352-53. Also see Oscar Schachter, "The Obligation to Implement the Covenant in Domestic Law", in Louis Henkin (ed.), *The International Bill of Rights :The Covenant on Civil and Political Rights* (New York : Columbia University Press, 1981), pp. 311-31.

4. See Abdulrahim P. Vijapur, "The Principle of Non-discrimination in International Human Rights Law: The Meaning and Scope of the Concept," *India Quarterly* (New Delhi), Vol. 49, no. 4, 1993, pp. 69-84.

5. For a detailed and scholarly analysis of this provision see Louis B. Sohn, "The Rights of Minorities", in Louis Henkin (ed.), *The International Bill of Rights—The Covenant on Civil and Political Rights* (New York : Columbia University Press, 1981), pp. 270-289 and 470-78.

6. For a brief history of the drafting of Article 27 and for a general discourse on the concept of "minority rights" See Abdulrahim P. Vijapur, "Approaching Minority Rights", *Alpjan* (New Delhi), Vol. 1, No. 1, Oct-Dec. 2000, pp. 5-17 and 26.

7. See *Ibid.*, pp. 13-14.

8. *Study on the Rights of Persons Belonging to Ethnic, Religious and Linguistic Minorities* by Francesco Capotorti (Special Rapporteur of the UN Sub-Commission on the Prevention of Discrimination and Protection of Minorities), UN Doc. E/CN.4/Sub.2/384/Rev.1 (1979) reprinted as UN Publications, E.78, xiv. 1, 1979, paras 206-210.

9. For a detailed study see Partick Thornberry, The UN Declaration on *Rights of Persons Belonging to National or Ethnic, Religious and Linguistic*

Minorities: Background, Analysis and Observations (London: Minority Rights Group, 1993).

10. For the text of paragraphs 1 and 7 to 13 of the General Comment 18(37) on Article 26 see Manual on Human Rights Reporting (Geneva: Office of the UN High Commissioner for Human Rights, 1997) UN Publication Sales No. GV. E. 97.0.16), pp. 252-54.

11. UN Doc. E. CN. 4/Sub. 2/1993/34, para. 172.

12. Will Kymlicka, *Multicultural Citizenship: A Liberal Theory of Minority Rights* (Oxford: Oxford University Press, 1995), p. 4.

13. Warwick McKean, *Equality and Discrimination in International Law* (Oxford : Clarendon Press, 1983), p. 159.

14. On the role and effectiveness of the Human Rights Committee See, Abdulrahim P. Vijapur, *The United Nations at Fifty--studies in Human Rights* (New Delhi: South Asian Publishers, 1996), pp. 82-93; Dominic McGoldrick, *The Human Rights Committee: Its Role in the Development of the International Covenant on Civil and Political Rights* (Oxford: Clarendon Press,1991), and Torkel Opsanl, "The Human Rights Committee", in Philip Alston (ed.), *The United Nations and Human Rights—A Critical Appraisal* (Oxford: Clarendon Press, 1992), pp. 369-443.

15. *Manual on Human Rights Reporting*, N. 6, pp. 259-60.

16. Second periodic report of India under ICCPR (CCPR/C/37/Add. 13, 5 October 1989), p. 3.

17. Third periodic report of India under ICCPR (CCPR/C/76/Add. 6, 17 June 1996), p. 4.

18. See the initial report of India to Human Rights Committee, UN Doc. CCPR/C/10/Add. 8, 13 July, 1983, p. 25.

19. For a detailed study on this aspect see M.R. Kazimi, "Judiciary and the Protection of the Rights of the Minorities in India," in Abdulrahim P. Vijapur and Kumar Suresh (Eds.) *Perspectives on Human Rights* (New Delhi: Manak Publications Pvt. Ltd., 1999), pp. 59-68.

20. See Soli J. Sorabjee, "Protection and Promotion of Fundamental Rights by Public Interest Litigation in India", *International Commission of Jurists - The Review* (Geneva), No. 51, 1983, pp. 31-37; Justice P.N. Bhagwati, "Judicial Activism and Public Interest Litigation," *Columbia Journal of Transnational Law* (New York), vol. 23, 1985, pp. 561-77; and Paramanand Singh, "Human Rights Protection Through Public Interest Litigation in India," *Indian Journal of Public Administration* (New Delhi), Vol. 45, No. 4, 1999, pp. 731-49.

21. For instance, explanation II in Article 25 of the constitution, section 2 of the Hindu Marriage Act, explanation to section 3 of the 1955 Untouchability (Offenses) Act and the Bombay Hindu Places of Public Worship (Entry Authorization) Act, 1956, construe persons professing the Buddhism, Jainism or Sikhism as Hindus.

22. For a discussion on the question of definition of Hindus appearing in official legal texts, See Marc Galanter, *Law and Society in Modern India*,

edited by Rajiv Dhawan (Delhi: Oxford University Press, 1989), pp. 241-49; J. Duncan M. Derrett, *Religion, Law and the State in India* (London: Faber and Faber, 1968), p. 44 and his article "The Definition of a Hindu", *Supreme Court Journal*, Vol. 2, 1966, pp. 67-74. Also see T.K. Oommen, "State and Religion in Multi-Religious Nation-states: The Case of South Asia", *South Asia Journal* (New Delhi), Vol. 4, no. 1, 1990, pp. 25-26.

23. D.D. Basu, *Human Rights in Constitutional Law* (New Delhi: Prentice-Hall of India, 1994), p. 20.

24. Erica-Irene A. Daes, *Status of the Individual and Contemporary International Law* (New York: UN Publications, 1992), p. 4.

25. *Ibid.*, p. 8.

26. CCPR/C/10/Add.8, 13 July 1983.

27. CCPR/C/37/Add. 13, 5 October 1989.

28. CCPR/C/76/Add. 6, 17 June 1996.

29. For a summary of discussion on India's initial report see *Report of the Human Rights Committee GAOR*, 39th Session Suppl. No. 40 (A/39/40), paras. 264, 267 and 283.

30. *Report of the HRC, GAOR*, Suppl. No. 40, A/46/40, para 308, and p. 76.

31. Cited in James Chiriyankandath, "Human Rights in India: Concepts and untexts", Contemporary South Asia (London), Vol. 2, No. 3, 1993, p. 253.

32. Amnesty International, *Amnesty International Report 1991* (London: Amnesty International, 1991), p. 114.

33. For a pioneering and first hand account of the origin, development, working, powers, functions, short-comings and handicaps of NCM since its inception in 1978 till 2001 see Tahir Mahmood, *Minorities Commission: Minor Role in Major Affairs* (New Delhi: Pharos Media and Publishing Ltd., 2001).

34. See *Report of the HRC*, Vol. 1. GAOR, Suppl. No. 40 (A/52/40), (4-8, 1997), p. 68.

35. See particularly Gopal Singh, *Report on Minorities*, Vols. I and II, High Power Panel on Minorities, Scheduled Castes, Scheduled Tribes and other Backward Sections (New Delhi: Ministry of Home Affairs, Government of India, 1983); Imtiaz Ahmad, "Muslim Educational Backwardness - An Inferential Analysis", *Economic and Political Weekly* (Bombay), Vol. 16 September 5, 1981, pp. 1457-65; R.N. Thakur, *Plight of Minorities—Problems and Grievances in Their Education* (New Delhi: Gyan Publishing House, 1999); Myron Weiner, "India's Minorities: Who are They? What do they Want?", in Partha Chatterjee (ed.), *State and Politics in India* (New Delhi : Oxford University Press, 1997), pp. 459-95; Abdulrahim P. Vijapur, "Minorities and Human Rights : A Comparative Perspective of International and Domestic law", in D.L. Sheth and Gurpreet Mahajan (eds.), *Minority Identities and the Nation State* (New Delhi : Oxford University Press, 1999), pp. 242-67 and Idem, "India:, in *Freedom of Religion or Belief : A*

World Report, edited by Kevin Boyle and Juliet Sheen (London/New York: Routledge, 1997), pp. [36]. Idem, "Plight of Education Among Indian Muslims--Problems and Prospects", in M.A. Jawaid & others (ed.), *Minorities of India in the 21st Century: Problems and Prospects* (New Delhi: Indian Council of Social Science Research/Manak Publications, 2002).

36. These data are taken from Iqbal A. Ansari's Article, "Federal Nation Building: Non-Regional Dimensions of Pluralism and Representation of Muslims in Elected Bodies", in Abdulrahim P. Vijapur (ed.), *Dimensions of Federal Nation Building* (New Delhi: Manak Publications, 1998), pp. 222-23.

37. Gopal Singh, *ibid.*, p. 31.

38. E/CN.4/1994/79, dated 20 January 1994.

39. *The Times of India* (New Delhi), 14 February 1994.

40. T.K. Oommen, "State and Religion in Multi-religions Nation-States: The Case of South Asia", *South Asia Journal* (New Delhi), Vol. 4, No. 1, 1990, p. 29.

41. *Rev. Stainislaus v. State of Madhya Pradesh*, AIR, 1977, Supreme Court, p. 908, paras, 19-20.

42. S. Natarajan, *A Century of Social Reform in India* (Bombay: Asia, 1959), p. 194.

43. Donald E. Smith, *India as a Secular State* (Princeton, NJ: Princeton University Press, 1963), p. 187.

44. CCPR/C/48/CRP.2/Rev.1, 20 July 1993.

45. *India Today* (New Delhi), 15 January 1990, p. 34.

46. For details see "Panel report on 1984 riots ready", *The Times of India*, 11 January 1994.

47. Peoples, Union of Democratic Rights and People's Union for Civil Rights (PUDR and PUCL), *Who are the Guilty*? Report of a Joint Enquiry into the Causes and Impact of the Riots in Delhi from 31 October to 10 November (New Delhi, 1984).

48. *Human Rights in India - The Updated Amnesty International Report* (New Delhi: Vistaar Publications, 1993), p. 44.

49. *Ibid.*, p. 45.

50. For a detailed report see M.J. Akbar, "Id: Day of Death", *Sunday* (Calcutta), 24 August 1980, pp. 6-11. Also see his *Riot after Riot* (New Delhi: Penguin, 1988).

51. Cited in *Amnesty International Report, n.* 26, and p. 76.

52. Cited in Javed Anand, "Minority Rights in India: Constitution and the Reality", In Sumanta Banerjee (ed.), *Shrinking Space: Minority Rights in South Asia* (Kathmandu, Nepal: South Asia Forum for Human Rights, 1999), p. 157.

53. S.C. Dube, *Indian Society* (New Delhi: National Book Trust of India, 1992), p. 60.

54. See G.V. Krishnan, "Hindu Munnani stir runs out of steam", *The Times of India*, 19 March 1994.

55. Asghar Ali Engineer, "Communalism, Communal Violence and

Human Rights" in Upendra Baxi (ed.), *The Right to be Human* (New Delhi: Lancers Books, 1986), p. 165.

56. For a detailed discussion on the changes made in history textbooks during the last three years (1999-2001) see *Communalisation of Education - The History Textbooks Controversy* (New Delhi: Delhi Historians' Group, C/122 Uttarakhand, Jawaharlal Nehru University, December 2001). This book is a compilation of articles on the subject by eminent historians such as Romila Thapar, Bipan Chandra, Irfan Habib, R.S. Sharma, Satish Chandra, Arjun Dev and Sumit Sarkar, Mridula Mukherjee and Aditya Mukherjee provide an overview of the textbooks controversy. One section of the book includes articles by Vir Sanghiv, Dileep Padgaonkar, Rajeev Dhavan, Anil Bordia, Subir Roy, Anjali Modi, Saba Naqui Bhaumik and the two editorials of *The Indian Express*. In the last section text of the deletions made from the NCERT books of Class VI (by Romila Thapar), Class VII (by Satish Chandra), two books of Class XI)by Arjun Dev and Indira Arjun Dev) and (R.S. Sharma).

57. See for a detailed analysis of the changes in history textbooks, Krishna Kumar, "Continued text," *Seminar* (New Delhi). No. 400, December 1992, pp. 16-20. Professor Krishna Kumar, an eminent educationalist of Delhi University, who got an access to these history books with the help of an official of the State Government was informed that an adjective meaning "innumerable" will be inserted before "Hindu public" and the clause "a temple" will ultimately read as "Ram temple". It is interesting that there is no intention, at least so far, the author was informed, of describing the temple as the birthplace of Lord Rama. Before these additional changes could be incorporated the State government was dismissed on 6 December 1992 following the demolition of Babri Mosque. At another place, Prof. Kumar describes how a newly prepared set of history textbooks (in 1992) by Bhartiya Vidya Bhavan for use in schools of BJP ruled States intends to inform the school children and create bias among them towards Muslims. In their textbooks: the revivalists depict the Mughals as foreigners and oppressors, and interpret Indian achievement of freedom from English rule as but the latest episode in a long ongoing struggle to free India from foreign influences. Muslims are, by this interpretation, the contemporary incarnation of the Mughal pattern of dominance. Krishna Kumar, "Hindu revivalism in north-central India", in M.E. Marty and R.S. Appleby (eds.), *Fundamentalism and Society* (Chicago, Ill.: University of Chicago Press, 1993), p. 555. Cited in Jagdish Gundara "Aspects of Religion in Secular Education", in *Education Rights and Minorities* (London: Minority Rights Group, 1994), p. 26.

58. R. Nath, "The Lost Statement", *The Times of India, Sunday Review* (New Delhi), 5 December 1993. This article reproduces the text of Babur's will.

59. Cited in Soli J. Sorabji, "Spirit of Tolerance—Indian Courts' proud record of safeguarding right of dissent", *The Indian Express* (New Delhi), 28 January 1994.

60. Cited in John Humphrey, *No Distant Millennium — The International Law of Human Rights* (Paris : UNESCO, 1989), p. 46.

APPENDICES

Appendix I

I
Excerpts from the Constitution of India

Preamble

We, the people of India, having solemnly resolved to constitute India into a Sovereign, Socialist, Secular, Democratic, Republic and to secure to all its citizens:

Justice—social, economic and political;

Liberty—of thought, expression, belief, faith and worship;

Equality—of status and of opportunity; and to promote among them all;

Fraternity—assuring the dignity of the individual and the unity and integrity of the Nation;

In our constituent Assembly this twenty-sixth day of November, 1949, do Hereby adopt, enact and give to ourselves this Constitution.

Part III
Fundamental Rights

General

12. Definition—In this Part, unless the context otherwise requires, "the State" includes the Government and Parliament of India and the Government and the Legislature of each of the States and all local or other authorities within the territory of India or under the control of the Government of India.

13. **Laws Inconsistent with or in Derogation of the Fundamental Rights**

1. All laws in force in the territory of India immediately before the commencement of this Constitution, in so far they are inconsistent with the provisions of this Part, shall, to the extent of such inconsistency, be void.
2. The State shall not make any law which takes away or abridges the rights conferred by this Part and any law made in contravention of this clause shall, to the extent of the

contravention, be void.

3. In this Article, unless the context otherwise requires-
   (a) "law" includes any Ordinance, order, bye-law, rule, regulation, notification, custom or usage having in the territory of India, the force of law;
   (b) "laws in force" includes laws passed or made by a Legislature or other competent authority in the territory of India before the commencement of this Constitution and not previously repeated notwithstanding that any such law or any part thereof may not be then in operation either at all or in particular areas.
4. Nothing in this Article shall apply to any amendment of this Constitution made under Article 368.

Right to Equality

14. Equality before Law

The State shall not deny to any person equality before the law or the equal protection of the laws within the territory of India.

15. Prohibition of Discrimination on Grounds of Religion, Race, Caste, Sex or Place of Birth

(i) The State shall not discriminate against any citizen on grounds only of religion, race, caste, sex, place of birth or any of them.

(ii) No citizen shall, on grounds only of religion, race, caste, sex, place of birth or any of them, be subject to any disability, liability, restriction or condition with regard to—
   (a) access to shops, public restaurants, hotels and places of public entertainment; or
   (b) the use of wells, tanks, bathing ghats, roads and places of public resort maintained wholly or partly out of State funds or dedicated to the use of general public.

(iii) Nothing in this Article shall prevent the State from making any special provision for women and children.

(iv) Nothing in this Article or in clause (2) of Article 29 shall prevent the State from making any special provision for the advancement of any socially and educationally backward classes of citizens or for the Scheduled Castes and the Scheduled Tribes.

16. Equality of Opportunity in Matters of Public Employment

(i) There shall be equality of opportunity for all citizens in matters relating to employment or appointment to any office under the State.

(ii) No citizen shall, on grounds only of religion, race, caste, sex, descent, place of birth, residence or any of them, be ineligible for, or discriminated against in respct of, any employment or office under the State.

(iii) Nothing in this Article shall prevent Parliament from making any law prescribing, in regard to a class or classes of employment or appointment to an office under the Government of, or any local or other authority within, a State or Union Territory, any requirement as to residence within that State or Union Territory prior to such employment or appointment.

(iv) Nothing in this Article shall prevent the State from making any provision for the reservation of appointments or posts in favour of any backward class of citizens which, in the opinion of the State, is not adequately represented in the services under the State.

(a) Nothing in this Article shall prevent the state from making any provision for reservation in matters of promotion to any class or classes of posts in the services under the state in favour of the Scheduled Castes and Scheduled Tribes which in the opinion of the States, are not adequately represented in the services under the State.

(v) Nothing in this Article shall affect the operation of any law which provides that the incumbent of an office in connection with the affairs of any religious or denominational institution or any member of the governing body there of shall be a person professing a particular religion or belonging to a particular denomination.

17. Abolition of Untouchability

"Untouchability" is abolished and its practice in any form is forbidden. The enforcement of any disability arising out of "Untouchability" shall be an offence punishable in accordance with law.

18. Abolition of Titles

(1) No title, not being a military or academic distinction, shall be conferred by the State.

(ii) No citizen of India shall accept any title from any foreign State.

(iii) No person who is not a citizen of India shall, while he holds any office of profit or trust under the State, accept without the consent of the President any title from any foreign State.

(iv) No person holding any office of profit or trust under the State shall, without the consent of the President, accept any present, emolument, or office of any kind from or under any foreign State.

Right to Freedom

19. Protection of Certain Rights Regarding Freedom of Speech, etc.

(i) All citizens shall have the right—

(a) to freedom of speech and expression;

(b) to assembly peaceably and without arms;

(c) to form associations or unions;

(d) to move freely throughout the territory of India;

(e) to reside and settle in any part of the territory of India; and

(f) to practise any profession, or to carry on any occupation, trade or business.

(ii) Nothing in sub-clause (a) of clause (1) shall affect the operation of any existing law, or prevent the State from making any law, in so far as such law imposes reasonable restrictions on the exercise of the right conferred by the said sub-clause in the interests of the sovereignty and integrity of India, the security of the State, friendly relations with foreign States, public order, decency or morality, or in relation to contempt of court, defamation or incitement to an offence.

(iii) Nothing in sub-clause (b) of the said clause shall affect the operation of any existing law in so far as it imposes, or prevent the State from making any law imposing, in the interest of the sovereignty and integrity of India or public order, reasonable restrictions on the exercise of the right conferred by the isaid sub- clause.

(iv) Nothing in sub-clause (c) of the said clause shall affect the operation of any existing law in so far as it imposes, or prevent the State from making any law imposing, in the interests of the sovereignty and integrity of India or public order or morality, reasonable restrictions on the exercise of the right conferred by the said sub-clause.

(v) Nothing in sub-clause (d) and (e) of the said clause shall affect the operation of any existing law in so far as it imposes, or prevent the State from making any law imposing, reasonable restrictions on the exercise of any of the rights conferred by the said sub-clauses either in the interests of the general public or for the protection of the interests of any Scheduled Tribe.

(vi) Nothing in sub-clause (f) of the said clause shall affect the operation of any existing law in so far as it imposes or prevent the State from making any law imposing, in the interests of the general public, reasonable restrictions on the exercise of the right conferred by the said sub-clause, and, in particular, nothing in the said sub-clause shall affect the operation of any existing law in so far as it relates to, or prevent the State from making any law relating to,—

(a) the professional or technical qualifications necessary for practising any profession or carrying on any occupation, trade or business, or

(b) the carrying on by the State, or by a corporation owned or controlled by the State, of any trade, business, industry or service, whether to the exclusion, complete or partial, of citizens or otherwise.

20. Protection in Respect of Conviction for Offences

(i) No person shall be convicted of any offence except for violation of a law in force at the time of the commission of the act charged as an offence, nor be subjected to a penalty greater than that which might have been inflicted under the law in force at the time of the commission of the offence.

(ii) No person shall be prosecuted and punished for the same offence more than once.

(iii) No person accused of any offence shall be compelled to be a witness against himself.

21. Protection of Life and Personal Liberty

(i) No person shall be deprived of his life or personal liberty except, according to procedure established by law.

22. Protection Against Arrest and Detention in Certain Cases

(i) No person who is arrested shall be detained in custody without being informed, as soon as may be, of the grounds for such arrest nor shall he be denied the right to consult, and to be defended by, a legal practitioner of his choice.

(ii) Every person who is arrested and detained in custody shall be produced before the nearest magistrate within a period of twenty-four hours of such arrest excluding the time necessary for the journey from the place of arrest to court of the magistrate and no such person shall be detained in custody beyond the said period without the authority of a magistrate.

(iii) Nothing in clauses (1) and (2) shall apply-

(a) to any person who for the time being is an enemy alien; or

(b) to any person who is arrested or detained under any law providing for preventive detention.

(iv) No law providing for preventive detention shall authorize the detention of a person for a longer period than three months unless—

(a) an Advisory Board consisting of persons who are, or have been, or are qualified to be appointed as, Judges of a High Court has reported before the expiration of the said period of three months that there is in its opinion sufficient cause for such detention:

Provided that nothing in this sub-clause shall authorize the detention of any person beyond the maximum period prescribed by any law made by Parliament under sub-clause (b) of clause (7); or

(b) such person is detained in accordance with the provisions of any law made by Parliament under sub-clauses (a) and (b) of clause (vii).

(v) When any person is detained in pursuance of an order made under any law providing for preventive detention, the authority making the order shall, as soon as may be, communicate to such person the grounds on which the order has been made and shall afford him the earliest opportunity of making a representation against the order.

(vi) Nothing in clause (v) shall require the authority making any such order as is referred to in that clause to disclose facts which such authority considers to be against the public interest to disclose.

(vii) Parliament may by law prescribe

(a) the circumstances under which, and the class or classes of cases in which, a person may be detained for a period longer than three months under any law providing for preventive detention without obtaining the opinion of an Advisory Board in accordance with the provisions of sub-clause (a) of clause (iv);

(b) the maximum period for which any person may in any class or classes of cases be detained under any law providing for preventive detention; and

(c) the procedure to be followed by an Advisory Board in an inquiry under sub-clause (a) of clause (iv).

Right Against Exploitation

23. Prohibition of Traffic in Human Beings and Forced Labour

(i) Traffic in human beings and begar and (other) similar forms of forced labour are prohibited and any contravention of this provision shall be an offence punishable in accordance with law.

(ii) Nothing in this Article shall prevent the State from imposing compulsory service for public purposes, and in imposing such service the State shall not make any discrimination on grounds only of religion, race, caste or class or any of them.

24. Prohibition of Employment of Children in Factories, etc.

No child below the age of fourteen years shall be employed to work in any factory or mine or engaged in any other hazardous employment.

Right to Freedom of Religion

25. Freedom of Conscience and free Profession, Practice and Propagation of Religion

(i) Subject to public order, morality and health and to the other provisions of this Part, all persons are equally entitled to freedom of conscience and the right freely to profess, practise and progagate religion.

(ii) Nothing in this Article shall affect the operation of any existing law or prevent the State from making any law

(a) regulating or restricting any economic, financial, political or other secular activity which may be associated with religious practice;

(b) providing for social welfare and reform or the throwing open of Hindu religious institutions of a public character to all classes and sections of Hindus.

Explanation 1—The wearing and carrying of *kirpans* shall be deemed to be included in the profession of the Sikh religion.

Explanation II—In sub-clause (ii), the reference to Hindus shall be construed as including, a reference to persons professing the Sikh, Jain or Buddhist religion, and the reference to Hindu religious institutions shall be construed accordingly.

26. Freedom to Manage Religious Affairs

(i) Subject to public order, morality and health, every religious denomination or any section thereof shall have the right

(i) to establish and maintain institutions for religious and charitable purpose;

(ii) to manage its own affairs in matters of religion;
(iii) to own and acquire movable and immovable property; and
(iv) to administer such property in accordance with law.

27. Freedom as to Payment of Taxes for Promotion of any Particular Religion

No person shall be compelled to pay any taxes, the proceeds of which are specifically appropriated in payment of expenses for the promotion or maintenance of any particular religion or religious denomination.

28. Freedom as to Attendance at Religious Instruction or Religious Worship in Certain Educational Institutions

(i) No religious instruction shall be provided in any educational institution wholly maintined out of State funds.
(ii) Nothing in clause (i) shall apply to an educational institution which is administered by the State but has been established under any endowment or trust which requires that religious instruction shall be imparted in such institution.
(iii) No person attending any educational institution recognized by the State or receiving aid out of State funds shall be required to take part in any religious instruction that may be imparted in such institution or to attend any religious worship that may be conducted in such institution or in any premises attached thereto unless such person or, if such person is a minor, his guardian has given his consent thereto.

Cultural and Educational Rights

29. Protection of Interests of Minorities

(i) Any section of the citizens residing in the territory of India or any part thereof having a distinct language, script or culture of its own shall have the right to conserve the same.
(ii) No citizen shall be denied admission into any educational institution maintained by the State or receiving aid out of State funds on grounds only of religion, race, caste, language or any of them.

30. Right of Minorities to Establish and Administer Educational Institutions

(i) All minorities, whether based on religion or language, shall have the right to establish and administer educational institutions of their choice.

(ii) A In making any law providing for the compulsory acquisition of any property of an educational institution established and administered by a minority, referred to in clause (i), the State shall ensure that the amount fixed by or determined under such law for the acquisition of such property is such as would not restrict or abrogate the right guaranteed under that clause.

(iii) The State shall not, in granting aid to educational institutions, discriminate against any educational institution on the ground that it is under the management of a minority, whether based on religion or language.

31 C. Saving of Laws giving Effect to Certain Directive Principles

Notwithstanding anything contained in Article 13, no law giving effect to the policy of the State towards securing all or any of the principles laid down in Part IV shall be deemed to be void on the ground that it is inconsistent with or takes away or abridges any of the rights conferred by Article 14 or Article 19; and no law containing a declaration that it is for giving effect to such policy shall be called in question in any court on the ground that it does not give effect to such policy...

Right to Constitutional Remedies

32. Remedies for Enforcement of Rights Conferred by this Part

(i) The right to move the Supreme Court by appropriate proceedings for the enforcement of the rights conferred by this Part is guaranteed.

(ii) The Supreme Court shall power to issue directions or orders or writs, including writs in the nature of *habeas corpus, mandamus,* prohibition, *quo warranto* and *certiorari,* whichever may be appropriate, for the enforcement of any of the rights conferred by this Part.

(iii) Without prejudice to the powers conferred on the Supreme Court by clauses (1) and (2), Parliament may by law empower any other court to exercise within the local limits of its jurisdiction all or any of the powers exercisable by the Supreme Court under clause (2).

(iv) The right guaranteed by this Article shall not be suspended except as otherwise provided for by this Constitution.

33. Power of Parliament to Modify the Rights Conferred by this Part in their Application to Forces, etc.

Parliament may, by law, determine to what extent any of the rights conferred by this part shall in their application to,

(a) the members of the Armed Forces; or
(b) the members of the Forces charged with the maintenance of public order; or
(c) persons employed in any bureau or other organization established by the State for purposes of intelligence or counter intelligence; or
(d) persons employed in, or in connection with, the telecommunication systems set up for the purposes of any Force, bureau or organization referrred to in clauses (a) to (c).

be restricted or abrogated so as to ensure the proper discharge of their duties and the maintenance of discipline among them.

34. Restriction on Rights Conferred by this Part while Martial Law is in force in any Area

Notwithstanding anything in the foregoing provisions of this Part, Parliament may by law indemnify any person in the service of the Union or of a State or any other person in respect of any act done by him in connection with the maintenance or restoration of order in any area within the territory of India where martial law was in force or validate any sentence passed, punishment inflicted, forfeiture ordered or other act done under martial law in such area.

III

Part IV
Directive Principles of State Policy

36. Definition

In this Part, unless the context otherwise requires, "the State" has the same meaning as in Part III.

37. Application of the Principles Contained in this Part

The provisions contained in this Part shall not be enforceable by any court, but the principles therein laid down are nevertheless fundamental in the governance of the country and it shall be the duty of the State to apply these principles in making laws.

38. State to Secure a Social Order for the Promotion of Welfare of the People

(i) The State shall strive to promote the welfare of the people by securing and protecting as effectively as it may a social order in which justice, social, economic and political, shall inform all the institutions of the national life.

(ii) The State shall, in particular, strive to minimize the inequalities in income, and endeavour to eliminate inequalities in status, facilities and opportunities, not only amongst individuals but also amongst groups of people residing in different areas or engaged in different vocations.

39. Certain Principles of Policy to be followed by the State

The State shall, in particular, direct its policy towards securing

(a) that the citizen, men and women equally, have the right to an adequate means of livelihood;

(b) that the ownership and control of the material resources of the community are so distributed as best to subserve the common good;

(c) that the operation of the economic system does not result in the concentration of wealth and means of production to the common detriment;

(d) that there is equal pay for equal work for both men and women;

(e) that the health and strength of workers, men and women, and the tender age of children are not abused and that citizens are not forced by economic necessity to enter avocations unsuited to their age or strength;

(f) that children are given opportunities and facilities to develop in a healthy manner and in conditions of freedom and dignity and that childhood and youth are protected against exploitation and against moral and material abandonment.

39. Equal Justice and Free Legal Aid

The State shall secure that the operation of the legal system promotes justice, on a basis of equal opportunity, and shall, in particular, provide free legal aid, by suitable legislation or schemes or in any other way, to ensure that opportunities for securing justice are not denied to any citizen by reason of economic or other disabilities.

40. Organisation of Village Panchayats

The State shall take steps to organize village panchayats and endow them with such powers and authority as may be necessary to enable them to function as units of self- government.

41. Right to work, to Education and to Public Assistance in Certain Cases

The State shall, within the limits of its economic capacity and development, make effective provision for securing the right to work, to education and to public assistance in cases of unemployment, old age, sickness and disablement, and in other cases of underserved want.

42. Provision for Just and Human Conditions of Work and Maternity Relief

The State shall make provision for securing just and humane conditions of work and for maternity relief.

43. Living Wage, etc., for Workers

The State shall endeavour to secure, by suitable legislation or economic organization or in any other way, to all workers agricultural, industrial or otherwise, work, a living wage, conditions of work ensuring a decent standard of life and full enjoyment of leisure and social and cultural opportunities and, in particular, the State shall endeavour to promote cottage industries on an individual or cooperative basis in rural areas.

43A. Participation of Workers in Management of Industries

The State shall take steps, by suitable legislation or in any other way, to secure the participation of workers in the management of undertakings, establishments or other organisations engaged in any industry.

44. Uniform Civil Code for the Citizens

The State shall endeavour to secure for the citizens a uniform civil code throughout the territory of India.

45. Provision for Free and Compulsory Education for Children

The State shall endeavour to provide, within a period, within a period of ten years from the commencement of this Constitution, for free and compulsory education for all children until they complete the age of fo·urteen years.

46. Promotion of Educational and Economic Interests of Scheduled Castes, Scheduled Tribes and other Weaker Sections

The State shall promote with special care the educational and economic interests of the weaker sections of the people, and in particular, of the Scheduled Castes and Scheduled Tribes, and shall protect them from social injustice and all forms of exploitation.

47. Duty of the State to Raise the Level of Nutrition and the Standard of Living and to Improve Public Health

The State shall regard the raising of the level of nutrition and the standard of living of its people and the improvement of public health as among its primary duties and, in particular, the State shall endeavour to bring about prohibition of the consumption except for medicinal purposes of intoxicating drinks and of drugs which are injurious to health.

48. Organization of Agriculture and Animal Husbandry

The State shall endeavour to organize agriculture and animal husbandry on modern and scientific lines and shall, in particular, take steps for preserving and improving the breeds, and prohibiting the slaughter of cows and calves and other milch and draught cattle.

48A. Protection and Improvement of Environment and Safeguarding of Forests and Wildlife

The State shall endeavour to protect and improve the environment and to safeguard the forests and wildlife of the country.

49. Protection of Monuments and Places and Objects of National Importance

It shall be the obligation of the State to protect every monument or place or object of artistic or historic interest, declared by or under law made by Parliament to be of national importance, from spoilation, disfigurement, destruction, removal, disposal or export as the case may be.

50. Separation of Judiciary from Executive

The State shall take steps to separate the judiciary from the executive in the public services of the State.

51. Promotion of International Peace and Security

The State shall endeavour to—

(a) promote international peace and security;

(b) maintain just and honourable relations between nations;

(c) foster respect for international law and treaty obligations in the dealings of organized people with one another; and

(d) encourage settlement of international disputes by arbitration.

IV
Part IV-A
Fundamental Duties

51 A. Fundamental Duties

It shall be the duty of every citizen of India

(a) to abide by the Constitution and respect its ideals and institutions, the National Flag and the National Anthem;

(b) to cherish and follow the noble ideals which inspired our national struggle for freedom;

(c) to uphold and protect the sovereignty, unity and integrity of India;

(d) to defend the country and render national service when called upon to do so;

(e) to promote harmony and the spirit of common brotherhood amongst all the people of India transcending religious, linguistic and regional or sectional diversities; to renounce practices derogatory to the dignity of women;

(f) to value and preserve the rich heritage of our composite culture;

(g) to protect and improve the natural environment including forests lakes, rivers and wildlife, and to have compassion for living creatures;

(h) to develop the scientific temper, humanism and the spirit of inquiry and reform;

(i) to safeguard public property and to abjure violence;

(j) to strive towards excellence in all spheres of individual and collective activity so that the nation constantly rises to higher levels of endeavour and achievement.

V
Some Other Provisions

Article 226. Power of High Courts to Issue Certain Writs

1. Notwithstanding anything in Article 32, every High Court shall have power, throughout the territories in relation to which it exercises jurisdiction, to issue to any person or authority, including in appropriate cases, any Government, within those territories directions, orders or writs, including writs in the nature of *habeas corpus, mandamus, prohibition, quo warranto* and

certiorari, or any of them, for the enforcement of any of the rights conferred by Part III and for any other purpose.

2. The power conferred by clause (I) issue directions, orders or writs to any Government, authority or person may also be exercised by any High Court exercising jurisdiction in relation to the territories within which the cause of action, wholly or in part, arises for the exercise of such power, notwithstanding that the seat of such Government or authority or the residence of such person is not within those territories.
3. Where any party against whom an interim order, whether by way of injunction or stay or in any other manner, is made on, or in any proceedings relating to, a petition under clause (i), without—
   (a) furnishing to such party copies of such petition and all documents in support of the pleas for such interim order; and
   (b) giving such party an opportunity of being heard, makes an application to the High Court for the vacation of such order and furnishes a copy of such application to the party in whose favour such order has been made or the counsel of such party, the High Court shall dispose of the application within a period of two weeks from the date on which it is received or from the date on which the copy of such application is so furnished, whichever is later, or where the High Court is closed on the last day of that period, before the expiry of he next day afterwards on which the High Court is closed on the last day of that period, before the expiry of the next day afterwards on which the High Court is open; and if the application is not so disposed of, the interim order shall, on the expiry of that period, or, as the case may be, the expiry of the said next day, stand vacated.
4. The power conferred on a High Court by this Article shall not be in derogation of the power conferred on the Supreme Court by clause (2) of Article 32.

Article 300A. Persons not to be deprived of property save by authority of law

No person shall be deprived of his property save by authority of law.

Article 325. No person to be ineligible for inclusion in, or to claim to be included in a special, electoral roll on grounds of religion, race, caste or sex

There shall be one general electoral roll for every territorial constituency for election to either House of Parliament or to the House or either House of the Legislature of a State and no person shall be ineligible for inclusion in any such roll or claim to be included in any special electoral roll for any such constituency on grounds only of religion, race, caste, sex or any of them.

Article 326. Elections to the House of the People and to the Legislative Assemblies of States to be on the basis of adult suffrage

The elections to the House of the People and to the Legislative Assembly of every State shall be on the basis of adult suffrage; that is to say, every person who is a citizen of India and who is not less than eighteen years of age on such date as may be fixed in that behalf by or under any law made by the appropriate Legislature and is not otherwise disqualified under this Constitution or any law made by the appropriate Legislature on the ground of non-residence, unsoundness of mind, crime or corrupt or illegal practice, shall be entitled to be registered as a voter at any such election.

Appendix II

Notes on: Constitution (Amendment) Acts (1951-2001)

1. *THE CONSTITUTION (FIRST AMENDMENT) ACT, 1951*

The Constitution had hardly become operative, when one of its inherent contradictions manifested itself— this contradiction emanated from the provisions of Chapter-III enshrining fundamental rights enforceable by law and those of Chapter-IV Directive Principles of State Policy, which are not enforceable by any court but are, nevertheless, fundamental... and lays down that it shall be the duty of the State to apply these principles in making laws. Thus, while several States pursuing these principles enacted legislation, but that came into conflict with the fundamental rights, for instance, Article 31 laid down: "No person is to be deprived of one's property saved by authority of law". It did provide for State taking over of property for public purposes but on payment of just compensation. Again, Article 19 provided for freedom to carry on any occupation, trade or business, of course, subject to reasonable restrictions in the interest of general public. Although the provision was wide enough to provide for, for instance, State taking over road transport system to the exclusion of private bus operators, but these laws were challenged in the court of law. Further, legislations relating to *zamindari* abolition, were declared ultra- vires by respective High Courts.

Hence, the Parliament considered it necessary to enact amendments to the Constitution to insert provisions fully securing the Constitutional validity of *zamindari* abolition laws in general and certain other legislations already enacted. Accordingly, the first amendment aimed at the visions of Articles 19 and 31 and to circumscription of Article 13. The new Article 31A and 31B were inserted and Ninth Schedule was added to the Constitution. These amendments listed a number of legislations already enacted in the Ninth Schedule and it was clearly specified that none of the Acts and Regulations listed therein, nor any of the provisions thereof shall be deemed to be void notwithstanding any udgement, decree or order by the Court or Tribunal to the contrary, which would be liable to be impugned under Articles 13 of the Constitution.

2. *THE CONSTITUTION (SECOND AMENDMENT) ACT, 1952*

The original Article 81 (1) (a) prescribed an absolute limit of 500 elected members in the House of People, Article 81 (1) (b) provided that the State shall be divided, grouped or formed into territorial constituencies and the number of members to be allotted to each constituency shall be so determined as to ensure that there shall be not less than one member for every 750,000 of the population and not more than one member of every 500,000 of the population. At first, seats were allotted in the House of People to Part A and Part B States on the basis of one member for every 7.2 lakh of the estimated population giving a total of 470 members to these States. The 1951 Census figures were, howerver, higher in all cases and in view of the overall limit of 500 members prescribed in Article 81 (1) (a), it was not possible to increase appreciably the total number of seats allotted to these States. It was accordingly necessary to reduce the representation from one member for every 7.2 lakhs to one member for every 7.5 lakhs of population. This figure of 7.5 lakhs was the maximum permissible under Article 81 (1) (b) as it stood; but even so, if the average population of a parliamentary constituency in any State was to be 750,000 it was obvious that the population of some constituencies would exceed that figure. It was, therefore, deemed necessary that Article 81 (1) (b) should be amended relaxing the limits prescribed therein so as to avoid a constitutional irregularity in delimiting the constituencies for the purpose of readjustment of representation in the House of the People as required under Article 81 (3) of the Constitution. The Act achieves this end.

3. *THE CONSTITUTION (THIRD AMENDMENT) ACT, 1954*

Entry 33 of the Concurrent List enables Parliament to legislate in respect of products of industries declared to be under Union control. In addition, Parliament was empowered by Article 369, for a period of five years, to legislate in respect of certain specified essential commodities. It was not considered advisable that after

Article 369 lapsed on 25th January, 1955, the Centre should be divested of all legal powers to control the production, supply and distribution of some of these essential commodities. The Bill sought to amplify entry 33 of the Concurrent List accordingly.

4. *THE CONSTITUTION (FOURTH AMENDMENT) ACT, 1955*

Some decisions of the Supreme Court had given a very wide meaning to clause (1) and (2) of Article 31. Despite the difference in the wording of the two clauses, they were regarded as dealing with the same subject. According to these decisions, even where deprivation of property was caused by a purely regulatory provision of law and was not accompanied by an acquisition or taking possession of that or any other property right by the State, the law, in order to be valid, had to provide for compensation under clause (2) of the Article. It was considered necessary, therefore, to re-state more precisely the State's power of compulsory acquisition and requisitioning of private property and distinguish it from cases where the operation of regulatory or prohibitory laws of the State resulted in "deprivation of property".

The scope of Article 31A also needed to be extended to cover certain categories of essential welfare legislation.

Finally, the judgment of the Supreme Court in *Saghir Ahmed* v *The State of U.P.* had raised the question whether an Act providing for a State monopoly in a particular trade or business conflicted with the freedom of trade and commerce guaranteed by Article 301, but had left the question undecided. The judgment had given rise to the impression that notwithstanding the clear authority of Parliament or of a State Legislature to introduce State monopoly in a particular sphere of trade or commerce [vide clause (6) of Article 19 as amended by the Constitution (First Amendment) Act, the law might have to be justified before the courts as being "in the pulbic interest in to a" under Article 3.1 or as amounting "reasonable restriction," under Article 304(b). It was felt necessary that Article 305 should be amended to make this clear.

The Act accordingly in the main, amends Articles 31, 31A and 305 and, as a corollary to the amendment of Article 31A augments the Ninth Schedule by the inclusion of some more Acts.

5. *THE CONSTITUTON (FIFTH AMENDMENT) ACT, 1955*

Under the proviso to Article 3 of the Constitution, as it stood before amendment, no Bill for the purpose of forming a new State, increasing or diminishng the area of any State or alltering the boundaries or name of any State should be introduced in the

Parliament, unless the views of the State Legislatures concerned with respect to the provisions of the Bill had been ascertained by the President. It was considered desirable that when a reference was made to the State Legislatures for the said purpose, the President should be able to prescribe the period within which the States should convey their views, and it should be open to the President to extend such period whenever he considered it necessary. It was also considered desirable to provide that the Bill would not be introduced until after the expiry of such period. The Act amends the proviso to Article 3 of the Constitution accordingly.

6. *THE CONSTITUTION (SIXTH AMENDMENT) ACT, 1956*

High judicial authorities had found the interpretation of the original Article 286 a difficult task and had expressed divergent views as to the scope and effect, in particular, of the explanation in clause (1) of Bombay is the United Motors (India) Ltd., was that sub-clause (a) and the and of clause (2). The majority view of Supreme Court in the *State of Bombay* v. *The United Motors (India) Litd.*, was that sub-clause (a) and the *Explanation* in clause (1) prohibited the taxation of a sale involving inter-State elements by all States except the State in which the goods were delivered for the purpose of consumption there in, and furthermore, that clause (2) did not affect the power of that State to tax the inter-State sale even though Parliament had not made a law removing the ban imposed by that clause. This resulted in dealers resident in one State being subjected to the sales tax jurisdiction and procedure of several other States with which they had dealings in the normal course of their business. Two-and-half years later, the second part of this decision was reversed by the Supreme Court in *Bengal Immunity Company Ltd.* v. *The State of Bihar* but here too the Court was not unanimous.

Further, in pursuance of clause (3) of the Article, Parliament passed an Act in1952 declaring a number of goods to be essential to the life of the community. Since this declaration would not affect pre- existing State laws imposing sales tax on these goods, the result was a wide disparity from State to State, not only in the range of exempted goods, but also in the rates applicable to them.

The Taxation Enquiry Commission, after examining the problem with great care and thoroughness, made certain recommendations which were generally accepted by all the State Governments.

The Act gives effect to the recommendations of the Commission as regards the amendment of the Constitutional provisions relating to sales tax.

7. *CONSTITUTION (SEVENTH AMENDMENT) ACT, 1956*

It was considered necessary to make numerous amendments in the Constitution in order to implement the scheme of State' reorganisation. The Act makes these amendments and also some other amendments to certain provisions of the Constitution relating to High Courts and High Court Judges, the executive power of the Union and the States, and a few entries in the legislative lists.

8. *THE CONSTITUTION (EIGHTH AMENDMENT) ACT, 1959*

The reasons which weighed with the Constituent Assembly of India in making provision for the reservation of seats for the Schedule Castes and Schedule Tribes and representation of the Anglo-Indian Community in the House of the People and the State Legislative Assemblies have not ceased to exist. The Act, therefore, makes the aforesaid reservation and nomination continue for another ten years.

9. *THE CONSTITUTION (NINTH AMENDMENT) ACT, 1960*

The Indo-Pakistan agreements dated September 10, 1950, October 23, 1959, and January 11, 1960, which settled certain boundary disputes relating to the borders of the State of Assam, Punjab and West Bengal, and the Union Territory of Tripura involved transfer of certain territories to Pakistan after demarcation. The Act amends the Constitution to give effect to the transfer of these territories.

10. *THE CONSTITUTION (TENTH AMENDMENT) ACT, 1961*

In deference to the desire and request of the people of Free Dadra and Nagar Haveli, embodied in a formal Resolution adopted by their Varishta Panchayat on June 12, 1961, for integration of their territories with the Union of India, the Government of India decided that these territories will form part of India as a specific Union Territory with effect from August 11,1961. The Act makes appropriate amendments to the Constitution of India.

11. *THE CONSTITUTION (ELEVENTH AMENDMENT)ACT, 1961*

The requirement of Article 66 (1) that members of the two Houses of Parliament should assemble at a joint sitting for the election of the Vice President seemed to be totally unnecessary and was also likely to cause practical difficulties. It was, therefore, proposed to amend the Article. Moreover, it was possible that the elections to the two Houses of Parliament might not always be completed before the election of the President or Vice President. It was, therefore, proposed to amend Article 71 pertaining to matters relating to the election of the President or Vice President. The Act gives effect to the two proposals.

12. THE CONSTITUTION (TWELFTH AMENDMENT) ACT, 1962

On the acquisition of the territories of Goa, Daman and Diu with effect from December 20, 1961, these territories had, by virtue of sub-clause (c) of clause (3) of Article 1 of the Constitution, been comprised within the territory by the President through an Administrator in accordance with Article 239 of the Constitution . It was, however, considered desirable that Goa, Daman and Diu should be specifically included as a Union Territory in the First Schedule to Constitution. It was also considered that clause (1) of Article 240 should be suitably amended to confer power on the President to make regulations for the peace, progress and good government of Goa, Daman and Diu. The Act makes the above mentioned provisions.

13. THE CONSTITUTION (THIRTEENTH AMENDMENT) ACT, 1962

An agreement in July 1960, between the Government of India and the leaders of the Naga People's Convention provided for the formation in the Union of India of a separate State of Naga Hills-Tuensang Area (Nagaland) - an erstwhile Part 'B' tribal area within the State of Assam. The agreement, *inter alia,* provided that the governor of Nagaland would be responsible (i) for law and order so long as the situation in the State continued to remain disturbed on account of the hostile activities inside the area; (ii) for the funds to be made available to the new State by the Government of India; and (iii) for the administration of Tuensang district for a period of ten years. It was also decided that the Acts of Parliament, in respect of certain specified subjects would not apply to Nagaland unless so decided by Nagaland Legislature.

As these matters were peculiar to the proposed new State of Nagaland, provision with respect thereto had to had to be made in the Constitution itself. The Act accordingly amends the Constitution by inserting new Article 371A to provide for the aforesaid and ancillary matters.

14. THE CONSTITUTION (FOURTHEENTH AMENDMENT) ACT, 1962

The French establishments of Pondicherry, Karikal, Mahe and Yanam became territories of the Indian Union with effect from the 16th August, 1962, when the "Treaty of Cession" was ratified by the Governments of India and France. This Act provides for these territories being specified in the Constitution as a Union Territory called

"Pondicherry". By appropriate amendments to Article 81 and the Fourth Scheme the Constitution Act further enables representation being given immediately to 'Pondicherry' in both the Houses of Parliament.

The Act also confers necessary legislature powers on Parliament through a new Article 239A to enact laws for creating Legislatures and Council of Ministers in certain Union Territories, broadly on the pattern of the scheme which was in force in some of the Part 'C' States before the reorganisation of the State. The new Article 239A follows generally the provisions of Article 241 as it stood before the reorganisation of the States.

15. THE CONSTITUTION (FIFTEENTH AMENDMENT) ACT, 1963

Several amendments to the Constitution had been under consideration of the Government of India for a long time. Proposals, *inter alia,* in respect of Article 297 dealing with territorial waters, Article 311 dealing with services and Article 316 dealing with Public Service Commissions were originally included in the Constitution (Fifth Amendment) Bill, 1955. Except for an amendment relating to Article 3 of the Constitution, which was effected by the Constitution (Fifth Amendment) Act, 1955, the Bill was allowed to lapse. Some of its provisions, with minor modifications, have been incorporated in the present Act. The Act also includes certain new provisions for amendment of the Constitution : (i) The Law Commission in their Fourteenth Report has recommended that the retiring age of the High Court Judges be raised to sixty-five years. On a careful consideration of the recommendation, it was decided to raise the retiring age to sixty two and to amend the Constitution accordingly, (ii) Whenever any question arose as to the correct age of a Judge of the Supreme Court or a High Court, the question had to be decided by the President. This position has been clarified by the present Act making a specific provision in that regard, (iii) It was considered desirable, in public interest, that Judges should be transferred from one High Court to another. Since a transfer was expected to impose some additional financial burden on the judge who was so transferred, the Act provides for the payment of some compensatory allowance to him. (iv) The seat of the Central Government being in New Delhi, the Punjab High Court alone had jurisdiction with respect to the Central Government. This involved considerable hardship to litigants from distant places. The Act, therefore, amends the provision in this respect to that when any relief is sought against some action taken by any Government authority or person, the High Court within whose jurisdiction the cause of action arises may also have jurisdiction to issue appropriate directions, orders or writs.

16. *CONSTITUTION (SIXTEENTH AMENDMENT) ACT, 1963*

The Committee on National Integration and Regionalism, appointed by the National Integration Council, recommended that Article 19 be so amended that adequate powers become available for the preservation and maintenance of the integrity and sovereignty of the Union. The Committee was further of the view that every candidate for the membership of a State Legislature or Parliament, and every aspirant to, and incumbent of, public office should pledge himself to uphold the Constitution and to preserve the integrity and sovereignty of the Union and, towards that end in view, desired that forms of oath in the Third Schedule to the Constitution should be suitably amended. The Act gives effect to these objects.

17. *THE CONSTITUTION (SEVENTEENTH AMENDMENT) ACT, 1964*

Article 31A of the Constitution provided that a law in respect of acquisition by the State of any estate would not be deemed to be void on the ground that it was inconsistent with Articles 14, 19 or 31. The expression "estate" had been defined differently in different States. As a result of the transfer of land from one State to another under the scheme of re-organisation of States, the expression came to have different connotations even in parts of the same State. The present Act, therefore, modifies the definition of "estate" in Article 31A and amends the Ninth Schedule by including there in certain State enactments.

18. *THE CONSTITUTION (EIGHTEENTH AMENDMENT) ACT,1966*

Article 3 of the Constitution provided for the formation of new States and alteration of areas, boundaries or names of existing States. By the Seventh Amendment of the Constitution in 1956, the concept of Union Territories" was introduced in the Constitution, but Article 3 was not amended to include the terms "Union Territories".

It was considered proper to amend this Article to make it clear that "State" in clauses (a) to (e) of that Article (but not in the proviso) includes "Union Territories").

It was also proposed to make it clear that power under clause (a) of Article 3 includes power to form a new State or Union Territory by uniting part of a State or Union Territory to another State or Union territory.

It was considered property to amend this Article to make it clear that "State" in clauses (a) to (e) of that Article (but not in the proviso) includes "Union territories".

It was also proposed to make it clear that power to form a new State or Union Territory by uniting part of a State or Union territory to another State or Union Territory.

The present Act achieves those objects.

19. THE CONSTITUTION (NINETEENTH AMENDMENT) ACT, 1966

The Act gives effect to the recommendation made by the Election Commission, in its Report on the Third General Elections in India 1962 relating to the abolition of election tribunals and trial of election petitions by High Courts.

20. THE CONSTITUTION (TWENTIETH AMENDMENT) ACT, 1966

According to the recent judgments of the Supreme Court appointment of district judges in Uttar Pradesh and a few other States were rendered invalid and illegal on the ground that such appointments were not made in accordance with the provisions of Article 233 of the Constitution. The Supreme Court also held that the power of posting a district Judge from one station to another and that the power of transfer of a district judge is vested in the High Court under Article 235. The present Act invalidates the judgments, decrees, orders and sentences passed or made theretofore by all such district judges in those States and also validates the appointment, posting, promotion and transfer of such district judges barring those few who were not eligible for appointment under Article 233.

21. THE CONSTITUTION (TWENTY-FIRST AMENDMENT) ACT, 1967

Following persistent demands from the Sindhi- speaking people and the recommendations of the Commissioner for Linguistic Minorities, Government, on November 4, 1966, announced its decision to include the Sindhi language in the Eighth Schedule to the Constitution. The present Act gives effect to that decision.

22. THE CONSTITUTION (TWENTY- SECOND AMENDMENT) ACT, 1969

On September 11, 1968, the Government of India announced the broad details of the Scheme for constituting within the State of Assam, an autonomous State comprising certain areas specified in Part A of the table appended to paragraph 20 of the Sixth Schedule of the Constitution. The Act amends the Constitution to enable Parliament to enact a law to give effect to the said scheme.

23. *THE CONSTITUTION (TWENTY-THIRD AMENDMENT) ACT, 1969*

More than ninety per cent of the population of the State of Nagaland, which came into being in 1963, is tribal. It would be anomalous to make provision for reservation for Scheduled Castes and Scheduled Tribes in Legislatures in the States where they are in a majority. It was, therefore, proposed, as desired by the Government of Nagaland, not to make any reservation for the Scheduled Tribes in Nagaland either in Lok Sabha or in the State Legislative Assembly.

Under Article 333 of the Constitution, the number of Anglo-Indians, who may be nominated to the State Legislative Assemblies, is left to the discretion of the Governor. It was proposed to amend that Article so as to provide that not more than one Anglo-Indian should be nominated by the Governor to any State Legislature Assembly.

Article 334 of the Constitution lays down that provisions of the Constitution relating to the reservation of seats for the Scheduled Castes and Sheduled Tribes and the representation of the Anglo-Indian community by nomination in the House of People and the Legislative Assemblies of the States shall cease to have effect on the expiration of a period of twenty years from the commencement of the Constitution. Although the Scheduled Castes and Scheduled Tribes have made considerable progress in last twenty years, the reasons, which weighted with the Constitutent Assembly in making provision with regard to the aforesaid reservation of seats and nomination of members, have not ceased to exist. It was, therefore, proposed to continue the reservation for them.

24. *THE CONSTITUTION (TWENTY-FOURTH AMENDMENT) ACT, 1971*

In the Golak Nath case [(1967) 2 S.C.R. 761], the Supreme Court reserved, by a narrow majority, its own earlier decisions upholding the power of Parliament to amend all parts of the Constitution including Part III relating to fundamental rights. The result of the judgment was that Parliament was considered to have no power to take away or curtail any of the fundamental rights even if became necessary to do so for the attainment of the objectives set out in the Preamble to the Constitution. The Act, therefore, amends the Constitution to provide expressly the Parliament power to amend any part of the Constitution.

25. *THE CONSTITUTION (TWENTY-FIFTH AMENDMENT) ACT, 1971*

Article 31 of the Constitution specifically provided that no law providing for the compulsory acquisition or requisitioning of property which either fixed the amount of compensation or specified the principles on which and the manner in which the compensation was to be determined and given could be called in question in any court on the ground that the compensation provided by that law was not adequate. In the Bank Nationalisation [(1970) 3 S. C. R. 830], the Supreme Court had held that the Constitution guaranteed right to compensation, that is, the equivalent in money of the property compulsorily acquired. Thus, in effect, the adequacy of compensation and the relevancy of the principles laid down by the Legislature for determining the amount of compensation had virtually become justiciable inasmuch as the court could go into the question whether the amount paid to the owner of the property was what might be regarded reasonbly as compensation for loss of property. In the same case, the court had also held that a law which sought to acquire or requisition property for a public purpose should also satisfy the requirements of Article 19 (1) (f).

The Act amends the Constitution to surmount the difficulties placed in the way of giving effect to the Directive Principles of State Policy by the aforesaid interpretation.

26. *THE CONSTITUTION (TWENTY-SIXTH AMENDMENT) ACT, 1971*

The concept of rulership, with privy purses and special privileges unrelated to any current functions and social purposes, was incompatible with an egalitarian social order. Government, therefore, decided to terminate the privy purses and privileges of the Rulers of former Indian States. It was necessary for this purpose, apart from amending the relevant provisions of the Constitution to insert a new Article therein so as to terminate expressly the recognition already granted to such Rulers and to abolish privy purses and extinguish all rights, liabilities and obligations in respect of privy purses. Hence this Act.

27. *THE CONSTITUTION (TWENTY-SEVENTH AMENDMENT) ACT, 1971*

As a part of the scheme of reorganisation of the north-eastern areas, it was proposed that the Union Territory of Mizoram contemplated under the scheme should have a legislature and a Council of Ministers. It was proposed to achieve this object by including the Union Territory of Mizoram in Article 239A of the Constitution.

The Study Team appointed by the Administrative Reforms Commission on the Administration of Union Territories and NEFA had recommended that the Administrator of a Union Territory with legislature might have the power to promulgate ordinances when the legislature was not in session. It was proposed to accept this recommendation and include a suitable provision in the Constitution conferring on such an Administrator the power to promulgate ordinances.

Under paragraph 18(2) of the Sixth Schedule to the Constitution read with Article 240 of the Constitution, the President is empowered to make regulations for the North-East Frontier Agency. It was proposed to continue these powers even after the Agency became the Union Territory of Arunachal Pradesh under the reorganisation scheme. It was also proposed to have similar powers with respect to the Union Territory of Mizoram.

When the legislature of a State is dissolved or its functioning is suspended by a proclamation under Article 356 of the Constitution, the Parliament is empowered to confer legislative powers on the President in respect of that State by passing a law under Article 357 (1). No such provision existed in the case of Union territories with legislatures, with the result that whenever the legislature of any Union Territory was dissolved or its functioning was suspended by an order of President, all legislation relating to that Union Territory had to be passed by the Parliament. It was proposed that in such circumstances, the regulation—making power under Article 240 should be avilable to the President.

Hill Areas of Manipur are predominantly inhabited by members of Scheduled Tribes. To safeguard their interests, special provisions were made in section 52 of the Government of Union Territories Act, 1963, for a committee of the Legislative Assembly of the Union territory of Manipur consisting of members from the Hill Areas. With the Union Territory of Manipur becoming a State under the re- organisation scheme, the said section 52 was to cease to be operative. It was proposed, as a part of the scheme of safeguards for the people of the Hill Areas, to continue this arrangement even after Manipur became a State. So, a specific provision was proposed to be made in the Constitution for the formation of such a committee.

This Act gives effect to the above proposals.

28. *THE CONSTITUTION (TWENTY-EIGHTH AMENDMENT) ACT, 1972*

Article 314 of the Constitution guaranteed to persons who were appointed by the Secretary of State or Secretary of State in Council to a civil service of the Crown in India and who continued to serve after the commencement of the Constitution under the Government of India or of a State, the same conditions of service as respects remuneration, leave and pension and the same rights as respects disciplinary matters or rights as similar thereto as changed circumstances may permit, as such persons were entitled to immediately before such commencement. The concept of a class of officers with immutable conditions of service was incompatible with the changed social order. It was, therefore, considered necessary to amend the Constitution to provide for the deletion of Article 314 and for the inclusion of new Article 312A which confers powers on Parliament to vary or revoke by law, the conditions of service of the officers aforesaid and contains appropriate consequential and incidental provisions. The Act gives effect to the above objects.

29. *THE CONSTITUTION (TWENTY-NINTH AMENDMENT) ACT, 1972*

The Kerala Land Reforms Act, 1963 (Act 1 of 1964), is the principal land reform law in the State of Kerala and was included in the Ninth Schedule to the Constitution. In the course of implementation, the State Government faced serious practical difficulties and to overcome them, that Act was extensively amended by the Kerala Land Reforms (Amendment) Act, 1969 (Act 35 of 1969) and by the Kerala Land Reforms (Amendment) Act, 1971 (Act 25 of 1971). Certain crucial provisions of the principal Act as amended were challenged in the High Court of Kerala and in the Supreme Court, creating a climate of uncertainty in the effective implementation of land reforms. Although the High Court of Kerala had generally upheld the scheme of land reforms envisaged in the principal Act as amended, a few vital provisions had been struck down by the High Court. Even in regard to the provisions upheld by the High Court, the affected parties had moved the Supreme Court in appeal. Some persons also moved the Supreme Court in (original petitions) challenging certain provisions of the Act. The Supreme Court in its judgments delivered on 26th and 28th April, 1972, generally upheld the scheme of land reforms as envisaged in the principal Act as amended but agreed with the High Court invalidating certain crucial provisions. It was feared that this could have far-reaching adverse effects on the implementation of the programme of land reforms in the State and thousands of tenants would be adversely affected by some of the provisions which had been either struck down or rendered ineffective. It was also apprehended that certain observations of the Supreme Court in the judgments might open the flood gates of litigation much to the detriment of thousands of Kudikidappukars in the State who would not be able to defend themselves in protracted legal proceedings. Further, appeals had been preferred against the judgment of the Kerala High Court invalidating certain important provisions of the principal Act as amended, e.g., sections 4A (1) (a) and (b), 7, 7B (1) and 106 and they were pending in the Supreme Court.

It was, therefore, proposed to include the Kerala Land Reforms (Amendment) Act, 1969 and the Kerala Land Reforms (Amendment) Act, 1971 in the Ninth Schedule to the Constitution so that they might have the protection under Article 31B and any uncertainty or doubt that might arise in regard to the validity of those Acts was removed. The Act achieves this object.

30. THE CONSTITUTION (THIRTIETH AMENDMENT) ACT, 1972

This Act gives effect to the recommendations of the Law Commission of India in its forty-fourth and forty-fifth reports on civil appeals to the Supreme Court on certificate of fitness. At present, an appeal lies to the Supreme Court, *inter alia*, on a certificate given by a High Court that the amount or the value of the subject- matter of dispute is not less than twenty thousand rupees or that the judgment, decree or final order involves, directly or indirectly, some claim or question respecting property of the like amount. The valuations cannot be the rational yard- stick for a right to appeal. An important question of law can arise even in suits of small value and the test of valuation results in cases without merit going up to the Supreme Court. The Law Commission recommended that clause (a) and (b) of Article 133(1) of the Constitution should be ommitted and that an appeal should lie to the Supreme Court only if the High Court certifies that the case involves a substantial question of law of general importance and that in the opinion of the High Court, the said question needs to be decided by the Supreme Court. The amendment of the Article accordingly would curtail the number of appeals which are filed in the Supreme Court merely on the valuation test being satisfied, without any merit in them. The Act achieves this object.

31. THE CONSTITUTION (THIRTY-FIRST AMENDMENT) ACT, 1973

Clause (1) of Article 81 of the Constitution provides that the House of the People shall consist of not more than 500 members to be chosen by direct election from territorial constituencies in the States and not more than 25 members to represent the Union Territories, chosen in such manner as Parliament may by law provide. As a result of the enactment of the North-Eastern Area (Reorganisation) Act, 1971 (81 of 1971), the total number offseats in the Lok Sabha allotted to the States increased to 506, six more than the permissible limit of 500 under Article 81. The actual total number of the present Lok Sabha is 522 (482 from the fifteen major States, 17 from six smaller States of Himachal Pradesh, Jammu and Kashmir, Manipur, Meghalaya, Nagaland and Tripura each of which has a population of less than six millions and 16 from the nine Union Territories).

Clause (2) of Article 81 of the Constitution lays down that for the purposes of sub-clause (a) of clause (1) there shall be allotted to each State a number of seats in the House of the People in such manner that the ratio between that number and the population of the State is, so far as practicable, the same for all States and that each State shall be divided into territorial constituencies in such manner that the ratio between the population of each constituency and the number of seats allotted to it is, so far as practicable, the same throughout the State. Under clause (3) of Article 81, the expression "population" means the population as ascertained in the last preceding census of which the relevant figures have been published. Article 82 enjoins that on the completion of each census, the allocation of seats in the House of the People to the States and the division of each State into territorial constituencies shall be re-adjusted by such authority and in such manner as Parliament may inlaw determine. In pursuance of Article 82, Parliament has enacted the Delimitation Act, 1972, and the Delimitation Commission has been constituted to undertake the necessary task of the re-adjustment envisaged in Article 82. It will be noticed that adherence to the principles laid down in clause (2) of Article 81 by the Delimitation

Commission in undertaking re- adjustment as enjoined by article 82 on the basis of the 1971 census, figures may have the effect of effecting the number of seats allotted to the States in the House of the People. It was felt that it would be better to ensure that any re-adjustment and consequent allocation of seats did not adversely affect the existing number of seats allotted to each State in the House of the People and to achieve this purpose, it would be necessary to increase the strength of the Lok Sabha suitably.

In order to ensure that there is no reduction in the existing representation in the House of the People in respect of any of the States, section 2 of the Act amends Article 81 so as to increase the upper limit for representation of the State from 500 to 525. The opportunity is taken to decrease the limit for the Union Territories from 25 to 20, as existing representation for Union Territories is only 16. Government also considered it necessary to make an amendment in clause (2) of Article 81 to provide that the provisions of sub-clause (a) of clause (2) of Article 81 shall not be applicable to any State so long as its population did not exceed six millions. This is to ensure that the existing representation in the Lok Sabha is maintained for the smaller States referred to above.

Article 330 of the Constitution relates to reservation of seats in the Lok Sabha for Scheduled Castes and Scheduled Tribes. The provisions of this Article have, however, been made inapplicable to the State of Nagaland on the ground that it has a predominantly tribal population. According to the 1971 census, 88.6 per cent of Nagaland's population belongs to the Scheduled Tribes. The corresponding figures for the State of Meghalaya and the Union Territories of Arunachal Pradesh and Mizoram are 80.5 per cent, 79.0 per cent and 94.3 per cent respectively. Government, therefore, considered that the provisions of Article 330 should not apply also to the predominantly tribal units of Meghalaya, Arunachal Pradesh and Mizoram. Similarly, it was considered that as in the case of Nagaland, there need to be no reservation of seats for Scheduled Tribes in the Legislative Assembly of the State of Meghalaya and that Article 332 of the Constitution might be amended suitably. Sections 3 and 4 of the Act achieve these objects.

32. *THE CONSTITUTION (THIRTY- SECOND AMENDMENT) ACT, 1973*

When the State of Andhra Pradesh was formed in 1956, certain safeguards were envisaged for the Telengana area in the matter of development and also in the matter of employment opportunities and educational facilities for the residents of that area. The provisions of clause (1) of Article 371 of the Constitution were intended to give effect to certain features of these safeguards. The Public Employment (Requirement as to Residence) Act, 1957, was enacted, *inter alia*, to provide for employment opportunities for residents of Telengana area. But in 1969, the Supreme Court held the relevant provision of the Act to be unConstitutional in so far as it related to the safeguards envisaged for the Telengana area. Owing to a variety of causes, the working of the safeguards gave rise to a certain amount of dissatisfaction some times in the Telengana area and some times in the other areas of the State. Measures were devised from time to time to resolve the problems. During 1973, several leaders of Andhra Pradesh made a concerted effort to analyse the factors which had been giving rise to the dissatisfaction and find enduring answers to the problems with a view to achieving fuller emotional integration of the people of Andhra Pradesh. On the 21st September, 1973, they suggested certain measures (generally known as the Six-Point Formula) indicating a uniform approach for promoting accelerated development of the backward areas of the State so as to secure the balanced development of the State as a whole and for providing equitable opportunities to different areas of the State in the matter of education, employment and career prospects in public services.This formula received wide support in Andhra Pradesh and was endorsed by the State Government.

The present Act provides the necessary Constitutional authority for giving effect to the Six- Point Formula in so far as it relates to the provision of equitable opportunities for people of different areas of the State in the matter of admission to educational institutions and public employment. The Act provides, *inter alia*, for the Constitution of an Administrative Tribunal to deal with certain disputes and grievances relating to public services. It also empowers Parliament to legislate for establishing a Central University in the State and contains provisions for the validation of certain appointments made in the past. As the Six- Point Formula provides for the discontinuance of the Regional Committees constituted under clause (1) of Article 371 of the Constitution, the Act also provides for the repeal of that clause.

33. *THE CONSTITUTION (THIRTY-THIRD AMENDMENT) ACT, 1974*

Article 101 (3) (b) and 190 (3) of the Constitution permit a member of either House of Parliament or a member of a House of Legislature of a State to resign his seat by writing under his hand addressed to the Speaker or the Chairman, as the case may be. In the recent past, there had been instances where coercive measures had been resorted for compelling members of a Legislative Assembly to resign their membership. If this was not checked, it might become difficult for legislature to function in accordance with the provisions of the Constitution. It was, therefore, proposed to amend the above two Articles to impose a requirement as to acceptance of the resignation by the Speaker or the Chairman and to provide that the resignation shall not be accepted by the Speaker or the Chairman if he was satisfied after making such inquiry as he thought fit that the resignation was not voluntary or genuine. The Act achieves the above object.

34. *THE CONSTITUTION (THIRTY-FOURTH AMENDMENT) ACT, 1974*

The Chief Ministers' Conference held on the 23rd July, 1972, had made important suggestions with regard to reduction in the level of ceiling on land holdings, application of ceiling on the basis of land held by a family and the withdrawing of exemptions. The suggestions of the Chief Ministers' Conference were accepted by the Government of India and necessary guidelines were issued to the State Governments for the revision of ceiling laws.

The present Act amends the Ninth Schedule to the Constitution to include therein the revised ceiling laws which had till then been enacted in broad conformity with the aforesaid guidelines so that they may have the protection under Article 31 B of the Constitution and any uncertainty or doubt regarding their validity is removed. The Act also extends similar protection to two State Acts dealing with the abolition of intermediary tenures.

35. *THE CONSTITUTION (THIRTY-FIFTH AMENDMENT) ACT, 1974*

In pursuance of the historic agreement of May 8, 1974 between the Chogyal, leaders of the political parties representing the people of Sikkim and the Government of India and of the unanimous desire of the members of the Sikkim Assembly expressed in the meetings of the Assembly held on the 11th May, 1974 for the progressive realisation of a fully responsible government of Sikkim and for furthering its close relationship with India, the Sikkim Assembly considered and passed the Government of Sikkim Bill, 1974, unanimously. The Chogyal promulgated this Bill on July 4, 1974 as the Government of Sikkim Act, 1974. For the speedy development of Sikkim in the social, economic and political fields, Section 30 of the Government of Sikkim Act, 1974, empowered the Government of Sikkim, *inter alia*, to seek participation and representation for the people of Sikkim in the political institutions of India. On the 28th June, 1974, after passing the Government of Sikkim Bill, the Sikkim Assembly resolved unanimously that measures should be taken amongst other things for seeking representation for the people of Sikkim in India's parliamentary system.

After the promulgation of the Government of Sikkim Act, the Chief Minister of Sikkim made formal requests to the Government of India through the Chief Executive requesting the Government of India to take such steps as may be legally or Constitutionally necessary to give effect to the Government of Sikkim Act, 1974 and the resolutions passed by the Assembly and particularly for providing for representation for the people of Sikkim in the Parliament.

With a view to giving effect to the wishes of the people of Sikkim and for strengthening Indo-Sikkim cooperation and inter-relationship, this Act sought to amend the Constitution to provide for the terms and conditions of association of Sikkim with the Union. The terms and conditions were set out in the Tenth Schedule added to the Constitution by clause 5 of the Act. Apart from referring to the responsibilities of the Government of India and the powers of the President in this regard, the Schedule provided for the allotment to Sikkim of one seat in the Council of States and one seat in the House of the People and for the election of the representatives of Sikkim in the Council of States and the House of the People by the members of the Sikkim Assembly.

36. THE CONSTITUTION (THIRTY-SIXTH AMENDMENT) ACT, 1975

The Sikkim Assembly unanimously adopted a resolution on the 10th April, 1975 which, *inter alia*, noted the persistent harmful activities of the Chogyal which were aimed at undermining the responsible democratic government set up under the provisions of the May 8 Agreement of 1973 and the Government of Sikkim Act, 1974. The resolution declared that the Assembly had satisfied itself that these activities of the Chogyal not only violated the objectives of the Agreement of May 8, 1973, but also ran counter to the wishes of the people of Sikkim and impeded their democratic development and participation in the political and economic life of India. Accordingly, the Assembly solemnly declared and resolved that "The institution of the Chogyal is hereby abolished and Sikkim shall henceforth be a constituent unit of India, enjoying a democratic and fully responsible Government".

The Assembly also resolved that this Resolution be submitted to the people of Sikkim forthwith for their approval. A special opinion poll conducted by the Government of Sikkim on the 14th April, 1975, resulted in a total of 59, 637 votes in favour and 1, 496 votes against the Resolution out of a total electorate of approximately 97,000.

The result of this poll was communicated to the Government of India by the Chief Minister of Sikkim on the 15th April, 1975. The Chief Minister on behalf of the Council of Ministers strongly requested the Government of India to make an immediate response and accept the above decision, taking as has been requested in the Assembly Resolution of the 10th April, 1975, such measures as may be necessary and appropriate to implement the decision as early as possible.

The Chief Minister and other Ministers of Sikkim also visited New Delhi on the 16th- 17th April, 1975 and urged the Government of India to take immediate action in this behalf.

Accordingly, it was proposed to include Sikkim as a full- fledged State in the First Schedule to the Constitution and to allot to Sikkim one seat in the Council of States and one seat in the House of the People. It is also proposed to insert a new Article containing the provisions considered necessary to meet the special circumstances and needs of Sikkim.

The Act sought to achieve the above objects.

37. *THE CONSTITUTION (THIRTY-SEVENTH AMENDMENT) ACT, 1975*

The Union Territory of Arunachal Pradesh is at present administered through a Chief Commissioner. It has a Pradesh Council, consisting mostly of representatives of Zila Parishads, which functions as an advisory body on important matters relating to the administration of the Union Territory.

Some members of the Pradesh Council are also associated with the Chief Commissioner in the day-to-day administration as Counsellors. It is proposed to replace the Pradesh Council by a Legislative Assembly and the Counsellors by a council of Ministers as in certain other Union Territores specified in Article 239A of the Constitution. The Act, therefore, seeks to include Arunachal Pradesh in that Article.

Under Article 240 of the Constitution, the President is empowered to make regulations for the Union Territory of Arunachal Pradesh. With the Constitution of a Legislative Assembly for the Union Territory, it is proposed to provide that, as in the case of other Union Territories with

Legislatures, this power may be exercised only when the Assembly is either dissolved or its functioning remains suspended. The Act seeks to amend Article 240 also to achieve this object.

38. THE CONSTITUTION (THIRTY-EIGHTH AMENDMENT) ACT, 1975

The Constitution (Thirty-eighth Amendment) Act, 1975 seeks to amend Articles 123, 213, 239B, 352, 356, 359 and 360 of the Constitution. Article 123 empowers the President to promulgate ordinances when both the Houses of Parliament are not in session if he is satisfied that circumstances exist rendering it necessary to take immediate action. Corresponding power have been conferred on the Administrator under Article 239B when the legislature of a Union Territory is not in session.

On the plain language of Articles 123, 213 and 239B there is no doubt that the satisfaction mentioned in those Articles is subjective satisfaction and that it is not justiciable. There is no doubt that this was also the intention of the makers of the Constitution. However, litigation is pending involving the justiciability of this issue and contentions are being raised that the issue is subject to judicial scrutiny. To place the matter beyond doubt, it is proposed to provide in the Constitution that the satisfaction of the President, Governor or the Administrator shall be final and conclusive and shall not be questioned in any court on any ground.

Article 352 empowers the President to declare Emergency if he is satisfied that the security of India or any part of it is threatened by war, external aggression or internal disturbance. Article 356 empowers the President to assume to himself the functions of the government of a State if the Constitutional machinery in any State fails and the government in the State cannot be carried on. Likewise Article 360 empowers the President to declare financial emergency if he is satisfied that the financial stability of India is threatened. Here again the issue regarding satisfaction is, on the face of the article, clearly not justiciable. However, as the validity of the proclamation issued under Article 352 has been challenged in several proceedings and as litigation of this nature involves waste of public money and time, it is proposed to amend these three Articles so as to make the satisfaction of the President final and conclusive and not justiciable on any ground.

In regard to Article 352 contentions have been raised in certain writ petitions that while the original proclamation of emergency is in operation no further proclamation could be made thereunder. In order to place the matter beyond doubt, it is proposed to make it clear in Article 352 that the President may issue different proclamations on different grounds whether or not there is a proclamation already in existence and in operation.

When a proclamation of emergency is in operation, the President is empowered under Article 350 of the Constitution to issue an order suspending the right to move any court for the enforcement of such of the rights conferred by Part III as may be mentioned in that order. It was intended that the powers conferred by this Article should be exercised during an emergency according to the needs of the situation. On the other hand, Article 358 renders the provisions of Article 19 automatically inoperative while the proclamation of emergency is in operation and the power to make any law or to take any executive action is not restricted by provisions of that Article. The intention underlying Article 359 appears to be that when an order made under clause (1) of that Article in relation to any of the rights conferred by Part III and mentioned in the orders, the orders so made would have for all practical purposes the same effect in relation to those rights as Article 358 has in relation to Article 19. It is, therefore, proposed not to have any difference in language between Article 358 and the language in respect of those rights only which may be mentioned in the presidential order under clause (1) of Article 359.

The Act seeks to achieve the aforesaid objects.

39. THE CONSTITUTION (THIRTY-NINTH AMENDMENT) ACT, 1975

Article 71 of the Constitution provides that disputes arising out of the election of the President or Vice-President shall be decided by the Supreme Court. The same Article provides that matters relating to their election shall be regulated by a parliamentary law. So far as the Prime Minister or Speaker are concerned, matters relating to their election are regulated by the provisions of Representation of the People Act, 1951. Under this Act the High Court has jurisdiction to try an election petition presented against either of them.

The President, the Vice-President, the Prime Minister or the Speaker are holders of High offices. The President is not answerable to a court of law for anything done while in office in the exercise of his powers. A fortiori, matters relation to his election should not be brought before a court of law but should be entrusted to a forum other than a court.

The same reasoning applies equally to the incumbents of the offices of Vice-President, Prime Minister and Speaker. It is accordingly, proposed to provide that disputes relating to the election of the President and Vice-President shall be determined by a forum as may be determined by a parliamentary law. Similar provisions proposed to be made in case of the election to either House of the Parliament or, as the case may be, to the House of the People of a person holding the office of Prime Minister or the Speaker. It is further proposed to render pending proceedings in respect of such election under the existing law null and void. The Act also provides that this parliamentary law creating a new forum for trial of election matters relating to the incumbents of the high offices above mentioned shall not be called in question in any Court.

Recourse was had in the past to the Ninth Schedule where ever it was found that progressive legislation conceived in the interests of the public was imperilled by litigation. It has become necessary to have course to this device once again now. Between 1971 and 1973, legislation was enacted for nationalising cooking coal and coal mines for conserving these resources in the interests of steel industry. The enactments have been brought before courts on the ground that they are unConstitutional. So is the case of sick textile undertakings which were nationalised in 1974. To prevent smuggling of goods and diversion of foreign exchange which affected national economy, Parliament enacted legislations which again have been challenged in the Supreme Court and the High Court. These and other important and special enactments which it is considered necessary should have the Constitutional protection under Article 31B are proposed to be included in the Ninth Schedule. Certain State legislations relating to land reform and ceiling on agricultural land holdings have already been included in the Ninth Schedule. Certain amendments made to these legislations also require protection of the provision of Article 31B.

The Act seeks to give effect to the above objects.

40. THE CONSTITUTION (FORTIETH AMENDMENT) ACT, 1976

Under Article 297 of the Constitution, all lands, minerals and other things of the value underlying the ocean within the territorial waters or the continental shelf of India vest in the Union to be held for the purposes of the Union. India has sovereign rights over the resources of the exclusive economic zone and is entitled to exercise jurisdiction in respect of certain other matters. It is proposed to amend Article 297 of the Constitution so as to provide that all lands, minerals and other things of value underlying the ocean within the exclusive economic zone of India shall also vest in the Union and be held for the purposes of the Union. At present, the limits of territorial waters and the continental shelf are determined by Proclamation issued by the President. It is proposed that the limits of the territorial waters, the continental shelf, the exclusive economic zone and the maritime zones of India shall be as specified from time to time by or under law made by Parliament.

Recourse was had in the past to the Ninth Schedule whenever it was found that progressive legislation conceived in the interest of the public was imperilled by litigation. Certain State legislations relating to land reforms and ceiling on agricultural land holdings have already been included in the Ninth Schedule. Certain amendments made to these legislations also require protection of the provisions of the Article 31B as much as in many cases, such enactments have been challenged in courts and courts have granted interim relief which has hampered the implementation of the national land reform policy.

Besides these Acts relating to land reforms certain State enactments relating to private forests require protection of Article 31B as these enactments to end the monopoly of vested interests and forest contractors. Some of such legislations have been challenged in courts and as the courts have granted interim reliefs staying the operation of these enactments, the State Governments have not been able to implement these legislations.

Certain Central laws like the Smugglers and Foreign Exchange Manipulatiors (Forfeiture of Property) Act, 1976, the Urban Land (Ceiling and Regulation) Act, 1976; the Essential Commodities Act, 1955 and certain provisions of the Motor Vehicles Act, 1939 require protection of Article 31B. If these legislations are allowed to be challenged in courts of law hereby delaying the implementation of these laws, the very purpose of enacting these laws would be frustrated and the national economy may be severely affected.These and other important and special enactments which it is considered necessary should have the Constitutional protection, are proposed to be included in the Ninth Schedule.

The Bill seeks to give effect to the above objects.

41. *THE CONSTITUTION (FORTY-FIRST AMENDMENT) ACT, 1976*

Article 316 (2) of the Constitution provides that the Chairman and Members of a State Public Service Commission or Joint Commission shall retire at 60 or hold office for a term of six years from the date on which they enter service, whichever is earlier. This was the position when the Constitution came into force. Subsequently, while the age of retirement of the High Court Judges was raised to 62, that of the Chairman and the Members of the State Public Service Commissions remained unchanged.

The same Article provides that one-half of the members of every Public Service Commission shall be employees of the Government of India or the Government of a State. The age of retirement of Government employees was 55 originally but was later raised to 58 in the case of All-India Services, Central Government servants and the Government servants of several States. Membership of the Commission is no attraction, therefore, to them as they will have only two years to serve on the Commission which position is not desirable from the point of view of the efficient functioning of the Commission.

Academicians like University Professors are eligible for appointment to the State Public Service Commissions. The age of retirement of University Professors has been recently raised to 60. It will not be attractive for these academicians to serve on a Public service Commission if the age of retirement remains sixty. The Chairman/ Members of a State Public Service Commission are forbidden to serve under the Government of India or a State Government after retirement. Consequently, no eminent academician will be eager to accept appointment on the Commission unless the age of retirement is raised to 62.

The proposal is to raise the age of retirement of the Chairman and Members of the State Public Service Commission to 62. The Bill seeks to give effect to this proposal.

42. *THE CONSTITUTION (FORTY-SECOND AMENDMENT) ACT, 1976*

A Constitution to be living must be growing . If the impediments to the growth of the Constitution are not removed, the Constitution will suffer a virtual atrophy. The question of amending the Constitution for removing the difficulties which have arisen in achieving the objective of socio-economic revolution, which would end poverty and ignorance and disease and inequality of opportunity, has been engaging the active attention of Government and the public for some years now.

The democratic institutions provided in the Constitution are basically sound and the path for progress does not lie in denigrating any of these institutions. However, there could be no denial that these institutions have been subjected to considerable stresses and strains and that vested interests have been trying to promote their selfish ends to the great detriment of public good.

It is, therefore, proposed to amend the Constitution to spell out expressly the high ideals of socialism, secularism and the integrity of the nation, to make the directive principles more comprehensive and give them precedence over those fundamental rights which have been allowed to be relied upon to frustrate socio-economic reforms for implementing the directive principles. It is also proposed to specify the fundamental duties of citizens and make special provisions for dealing with anti-national activities, whether by individuals or associations.

Parliament and the State Legislatures embody the will of the people and the essence of democracy is that the will of the people should prevail. Even though Article 368 of the Constitution is clear and categoric with regard to all inclusive nature of the amending power, it is considered necessary to put the matter beyond doubt. It is proposed to strengthen the presumption in favour of the constitutionality of legislation enpacted by Parliament and State Legislature by providing for a requirement as to the minimum number of Judges for determining questions as to the Constitutionality of laws and for a special majority of not less than two-thirds for declaring any law to be constitutionally invalid. It is also proposed to take away the jurisdiction of High Courts with regard to determination of Constitutional validity of central laws and confer exclusive jurisdiction in this behalf on the Supreme Court so as to avoid multiplicity of proceedings with regard to validity of the some Central laws in different High Courts and the consequent possibility of the Central law being valid in one State and in valid in another State.

To reduce the mounting arrears in High Courts and to secure the speedy disposal of service matters, revenue matters and certain other matters of special importance in the context of the socio-economic development and progress. It is considered expedient to provide for administrative and other tribunals for dealing with such matters while preserving the jurisdiction of the Supreme Court in regard to such matters under Article 136 of the Constitution. It is also necessary to make certain modifications in the writ jurisdiction of the High Courts under Article 226.

43. *THE CONSTITUTION (FORTY-THIRD AMENDMENT) ACT, 1977*

The Constitution (Forty-second Amendment) Act, 1976, inserted various Articles in the Constitution to curtail, both directly and indirectly, the jurisdiction of the Supreme Court and the High Courts to review the Constitutionality of laws. Article 32A barred the Supreme Court from considering the Constitutional validity of any State law in proceedings for the enforcement of fundamental rights unless the Constitutional validity of any Central law was also in issue in such proceedings. Article 131A gave to the Supreme Court exclusive jurisdiction to decide the Constitution validity of a Central law and thus deprived the High Courts of their jurisdiction in respect of the same. Article 144 A provided that the minimum number of Judges of the Supreme Court who shall sit for the purpose of determining the Constitutional validity of any Central law or State law shall be seven and required a special majority of two-thirds for the invalidation of such law. Article 226A barred the High Courts from deciding the validity of any Central law and Article 228A required that there should be a Bench of at least five Judges for determining the constitutional validity of any State law and prescribed a special majority for a judgment invalidating such a law.

It is considered that Articles 32A, 131A and 228A cause hardship to persons living in distant parts in India. Further, Article 32A would lead to multiplicity of proceedings as ceases relating to the validity of a State law which could be disposed of by the Supreme Court itself have to be heard first by the High Court. The minimum number of Judges in every case wherein the Constitutional validity of a law is involved, however, unsubstantial the challenge might be, results in valuable judicial time being lost in hearing and rejecting submissions that have no substance. The Supreme Court has, in *M/s Mistrilal Jain* v. *The State of Orissa* and others (AIR 1977 SC 1686) expressed the hope that Article 144 A would engage the prompt attention of Parliament and would be amended so as to leave to the court itself the duty to decide how large a Bench should decide any particular case. In fact, a number of cases have been held up in the Supreme Court and High Courts as a result of the aforementioned Articles.

It is, therefore, proposed to omit Articles 32A, 131A, 144A, 226A and 228A. It is also proposed to make special provisions to enable the Supreme Court and the High Courts to deal with pending cases in the same manner as if the said Articles had been omitted with effect from the Ist February, 1977 (viz., the date on which those Articles were brought into force). Necessary consequential amendments to Articles 145, 228 and 366 are also proposed to be made.

Article 31 D confers special power on Parliament to enact certain laws in respect of anti-national activities. It is considered that these powers of Parliament to make laws for dealing with anti- national activities and anti-national associations are of a sweeping nature and are capable of abuse. It is, therefore, proposed to omit Article 31D.

The Bill seeks to achieve the above objects.

44. *THE CONSTITUTION (FORTY-FORTH AMENDMENT) ACT, 1978*

Recent experience has shown that the fundamental rights, including those of life and liberty, granted to citizens by the Constitution are capable of being taken away by a transient majority. It is, therefore, necessary to provide adequate safeguards against the recurrence of such a contingency in the future and to ensure to the people themselves an effective voice in determining the form of government under which they are to live. This is one of the primary objects of this Bill.

2. It is, therefore, proposed to provide that certain changes in the Constitution which would have the effect of impairing its secular or democratic character, abridging or taking away fundamental rights prejudicing or impeding free and fair elections on the basis of adult suffrage and compromising the independence of judiciary, can be made only if they are approved by the people of India by a majority of votes at a referendum in which at least fifty-one per cent, of the electorate participate. Article 368 is being amended to ensure this.

In view of the special position sought to be given to fundamental rights, the right to property, which has been the occasion for more than one amendment of the Constitution, would cease to be a fundamental right and become only a legal right. Necessary amendments for this purpose are being made to Article 19 and Article 31, is being deleted. It would, however, be ensured that the removal of property from the list of fundamental rights would not affect the right of minorities to establish and administer educational institutions of their choice.

Similarly, the right of persons holding land for personal cultivation and within the ceiling limit to receive compensation at the market value would not be affected. Property, while ceasing to be a fundamental right, would, however, be given express recognition as a legal right, provision being made that no person shall be deprived of his property save in accordance with law.

A Proclamation of Emergency under Article 352 has virtually the effect of amending the Constitution by converting it for the education into that of a Unitary State and enabling the rights of the citizen to move the courts for the enforcement of fundamental rights- including the right to life and liberty - to be suspended. Adequate safeguards are, therefore, necessary to ensure that this power is properly exercised and is not abused. It is, therefore, proposed that a Proclamation of Emergency can be issued only when the security of India or any part of its territory threatened by war or external aggression or by armed rebellion. Internal disturbance not amounting to armed rebellion would not be a ground for the issue of a Proclamation.

Further, in order to ensure that a Proclamation is issued only after due consideration, it is sought to be provided that Emergency can be proclaimed only on the basis of written advice tendered to the President by the Cabinet. In addition, as a Proclamation of Emergency virtually has the effect of amending the Constitution, it is being provided that the proclamation would have to be approved by the two Houses of Parliament same majority which is necessary to amend the Constitution and such approval would have to be given within a period of one month. Any such Proclamation would be in force only for a period of six months and can be continued only by further resolutions passed by the same majority. The Proclamation would also cease to be in operation if a resolution disapproving the continuance of the Proclamation is passed by Lok Sabha. Ten per cent or more of the members of Lok Sabha can requisite a special meeting for considering a resolution for disapproving Proclamation.

As a further check against the misuse of the Emergency provisions and to put the right to life and liberty on a secure footing, it would be provided that the power to suspend the right to move the Court for the enforcement of a fundamental right cannot be exercised in respect of the fundamental right to life and liberty. The right to liberty is further strengthened by the provision that a law for preventive detention cannot authorise, in any case, detention for a longer period than two months, unless an Advisory Board has reported that there is sufficient cause for such detention.

An additional safeguard would be provided by the requirement that the Chairman of an Advisory Board shall be a serving Judge of the appropriate High Court and that the Board shall be constituted in accordance with the recommendation of the Chief Justice of High Court.

A special provision being made guaranteeing the right of the media to report freely and without censorship the proceedings in Parliament and the State Legislatures. The provision with regard to the breakdown of the Constitutional machinery in the States is being amended so as to provide that a Proclamation issued under Article 356 would be in forece only for a period of six months in the instance and that it cannot exceed one year ordinarily. However, if a Proclamation of Emergency is in forece operation and the Election Commission certifies that the extension of the President's rule beyond a period of one year is necessary on account of difficulties in holding elections to the Legislative Assembly of the State concerned, the period of operation of the Proclamation can be extended beyond one year. This is subject to the existing limit of three years. These changes would ensure that democratic rule is restored to a State after the minimum period which will be necessary for holding elections.

With a view to avoiding delays. It is proposed to amend Articles 132, 133 and 134 and insert a new Article 134A to provide that a High Court should consider the question of granting a certificate for appeal to Supreme Court immediately after the delivery of the judgments, decree, final order or sentence concerned on the basis of an oral application by a party or, if the High Court deems fit so to do so, on its own motion. Cases of special leave to appeal by Supreme Court will be left to be regulated exclusively by Article 136.

The other amendments proposed in the Bill are mainly for removing or correcting the distortions which came into the Constitution by reason of amendments enacted during the period of the internal Emergency.

The Bill seeks to achieve the above objects.

45. THE CONSTITUTON (FORTY-FIFTH AMENDMENT) ACT, 1980

Article 334 of the Constitution lays down that the provisions of the Constitution relating to the reservation of seats for the

Scheduled Castes and Scheduled Tribes and the representation of the Anglo- Indian community by nomination in the Lok Sabha and in the Legislative Assemblies of the State shall cease to have effect on the expiration of a period of thirty years from the commencement of the Constitution. Although the Scheduled Castes and the Scheduled Tribes have made considerable progress in the last thirty years, the reasons which weighed the Constituent Assembly in making provisions with regard to the aforesaid reservation of seats and nomination of members, have not ceased to exist. It is, therefore, proposed to continue the reservation for the Scheduled Castes and Scheduled Tribes and the representation of the Anglo-Indians by nomination for a further period of ten years.

The Bill seeks to achieve the above object.

46. THE CONSTITUTION (FORTY- SIXTH AMENDMENT) ACT, 1982

Sales tax laws enacted in pursuance of the Government of India Act, 1935 as also the laws relating to sales tax passed after the coming into force of the Constitution proceeded on the footing that the expression "sale of goods", having regard to the rule as to broad interpretation of entries in the legislative lists, would be given a wider connotation. However, in Gannon Dunkerley's case (AIR 1958 SC 560). The Supreme Court held that the expression "sale of goods" as used in the entries in the Seventh Schedule to the Constitution has the same meaning as in the Sale of Goods Act, 1930. This decision related to works contracts.

2. By a series of subsequent decision, the Supreme Court has, on the basis of the decision in Gannon Dunkerley's case, held various other transactions which resemble, in substance, transactions by way of sales, to be not liable to sales tax. As a result of these decisions, a transaction, in order to be subject to the levy of sales tax under entry 92 A of the Union List or entry 54 of the State List, should have the following ingredients. namely, parties competent to contract, mutual assent and transfer of property in goods from one of the parties to the contract to the other party thereto for a price.
3. This position has resulted in scope for avoidance of tax in various ways. An example of this is the practice of inter-State consignment transfers, i.e., transfer of goods from head office or a principle in one State to a Branch or agent in another State

or *vice versa* or transfer of goods on consignment account, to avoid the payment of sales tax on Inter-State sales under the Central Sales Tax Act. While in the case of a works contract, if the contract treats the sale of materials separately from the cost of the labour, the sale of materials would be taxable, but in the case of an indivisible works contract, it is not possible to levy sales tax on the transfer of property in the goods involved in the execution of such contract as it has been held that there is no sale of the materials as such and the property in them does not pass as movables. Though practically the purchaser in a hire- purchase agreement gets the goods on the date of the hire-purchase, it has been held that there is sale only when the purchaser exercises the option to purchase at a much later date and therefore only the depreciated value of he goods involved in such transaction at the time, the option to purchase is exercised becomes assessable to sales tax. Similarly, while sale by a registered club or other association of persons (the club or association of persons having corporate status) to its members is taxable, sales by an unincorporated club or association of persons to its members is not taxable as such club or association, in law, has no separate existence from hat of the members. In the *Associated Hotels of India* case (AIR 1972 SC 1131), the Supreme Court held that there is no sale involved in the supply of food or drink by a hotelier to a person lodged in the Hotel.

4. In the *New India Sugar Mills* case, AIR 1963 SC 1207, the Supreme Court took the view that in the transfer of controlled commodities in pursuance of a direction under a Control Order, the element of volition by the seller, or mutual assent, is absent and , therefore, there is no sale as defined in the Sale of Goods Act, 1930. However, in *Oil and Natural Gas Commission* v *State of Bihar* AIR 1976 SC 2470, the Supreme Court had occasion to consider its earlier decisions with regard to the liability of transfers of controlled commodities to be charged to sales tax. The Supreme Court held that where there are any statutory compulsions, the statute itself should be treated as supplying the consensus and furnishing the modality of the consensus. In *Vishnu Agencies* v *Commercial Tax Officer* AIR 1978 SC 449, six of the seven Judges concurrred in over-ruling the decision in New India Sugar Mills case while the seventh Judge held

the case to be distinguishable. It is, therefore, considered desirable to put the matter beyond any doubt.

5. The various problems connected with the power of the States to levy a tax on the sale of goods and with the Central Sales Tax Act, 1956 were referred to the Law Commission of India. The Commission considered these matters in their Sixty-first Report and, recommended *inter alia* certain amendments in the Constitution if as a matter of administative policy, it is decided to levy tax on transactions of the nature mentioned in the preceding paragraphs.
6. Device by way of lease of films has also been resulting in avoidance of sales tax. The main right in regard to a film relates to its exploitation and after exploitation for a certain period of time, in most cases, the film ceases to have any value. It is, therefore, seen that instead of resorting to the outright sale of a film, only a lease or transfer of the right to exploitation is made.
7. There were reports from State governments to whom revenues from sales tax have been assigned, as to the large scale avoidance of Central sales tax levable on inter- State sale of goods through the device of consignment of goods from one State to another and as to the leakage of local sales tax in works contracts, hire purchase transactions, lease of films, etc. Though Parliament could levy a tax on these transactions, as tax on sales has all along been treated as an item of revenue to be assigned to the States, in regard to these transactions which resemble sales also, it is considered that the same policy should be adopted.
8. Besides the above mentioned matters, a new problem has arisen as a result of the decision of the Supreme Court in *Northern India Caterers (India) Ltd.* vs. *Lt. Governor of Delhi* AIR 1978 SC 1591 States have been proceeding on the basis that the *Associated Hotels of India* case was applicable only to supply of food or drink by a hotelier to a person, lodged in the hotel and that tax was leviable on the sale of foodstuffs by a restaurant. But over ruling the decision of the Delhi High Court, the Supreme Court has held in the above case that service of meals whether in a hotel or restaurant does not constitute a sale of food for the purpose of lavy of sales tax but must be regarded as the rendering of a service in the satisfaction of a human need or ministering to the bodily want of human beings. It

would not make any difference whether the visitor to the restaurant is charged for the meal as a whole or according to each dish separately.

9. It is, therefore, proposed to suitably amend the Constitution to include in Article 366 a definition of "tax on the sale or purchase of goods" by inserting a new clause (29A). The definition would specifically include within the scope of that expression tax on—
   (i) transfer for consideration of controlled commodities;
   (ii) the transfer of property in goods involved in the execution of a works contract;
   (iii) delivery of goods on hire-purchase or any system of payment by instalments;
   (iv) transfer of the right to use any goods for any purchase for cash, deferred payment or other valuable consideration;
   (v) the supply of goods by an unincorporated associated or body of persons to a member thereof for cash, deferred payment or other valuable consideration,
   (vi) for supply, by way of or as part of any service, of food or any drink for cash, deferred payment or other valuable consideration. (See clause 4).
10. A new entry is sought to be inserted in the Union List in the Seventh Schedule, as entry 92-B to enable the levy of tax on the consignment of goods where such consignment takes place in the course of inter- State trade or commerce. (See clause 5).
11. Clause (1) of Article 269 is proposed to be amended so that the tax levied on the consignment of goods in the course of inter-state trade of commerce shall be assigned to the States. Clause (3) of that Article is proposed to be amended to enable Parliament to formulate by law principles for determining when a consignment of goods takes place in the course of inter- state trade or commerce. (See clause 2).
12. Clause (3) of Article 286 is proposed to be amended to enable Parliament to specify, by law, restrictions and conditions in regard to the system of levy, rates and other incidents of the tax on the transfer of goods involved in the execution of a works contract, on the delivery of goods on hire purchase or any system of payment by instalments and on the right to use any goods. (See clause 3).

13. The proposed amendments would help in the augmentation of the State revenues to a considerable extent. Clause 6 of the Bill seeks to validate laws levying tax on the supply of food or drink for consideration and also the collection or recoveries made by way of tax under any such law. However, no sales tax will be payable on food or drink supplied by a hotelier to a person lodged in the hotel during the period from the date of the judgement in the *Associated Hotels of India* case and the commencement of the present Amendment Act if the conditions mentioned in sub- clause (2) of clause 6 of the Bill are satisfied. In the case of food or drink supplied by restaurants, this relief will be available only in respect of the period after the date of judgement in the Northern India Caterers (India) Limited case and the commencement of the present Amendment Act.
14. The Bill seeks to achieve the above objects.

48. THE CONSTITUTION (FORTY-EIGHTH AMENDMENT) ACT, 1984

The Proclamation issued by the President under Article 356 of the Constitution on the 6th day of October,1983 with respect to the State of Punjab cannot be continued in force for more than one year unless the special conditions mentioned in clause (5) of Article 356 of the Constitution are satisfied. Although he Legislative Assembly is in suspended animation and a popular government can be installed, having regard to the prevailing situation in the State, the continuance of the Proclamation beyond 5th October, 1984, it is necessary to amend Article 356 of the Constitution. It is, therefore, proposed to amend clause (5) of Article 356 so as to make the conditions mentioned therein applicable for the purposes of the continuance in force of the said Proclamation up to a period of two years from the date of its issue.

49. THE CONSTITUTION (FORTY-NINTH AMENDMENT) ACT, 1984

The Tripura Legislative Assembly passed a resolution on the 19th March,1982 and again on the 11th February, 1983, urging the Government of India to apply for provisions of the Sixth Schedule to the Constitution to the tribal areas of the State of Tripura. The State Government of Tripura, therefore, recommended amendment of the Constitution for the purpose. Though under the Tripura Tribal Areas Autonomous District Council Act, 1979, an autonomous District council has been functioning in the State, it was considered necessary to give it Constitutional sanctity with a view to meet the aspirations of the tribal population. The Council is expected to ensure rapid development of tribal areas and self-governance by the tribals.

50. THE CONSTITUTION (FIFTIETH AMENDMENT) ACT, 1984

By Article 33 of the Constitution Parliament is empowered to enact laws determining to what extent any of the rights conferred by Part III of the Constitution shall, in their application to the members of the Armed Forces or the Forces charged with the maintenance of public order, be restricted or abrogated soas to ensure the proper discharge of their duties and the maintenance of discipline among them.

2. It is proposed to amend Article 33 so as to bring within its ambit—
   (i) the members of the Forces charged with the protection of property belonging to or in charge or possession of the State; or
   (ii) persons employed in any bureau or other organisation established by the State for purposes of intelligence or counter-intelligence; or
   (iii) persons employed in, or in connection with, the telecommunication systems set up for the purposes of any Force, bureau or organisation.

Experience has revealed that the need for ensuring proper discharge of their duties and the maintenance of discipline among them is of paramount importance in the national interest.

3. The Bill seeks to achieve the above object.

52. THE CONSTITUTION (FIFTY-SECOND AMENDMENT) ACT, 1984

The evil of political defections has been a matter of national concern. If it is not combated, it is likely to undermine the very foundations of our democracy and the principles which sustain it. With this object, an assurance was given in the address by the president to Parliament that the Government intended to introduce in the current session of Parliament an anti-defection Bill. The Bill is meant for outlawing defection and fulfilling the above assurance.

2. The Bill seeks to amend the Constitution to provide that an

elected member of Parliament or a State Legislature, who has been elected as a candidate set up by a political party and a nominated member of Parliament or a State Legislature who is a member of a political party at the time he takes his seat or who becomes a member of political party within six months after he takes his seat would be disqualified on the ground of defection if he voluntarily relinquishes his membership of such plitical party or votes or abstains from voting in such House contrary to any direction of such party or is expelled from such party. An independent member of Parliament or a State Legislature should also be disqualified if he joins any political party after his election. A nominated member of Parliament or a State legislature who is not a member of political party at the time of his nomination and who has not become a member of any political party before the expiry of six months from the date on which he takes his seat shall be disqualified if he joins any political party after the expiry of the said period of six months. The Bill also makes suitable provisions with respect to splits in, and mergers of political parties. A special provision has been included in the Bill to enable a person who has been elected as the presiding officer of a House to sever his connections with his political party. The question as to whether a member of a House of Parliament or State Legislature has become subject to the proposed disqualification will be determined by the presiding officer of the House; where the questions with reference to the presiding officer himself, it will be decided by a member of the House elected by the House in that behalf.

3. The Bill seeks to achieve the above objects.

53. *THE CONSTITUTION (FIFTY-THIRD AMENDMENT) ACT, 1986*

On the 30th June,1986, a Memorandum of Settlement on Mizoram was signed by the Government of India and the Government of Mizoram with the Mizo National Front which envisages among other things, the conferment of statehood on the Union Territory of Mizoram subject to the other stipulations contained in the Memorandum. Paragraph 1.2 of the Memorandum provides that to give effect to the decision "all the necessary legislative and administrative measures will be undertaken, including those for the enactment of Bills for the amendment of the Constitution and other laws for the conferment of statehood as aforesaid, to come into effect on a date to be notified by the Central Government."

2. Paragraph 1.3 of the Memorandum provides as follows:—

Acts of Parliament shall not apply to the new State of Mizoram unless so decided by the Mizora Legislature with regard to—

(i) religious or social practices of Mizos;

(ii) Mizo customary law and procedure;

(iii) administration of civil and criminal justice involving decisions according to Mizo customary law;

(iv) ownership and transfer of land.

The above provision will not, however, apply in the case of Central Acts which are in force in the Union Territory of Mizoram immediately before the date on which the Constitution (Amendment) Act comes into force.

3. The Memorandum also provides that the Legislative Assembly of the proposed new State of Mizoram will consist of not less than forty members.

4. As the matters specified in Paragraph 2 & 3 are peculier to the proposed new State of Mizoram, provisions with respect thereto have to be made in the Constitution itself. This Bill accordingly seeks to amend the Constitution to provide for the aforesaid matters. A separate Bill for the establishment of the new State relatable to Article 2 is also being introduced.

54. *THE CONSTITUTION (FIFTY FOURTH AMENDMENT) ACT, 1986*

The salaries of Judges of the Supreme Court and the High Courts are governed by the provisions of Part D of the Second Schedule to the Constitution of India as indicated below:

Chief Justice of India	Rs. 5,000 per month
Judges of the Supreme Court	Rs. 4, 000 per month
Chief Justice of a High Court	Rs. 4, 000 per month
Judges of a High Court	Rs. 3, 500 per month

2. These salaries have remained static since 1950, despite high inflation and price rise that has taken place during all these years. The Joint Conference of Chief Justices, Chief Ministers and Law Ministers of the States held on 31st August and 1st September, 1985, *inter alia,* discussed and recommended improvement in service conditions of Judges including increase in their salaries, not only to minimise the inflationary pressures

on them but also to attract best talents in the country to man the judicial posts.

3. Having considered all aspects of the matters, it is proposed to increase the salaries of the Judges as detailed below:

Chief Justice of India	Rs. 10,000 per month
Judges of the Supreme Court	Rs. 9,000 per month
Chief Justice of a High Court	Rs. 9,000 per month
Judges of a High Court	Rs. 8,000 per month

4. This Bill seeks to amend Part D of Second Schedule to the Constitution to give effect to the above increases in the salaries of Judges and to make an enabling provision in Articles 125 and 221 to provide for changes in the salaries of Judges in future by Parliament by law.

55. THE CONSTITUTION (FIFTY-FIFTH AMENDMENT) ACT, 1986

The Government of India have proposed to confer statehood on the Union Territory of Arunachal Pradesh. It has also been proposed as follows:—

(i) Having regard to the sensitive location of Arunachal Pradesh, the Governor of the proposed new State shall have special responsibility with respect to law and order in the State and in the discharge of his functions thereto, the Governor shall, after consulting Council of Ministers, exercise his individual judgement as to the action to be taken and this special responsibility of the Governor shall cease when the President by order so directs;

(ii) The Legislative Assembly of the new State of Arunachal Pradesh shall consist of forty members. But as it is proposed to make the existing thirty member Legislative Assembly of the Union Territory of Arunachal Pradesh to be the provisional Legislative Assembly for the new State of Arunachal Pradesh until elections are held on the expiry of the five year term of the existing Assembly, it is proposed to provide that the Legislative Assembly of the new State of Arunachal Pradesh shall consist of not less than thirty members.

2. In order to give effect to the above proposals, it is necessary to make special provisions in the Constitution. The Bill accordingly seeks to amend the Constitution to provide for the aforesaid matters. A separate Bill for the establishment of the new State relatable to Article 2 is also being introduced.

56. *THE CONSTITUTION (FIFTY-SIXTH AMENDMENT) ACT, 1987*

The Government of India have decided to constitute the territories comprised in the Goa district of the Union Territories of Goa, Daman and Diu as the State of Goa and the territories comprised in the Daman and Diu districts of that Union Territory as a new Union Territory of Daman and Diu. In this context, it has been decided that the Legislative Assembly of the new State of Goa shall consist of forty members. The existing Legislative Assembly of the Union Territory of Goa, Daman and Diu has thirty elected members and three nominated members. It is intended to make this Assembly with the exclusion of two members representing Daman and Diu Districts, the provisional Legislative Assembly for the new State of Goa until elections are held on the expiry of the five-year term of the existing Assembly. It is, therefore, necessary to provide that the Legislative Assembly of the new State of Goa shall consist of not less than 30 members.

57. *THE CONSTITUTION (FIFTY-SEVENTH AMENDMENT) ACT, 1987*

The Constitution (Fifty-first Amendment) Act, 1984 was enacted to provide for reservation of seats in the House of the People for the Scheduled Tribes in Nagaland, Meghalaya, Mizoram and Arunachal Pradesh and also for reservation of seats for Scheduled Tribes in Legislative Assemblies of Nagaland and Meghalaya by suitably amending Articles 330 and 332. Even though these States are predominantly tribal areas, the underlying objective of the aforesaid Act was to ensure that the members of the Scheduled Tribes in these areas do not fail to secure a minimal representation because of their inability to compete with the advanced sections of the people.

The Constitution (Fifty- first Amendment) Act, though formally enforced, cannot be fully implemented unless parallel action is taken to determine the seats which are to be reserved for Scheduled Tribes in these areas. The number of seats reserved for Scheduled Castes and Scheduled Tribes in the Legislative Assembly of any state under Article 332 of the Constitution will have to be determined having regard to the provisions of Article 332(3) of the Constitution. However, in view of the historical background with respect to the areas comprised in the North-Eastern States, the circumstances obtaining in these areas in the State of development of the Scheduled Tribes in these areas and other relevant considerations, it is considered necessary to provide for special arrangements with regard to the reservation for Scheduled Tribes in these areas for a temporary period so as to facilitate easy transition of these areas to the normal arrangements as envisaged in the Constitution. Hence this Act to further Article 332 of the Constitution for making temporary provision, until the re-adjustment of seats on the basis of the first census after the year 2000 under Article 170 of the Constitution for these States, for the determination of the number of seats reserved for Scheduled Tribes.

58. THE CONSTITUTION (FIFTY-EIGHTH AMENDMENT) ACT, 1987

The Constitution of India was adopted by the Constituent Assembly in English. A Hindi translation of the Constitution, signed by the members of the Constituent Assembly, was also published in 1950 under the authority of the President of the Constituent Assembly in accordance with a resolution adopted by that Assembly.

2. There has been a general demand for the publication of an authoritative text of the Constitution in Hindi incorporating there in all the subsequent amendments. It is also imperative to have an authoritative text of the Constitution for facilitating its use in the legal process. Any Hindi version of the Constitution should not only conform to the Hindi translation published by the Constituent Assembly, but should also be in conformity with the language, style and terminology adopted in the authoritative texts of Central Acts in Hindi. It is, therefore, proposed to amend the Constitutions so as to empower the president of India to publish under his authority the translation of the Constitution in Hindi signed by the members of the Constituent Assembly with such modifications as may be necessary to bring it in conformity with the language, style and terminology adopted in the authoritative texts of Central Acts in the Hindi language. The President would also be authorised to publish the translation in Hindi of every amendment of the Constitution made in English.

3. The Bill seeks to achieve the aforesaid objects.

59. THE CONSTITUTION (FIFTY-NINTH AMENDMENT) ACT, 1988

Unless clause (51 of Article 356 of the Constitution, a resolution approving the continuance in force of a Presidential Proclamation issued under clause (1) of that Article beyond a period of one year cannot be passed by either House of Parliament unless the two conditions specified in that cluase are met. The one year period in the case of the Proclamation made with respect to the State of Punjab is due to expire on the 10th May, 1988. In view of the continued disturbed situation in Punjab, escalation in the activities of terrorists and anti-national forces resulting in the death of innocent men, women and children and of the fact that the Punjab State Legislative Assembly had to be dissolved because of the virtual impossibility of forming a popular government in the prevailing circumstances, the continuance in force of the said Proclamation beyond the period of one year may be necessary in Punjab. Article 356 (5) of the Constitution is therefore, proposed to be amended so as to facilitate the extension of the said Proclamation, if necessary, up to a period of three years as permissible under clause (4) of that Article.

The continuance of the Proclamation after the 10th May, 1988 may not, it is felt, be effective as terrorist activities had been on the increase. It may be necessary to invoke the provisions of Article 352 of the Constitution to declare a partial Emergency either in the whole of the State of Punjab or in particular districts of the State. If such a situation arises, the expression "armed rebellion" included in that Article as one of the grounds for declaration of Emergency (which alone could be resorted to in the case of an Internal Emergency) may not be appropriate in the prevailing situation in Punjab to declare a Proclamation in the State. It is, therefore, felt that Article 352 may be suitably amended in its application to the state of Punjab to include "internal disturbance" as one of the grounds that the integrity of India is threatened by internal disturbance in any part of the territory of, India so as to facilitate the taking of action under that Article if it becomes necessary at a future date. The expression "internal disturbance" was one of the grounds included in that Article from the commencement of the Constitution till it was amended by the Constitution (Forty-fourth Amendment) Act, 1978. Consequentially, Articles 358 and 359 are also proposed to be amended so as to provide for the automatic suspension of Article 19 of the Constitution and the issuing of an order by the President suspending the operation of any of the Constitution and the other provisions contained in Part III (except Article 20) under Article 359, if and when a Proclamation of Emergency on the ground of internal disturbance is issued in relation to the whole or any part of the State of Punjab.

As the proposed amendments are only for the purpose of curbing the terrorist activities in the State of Punjab more effectively, the powers that are proposed to be conferred by these amendments would not be resorted to for any period beyond what is absolutely necessary for achieving the aforesaid object. Accordingly, the amendments proposed in Articles 352, 358 and 359 have been made to be operative only for a period of two years from the commencement of this Amendment.

The Bill seeks to achieve the aforesaid objects.

60. THE CONSTITUTION (SIXTIETH AMENDMENT) ACT, 1988

Clause (2) of Article 276 of the Constitution specified that the total amount payable in respect of any one person to the State or to any one municipality, district board, local board or other local authority in a State by way of taxes on professions, trades, callings and employments leviable by a State Legislature under clause (1) of that Article shall not exceed two hundred and fifty rupees per annum. The proviso to that clause, however, enables the continuance of the levy of such tax at a rate exceeding two hundred and fifty rupees per annum in any State, municipality, etc., if in the financial year immediately preceding the commencement of the Constitution there was in force in that State, municipality, etc., any such tax exceeding that rate.

2. Some of the State Governments have represented that this ceiling of two hundred and fifty rupees which was fixed in 1949, needs to be revised upwards taking into consideration the price rise and other factors. It is also pointed out that the profession tax has, at present, become almost regressive because of the ceiling since even people with high salaries have to pay this tax at only the maximum amount of two hundred and fifty rupees per annum. The upward revision of profession tax will also help the State Governments in raising additional resources.

3. It is accordingly proposed to amend clause (2) of Article 276 of the Constitution to increase the ceiling of profession tax from

two hundred and fifty rupees per annum to two thousand and five hundred rupees per annum. As the proviso to this clause is no longer relevant, it is proposed to omit it.

4. The Bill seeks to achieve the above objects.

61. *THE CONSTITUTION (SIXTY-FIRST AMENDMENT) ACT, 1988*

Article 326 of the Constitution provides that the elections to the House of the People and to the Legislative Assembly of every State shall be on the basis of adult suffrage, that is to say, a person should not be less than 21 years of age. It has been found that many of the countries have specified 18 years as the voting age. In our country some of the State Governments have adopted 18 years of age for elections to the local authorities. The present-day youth are literate and enlightened and the lowering of the voting age would provide to the unrepresented youth of the country an opportunity to give vent to their feelings and help them become a part of the political process. The present-day youth are very much politically conscious. It is, therefore, proposed to reduce the voting age from 21 years to 18 years.

2. The Bill seeks to achieve the above object.

62. *THE CONSTITUTION (SIXTY-SECOND AMENDMENT) ACT, 1989*

Article 334 of the Constitution lays down that the provisions of the Constitution relating to the reservation of seats for the Scheduled Castes and the Scheduled Tribes and the representation of the Anglo-Indian community by nomination in the Lok Sabha and in the Legislative Assemblies of the States shall cease to have effect on the expiration of a period of forty years from the commencement of the Constitution. Although the Scheduled Castes and the Scheduled Tribes have made some progress in the last forty years, the reasons which weighed with the Constituent Assembly in making provisions with regard to the aforesaid reservation of seats and nomination of members, have not creased to exist. It is, therefore, proposed to continue the reservation for the Scheduled Castes and the Scheduled Tribes and the representation of the Anglo Indians by nomination for a further period of ten years.

2. The Bill seeks to achieve the above object.

63. *THE CONSTITUTION (SIXTY-THIRD AMENDMENT) ACT, 1989*

The Constitution (Fifty-ninth Amendment) Act, 1988 was passed in March 1988, making certain changes in regard to making a Proclamation of Emergency in Punjab and to the duration of President's rule in that State.

2. On reconsideration, the Government is of the view that there is no need for the special powers in regard to the Proclamation of Emergency in Punjab as envisaged in the amendment. It is also considered that the amendment to Article 356 made by the said Act is no longer needed. It is, therefore, considered that the amendments made by the aforesaid Act should be repealed.

3. As regards President's Proclamation issued on 11. 5. 1987 under clause (1) of Article 356 of the Constitution, this has been approved by both the Houses of Parliament in October, 1989. The Bill seeks to achieve the above objects.

64. *THE CONSTITUTION (SIXTY-FOURTH AMENDMENT) ACT, 1990*

Under clause (4) of Article 456 of the Constitution, no Proclamation issued under that Article and approved by both the Houses of Parliament shall remain in force for more than three years. However, under clause (5) of the said Article a resolution approving the continuance in force of a Proclamation issued under clause (1) of that Article beyond a period of one year cannot be passed by either House of Parliament unless the two conditions relating to a Proclamation of Emergency being in operation in whole or any part of the State and the certificate by the Election Commission that the continuation of the Proclamation issued under clause (1) is necessary on account of difficulties in holding general elections to the Legislative Assembly of the State as specified in that clause are met. The three year period in the case of Proclamation issued on 11th May, 1987 with respect to the State of Punjab would be over on 10th May, 1990 and the said two conditions are also not fulfilled. The prevailing circumstances in the State do not hold out good prospects for free and peaceful elections to the State Legislative Assembly. The representatives of various political parties who attended the All-Party Meeting convened by the Governor of Punjab at Chandigarh recently were also of the view that congenial conditions should be created first before holding the elections to the State Legislative Assembly. Clause (4) and (5) of Article 356 of the Constitution are, therefore, proposed to be amended so as to facilitate the extension of the said Proclamation upto a total period of three years and six months in relation to the State of Punjab.

2. The Bill seeks to achieve the above objects.

65. *THE CONSTITUTION (SIXTY-FIFTH AMENDMENT) ACT, 1990*

Article 338 of the Constitution provides for a Special Officer for the Scheduled Castes and Schedules Tribes under the Constitution and to report to the President on their working. It is felt that a high level five member Commission under Article 338 will be a more effective arrangement in respect of the Constitutional safeguards for Scheduled Castes and Scheduled Tribes than a single Special Officer as at present. It is also felt that it is necessary to elaborate the functions of the said Commission so as to cover measures that should be taken by the Union or any State for the effective implementation of those safeguards and other measures for the protecton, welfare and socio- economic development of the Scheduled Castes and Scheduled Tribes and to entrust to the Commission such other functions in relation to the protection, welfare and development and advancement of the Scheduled Castes and Scheduled Tribes as the President may, subject to any law made by Parliament , by rule specify. It is also felt that the report of the said Commission shall be laid before Parliament and the Legislature of the States.

2. The Bill seeks to achieve the aforesaid objects.

66. *THE CONSTITUTION (SIXTY- SIXTH AMENDMENT) ACT, 1990*

Article 31B of the Constitution confers on the enactments included in the Ninth Schedule to the Constitution, immunity from legal challenge on the ground that they violate the fundamental rights enshrined in Part III of the Constitution.

2. In the past, whenever it was found that progressive legislation, conceived in the interest of the public was imperilled by litigation, recourse was taken to the Ninth Schedule. Several

State enactments relating to land reforms and ceiling on agricultural land holdings have already been included in the Ninth Schedule. Since the government is commited to give importance to land reforms, it is decided to include all land reforms laws in the Ninth Schedule so that they are not challenged before the courts. The State Governments of Andhra Pradesh, Bihar, Gujarat, Himachal Pradesh, Karnataka, Kerala, Madhya Pradesh, Maharashtra, Orissa, Rajasthan, Uttar Pradesh, West Bengal, Tamil Nadu and administration of the Union Territory of Pondicherry have suggested the including of some of their Acts relating to land reforms in the Ninth Schedule.

3. Since the amendment to Acts which are already placed in the Ninth Schedule are not automatically immunized from legal challenge, some amending Acts are also proposed to be included in the Ninth Schedule. The Acts which are proposed to be included in the Ninth Schedule have been examined. In order to ensure that implementation of these Acts is not adversely affected by litigation, it is proposed to include them in the Ninth Schedule.
4. The Bill seeks to achieve the above object.

67. *THE CONSTITUTION (SIXTY-SEVENTH AMENDMENT) ACT, 1990*

Under clause (4) of Article 356 of the Constitution, no Proclamation issued under that Article and approved by both the Houses of Parliament shall remain in force for more than three years. However, under clause (5) of the said Article, a resolution approving the continuance in force of a Proclamation issued under clause (1) of that Article beyond a period of one year cannot be passed by either House of Parliament unless the two conditions relating to a Proclamation of Emergency being in operation in the whole or any Proclamation issued under clause (1) is necessary on account of difficulties in holding general elections to the Legislative Assembly of the State as specified in that clause are met. The three year period in the case of Proclamation issued on 11th May, 1987 with respect to the State of Punjab was extended to three years and six months by the Constitution (Sixty-fourth Amendment) Act, 1990 and clause (5) of Article 356 was also suitably amended by that Act in the expectation that it would be possible to hold elections to the Legislative Assembly of the State. The prevailing circumstances in the State, however, stall do not hold out prospects for free and peaceful elections to the State Legislative Assembly. Clause (4) of Article 356 of the Constitution is, therefore, proposed to be amended so as to facilitate the extension of the said, Proclamation upto a total period of four years in relation to the State of Punjab.

2. The Bill seeks to achieve the above objects.

68. THE CONSTITUTION (SIXTY-EIGHTH AMENDMENT) ACT, 1991

Under clause (4) of Article 356 of the Constitution, no Proclamation issued under that Article and approved by both the Houses of Parliament shall remain in force for more than three years. However, under clause (5) of the said Article, a resolution approving the continuance in force of a Proclamation issued under clause (1) of that Article beyond a period of one year cannot be passed by either House of Parliament unless the two conditions relating to a Proclamation of Emergency being in operation in the whole or any part of the State and the certificate by the Election Commission that the continuation of the Proclamation issued under clause (1) is necessary on account of difficulties in holding general elections to the Legislative Assembly of the State as specified in that clause are met. The three years was extended to three years and six months by the Constitution (Sixty-fourth Amendment) Act, 1990 and clause (5) of Article 356 was also suitably amended by that Act in the expectation that it would be possible to hold elections to the Legislative Assembly of that State. In October, 1990, it was felt that it was not conducive to hold free and fair elections to the Punjab State Legislative Assembly. Therefore, clause (4) of Article 356 was again amended by the Constitution (Sixty-seventh) Amendment Act, 1990 to enable extension of President's proclamation issued on 11th May 1987 for a total period of four years.

2. Despite pressure from the security forces, the terrorist violence has been continuing in Punjab. Therefore, the prevailing circumstances, still do not hold out prospects for fair, free and peaceful elections to the Legislative Assembly of Punjab. Clause

(4) of Article 356 of the Constitution is, therefore, proposed to be amended so as to facilitate the extension of the said Proclamation up to a total period of five years in relation to the State of Punjab.

3. The Bill seeks to achieve the above objects.

69. *THE CONSTITUTION (SIXTY-NINTH AMENDMENT) ACT, 1991*

The question of re-organisation of the administrative set-up in the Union Territory of Delhi has been under the consideration of the Government for some time. The Government of India appointed on 24.12.1987 a Committee to go into the various issues connected with the administration of Delhi and to recommend measures *inter alia* for the streamlining of the administrative set up. The Committee went into the matter in great detail and considered the issues after holding discussions with various individuals, associations, political parties and other experts and taking into account the arrangements in the national capitals of other countries with a federal set-up and also the debates in the Constituent Assembly as also the reports by earlier Committees and Commissions. After such detailed inquiry and examination, it recommended that Delhi should continue to be a Union Territory and provided with a Legislative Assembly and a Council of Ministers responsible to such Assembly with appropriate powers to deal with matters of concern to the common man. The Committee also recommended that with a view to ensuring stability and permanence the arrangements should be incorporated in the Constitution to give the National Capital a special status among the Union Territories.

2. The Bill seeks to give effect to the above proposals.

70. The Constitution (Seventieth Amendment) Act, 1992

While considering the Constitution (Seventy-fourth Amendment) Bill, 1991 and the Government of National Capital Territory Bill, 1991, views were expressed in both the Houses of Parliament in favour of including also the elected members of the Legislative Assemblies of Union Territories in the electoral college for the election of the President under Article 54 of the Constitution. At present, Article 54 relating to the election of the President provides for an electoral college consisting of only the elected members of Parliament as well as the Legislative Assemblies of the State (not Union Territories). Similarly, Article 55 providing for the manner of such election also speaks of Legislative Assemblies of States. Accordingly, an Explanation is sought to be inserted in Article 54 to provide that reference to "State" in Articles 54 and 55 would include the National Capital Territory of Delhi and the Union Territory of Pondicherry for constituting the electoral college for election of the President. This would enable the elected members of the Legislative Assembly created for the Union Territory of Pondicherry under the provisions of Article 239-A and of the proposed Legislative Assembly of the National Capital Territory of Delhi under Article 239-AA to be included in the electoral college.

2. The Constitution (Seventy-fourth Amendment) Bill, 1991 received assent of the President on 21st December, 1991. The said Bill as originally introduced in the Lok Sabha sought to incorporate in Article 239-AA a sub-clause (b) to clause (7). This proposed sub-clause was subsequently dropped since inclusion of the said sub-clause would have necessitated ratification of the bill by Legislatures of not less than one-half of the State and thereby delayed the early Constitution of a Legislative Assembly for the Union Territory of Delhi. The sub-clause (Clause 3 of the present Bill) is sought to be inserted in the present Constitution (Amendment) Bill with retrospective effect, i.e., from 21st December, 1991. Ratification by States is also proposed to be obtained for the clause along with ratification for the other clause of the Bill which seeks to amend Article 54.

3. The Bill seeks to give effect to the above proposals.

71. THE CONSTITUTION (SEVENTY-FIRST AMENDMENT) ACT, 1992

There have been demands for inclusion of certain languages in the Eighth Schedule to the Constitution. It is proposed to include Konkani, Manipuri and Nepali languages in the Eighth Schedule to the Constitution. The Bill seeks to give effect to this decision.

2. The Nepali language is also known in some areas as 'Gorkha Bhasa'. In the Census operations, other nomenclatures such as 'Gurkhiya' or 'Nepali' have also been used.

72. *THE CONSTITUTION (SEVENTY-SECOND AMENDMENT) ACT, 1992*

A Memorandum of Settlement was signed by the Government of India with Tripura National Volunters on the 12th August, 1988. The said document provides for a greater share of tribals in the governance of the State and envisages amendment of the Constitution to provide that, notwithstanding anything contained in the Constitution, the number of seats in the Legislative Assembly of the State of Tripura reserved for Scheduled Tribes shall be increased and number of seats in the existing Assembly of the State shall not be disturbed at any cost until its dissolution.

2. A Government Bill namely the Constitution (Sixty-ninth Amendment) Bill, 1990 to give effect all the above mentioned provisions was introduced in the Ninth Lok Sabha but it lapsed due to the dissolution of the Ninth Lok Sabha.

3. In order to implement the said Memorandum and also to restore confidence amongst tribal people, immediate measures are to be taken by providing minimum number of seats for Scheduled Tribes in the Legislative Assembly of the State of Tripura. immediate measures are to be taken by providing minimum number of seats for Scheduled Tribes in the Legislative Assembly of the State of Tripura.

4. The Bill seeks to achieve the aforesaid object.

73. *THE CONSTITUTION (SEVENTY-THIRD AMENDMENT) ACT*

Though the Panchayati Raj Institutions have been in existence for a long time, it has been observed that these institutions have not been able to acquire the status and dignity of viable and responsive people's bodies due to a number of reasons including absence of regular elections, prolonged supersessions, insufficient representation of weaker sections like Scheduled Castes, Scheduled Tribes and women, inadequate devolution of powers and lack of financial resources.

2. Article 40 of the Constitution which enshrines one ot the Directive Principles of State Policy lays down that the States shall take steps to organise village panchayats and endow them with such powers and authority as may be necessary to

enable them to function as units of self-government. In the light of the experience in the last forty years and in view of the short-comings which have been observed , it is considered that there is an imperative need to enshrine in the Constitution certain basic and essential features of Panchayati Raj Institutions to impact certainty continuity and strength to them.

3. Accordingly, it is proposed to add a new Part relating to Panchayats in the Constitution to provide for among other things, Gram Sabha in a village or group of villages; Constitution of Panchayats at village and other level or levels; direct elections to all seats in Panchayats at the village and intermediate level, if any, and to the offices of Chairpersons of Panchayats at such levels; reservation of seats for the Scheduled Castes and Schedules Tribes in proportion to their population for membership of Panchayats and office of Chairpersons in Panchayats at each level; reservation of not less than one-third of the seats for women; fixing tenure of 5 years for Panchayats and holding elections within a period of 6 months in the event of supersession of any Panchayat; disqualifications for membership of Panchayats; devolution by the State Legislature of powers and responsibilities upon the Panchayats with respect to the preparation of plans for economic development and social justice and for the implementation of development schemes; sound finance of the Panchayats by securing authorisation from State Legislatures for grants-in-aid to the Panchayats from the Consolidated Fund of the State, as also assignment to, or appropriation by, the Panchayats of the revenues of designated taxes, duties, tolls and fees, setting up of a Finance Commission within one year of the proposed amendment and thereafter every 5 years to review the financial position of Panchayats; auditing of accounts of the Panchayats; powers of State Legislature, to make superintendence, direction and control of the chief electoral officer of the State; application of the provisions of the said Part to Union territories; excluding certain States and areas from the application of the provisions of the said Part; continuance of existing laws and Panchayats until one year from the commencement of the proposed amendment and barring interference by courts in electoral matters relating to Panchayats

4. The Bill seeks to achieve the aforesaid objectives. aforesaid objectives.

74. THE CONSTITUTION (SEVENTY-FOURTH AMENDMENT) ACT

In many States local bodies have become weak and ineffective on account of a variety of reasons, including the failure to hold regular elections, prolonged supersessions and inadequate devolution of powers and functions. As a result, Urban Local Bodies are not able to perform effectively as vibrant democratic units of self-government.

2. Having regard to these inadequacies, it is considered necessary that provisions relating to Urban Local Bodies are incorporated in the Constitution particularly for—

(i) putting on a firmer footing the relationship between the State Government and the urban Local Bodies with respect to—
   (a) the functions and taxation powers; and
   (b) arrangements for revenue sharing;
   (ii) ensuring regular conduct of elections;
   (iii) ensuring timely elections in the case of supersession; and
   (iv) providing adequate representation for the weaker sections like Scheduled Castes, Scheduled Tribes and women.

3. Accordingly, it is proposed to add a new part relating to the Urban Local Bodies in the Constitution to provide for—
   (a) Constitution of three types of Municipalities:
   (i) Nagar Panchayats for areas in transition from a rural area to urban area;
   (ii) Municipal Councils for smaller urban areas;
   (iii) Municipal Corporations for larger urban areas;

   The broad criteria for specifying the said areas is being provided in the proposed Article 243 Q;

   (b) composition of Municipalities, which will be decided by the Legislature of a State, having the following features:
   (i) persons to be chosen by direct election;
   (ii) representation of Chairpersons of Committees, if any, at ward or other levels in the Municipalities;
   (iii) representation of persons having special knowledge or experience of Municipal Administration in Municipalities (without voting rights);
   (c) election of Chairpersons of a Municipality in the manner specified in the State law;

(d) Constitution of committees at ward level or other level or levels within the territorial area of a Municipality as may be provided in the State law;

(e) reservation of seats in every Municipality—

(i) for Scheduled Castes and Scheduled Tribes in proportion to their population of which not less than one-third shall be for women;

(ii) for women which shall not less than one-third of the total number of seats;

(iii) in favour of backward class of citizens if so provided by the Legislature of the State;

(iv) for Scheduled Castes, Scheduled Tribes and women in the office of Chairpersons as may be specified in the State law;

(f) fixed tenure of 5 years for the Municipality and re-election within six months of end of tenure. If a Municipality is dissolved before expiration of its duration, elections to be held within a period of six month of its dissolution;

(g) devolution by the State Legislature of powers and responsibilities upon the Municipalities with respect to preparation of plans for economic development and social justice, and for the implementation of development schemes as may be required to enable them to function as institutions of self-government;

(h) levy of taxes and duties by Municipalities, assigning of such taxes and duties to Municipalities by State Governments and for making grants- in-aid by the State to the Municipalities as may be provided in the State law;

(i) a Finance Commission to review the finances of the Municipalities and to recommend principles for—

(1) determining the taxes which may be assigned to the Municipalities;

(2) sharing of taxes between the State and Municipalities;

(3) grants-in-aid to the Municipalities from the Consolidated Fund of the State;

(j) audit of accounts of the Municipal Corporation by the Comptroller and Auditor- General of India and laying of reports before the Legislature of the State and the Municipal Corporation concerned;

(k) making of law by a State Legislature with respet to elections to the Municipalities to be conducted under the superintendence, direction and control of the chief electoral officer of the State;

(l) application of the provisions of the Bill to any Union Territory or part thereof with such modifications as may be specified by the President;

(m) exempting Scheduled areas referred to in clause (1), and tribal areas referred to in clause (2) , of Article 244, from the application of the provisions of the Bill . Extension of provisions of the Bill to such areas may be done by Parliament by law;

(n) disqualifications for membership of a Municipality;

(o) bar of jurisdiction of Courts in matters relating to elections to the Municipalities.

4. The Bill seeks to achieve the aforesaid objectives.

75. *THE CONSTITUTION (SEVENTY-FIFTH AMENDMENT) ACT, 1993*

The operation of the Rent control Legislations, as are today in various States, suffers from major weaknesses and has led to various unintended consequences. Some of the deterious legal consequences include mounting and unending litigation, inability of the courts to provide timely justice, evolution of practices and systems to bypaŝs the operations of rent legislations and steady shrinkage of rental housing market.

2. The Supreme Court, taking note of the precarious state of rent litigation in the country, in the case of *Prabhakaran Nair and others* v *State of Tamil Nadu* (Civil Writ Petition 506 of 1986 and other writs) observed that the Supreme Court and the High Courts should be relieved of the heavy burden of rent litigation. Tiers of appeals should be curtailed. Laws should be simple, rational clear. Litigations must come to end quickly. The idea of a National Rent Tribunal on an all-India basis with quicker procedure should be examined.

3. It is proposed to amend Article 323B in Part XIVA of the Constitution so as to give timely relief to the rent litigants by providing for setting up of State- level Rent Tribunals in order to reduce the tiers of appeals and to exclude the jurisdiction of all courts, except that of the Supreme Court, under Article 136 of the Constitution.

4. The Bill seeks to achieve the aforesaid objects.

76. *THE CONSTITUTION (SEVENTY-SIXTH AMENDMENT) ACT, 1994*

The policy of reservation of seats in Educational Institutions and reservation of appointments or posts in public services for Backward Classes, Scheduled Castes and Scheduled Tribes has had a long history in Tamil Nadu dating back to the year 1921. The extent of reservation has been increased by the State Government from time to time, consistent with the needs of the majority of the people and it has now reached the level of 69 per cent (18 per cent; Scheduled Castes, 1 per cent: Scheduled Tribes and 50 per cent: Other Backward Classes).

2. The Supreme Court delivered its judgment in *Indira Sawhney and Other* v *Union of India and Others* (AIR 1993 SC 477) on 16th November, 1992, holding that the total reservations under Article 16(4) should not exceed 50 per cent.
3. The issue of admission to educational institutions for the academic year 1993-94 came up before the High Court of Madras in a writ petition. The High Court of Madras held that the Tamil Nadu Government could continue its reservation policy as hitherto followed during that academic year and that the quantum of reservation should be brought down to 50 per cent during the academic year 1994-95 . The Government of Tamil Nadu had filed a Special Leave Petition against the decision of the High Court of Madras in order that the present reservation policy of he State Government should be reaffirmed so as to ensure to continue advancement of the Backward classes. However, the Supreme Court of India passed an interim order reiterating that the reservation should not exceed 50 per cent in the matter of admission to educational institutions.
4. In the special Session of Tamil Nadu Legislative Assembly held on 9th November 1993, it had been unanimously resolved to call upon the Central Government to take steps immediately to bring a suitable amendment to the Constitution of India as to enable the Government of Tamil Nadu to continue its policy of 69 per cent reservation in Government Services and for admission in Educational Institutions as at present. An all parties meeting had also been held on 26th November, 1993 in Tamil Nadu urging that there should not be any doubt or delay

in ensuring the continued implementation of 69 per cent reservation for the welfare and advancement of the backward classes.

5. The Tamil Nadu Government enacted a legislation namely Tamil Nadu Backward Classes, Scheduled Castes and Scheduled Tribes (Reservation of Seats in Educational Institutions and of appointments or posts in the Service under the State) Bill, 1993 and forwarded it to the Government of India for consideration of the President of India in terms of Article 31C of the Constitution.
6. In view of the importance and sensitive nature of the matter, the Union Home Minister held meetings with the leaders of Political Parties on 13th July, 1994 to discuss the provisions of the Bill. The general consensus among the leaders was that the Bill should be assented to. Accordingly, the President gave his assent to the Bill on 19th July, 1994.
7. The Tamil Nadu Government accordingly notified the Tamil Nadu Backward Classes, Scheduled Castes and Scheduled Tribes (Reservation of Seats in Educational Institutions and of appointments or posts in the Services under the State) Act, 1993 as Act No. 45 of 1994 on 19th July, 1994.
8. The Tamil Nadu Government requested the Government of India on 22nd July, 1994 that the aforementioned Tamil Nadu Act 45 of 1994 be included in the Ninth Schedule to the Constitution of India for the reasons given below:—

"The said Act attracts Article 31C of the Constitution, as falling within the purview of clauses (b) and (c) of Article 39, Articles 38 and 46 of the Constitution—*vide* section 2 of the Act. The Act has been passed relying on the directive principles of State Policy enshrined in Part IV of the Constitution and in particular, Articles 38, 39 (b) and (c) and 46 of the Constitution. As the Act is to give effect to the directive principles of State policy contained, *inter alia,* in Article 39 (b) and (c), the said Act will get the protection of Article 31C of the Constitution and therefore, cannot be challenged under Articles 14 and 19 of the Constitution, with reference to which Article 14, the reservation exceeding 50 per cent has been struck down by the Supreme Court. Now it has been decided to address the Government of India for including the Act in the Ninth Schedule to the Constitution, so that the law cannot be challenged as violative of any of the fundamental rights contained in Part III of the Constitution including Articles 15 and 16, and gets protection under Article 31B of the Constitution."

9. The Government of India has already supported the provision of the State legislation by giving the President's assent to the Tamil Nadu Bill. As a corollary to this decision, it is now necessary that the Tamil Nadu Act 45 of 1994 is brought within the purview of the Ninth Schedule to the Constitution so that it gets protection under Article 31B of the Constitution in regard to judicial review.
10. The Bill seeks to achieve the aforementioned objective.

77. *The Constitution (Seventy- Seventh Amendment) Act, 1995*

The Scheduled Castes and the Scheduled Tribes have been enjoying the facility of reservation in promotion since 1955. The Supreme Court in its judgment dated 16th November, 1992 in the case of *Indira Sawhney and others* v *Union of India and others*, however, observed that reservation of appointments or posts under Article 16 (4) of the Constitution is confined to initial appointment and cannot extend to reservation in the matter of promotion. This ruling of the Supreme Court will adversely affect the interests of the Scheduled Castes and the Scheduled Tribes. Since the representation of the Scheduled Castes and the Scheduled Tribes in services in the States have not reached the required level, it is necessary to continue the existing dispensation of providing reservation in promotion in the case of Scheduled Castes and the Scheduled Tribes. In view of the commitment of the Government to protect the interests of the Scheduled Castes and the Scheduled Tribes, the Government have decided to continue the existing policy of reservation in promotion for the Scheduled Castes and the Scheduled Tribes. To carry out this, it is necessary to amend Article 16 of the Constitution by inserting a new clause (4A) in the said Article to provide for reservation in promotion for the Scheduled Castes and the Scheduled Tribes.

2. The Bill seeks to achieve the aforesaid object.

78. *THE CONSTITUTION (SEVENTY-EIGHTH AMENDMENT) ACT, 1995*

Article 31B of the Constitution confers on the enactments

included in the Ninth Schedule to the Constitution immunity from legal challenge on the ground that they violate the fundamental rights enshrined in Part III of the Constitution. The Schedule consists of list of laws enacted by various State Governments and Central Government which *inter alia* affect rights and interest in property including land.

As such, following the First Amendment Act (1951), which appended Ninth Schedule to the Constitution, opened the door to escape judicial secrutiny. As and when it was apprehended that certain legislation conceived in public interest was likely to be imperilled by litigation, recourse was taken to the Ninth Schedule; thereby raising the number of legislation listed in the Ninth Schedule to 284.

The Constitution (Seventy-Ninth Amendment) Act, 1999

When the Constitution was initially adopted with provisions relating to reservations for Scheduled Castes, Scheduled Tribes, Anglo-Indian Communities etc., were to hold good for 10 years, it was expected that by 1960 the progress of so-called backward classes would reach a certain levelling. As such, Article 334 of the Constitution provided that thesé reservations shall cease to affect on the expiration of a period of 10 years from the commencement of the Constitution. From then on, dates of expiry of reservations have been extended , as noted earlier, periodically; in 1989 the Constitution 62nd Amendment Act raised the periodicity to 50 years. This Seventy- ninth Amendment provided to substitute "fifty years" by the words "sixty years".

The Constitution (Eightieth Amendment) Act, 2000

This amendment brought about changes in Article 270 relating to taxes levied and distributed between the Union and the States. Article 272 was found to be obsolete and the amendment deleted Article 272.

The Constitution (Eighty-First Amendment) Act, 2000

This amendment further modified Article 16 relating to right to equality of opportunity and employment in public offices to provide additional protective measures for Scheduled Castes, Scheduled Tribes or any other backward class of citizens by adding Article (4B) after Article (4A) to read as follows:

"(4B) Nothing in this Article shall prevent the State from

considering any unfilled vacancies of a year which are reserved for being filled up that year in accordance with any provision for reservation made under clause (4) or clause (4A) as a separate class of vacancies to be filled up in any succeeding year or years and such class of vacancies shall not be considered together with the vacancies of the year in which they are being filled up for determining 50 per cent reservation on number of vacancies in that year".

The Constitution (Eighty-Second Amendment) Act, 2000

This Act effected an amendment of Article 335 of the Constitution by providing relaxation in favour of the members of the Scheduled Castes and Scheduled Tribes in qualifying marks in any examination or lowering the standards of evaluation, for reservation in matters of promotion to any class or classes of services or posts in connection with the affairs of the Union or of a State.

The Constitution (Eighty-Third Amendment) Act, 2000

As noted earlier, the Constitution makes special provisions for the administration of certain areas callled "Scheduled Areas" situated within a State or Union Territory [Art, 244(1)] presumably because of the backwardness of the people of these areas. These Areas and special provisions are listed in the Fifth Schedule and Articles 243-244A.

This Act amended Article 243M of the Constitution by inserting, after clause (3), the following:

"(3A) Nothing in Article 243 D, relating to reservation of seats for the Scheduled Castes, shall apply to the State of Arunachal Pradesh."

The Constitution (Eighty-Fourth Amendment) Act, 2001

Provisos to Articles 82 and 170(3) of the Constitution provide that no fresh readjustment of constituencies can be undertaken until the figures of the first census taken after the year 2000 are published. These provisos were inserted by the Constitution (Forty-Second Amendment) Act, 1976 as a measure to boost family planning norms. It may be noted here that States like Kerala where family planning was quite successful, the increase in the population of the State was minimum, but in State like Bihar and U.P. the increase was by leaps and bounds. Hence, the amendment of 1976 attempted to remove the imbalance caused due to uneven growth of population/ electorate in different constituencies.

Since the first census after the year 2000 was initiated, it was expected that the Constitutional embargo on undertaking fresh delimitation will lapse as soon as the figures of this census were published. Hence, the need of amending the Constitution.

Accordingly, Eighty-fourth Amendment provides that as and where the figures of the "year 2000" were mentioned in Articles 55, 70, 82, 330 and 332 of the Constitution the figures "2000" be substituted by the figures "2026."

The Constitution (Eighty-Fifth Amendment) Act, 2001

This Act further amended Article 16 to insert in clause (4A) for the words "in matters of promotion to any class" the words "in matters of promotion, with consequential seniority, to any class."

Appendix III

Universal Declaration of Human Rights

Preamble

Whereas recognition of the inherent dignity and of the equal and inalienable rights of all members of the human family is the foundation of freedom, justice and peace in the world,

Whereas disregard and contempt for human rights have resulted in barbarous acts which have outraged the conscience of mankind, and the advent of a world in which human beings shall enjoy freedom of speech and belief and freedom from fear and want has been proclaimed as the highest aspiration of the common people,

Whereas it is essential, if man is not to be compelled to have recourse, as a last resort, to rebellion against tyranny and oppression, that human rights should be protected by the rule of law,

Whereas it is essential to promote the development of friendly relations between nations,

Whereas the peoples of the United Nations have in the Charter reaffirmed their faith in fundamental human rights, in the dignity and worth of the human person and in the equal rights of men and women and have determined to promote social progress and better standards of life in larger freedom,

Whereas Member States have pledged themselves to achieve, in cooperation with the United Nations, the promotion of universal respect for the observance of human rights and fundamental freedoms,

Where as a common understanding of these rights and freedoms is of the greatest importance for the full realization of this pledge,

Now, therefore,

The General Assembly Proclaims

This Universal Declaration of Human Rights as a common standard of achievement for all peoples and all nations, to the end that every individual and every organ of society, keeping this Declaration constantly in mind, shall strive by teaching and education to promote respect for these rights and freedoms and by progressive measures, national and international, to secure their universal and effective recognition and observance, both among the peoples of Member States themselves and among the peoples of territories under their jurisdiction.

Article 1

All human beings are born free and equal in dignity and rights. They are endowed with reason and conscience and should act towards one another in a spirit of brotherhood.

Article 2

Everyone is entitled to all the rights and freedoms set forth in this Declaration, without distinction of any kind, such as race, colour, sex, language, religion, political or other opinion, national or social origin, property, birth or other status.

Furthermore, no distinction shall be made on the basis of the political, jurisdictional or international status of the country or territory to which a person belongs, whether it be independent, trust, non-self-governing or under any other limitation of sovereignty.

Article 3

Everyone has the right to life, liberty and the security of person.

Article 4

No one shall be held in slavery or servitude; slavery and the slave trade shall be prohibited in all their forms.

Article 5

No one shall be subjected to torture or to cruel, inhuman or degrading treatment or punishment.

Article 6

Everyone has the right to recognition everywhere as a person before the law.

Article 7

All are equal before the law and are entitled without any discrimination to equal protection of the law. All are entitled to equal protection against any discrimination in violation of this Declaration and against any incitement to such discrimination.

Arrticle 8

Everyone has the right to an effective remedy by the competent national tribunal for acts violating the fundamental rights granted to him by the Constitution or by law.

Article 9

No one shall be subjected to arbitrary arrest, detention or exile.

Article 10

Everyone is entitled in full equality to a fair and public hearing by an independent and impartial tribunal, in the determination of his rights and obligations and of any criminal charge against him.

Article 11

1. Everyone charged with a penal offence has the right to be presumed innocent until proved guilty according to law in a public trial at which he has had all the guarantees necessary for his defence.
2. No one shall be held guilty of any penal offence on account of any act or omission which did not constitute a penal offence, under national or international law, at the time when it was committed. Nor shall a heavier penalty be imposed than the one that was applicable at the time the penal offence was committed.

Article 12

No one shall be subjected to arbitrary interference with his privacy, family, home or correspondence, nor to attacks upon his honour and reputation. Everyone has the right to the protection of the law against such interference or attacks.

Article 13

1. Everyone has the right to freedom of movement and residence within the borders of each State.
2. Everyone has the right to leave any country, including his own, and to return to his country.

Article 14

1. Everyone has the right to seek and to enjoy in other countries asylum from persecution.
2. This right may not be involved in the case of prosecutions genuinely arising from non- political crimes or from acts contrary to the purposes and principles of the United Nations.

Article 15

1. Everyone has the right to a nationality.
2. No one shall be arbitrarily deprived of his nationality nor denied the right to change his nationality.

Article 16

1. Men and women of full age, without any limitation due to race, nationality or religion, have the right to marry and to found a family. They are entitled to equal rights as to marriage, during marriage and at its dissolution.

2. Marriage shall be entered into only with the free and full consent of the intending spouses.
3. The family is the natural and fundamental group unit of society and is entitled to protection by society and the State.

Article 17

1. Everyone has the right to own property alone as well as in association with others.
2. No one shall be arbitrarily deprived of his property.

Article 18

Everyone has the right to freedom of thought, conscience and religion; this right includes freedom to change his religion or belief, and freedom, either alone or in community with others and in public or private, to manifest his religion or belief in teachihng, practice, worship and observance.

Article 19

Everyone has the right to freedom of opinion and expression; this right includes freedom to hold opinions without interference and to seek, receive and impart information and ideas through any media and regardless of frontiers.

Article 20

1. Everyone has the right to freedom of peaceful assembly and association.
2. No one may be compelled to belong to an association.

Article 21

1. Everyone has the right to take part in the government of his country, directly or through freely chosen representatives.
2. Everyone has the right of equal access to public service in his country.
3. The will of the people shall be the basis of the authority of government; this will shall be expressed in periodic and genuine elections which shall be by universal and equal suffrage and shall be held by secret vote or by equivalent free voting procedures.

Article 22

Everyone, as a member of society, has the right to social secrurity and is entitled to realization, through national effort and international cooperation and in accordance with the organization and resources of each State, of the economic, social and cultural rights indispensable for his dignity and the free development of his personality.

Article 23

1. Everyone has the right to work, to free choice of employment, to

just and favourable conditions of work and to protection against unemployment.

2. Everyone, without any discrimination, has the right to equal pay for equal work.
3. Everyone who works has the right to just and favourable remuneration ensuring for himself and his family an existence worthy of human dignity, and supplemented, if necessary, by other means of social protection.
4. Everyone has the right to form and to join trade unions for the protection of his interests.

Article 24

Everyone has the right to rest and leisure, including reasonable limitation of working hours and periodic holiday with pay.

Article 25

1. Everyone has the right to a standard of living adequate for the health and well-being of himself and of his family, including food, clothing, housing and medical care and necessary social services, and the right to security in the event of unemployment, sickness, disability, widowhood, old age or other lack or livelihood in circumstances beyond his control.
2. Motherhood and childhood are entitled to special care and assistance. All children, whether born in or out of wedlock, shall enjoy the same social protection.

Article 26

1. Everyone has the right to education. Education shall be free, at least in the elementary and fundamental stages. Elementary education shall be compulsory. Technical and professional education shall be made generally available and higher education shall be equally accessible to all on the basis of merit.
2. Education shall be directed to the full development of the human personality and to the strengthening of respect for human rights and fundamental freedoms. It shall promote understanding, tolerance and friendship among all nations, racial or religious groups, and shall further the activities of the United Nations for the maintenance of peace.
3. Parents have a prior right to choose the kind of education that shall be given to their children.

Article 27

1. Everyone has the right to freely participate in the cultural life of the community, to enjoy the arts and to share in scientific advancement

and its benefits.

2. Everyone has the right to the protection of the moral and material interests resulting from any scientific, literary or artistic production of which he is the author.

Article 28

Everyone is entitled to a social and international order in which the rights and freedoms set forth in this Declaration can be fully realized.

Article 29

1. Everyone has duties to the community in which alone the free and full development of his personality is possible.
2. In the exercise of his rights and freedoms, everyone shall be subject only to such limitations as are determined by law solely for the purpose of securing due recognition and respect for the rights and freedom of others and of meeting the just requirements of morality, public order and the general welfare in a democratic society.
3. These rights and freedoms may in no case be exercised contrary to the purpose and principles of United Nations.

Article 30

Nothing in this Declaration may be interpreted as implying for any State, group or person any right to engage in any activity or to perform any act aimed at the destruction of any of the rights and freedoms set forth herein.

Appendix IV

International Covenant on Economic, Social and Cultural Rights

Preamble

The States Parties to the Present Covenant,

Considering that, in accordance with the principles proclaimed in the Charter of the United Nations, recognition of the inherent dignity and of the equal and inalienable rights of all members of the human family is the foundation of freedom, justice and peace in the world, *Recognizing* that these rights derive from the inherent dignity of the human person,

Recognizing that, in accordance with the Universal Declaration of Human Rights, the ideal of free human being enjoying freedom from fear and want can only be achieved if conditions are created whereby everyone may enjoy his economic, social and cultural rights, as well as his civil and political rights,

Considering the obligation of States under the Charter of the United Nations to promote universal respect for, and observance of, human rights and freedoms,

Realizing that the individual, having duties to other individuals and to the community to which he belongs, is under a responsibility to strive for the promotion and observance of the rights recognized in the present Covenant,

Agree upon the following Articles:

Part

Article 1

1. All people have the right of self-determination. By virtue of that right they freely determine their political status and

freely pursue their economic, social and cultural development.

2. All peoples may, for their own ends, freely dispose of their natural wealth and resources without prejudice to any obligations arising out of international economic cooperation, based upon the principle of mutual benefit, and international law. In no case may a people be deprived of its own means of subsistence.
3. The States parties to the present Covenant, including those having responsibility for the administration of Non-Self-governing and Trust Territories, shall promote the realization of the right of self-determination, and shall respect that right, in conformity with the provisions of the Charter of the United Nations.

Part II

Article 2

1. Each State Party to the present Covenant undertakes to take steps, individually and through international assistance and cooperation, especially economic and technical, to the maximum of its available resources, with a view to achieving progressively the full realization of the rights recognized in the present Covenant by all appropriate means, including particularly the adoption of legislative measures.
2. The States Parties to the present Covenant undertake to guarantee that the rights enunciated in the present Covenant will be exercised without discrimination of any kind as to race, colour, sex, language, religion, political or other opinion, national or social origin, property, birth or other status.
3. Developing countries, with due regard to human rights and their national economy, may determine to what extent they would guarantee the economic rights recognized in the present Covenant, to non-nationals.

Article 3

The States Parties to the present Covenant undertake to ensure the equal right of men and women to the enjoyment of all economic, social and cultural rights set forth in the present Covenant.

Article 4

The States Parties to the present Covenant recognize that, in the enjoyment of those rights provided by the State in conformity with the present Covenant, the State may subject such rights only to such limitations as are determined by law only in so far as this may be compatible with the nature of these rights and solely for the purpose of promoting the general welfare in a democratic society.

Article 5

1. Nothing in the present Covenant may be interpreted as implying for any State, group or person any right to engage in any activity or to perform any act aimed at the destruction of any of the rights or freedoms recognized herein, or at their limitation to a greater extent than is provided for in the present Covenant.
2. No restriction upon or derogation from any of the fundamental human rights recognized or existing in any country in virtue of law, conventions, regulations or custom shall be admitted on the pretext that the present Covenant does not recognize such rights or that it recognizes them to a lesser extent.

Part III

Article 6

1. The States Parties to the present Covenant recognize the right to work, which include the right of everyone to the opportunity to gain his living by work which he freely chooses or accepts, and will take appropriate steps to safeguard this right.
2. The steps to be taken by a State Party to the present Covenant to achieve the full realization of this right shall include technical and vocational guidance and training programmes, policies and techniques to achieve steady economic, social and cultural development and full and productive employment under conditions safeguarding fundamental political and economic freedoms to the individual.

Article 7

The States Parties to the present Covenant recognize the right of everyone to the enjoyment of just and favourable conditions of work which ensure, in particular:

(a) Remuneration which provides all workers, as a

minimum, with:

(i) Fair wages and equal remuneration for work of equal value without distinction of any kind, in particular women being guaranted conditions of work not inferior to those enjoyed by men, with equal pay for equal work;

(ii) A decent living for themselves and their families in accordance with the provisions of the present Covenant;

(b) Safe and healthy working conditions;

(c) Equal opportunity for everyone to be promoted in his employment to an appropriate higher level, subject to no considerations other than those of seniority and competence;

(d) Rest, leisure and reasonable limitation of working hours and periodic holidays with pay, as well as remuneration for public holidays.

Article 8

1. The States Parties to the present Covenant undertake to ensure:

(a) The right of everyone to form trade unions and join the trade union of his choice, subject only to the rules of the organization concerned, for the promotion and protection of his economic and social interests. No restrictions may be placed on the exercise of this right other than those prescribed by law and which are necessary in a democratic society in the interests of national security or public order or for the protection of the rights and freedoms of others;

(b) The right of trade unions to establish national federations or confederations and the right of the latter to form or join international trade union organizations;

(c) The right of trade unions to function freely subject to no limitations other than those prescribed by law and which are necessary in a democratic society in the interests of national security or public order or for the protection of the rights and freedoms of others;

(d) The right to strike, provided that it is exercised in conformity with the laws of the particular country.

2. This Article shall not prevent the imposition of lawful restrictions on the exercise of these rights by members of the armed forces or of the police or of the administration of the State.
3. Nothing in this Article shall authorize States Parties to the International Labour Organisation Convention of 1948 concerning Freedom of Association and protection of the Right to Organise to take legislative measures which would prejudice, or apply the law in such a manner as would prejudice, the guarantees provided for in that Convention.

Article 9

The States Parties to the present Covenant recognize the right of everyone to social security, including social insurance.

Article 10

The States Parties to the present Covenant recognize that:

1. The widest possible protection and assistance should be accorded to the family, which is the natural and fundamental group unit of society, particularly for its establishment and while it is responsible for the care and education of dependent children. Marriage must be entered into with the free consent of the intending spouses.
2. Special protection should be accorded to mothers during a reasonable period before and after childbirth. During such period working mothers should be accorded paid leave or leave with adequate social security benefits.
3. Special measures of protection and assistance should be taken on behalf of all children and young persons without any discrimination for persons of parentage or other conditions. Children and young persons should be protected from economic and social exploitation. Their employment in work harmful to their morals or health or dangerous to life or likely to hamper their normal development should be punishable by law. States should also set age limits below which the paid employment of child labour should be prohibited and punishable by law.

Article 11

1. The States Parties to the present Covenant recognize the right of everyone to an adequate standard of living for himself and his family, including adequate food, clothing

and housing, and to the continuous improvement of living conditions. The States Parties will take appropriate steps to ensure the realization of this right, recognizing to this effect the essential importance of international cooperation based on free consent.

2. the States Parties to the present Covenant, recognizing the fundamental right of everyone to be free from hunger, shall take,
individually and through international cooperation, the measures, including specific programmes, which are needed:
   (a) To improve methods of production, conservation and distribution of food by making full use of technical and scientific knowledge, by disseminating knowledge of the principles of nutrition and by developing or reforming agrarian systems in such a way as to achieve the most efficient development and utilization of natural resources;
   (b) Taking into account the problems of both food-importing and food-exporting countries, to ensure an equitable distribution of world food supplies in relation to need.

Article 12

1. The States Parties to the present Covenant recognize the right of everyone to the enjoyment of the highest attainable standard of physical and mental health.
2. The steps to be taken by the States Parties to the present Covenant to achieve the full realization of this right shall include those necessary for:
   (a) The provision for the reduction of the stillbirth rate and of infant mortality and for the healthy development of the child;
   (b) The improvement of all aspects of environmental and industrial hygiene;
   (c) The prevention, treatment and control of epidemic, endemic, occupational and other diseases;
   (d) The creation of conditions which would assure to all medical service and medical attention in the event of sickness.

Article 13

1. The States Parties to the present Covenant recognize the

right of everyone to education. They agree that education shall be directed to the full development of the human personality and the sense of its dignity, and shall strengthen the respect for human rights and fundamental freedoms. They further agree that education shall enable all persons to participate effectively in a free society, promote understanding, tolerance and friendship among all nations and all racial, ethnic or religious groups, and further the activities of the United Nations for the maintenance of peace.

2. The States Parties to the present Covenant recognize that, with a view to achieving the full realization of this right:
   (a) Primary education shall be compulsory and available free to all;
   (b) Secondary education in its different forms, including technical and vocational secondary education, shall be made generally available and accessible to all by every appropriate means, and in particular by the progressive introduction of free education;
   (c) Higher education shall be made equally accessible to all, on the basis of capacity, by every appropriate means, and in particular by the progressive introduction of free education;
   (d) Fundamental education shall be encouraged or intensified as far as possible for those persons who have not received or completed the whole period of their primary education;
   (e) The development of a system of school at all levels shall be actively pursued, an adequate fellowship system shall be established, and the material conditions of teaching staff shall be continuously improved.
3. The States Parties to the present Covenant undertake to have respect for the liberty of parents and, when applicable, legal guardians to choose for their children schools, other than those established by the public authorities, which conform to such minimum educational standards as may be laid down or approved by the State and to ensure the religious and moral education of their children in conformity with their own convictions.

4. No part of this Article shall be construed so as to interfere with the liberty of individuals and bodies to establish and direct educational institutions, subject always to the observance of the principles set forth in paragraph 1 of this Article and to the requirement that the education given in such institutions shall conform to such minimum standards as may be laid down by the State.

Article 14

Each State Party to the present Covenant which, at the time of becoming a Party, has not been able to secure in its metropolitan territory or other territories under jurisdiction compulsory primary education, free of charge, undertakes, within two years, to work out and adopt a detailed plan of action for the progressive implementation, within a reasonable number of years, to be fixed in the plan, of the principle of compulsory education free of charge for all.

Article 15

1. The States Parties to the present Covenant recognize the right of everyone:
   (a) To take part in cultural life;
   (b) To enjoy the benefits of scientific progress and its applications;
   (c) To benefit from the protection of the moral and material interests resulting from any scientific, literary or artistic production of which he is the author.
2. The steps to be taken by the States Parties to the present Covenant to achieve the full realisation of this right shall include those necessary for the conservation, the development and the diffusion of science and culture.
3. The States Parties to the present Covenant undertake to respect the freedom indispensable for scientific research and creative activity.
4. The States Parties to the present Covenant recognize the benefits to be derived from the encouragement and development of international contacts and cooperation in the scientific and cultural fields.

Part IV

Article 16

1. The States Parties to the present Covenant undertake to submit in conformity with this part of the Covenant reports

on the measures which they have adopted and the progress made in achieving the observance of the rights recognized herein.

2. (a) All reports shall be submitted to the Secretary-General of the United Nations, who shall transmit copies to the Economic and Social Council for consideration in accordance with the provisions of the present Covenant;

   (b) The Secretary-General of the United Nations shall also transmit to the specialized agencies copies of the reports, or any relevant parts therefrom, from States Parties to the present Covenant which are also members of these specialized agencies in so far as these reports, or parts therefrom, relate to any matters which fall within the responsibilities of the said agencies in accordance with their Constitutional instruments.

Article 17

1. The States Parties to the present Covenant shall furnish their reports in stages, in accordance with a programme to be established by the Economic and Social Council within one year of the entry into force of the present convenant after consultation with the States Parties and the specialized agencies concerned.
2. Reports may indicate factors and difficulties affecting the degree of fulfilment of obligations under the present Covenant.
3. Where relevant information has previously been furnished to the United Nations or to any specialized agency by any State Party to the present Covenant, it will not be necessary to reproduce that information, but a precise reference to the information so furnished will suffice.

Article 18

Pursuant to its responsibilities under the Charter of the United Nations in the field of human rights and fundamental freedoms, the Economic and Social Council may make arrangements with the specialized agencies in respect of their reporting to it on the progress made in achieving the observance of provisions of the present Covenant falling within the scope of their activities. These reports may include particulars of decisions and recommendations on such implementation adopted by their competent organs.

Article 19

The Economic and Social Council may transmit to the Commission on Human Rights for study and general recommendation or, as appropriate, for information the reports concerning human rights submitted by States in accordance with Articles 16 and 17, and those concerning human rights submitted by the specialized agencies in accordance with Article 18.

Article 20

The States Parties to the present Covenant and the specialised agencies concerned may submit comments to the Economic and Social Council on any general recommendation under Article 19 or refrence to such general recommendation in any report of the Commission on Human Rights or any documentation referred to therein.

Article 21

The Economic and Social Council may submit from time to time to the General Assembly reports with recommendations of a general nature and a summary of the information received from the States Parties to the present Covenant and the specialized agencies on the measures taken and the progress made in achieving general observance of the rights recognized in the present Covenant.

Article 22

The Economic and Social Council may bring to the attention of other organs of the United Nations, their subsidiary organs and specialized agencies concerned with furnishing technical assistance any matters arising out of the reports referred to in this part of the present Covenant which may assist such bodies in deciding, each within its field of competence, on the advisability of international measures likely to contribute to the effective progressive implementation of the present Covenant.

Article 23

The States Parties to the present Covenant agree that international action for the achievement of the rights recognized in the present covenant includes such methods as the conclusion of conventions, the adoption of recommendations, the furnishing of technical assistance and the holding of regional meetings and technical meetings for the purpose of consultation and study organized in conjunction with the Governments concerned.

Article 24

Nothing in the present Covenant shall be interpreted as impairing the provisions of the Charter of the United Nations and of the Constitutions of the specialized agencies which define the respective responsibilities of the various organs of the United Nations and of the specialized agencies in regard to the matters dealt with in the present Covenant.

Article 25

Nothing in the present covenant shall be interpreted as impairing the inherent right of all peoples to enjoy and utilize fully and freely their natural wealth and resources.

Part V

Article 26

1. The present Covenant is open for signature by any State Member of the United Nations or member of any of its specialized agencies, by any State Party to the Statute of the International Court of Justice and by any other State which has been invited by the General Assembly of the United Nations to become a party to the present Covenant.
2. The present Covenant is subject to ratification. Instruments of ratification shall be deposited with the Secretary-General of the United Nations.
3. The present Covenant shall be open to accession by any State referred to in paragraph 1 of this Article.
4. Accession shall be effected by the deposit of an instrument of accession with the Secretary-General of the United Nations.
5. The Secretary-General of the United Nations shall inform all States which have signed the present Covenant or acceded to it of the deposit of each instrument of ratification or accession.

Article 27

1. The present Covenant shall enter into force three months after the date of the deposit with the Secretary-General of the United Nations of the thirty-fifth instrument of ratification or instrument of accession.

2. For each State ratifying the present Covenant or acceding to it after the deposit of the thirty-fifth instrument of ratification or instrument of accession, the present Covenant shall enter into force three months after the date of the deposit of its own instrument of ratification or instrument of accession.

Article 28

The provisions of present Covenant shall extend to all parts of federal States without any limitations or exceptions.

Article 29

1. Any State Party to the present Convenant may propose an amendment and file it with the Secretary-General of the United Nations. The Secretary-General shall thereupon communicate any proposed amendments to the States Parties to the present Covenant with a request that they notify him whether they favour a conference of States Parties for the purpose of considering and voting upon the proposals. In the event that at least one- third of the States Parties favours such a conference, the Secretary-General shall convene the conference under the auspices of the United Nations. Any amendment adopted by a majority of the States Parties present and voting at the conference shall be submitted to the General Assembly of the United Nations for approval.
2. Amendments shall come into force when they have been approved by the General Assembly of the United Nations and accepted by a two-thirds majority of the States Parties to the present Covenant in accordance with their respective Constitutional processes.
3. When amendments come into force they shall be binding on those States Parties which have accepted them, other States Parties still being bound by the provisions of the present Covenant and any earlier amendment which they have accepted.

Appendix V

International Covenant on Civil and Political Rights

Preamble

The States Parties to the Present Covenant,

Considering that, in accordance with the principles proclaimed in the Charter of the United Nations, recognition of the inherent dignity and of the equal and inalienable rights of all members of the human family is the foundation of freedom, justice and peace in the world,

Recognizing that these rights derive from the inherent dignity of the human person,

Recognizing that, in accordance with the Universal Declaration of Human Rights, the ideal of free human beings enjoying freedom from fear and want can only be achieved if conditions are created whereby everyone may enjoy his economic, social and cultural rights, as well as his civil and political rights,

Considering the obligation of States under the Charter of the United Nations to promote universal respect for, and observance of, human rights and freedoms,

Realizing that the individual, having duties to other individuals and to the community to which he belongs, is under a responsibility to strive for the promotion and observance of the rights recognized in the present Covenant,

Agree upon the following Articles:

Part I

Article 1

1. All peoples have the right of self-determination. By virtue of having responsibility for the administration of Non-Self-

Governing and Trust Territories, shall promote the realization of the right of self-determination, and shall respect that right, in conformity with the provisions of the Charter of the United Nations.

Part II

Article 2

1. Each State Party to the present Covenant undertakes to respect and to ensure to all individuals within its territory and subject to its jurisdiction the rights recognized in the present Covenant, without distinction of any kind, such as race, colour, sex, language, religion, political or other opinion, national or social origin, property, birth or other status.
2. Where not already provided for by existing legislative or other measures, each State Party to the present Covenant undertakes to take the necessary steps, in accordance with its Constitutional processes and with the provisions of the present Covenant to adopt such legislative or other measures as may be necessary to give effect to the rights recognized in the present Covenant.
3. Each State Party to the present Covenant, undertakes:-
   (a) To ensure that any person whose rights or freedoms as herein recognized are violated shall have an effective remedy, notwithstanding that the violation has been committed by persons acting in an official capacity;
   (b) To ensure that any person claiming such a remedy shall have his right thereto determined by competent judicial, administrative or legislative authorities, or by any other competent authority provided for by the legal system of the State, and to develop the possibilities of judicial remedy;
   (c) To ensure that the competent authorities shall enforce such remedies when granted.

Article 3

The States Parties to the present Covenant undertake to ensure the equal right of men and women to the enjoyment of all civil and political rights set forth in the present Covenant.

Article 4

1. In time of public emergency which threatens the life of the nation and the existence of which is officially proclaimed, the States Parties to the present Covenant may take measures derogating from their obligations under the present Covenant to the extent strictly required by the exigencies of the situation, provided that such measures are not inconsistent with their other obligations under international law and do not involve discrimination solely on the ground of race, colour, sex, language, religion or social origin.
2. No derogation from Articles 6, 7, 8 (paragraphs 1 and 2), 11, 15, 16 and 18 may be made under this provision.
3. Any State Party to the present Covenant availing itself of the right of derogation shall immediately inform the other States Parties to the present Covenant, through the intermediary of the Secretary-General of the United Nations, of the provisions from which it has derogated and of the reasons by which it was actuated. A further communication shall be made, through the same intermediary, on the date on which it terminates such derogation.

Article 5

1. Nothing in the present Covenant may be interpreted as implying for any State, group or person any right to engage in any activity or perform any act aimed at the destruction of any of the rights and freedoms recognized herein or at their limitation to a greater extent than is provided for in the present Covenant.
2. There shall be no restriction upon or derogation from any of the fundamental human rights recognized or existing in any State Party to the present Covenant pursuant to law, conventions, regulations or custom on the pretext that the present Covenant does not recognize such rights or that it recognizes them to a lesser extent.

Part III

Article 6

1. Every human being has the inherent right to life. This right shall be protected by law. No one shall be arbitrarily deprived of his life.

2. In countries which have not abolished the death penalty, sentence of death may be imposed only for the most serious crimes in accordance with the law in force at the time of the commission of the crime and not contrary to the provisions of the present Covenant and to the Convention on the Prevention and Punishment of the Crime of Genocide. This penalty can only be carried out pursuant to a final judgement rendered by a competent court.
3. When deprivation of life constitutes the crime of genocide, it is understood that nothing in this Article shall authorize any State Party to the present Covenant to derogate in any way from any obligation and Punishment of the Crime of Genocide.
4. Anyone sentenced to death shall have the right to seek pardon or commutation of the sentence. Amnesty, pardon or commutation of the sentence of death may be granted in all cases.
5. Sentence of death shall not be imposed for crimes committed by persons below eighteen years of age and shall not be carried out on pregnant women.
6. Nothing in this Article shall be invoked to delay or to prevent the abolition of capital punishment by any State Party to the present Covenant.

Article 7

No one shall be subjected to torture or to cruel, inhuman or degrading treatment or punishment. In particular, no one shall be subjected without his free consent to medical or scientific experimentation.

Article 8

1. No one shall be held in slavery; slavery and the slave-trade in all their forms shall be prohibited.
2. No one shall be held in servitude.
3. (a) No one shall be required to perform forced or compulsory labour;

   (b) Paragraph 3 (a) shall not be held to preclude, in countries where imprisonment with hard labour may be imposed as a punishment for a crime, the performance of hard labour in pursuance of a sentence to such punishment by a competent court;

(c) For the purpose of this paragraph the term "forced or compulsory labour" shall not include:

(i) Any work or service, not referred to in subparagraph (d) normally required of a person who is under detention in consequence of a lawful order of a court, or of a person during conditional release from such detention;

(ii) Any service of a military character and, in countries where conscientious objection is recognized, any national service required by law of conscientious objectors;

(iii) Any service exacted in cases of emergency or calamity threatening the life or well being of the community;

(iv) Any work or service which forms part of normal civil obligations.

Article 9

1. Everyone has the right to liberty and security of person. No one shall be subjected to arbitrary arrest or detention. No one shall be deprived of his liberty except on such grounds and in accordance with such procedure as are established by law.
2. Anyone who is arrested shall be informed, at the time of arrest, of the reasons for his arrest and shall be promptly informed of any charges against him.
3. Anyone arrested or detained on a criminal charge shall be brought promptly before a judge or other officer authorized by law to exercise judicial power and shall be entitled to trial within a reasonable time or to release. It shall not be the general rule that persos awaiting trial shall be detained in custody, but release may be subject to guarantees to appear for trial, at any other stage of the judicial proceedings, and should occasion arise, for execution of the judgement.
4. Anyone who is deprived of his liberty by arrest or detention shall be entitled to take proceedings before a court, in order that court may decide without delay on the lawfulness of his detention and order his release if the detention is not lawful.
5. Anyone who has been the victim of unlawful arrest or detention shall have an enforceable right to compensation.

Article 10

1. All persons deprived of their liberty shall be treated with humanity and with respect for the inherent dignity of the human person.
2. (a) Accused persons shall, save in exceptional circumstances, be segregated from convicted persons and shall be subject to separate treatment appropriate to their status as unconvicted persons;
   (b) Accused juvenile persons shall be separated from adults and brought as speedily as possible for adjudication.
3. The penitentiary system shall comprise treatment of prisoners the essential aim of which shall be their reformation and social rehabilitation. Juvenile offenders shall be segregated from adults and be accorded treatment appropriate to their age and legal status.

Article 11

No one shall be imprisoned merely on the ground of inability to fulfill a contractual obligation.

Article 12

1. Everyone lawfully within the territory of a State shall, within that territory, have the right to liberty of movement and freedom to choose his residence.
2. Everyone shall be free to leave any country, including his own.
3. The above-mentioned rights shall not be subject to any restrictions except those which are provided by law, are necessary to protect national security, public order (order public) public health or morals or the rights and freedoms of others, and are consistent with the other rights recognized in the present Covenant.
4. No one shall be arbitrarily deprived of the right to enter his own country.

Article 13

An alien lawfully in the territory of a State Party to the present Covenant may be expelled therefrom only in pursuance of a decision reached in accordance with law and shall, except where compelling reasons of national security otherwise require, be allowed to submit the reasons against his expulsion and to have his case reviewed by, and be represented for the purpose before, the competent authority or a person or persons especially designated by the competent authority.

Article 14

1. All persons shall be equal before the courts and tribunals. In the determination of any criminal charge against him, or of his rights and obligations in a suit at law, everyone shall be entitled to a fair and public hearing by a competent, independent and impartial tribunal established by law. The Press and the public may be excluded from all or part of a trial for reasons, morals, public order (*ordre public*) or national security in a democratic society, or when the interest of the private lives of the parties so requires, or to the extent strictly necessary in the opinion of the court in special circumstances where publicity would prejudice the interests of justice; but any judgement rendered in a criminal case or in a suit at law shall be made public except where the interest of juvenile persons otherwise requires or the proceedings concern matrimonial disputes or the guardianship of children.
2. Everyone charged with a criminal offence shall have the right to be presumed innocent until proved guilty according to law.
3. In the determination of any criminal charge against him, everyone shall be entitled to the following minimum guarantees, in full equality:
   (a) To be informed promptly and in detail in a language which he understands of the nature and cause of the charge against him;
   (b) To have adequate time and facilities for the preparation of his defence and to communicate with counsel of his own choosing;
   (c) To be tried wothout undue delay;
   (d) To be tried in his presence, and to defend himself in person or through legal assistance of his own choosing; to be informed, if he does not have legal assistance, of this right; and to have legal assistance

assigned to him, any case where the interests of justice so require, and without payment by him in any such case if he does not have sufficient means to pay for it;

(e) To examine, or have examined, the witnesses against him and to obtain the attendance and examination of witnesses on his behalf under the same conditions as witnesses against him;

(f) To have the free assistance of an interpreter if he cannot understand or speak the language used in court;

(g) Not to be compelled to testify against himself or to confess guilt.

4. In the case of juvenile persons, the procedure shall be such as will take account of their age and the desirability of promoting their rehabilitation.
5. Everyone convicted of a crime shall have the right to his conviction and sentence being reviewed by a higher tribunal according to law.
6. When a person has by a final decision been convicted of a criminal offence and when subsequently his conviction has been reversed or he has been pardoned on the ground that a new or newly discovered fact shows conclusively that there has been a miscarriage of justice, the person who has suffered punishment as a result of such conviction shall be compensated according to law, unless it is proved that the non-disclosure of the unknown fact in time is wholly or partly attributable to him.
7. No one shall be liable to be tried or punished again for an offence for which he has already been finally convicted or acquitted in accordance with the law and penal procedure of each country.

Article 15

1. No one shall be held guilty of any criminal offence on account of any act or omission which did not constitute a criminal offence, under national or international law, at the time when it was committed. Nor shall a heavier penalty be imposed than the one that was applicable at the time when the criminal offence was committed. If subsequent to the commisson of the offence, provision is

made by law for the imposition of a lighter penalty, the offender shall benefit thereby.

2. Nothing in this Article shall prejudice the trial and punishment of any person for any act or omission which, at the time when it was committed, was criminal according to the general principles of law recognised by the community of nations.

Article 16

Everyone shall have the right to recognition everywhere as a person before the law.

Article 17

1. No one shall be subjected to arbitrary or unlawful interference with his privacy, family, home or correspondence, nor to unlawful attacks on his honour and reputation.
2. Everyone has the right to the protection of the law against such interference or attacks.

Article 18

1. Everyone shall have the right to freedom of thought, conscience and religion. This right shall include freedom to have or to adopt a religion or belief of his choice, and freedom, either individually or in community with others and in public or private, to manifest his religion or belief in worship, observance, practice and teaching.
2. No one shall be subject to coercion which would impair his freedom to have or to adopt a religion or belief of his choice.
3. Freedom to manifest one's religion or beliefs may be subject only to such limitations as are prescribed by law and are necessary to protect public safety order, health, or morals or the fundamental rights and freedoms of others.
4. The States Parties to the present Covenant undertake to have respect for the liberty of parents and, when applicable, legal guardians to ensure the religious and moral education of their children in conformity with their own convictions.

Article 19

1. Everyone shall have the right to hold opinions without interference.

2. Everyone shall have the right to freedom of expression; this right shall include freedom to seek, receive and impart information and ideas of all kinds, regardless of frontiers, either orally, in writing or in print, in the form of art, or through any other media of his choice.
3. The exercise of the rights provided for in paragraph 2 of this Article carries with it special duties and responsibilities. It may therefore be subject to certain restrictions, but these shall only be such as are provided by law and are necessary:
   (a) For respect of the rights or reputations of others;
   (b) For the protection of national security or of public order (*ordre public*) or of public health or morals.

Article 20

1. Any propaganda for war shall be prohibited by law.
2. Any advocacy of national, racial or religious hatred that constitutes incitement to discrimination, hostility or violence shall be prohibited by law.

Article 21

The right of peaceful assembly shall be recognized. No restrictions may be placed on the exercise of this right other than those imposed in conformity with the law and which are necessary in a democratic society in the interests of national security of public safety, public order (*ordre public*), the protection of public health or morals or the protection of the rights and freedom of others.

Article 22

1. Everyone shall have the right to freedom of association with others, including the right to form and join trade unions for the protection of his interests.
2. No restrictions may be placed on the exercise of this right other than those which are prescribed by law and which are necessary in a democratic society in the interests of national security or public safety, public order (*ordre public*), the protections of public health or morals or the protection of the rights and freedoms of others. This Article shall not prevent the imposition of lawful restrictions on members of the armed forces and of the police in their exercise of this right.

3. Nothing in this Article shall authorize States Parties to the International Labour Organisation Convention of 1948 concerning Freedom of Association and Protection of the Right to Organise to take legislative measures which would prejudice, or to apply the law in such a manner as to prejudice, the guarantees provided for in that Convention.

Article 23

1. The family is the natural and fundamental group unit of society and is entitled to protection by society and the State.
2. The right of men and women of marriageable age to marry and to found a family shall be recognized.
3. No marriage shall be entered into without the free and full consent of the intending spouses.
4. States Parties to the present Covenant shall take appropriate steps to ensure equality of rights and responsibilities of spouses as to marriage, during marriage and at its dissolution. In the case of dissolution, provision shall be made for the necessary protection of any children.

Article 24

1. Every child shall have, without any discrimination as to race, colour, sex, language, religion, national or social origin, property or birth the right to such measures of protection as are required by his status as a minor, on the part of his family, society and the State.
2. Every child shall be registered immediately after birth and shall have a name.
3. Every child has the right to acquire a nationality.

Article 25

Every citizen shall have the right and the opportunity, without any of the distinctions mentioned in Article 2 and without unreasonable restrictions:

(a) To take part in the conduct of public affairs, directly or through freely chosen representatives;

(b) To vote and to be elected at genuine periodic elections which shall be by universal and equal suffrage and shall be held by secret ballot, guaranteeing the free expression of the will of the electors;

(c) To have access, on general terms of equality, to public service in his country.

Article 26

All persons are equal before the law and are entitled without any discrimination to the equal protection of the law. In this respect, the law shall prohibit any discrimination and guarantee to all persons equal and effective protection against discrimination on any ground such as race, sex, language, religion, political or other opinion, national or social origin, property, birth or other status.

Article 27

In those States in which ethnic, religious or linguistic minorities exist, persons belonging to such minorities shall not be denied the right, in community with the other members of their group, to enjoy their won culture, to profess and practise their own religion, or to use their own language.

Part IV

Article 28

1. There shall be established a Human Rights Committee (hereafter referred to in the present Covenant as the Committee). It shall consist of eighteen members and shall carry out the functions hereinafter provided.
2. The Committee shall be composed of nationals of the States Parties to the present Covenant who shall be persons of high moral character and recognized competence in the field of human rights, consideration being given to the usefulness of the participation of some persons having legal experience.
3. The members of the Committee shall be elected and shall serve in their personal capacity.

Article 29

1. The members of the Committee shall be elected by secret ballot from a list of persons possessing the qualifications prescribed in Article 28 and nominated for the purpose by the States Parties to the present Covenant.
2. Each State Party to the present Covenant may nominate not more than two persons. These persons shall be nationals of the nominating State.
3. A person shall be eligible for renomination.

Article 30

1. The initial election shall be held no later than six months after the date of the entry into force of the present Covenant.
2. At least four months before the date of each election to the Committee, other than an election to fill a vacancy declared in accordance with Article 34, the Secretary-General of the United Nations shall address a written invitation to the States Parties to the present Covenant to submit their nominations for membership of the Committee within three months.
3. The Secretary-General of the United Nations shall prepare a list in alphabetical order of all the persons thus nominated, with an indication of the States Parties which have nominated them, and shall submit it to the States Parties to the present Covenant no later than one month before the date of each election.
4. Elections of the members of the Committee shall be held at a meeting of the States Parties to the present Covenant convened by the Secretary-General of the United Nations at the Headquarters of the United Nations. At that meeting, for which two-thirds of the States Parties to the present Covenant shall constitute a quorum, the persons elected to the Committee shall be those nominees who obtain the largest number of votes and an absolute majority of the votes of the representatives of States Parties present and voting.

Article 31

1. The Committee may not include more than one national of the same State.
2. In the election of the Committee, consideration shall be given to equitable geographical distribution of membership and to the representation of the different forms of civilization and of the principal legal systems.

Article 32

1. The members of the Committee shall be elected for a term of four years. They shall be eligible for re-election if renominated. However, the terms of nine of the members elected at the first election shall expire at the end of two years; immediately after the first election, the names of these

nine members shall be choosen by lot by the Chairman of the meeting referred to in Article 30, paragraph 4.

2. Elections at the expiry of office shall be held in accordance with the preceding Articles of this part of the present Covenant.

Article 33

1. If, in the unanimous opinion of the other members, a member of the Committee has ceased to carry out his functions for any cause other than absence of a temporary character, the Chairman of the Committee shall notify the Secretary-General of the United Nations, who shall then declare the seat of that member to be vacant.
2. In the event of the death or the resignation of a member of the Committee, the Chairman shall immediately notify the Secretary-General of the United Nations, who shall declare the seat vacant from the date of death or the date on which the resignation takes effect.

Article 34

1. When a vacancy is declared in accordance with Article 33 and if the term of office of the member to be replaced does not expire within six months of the declaration of the vacancy, the Secretary-General of the United Nations shall notify each of the States Parties to the present Covenant, which may within two months submit nominations in accordance with Article 29 for the purpose of filling the vacancy.
2. The Secretary-General of the United Nations shall prepare a list in alphabetical order of the persons thus nominated and shall submit it to the States Parties to the present Covenant. The election to fill the vacancy shall then take place in accordance with the relevant provisions of this part of the present Covenant.
3. A member of the Committee elected to fill a vacancy declared in accordance with Article 33 shall hold office for the remainder of the term of the member who vacated the seat on the Committee under the provisions of that Article.

Article 35

The members of the Committee shall, with the approval of the General Assembly of the United Nations, receive emoluments from United Nations resources on such terms and conditions as the General Assembly may decide, having regard to the importance of the Committee's responsibilities.

Article 36

The Secretary-General of the United Nations shall provide the necessary staff and facilities for the effective performance of the functions of the Committee under the present Covenant.

Article 37

1. The Secretary-General of the United Nations shall convene the initial meeting of the Committee at the Headquarters of the United Nations.
2. After its initial meeting, the Committee shall meet at such times as shall be provided in its rules of procedure.
3. The Committee shall normally meet at the Headquarters of the United Nations or at the United Nations Office at Geneva.

Article 38

Every member of the Committee shall, before taking up his duties, make a solemn declaration in open committee that he will perform his functions impartially and conscientiously.

Article 39

1. The Committee shall elect its officers for a term of two years. They may be reelected.
2. The Committee shall establish its own rules of procedure, but there rules shall provide, *inter alia*, that:
   (a) Twelve members shall constitute a quorum;
   (b) Decisions of the Committee shall be made by a majority vote of the members present.

Article 40

1. The States Parties to the present Covenant undertake to submit reports on the measures they have adopted which give effect to the rights recognized here in and on the progress made in the enjoyment of those rights;
   (a) Within one year of the entry into force of the present Covenant for the States Parties concerned;
   (b) Thereafter whenever the Committee so requests.
2. All reports shall be submitted to the Secretary-General of

the United Nations, who shall transmit them to the Committee for consideration. Reports shall indicate the factors and difficulties, if any, affecting the implementation of the present Covenant.

3. The Secretary-General of the United Natons may, after consultation with the Committee, transmit to the specialized agencies concerned copies of such parts of the reports as may fall within their field of competence.
4. The Committee shall study the reports submitted by the States Parties to the present Covenant. It shall transmit is reports, and such general comments as it may consider appropriate, to the States Parties. The Committee may also transmit to the Economic and Social Council these comments along with the copies of the reports it has received from States Parties to the present Covenant.
5. The States Parties to the present Covenant may submit to the Committee observations on any comments that may be made in accordance with paragraph 4 of this Article.

Article 41

1. A State Party to the present Covenant may at any time declare under this Article that it recognizes the competence of the Committee to receive and consider communications to the effect that a State Party claims that another State Party is not fulfilling its obligations under the present Covenant. Communications under this Article may be received and considered only if submitted by a State Party which has made a declaration recognizing in regard to itself the competence of the Committee. No communication shall be received by the Committee if it concerns a State Party which has not made such a declaration Communications received under this Article shall be dealt with in accordance with the following procedure:
   (a) If a State Party to the present Covenant considers that another State Party is not giving effect to the provisions of the present Covenant, it may, by written communication, bring the matter to the attention of that State Party. Within three months after the receipt of the communication, the receiving State shall afford the State which sent the communication an

explanation or any other statement in writing clarifying the matter, which should include, to the extent possible and pertinent, reference to domestic procedures and remedies taken, pending, or available in the matter.

(b) If the matter is not adjusted to the satisfaction of both States Parties concerned within six months after the receipt by the receiving State of the initial communication, either State shall have the right to refer the matter to the Committee, by notice given to the Committee and to the other State.

(c) The Committee shall deal with a matter referred to it only after it has ascertained that all available domestic remedies have been invoked and exhausted in the matter, in conformity with the generally recognized principles of international law. This shall not be the rule where the application of the remedies is unreasonably prolonged.

(d) The Committee shall hold closed meetings when examining communications under this Article.

(e) Subject to the provisions of subparagraph (c), the Committee shall make available its good offices to the States Parties concerned with a view to a friendly solutions of the matter on the basis of respect for human rights and fundamental freedoms as recognized in the present Covenant.

(f) In any matter referred to it, the Committee may call upon the States Parties concerned, referred to in subparagraph (b), to supply any relevant information.

(g) The States Parties concerned, referred to in sub paragraph (b), shall have the right to be represented when the matter is being considered in the Committee and to make submissions orally and/or in writing.

(h) The Committee shall, within twelve months after the date of receipt of notice under subparagraph (b), submit a report:

(i) If a soultion within the terms of subparagraph (e) is reached, the Committee shall confine its report to a brief statement of the facts and of the solution reached;

(ii) If a solution within the terms of subparagraph (e) is not reached, the Committee shall confine its report to a brief statement of the facts; the written submissions and record of the oral submissions made by the States Parties concerned shall be attached to the report.

In every matter, the report shall be communicated to the States Parties concerned.

2. The provisions of this Articles shall come into force when ten States Parties to the present Covenant have made declarations under paragraph 1 of this Article. Such declarations shall be deposited by the States Parties with the Secretary-General of the United Nations, who shall transmit copies there of to the other State Parties. A declaration may be withdrawn at any time by notification to the Secretary General. Such a withdrawal shall not prejudice the consideration of any matter which is the subject of a communication already transmitted under this Article; no further communication by any State Party shall be received after the notification of withdrawal of the declaration has been received by the Secretary-General, unless the State Party concerned has made a new declaration.

Article 42

1. (a) If a matter referred to the Committee in accordance with Article 41 is not resolved in the satisfaction of the States Parties concerned, the Committee may, with the prior consent of the States Parties concerned, appoint an ad hoc Conciliation Commission (hereinafter referred to as the Commission). The good offices of the Commission shall be made available to the States Parties concerned with a view to an amicable solution of the matter on the basis of respect for the present Covenant;

(b) The Commission shall consist of five persons acceptable to the States Parties concerned. If the States Parties concerned fail to reach agreement within three months on all or part of the composition of the Commission, the members of the Commission concerning whom no agreement has been reached shall be elected by secret ballot by a two-thirds majority vote of the Committee from among its members.

2. The members of the Commission shall serve in their personal capacity. They shall not be nationals of the States Parties concerned, or of a State not party to the present Covenant, or of a State Party which has not made a declaration under Article 41.
3. The Commission shall elect its own Chairman and adopt its own rules of procedure.
4. The meetings of the Commission shall normally be held at the Headquarters of the United Nations or at the United Nations Office at Geneva. However, they may be held at such other convenient places as the Commission may determine in consultation with the Secretary- General of the United Nations and the States Parties concerned.
5. The secretariat provided in accordance with Article 36 shall also service the commissions appointed under this Article.
6. The information received and collected by the Committee shall be made available to the Commission and the Commission may call upon the States Parties concerned to supply any other relevant information.
7. When the Commission has fully considered the matter, but in any event no later than twelve months after having been seized of the matter, it shall submit to the Chairman of the Committee a report for Communication to the States Parties concerned:
   (a) If the Commission is unable to complete its consideration of the matter within twelve months, it shall confine its reports to a brief statement of the status of its consideration of the matter;
   (b) If an amicable solution to the matter on the basis of respect for human rights as recognized in the present Covenant is reached, the Commission shall confine its report to a brief statement of the facts and of the solution reached;
   (c) If a solution within the terms of subparagraph (b) is not reached, the Commission's report shall embody its findings on all questions of fact relevant to the issues between the States Parties concerned, and its

views on the possibilities of an amicable solution of the matter. This report shall also contain the written submissions and a record of the oral submissions made by the States Parties concerned;

(d) If the Commission's report is submitted under subparagraph (c), the States Parties concerned shall, within three months of the receipt of the report, notify the Chairman of the Committee whether or not they accept the contents of the report of the Commission.

8. The provisions of this Article are without prejudice to the responsibilities of the Committee under Article 41.
9. The States Parties concerned shall share equally all the expenses of the members of the Commission in accordance with estimates to be provided by the Secretary General of the United Nations.
10. The Secretary-General of the United Nations shall be empowered to pay the expenses of the members of the Commission, if necessary, before reimbursement by the States Parties concerned, in accordance with paragraph 9 of this Article.

Article 43

The members of the Committee, and of the *ad hoc* conciliation commissions which may be appointed under Article 42, shall be entitled to the facilities, privileges and immunities of experts on mission for the United Nations as laid down in the relevant sections of the Convention on the Privileges and Immunities of the United Nations.

Article 44

The provisions for the implementation of the present Covenant shall apply without prejudice to the procedures prescribed in the field of human rights by or under the constituent instruments and the conventions of the United Nations and of the specialized agencies and shall not present the States Parties to the present Covenant from having recourse to other procedures for settling a dispute in accordance with general or special international agreements in force between them.

Article 45

The Committee shall submit to the General Assembly of

the United Nations, through the Economic and Social Council, an annual report on its activities.

Part V

Article 46

Nothing in the present Covenant shall be interpreted as impairing the provisions of the Charter of the United Nations and of the Constitutions of the specialized agencies which define the respective responsibilities of the various organs of the United Nations and of the specialized agencies in regard to the matters dealt with in the present Covenant.

Article 47

Nothing in the present Covenant shall be interpreted as impairing the inherent right all peoples to enjoy and utilize fully and freely their natural wealth and resources.

Part VI

Article 48

1. The present Covenant is open for signature by any State Member of the United Nations or member of any of its specialized agencies, by any State Party to the Statute of the International Court of Justice, and by any other State which has been invited by the General Assembly of the United Nations to become a party to the present Covenant.
2. The present Covenant is subject to ratification. Instruments of ratification shall be deposited with the Secretary-General of the United Nations.
3. The present Covenant shall be open to accession by any State referred to in paragraph 1 of this Article.
4. Accession shall be effected by the deposit of an instrument of accession with the Secretary- General of the United Nations.
5. The Secretary-General of the United Nations shall inform all States which have signed this Covenant or acceded to it of the deposit of each instrument of ratification or accession.

Article 49

1. The present Covenant shall enter into force three months after the date of the deposit with the Secretary- General of

the United Nations of the thirty-fifth instrument of ratification or instrument of accession.

2. For each State ratifying the present Covenant or acceding to it after the deposit of the thirty-fifth instrument of ratification or instrument of accession, the present Covenant shall enter into force three months after the date of the deposit of its own instrument of ratification or instrument of accession.

Article 50

The provisions of the present Covenant shall extend to all parts of federal States without any limitations or exceptions.

Article 51

1. Any State Party to the present Covenant may propose an amendment and file it with the Secretary-General of the United Nations. The Secretary-General of the United Nations shall there- upon communicate any proposed amendments to the States Parties to the present Covenant with a request that they notify him whether they favour a conference of States Parties for the purpose of considering and voting upon the proposals. In the event that at least one-third of the States Parties favours such a conference, the Secretary- General shall convene the conference under the auspices the United Nations. Any amendment adopted by a majority of the States Parties present and voting at the conference shall be submitted to the General Assembly of the United Nations for approval.
2. Amendments shall come into force when they have been approved by the General Assembly of the United Nations and accepted by a two-thirds majority of the States Parties to the present Covenant in accordance with their respective Constitutional processes.
3. When amendments come into force, they shall be binding on those States Parties which have accepted them, other States Parties still being bound by the provisions of the present Covenant and any earlier amendment which they have accepted.

Article 52

Irrespective of the notifications made under Article 48, paragraph 5, the Secretary-General of the United Nations shall inform all States referred to in paragraph 1 of the same Article of the following particulars:

(a) Signatures, ratifications and accessions under Article 48;

(b) The date of the entry into force of the present Covenant under Article 49 and the date of the entry into force of any amendments under Article 51.

Article 53

1. The present Covenant, of which the Chinese, English, French, Russian and Spanish texts are equally authentic, shall be deposited in the Archives of the United Nations.
2. The Secretary-General of the United Nations shall transmit certified copies of the present Covenant to all States referred to in Article 48.

Appendix VI

Convention on the Rights of the Child

Reproduced below are parts of this *Convention* which was adopted by the General Assembly of the United Nations on 20th November, 1989 and came in force on 2nd September, 1990.

Preamble

The States Parties to the Present Convention

Considering that, in accordance with the principles proclaimed in the Charter of the United Nations, recognition of the inherent dignity and of the equal and inalienable rights of all members of the human family is the foundation of freedom, justice and peace in the world,

Bearing in mind that the peoples of the United Nations have, in the Charter, reaffirmed their faith in fundamental human rights and in the dignity and worth of the human person, and have determined to promote social progress and better standards of life in larger freedom,

Recognizing that the United Nations has, in the Universal Declaration of Human Rights and in the International Covenants on Human Rights, proclaimed and agreed that everyone is entitled to all the rights and freedoms set forth therein, without distinction of any kind, such as race, colour, sex, language, religion, political or other opinion, national or social origin, property, birth or other status,

Recalling that, in the Universal Declaration of Human Rights, the United Nations has proclaimed that childhood is entitled to special care and assistance,

Convinced that the family, as the fundamental group of society and the natural environment for the growth and well-being of all its members and particularly children, should be afforded the necessary protection and assistance so that it can fully assume its responsibilities within the community,

Recognizing that the child, for the full and harmonious development of his or her personality, should grow up in a family environment, in an atmosphere of happiness, love and understanding.

Considering that the child should be fully prepared to live an individual life in society, and brought up in the spirit of the ideals proclaimed in the Charter of the United Nations, and in particular in the spirit of peace, dignity, tolerance, freedom, equality and solidarity,

Bearing in mind that the need to extend particular care to the child has been stated in the Geneva Declaration of the Rights of the Child of 1924 and in the Declaration of the Rghts of the Child adopted by the General Assembly on 20th November, 1959 and recognized in the Universal Declaration of Human Rights, in the International Covenant on Civil and Political Rights (in particular in Articles 23 and 24, in the International Covenant on Economic, Social and Cultural Rights (in particular in Article 10) and in the status and relevant instruments of specialized agencies and international organizations concerned with the welfare of children,

Bearing in mind that, as indicated in the Declaration of the Rights of the Child, "the child, by reason of his physical and mental immaturity, needs special safeguards and care, including appropriate legal protection, before as well as after birth",

Recalling the Provisions of the Declaration on Social and Legal Principles relating to the Protection and Welfare of Children, with Special Reference to Foster Placement and Adoption Nationally and Internationally, the United Nations Standard Minimum Rules for the administration of Juvenile Justice (The Beijing Rules); and the Declaration on the Protection of Women and Children in Emergency and Armed Conflict.

Recognizing that, in all countries in the world, there are children living in exceptionally difficult conditions, and that such children need special consideration.

Taking due account of the importance of the traditions and cultural values of each people for the protection and harmonious development of the child.

Recognizing the importance of International Cooperation for improving the living conditions of children in every country, in particular in the developing countries.

Have agreed as follows:

Part I

Article 1

For the purposes of the present Convention, a child means every human being below the age of eighteen years unless, under the law applicable to the child, majority is attained earlier.

Article 2

1. State Parties shall respect and ensure the rights set forth in the present Convention to each child within their jurisdiction without discrimination of any kind, irrespective of the child's or his or her parent's or legal guardian's race, colour, sex, language, religion, political or other opinion, national, ethnic or social origin, property, disability, birth or other status.
2. States Parties shall take all appropriate measures to ensure that the child is protected against all forms of discrimination or punishment on the basis of the status, activities, expressed opinions, or beliefs of the child's parents, legal guardians, or family members.

Article 3

1. In all actions concerning children, whether undertaken by public or private social welfare institutions, courts of law, administrative authorities or legislative bodies, the best interests of the child shall be a primary consideration.
2. States Parties undertake to ensure the child such protection and care as is necessary for his or her well-being, taking into account the rights and duties of his or her parents, legal guardians, or other individuals legally responsible for him or her, and, to this end, shall take all appropriate legislative and administrative measures.

Article 5

States Parties shall respect the responsibilities, rights and duties of parents or, where applicable, the members of the extended family or community as provided for by local custom, legal guardians or other persons legally responsible for the child, to provide, in a manner consistent with the evolving capacities of the child, appropriate direction and guidance in the exercise by the child of the rights recognized in the present Convention.

Article 6

1. States Parties recognize that every child has the inherent right to life.
2. States Parties shall ensure to the maximum extent possible the survival and development of the child.

Article 7

1. The child shall be registered immediately after birth and shall have the right from birth to a name, the right to acquire a nationality and, as far as possible, the right to know and be cared for by his or her parents.

Article 9

1. States Parties shall ensure that a child shall not be separated from his or her parents againt their will, except when competent authorities subject to judicial review determine, in accordance with applicable law and procedures, that such separation is necessary for the best interests of the child. Such determination may be necessary in a particular case such as one involving abuse or neglect of the child by the parents, or one where the parents are living separately and a decision must be made as to the child's place of residence.

Article 11

1. States Parties shall take measures to combat the illicit transfer and non-return of children abroad.
2. To this end, States Parties shall promote the conclusion of bilateral or multilateral agreements or accession to existing agreements.

Article 12

1. States Parties shall assure to the child who is capable of forming his or her own views the right to express those views freely in all matters affecting the child, the views of

the child being given due weight in accordance with the age and maturity of the child.

Article 13

1. The child shall have the right to freedom of expression; this right shall include freedom to seek, receive and impart information and ideas of all kinds, regardless of frontiers, either orally, in writing or in print, in the form of art, or through any other media of the child's choice.

Article 14

1. States Parties shall respect the right of the child to freedom of thought, conscience and religion.
2. States Parties shall respect the rights and duties of the parents and, when applicable, legal guardians, to provide direction to the child in the exercise of his or her right in a manner consistent with the evolving capacities of the child.
3. Freedom to manifest ones religion or beliefs may be subject only to such limitations as are prescribed by law and are necessary to protect public safety, order, health or morals, or the fundamental rights and freedoms of others.

Article 15

1. States Parties recognize the rights of the child to freedom of association and to freedom of peaceful assembly.
2. No restrictions may be placed on the exercies of these rights other than those imposed in conformity with the law and which are necessary in a democratic society in the interests on national security or public safety, public order (*ordre public*), the protection of public health or morals or the protection of the rights and freedoms of others.

Article 16

1. No child shall be subjected to arbitrary or unlawful interference with his or her privacy, family, home or correspondence, nor to unlawful attacks on his or her honour and reputation.
2. The child has the right to the protection of the law against such interference or attacks.

Article 17

States Parties recognize the important function performed

by the mass media and shall ensure that the child has access to information and material from a diversity of national and international sources, especially those aimed at the promotion of his or her social, spiritual and moral well- being and physical and mental health. To this end, States Parties shall:

(a) encourage the mass media to disseminate information and material of social and cultural benefit to the child and in accordance with the spirit of Article 29;

(b) encourage international cooperation in the production, exchange and dissemination of such information and material from a diversity of cultural, national and international sources;

(c) encourage the production and dissemination of children's books;

(d) encourage the mass media to have particular regard to the lingustic needs of the child who belongs to a minority group or who is indigenous;

(e) encourage the development of appropriate guidelines for the protection of the child from information and material injurious to his or her well-being, bearing in mind the provisions of Articles 13 and 18.

Article 18

1. States Parties shall use their best efforts to ensure recognition of the principle that both parents have common responsibilities for the upbringing and development of the child. Parents or, as the case may be, legal guardians, have the primary responsibility for the upbringing and development of the child. The best interests of the child will be their basic concern.
2. For the purpose of guaranteeing and promoting the rights set forth in the present Convention, States Parties shall render appropriate assistance to parents and legal guardians in the performance of their child-rearing responsibilities and shall ensure the development of institutions, facilities and services for the care of children.
3. States Parties shall take all appropriate measures to ensure that children of working parents have the right to benefit from child care services and facilities for which they are eligible.

Article 19

1. States Parties shall take all appropriate legislative, administrative, social and educational measures to protect the child from all forms of physical or mental violence, injury, or abuse, neglect or negligent treatment, maltreatment or exploitation, including sexual abuse, while in the care of parent(s) legal guardian(s) or any other person who has the care of the child.

Article 20

1. A child temporarily or permanently deprived of his or her family environment, or in whose own best interest cannot be allowed to remain in that environment, shall be entitled to special protection and assistance provided by the State.

Article 21

1. States Parties that recognize and/or permit the system of adoption shall ensure that the best interests of the child shall be the paramount consideration...

Article 23

1. States Parties recognize that a mentally or physically disabled child should enjoy a full and decent life, in conditions which ensure dignity, promote self-reliance and facilitate the child's active participation in the community.
2. States Parties recognize the right of the disabled child to special care and shall encourage and ensure the extension, subject to available resources, to the eligible child and those responsible for his or her care, of assistance for which application is made and which is appropriate to the child's condition and to the circumstances of the parents or others caring for the child.
3. Recognizing the special needs of a disabled child, assistance extended in accordance with paragraph-2 of the present Article shall be provided free of charge, whenever possible , taking into account the financial resources of the parents or others caring for the child, and shall be designed to ensure that the disabled child has effective access to and receives education, training, health care services, rehabilitation services, preparation for employment and recreation opportunities in a manner conducive to the child's achieving the fullest possible social integration and

individual development, including his or her cultural and spiritual development.

4. States Parties shall promote, in the spirit of international cooperation, the exchange of appropriate information in the field of preventive health care and of medical, psychological and functional treatment of disabled children, including dissemination of and access to information concerning methods of rehabilitation, education and vocational services, with the aim of enabling States Parties to improve their capabilities and skills and to widen their experience in these areas. In this regard, particular account shall be taken of the needs of developing countries.

Article 24

1. States Parties recognize the right of the child to the enjoyment of the highest attainable standard of health and to facilities for the treatment of illness and rehabilitation of health. States Parties shall strive to ensure that no child is deprived of his or her right of access to such health care services.
2. States Parties shall pursue full implementation of this right and, in particular, shall take appropriate measures:
   (a) to diminish infant and child mortality;
   (b) to ensure the provision of necessary medical assistance and health care to all children with emphasis on the development of primary health care;
   (c) to combat disease and malnutrition, including within the framework of primary health care, through, inter alia, application of readily available technology and through the provision of adequate nutritious foods and clean drinking water, taking into consideration the dangers and risks of environmental pollution;
   (d) to ensure appropriate pre-natal and post-natal health care for mothers;
   (e) to ensure that all segments of society, in particular parents and children, are informed, have access to education and are supported in the use of basic knowledge of child health and nutrition, the advantages of breast- feeding, hygiene and environmental sanitation and the prevention of accidents;

(f) to develop preventive health care, guidance for parents and family planning education and services.

3. States Parties shall take all effective and appropriate measures with a view to abolishing traditional practices prejudicial to the health of children.
4. States Parties undertake to promote and encourage international cooperation with a view to achieving progressively the full realization of the right recognized in the present Article. In this regard, particular account shall be taken of the needs of developing countries.

Article 27

1. States Parties recognize the right of every child to a standard of living adequate for the child's physical, mental, spiritual, moral and social development.
2. The parent(s) or others responsible for the child have the primary responsibility to secure, with their abilities and financial capacities, the conditions of living necessary for the child's development.
3. States Parties, in accordance with national conditions and within their means, shall take appropriate measures to assist parents and others responsible for the child to implement this right and shall in case of need provide material assistance and support programmes, particularly with regard to nutrition, clothing and housing.

Article 28

States Parties recognize the right of the child to education, and with a view to achieving this right progressively and on the basis of equal opportunity, they shall, in particular:

(a) make primary education compulsory and available free to all;

(b) encourage the development of different forms of secondary education, including general and vocational education, make them available and accessible to every child, and take appropriate measures such as the introduction of free education and offering financial assistance in case of need;

(c) make higher education accessible to all on the basis of capacity by every appropriate means;

(d) make educational and vocational information and

guidance available and accessible to all children;
(e) take measures to encourage regular attendance at schools and the reduction of drop-out rates.

2. States Parties shall take all appropriate measures to ensure that school discipline is administered in a manner consistent with the child's human dignity and in conformity with the present Convention.
3. States Parties shall promote and encourage international cooperation in matters relating to education, in particular with a view to contributing to the elimination of ignorance and illiteracy throughout the world and facilitating access to scientific and technical knowledge and modern teaching methods. In this regard, particular account shall be taken of the needs of developing countries.

Article 29

1. States Parties agree that the education of the child shall be directed to:
   (a) the development of the child's personality, talents and mental and physical abilities to their fullest potential;
   (b) the development of respect for human rights and fundamental freedoms, and for the principles enshrined in the Charter of the United Nations;
   (c) the development of respect for the child's parents, his or her own cultural identity, language and values, for the national values of the country in which the child is living the country from which he or she may originate, and for civilizations different from his or her own;
   (d) the preparation of the child for responsible life in a free society, in the spirit of understanding, peace, tolerance, equality of sexes, and friendship among all peoples, ethnic, national and religious groups and persons of indigenous origin;
   (e) the development of respect for the natural environment.
2. No part of the present Article or Article 28 shall be construed so as to interfere with the liberty of individuals and bodies to establish and direct educational institutions, subject always to the observance of the principles set forth in paragraph 1 of the present Article and to the requirements that the education given in such institutions shall conform to such minimum standards as may be laid down by the State.

Article 30

1. In those States in which ethnic, religious or linguistic minorities or persons of tridigenous origin exist, a child belonging to such a minority or who is indigenous shall not be denied the right, in community with other members of his or her group, to enjoy his or her own culture, to profess and practise his or her own religion, or to use his or her own language.

Article 31

1. States Parties recognize the right of the child to rest and leisure to engage in play and recreational activities appropriate to the age of the child and to participate freely in cultural life and the arts.
2. States Parties shall respect and promote the right of the child to participate fully in cultural and artistic life and shall encourage the provision of appropriate and equal opportunities for cultural, artistic, recreational and leisure activity.

Article 32

1. States Parties recognize the right of the child to be protected from economic exploitation and from performing any work that is likely to be hazardous or to interfere with the child's education, or to be harmful to the child's health or physical, mental, spiritual, moral or social development.
2. States Parties shall take legislative, administrative, social and educational measures to ensure the implementation of the present Article. To this end, and having regard to the relevant provisions of other international instruments. States Parties shall in particular;
   (a) provide for a minimum age or minimum ages for admission to employment:
   (b) provide for appropriate regulations of the hours and conditions of employment;
   (c) provide for appropriate penalties or other sanctions to ensure the effective enforcement of the present Article.

Article 33

States Parties shall take all appropriate measures, including legislative, administrative, social and educational measures, to protect children from the illicit use of narcotic drugs and psychotropic substances as defined in the relevant international treaties, and to prevent the use of children in the illicit production and trafficking of such substances.

Article 34

States Parties undertake to protect the child from all forms of sexual exploitation and sexual abuse. For these purposes, States Parties shall in particular take all appropriate national, bilateral and multilateral measures to prevent:

(a) the inducement or coercion of a child to engage in any unlawful sexual activity;

(b) the exploitative use of children in prostitution or other unlawful sexual practices;

(c) the exploitative use of children in pornographic performances and materials.

Article 35

States Parties shall take all appropriate national, bilateral and multilateral measures to prevent the abduction of, the sale of or traffic in children for any purpose or in any form.

Article 36

States Parties shall protect the child against all other forms of exploitation prejudicial to any aspects of the child's welfare.

Article 37

States Parties shall ensure that:

(a) no child shall be subjected to torture or other cruel, inhuman or degrading treatment or punishment. Neither capital punishment nor life imprisonment without possibility of release shall be imposed for offenses committed by persons below eighteen years of age;

(b) no child shall be deprived of his or her liberty unlawfully or arbitrarily. The arrest, detention or imprisonment of a child shall be in conformity with the law and shall be used only as a measure of last resort and for the shortest appropriate period of time;

(c) every child deprived of liberty shall be treated with humanity and respect for the inherent dignity of the human person, and in a manner which takes into account the needs of persons of his or her age. In particular, every child deprived of liberty shall be separated from adults unless it is considered in the child's best interest not to do so and shall have the right to maintain contract with his or her family through correspondence and visits, save in exceptional circumstances;

(d) every child deprived of his or her liberty shall have the right to prompt access to legal and other appropriate assistance, as well as the right to challenge the legality of the deprivation of his or her liberty before a court or other competent, independent and impartial authority, and to a prompt decision on any such action.

Article 38

1. States Parties undertake to respect and to ensure respect for rules of international humanitarian law applicable to them in armed conflicts which are relevant to the child.
2. States Parties shall take all feasible measures to ensure that persons who have not attained the age of fifteen years do not take a direct part in hostilities.
3. States Parties shall refrain from recruiting any person who has not attained the age of fifteen years into their armed forces...
4. In accordance with their obligations under international humanitarian law to protect the civilian population in armed conflicts, States Parties shall take all feasible measures to ensure protection and care of children who are affected by an armed conflict.

Article 39

1. States Parties shall take all appropriate measures to promote physical and psychological recovery and social reintegration of a child victim of any form of neglect, exploitation, or abuse; torture or any other form of cruel, inhuman or degrading treatment or punishment; or armed conflicts. Such recovery and reintegration shall take place in an environment which fosters the health, self-respect and dignity of the child.

Part 2

Article 42

1. States Parties undertake to make the principles and provisions of the Convention widely known, by appropriate and active means, to adults and children alike.

Appendix VII

Status of International Instruments Relating to Human Rights (As on 15th February, 2002)

S. No.	*International Instruments (Date of Entry into Force)*	*Total No. of State Parties*	*Total No. of Asian States*	*Ratification, Accession, Notification of Succession, Acceptance by Asian States*
1.	International Covenant on Economic, Social and Cultural Rights (3rd January, 1976)	145	30	Afghanistan, Armenia, Azerbaijan, Bangladesh, Cambodia, China, India, Iran, Iraq, Israel, Japan, Jordan, Democratic Peoples Republic of Korea (North, Kuwait, Kyrgyzstan, Lebanon, Muritius, Mongolia, Nepal, Philippines, Republic of Korea (South), Solomon Islands, Sri Lanka, Syria, Tajikistan, Thailand, Turkmenistan, Uzbekistan, Vietnam, Yemen.

S. No.	*International Instruments (Date of Entry into Force)*	*Total No. of State Parties*	*Total No. of Asian States*	*Ratification, Accession, Notification of Succession, Acceptance by Asian States*
2.	International Covenant on Civil and Political Rights (23rd March, 1976)*	148	28	Afghanistan, Armenia, Azerbaijan, Bangladesh, Cambodia, ***India***, Iran, Iraq, Israel, Japan, Jordan, Democratic Peoples Republic of Korea (North, Kuwait, Kyrgyzstan, Lebanon, Muritius, Mongolia, Nepal, Philippines, Republic of Korea (South), Sri Lanka, Syria, Tajikistan, Thailand, Turkmenistan, Uzbekistan, Vietnam, Yemen.
3.	Optional Protocol to Internatioal Covenant on	98	11	Armenia, Kyrgyzstan, Mauritius, Mongolia, Nepal, Philippines, Republic of Korea (South), Sri Lanka,

*Following 46 State-parties have so far made declarations recognizing the competence of Human Rights Committee under Article 41 of the Covenant (State to State complaint system): Algeria, Argentina, Austria, Australia, Belarus, Belgium, Bosnia-Herzegovina, Bulgaria, Canada, Chile, Congo, Croatia, Czech Republic, Denmark, Ecuador, Finland, Gambia, Germany, Guyana, Hungary, Iceland, Ireland, Italy, Luxembourg, Malta, Netherlands, New Zealand, Norway, Peru, Philippines, Poland, Republic of Korea, Russian Federation, Senegal, Slovak Republic, Slovenia, South Africa, Spain, Sri Lanka, Sweden, Switzerland, Tunisia, Ukraine, UK, USA and Zimbabwe.

S. No.	*International Instruments (Date of Entry into Force)*	*Total No. of State Parties*	*Total No. of Asian States*	*Ratification, Accession, Notification of Succession, Acceptance by Asian States*
	Civil and Political Rights (Individual Petitions Against State) (23rd March, 1976)			Tajikistan, Turkmenistan, Uzbekistan.
4.	Second Optional Protocol to the International Covenant on Civil and Political Right aiming at the Abolition of the Death Penalty (11th July, 1991)	44	2	Nepal, Turkmenistan.
5.	Convention on the Prevention and Punishment of the Crime of Genocide (12th January, 1951)	132	36	Afghanistan, Armenia, Azerbaijan, Bahrain, Bangladesh, China Cambodia, Democratic Peoples Republic of Korea (North), Fiji, ***India***, Iran, Iraq, Israel, Jordan, Kazakstan, Kuwait, Kyrgyzstan, Laos Lebanon, Maldives, Mongolia, Malaysia,

S. No.	*International Instruments (Date of Entry into Force)*	*Total No. of State Parties*	*Total No. of Asian States*	*Ratification, Accession, Notification of Succession, Acceptance by Asian States*
				Myanmar, Nepal, Pakistan, Pupua New Guinea, Philippines, Republic of Korea (South), Singapore, Saudi Arabia, Sri Lanka, Syria, Tonga, Uzbekistan, Vietnam, Yemen.
6.	Convention on the Non-Ap plicability of Statutory Limi tations to War Crimes Against Humanity (11th November, 1970)	44	11	Afghainstan, Armenia, Azerbaijan, Democratic Peoples Republic of Korea (North) India, Laos, Mongolia, Philippines, Kuwait, Vietnam, Yemen.
7.	International Covention on the Elimination of All Forms of Racial Discriminations (4th January, 1969)*	158	39	Afghanistan, Armenia, Azerbaijan, Bahrain, Bangladesh, China, Cambodia, Fiji, ***India***, Indonesia, Iran,

*Following 34 State-parties have so far made declarations recognizing the competence of the Committee on the Elimination of Racial Discrimination under Article 14 of the Convention: Algeria, Australia, Belgium, Bulgaria, Chile, Costa Rica, Cyprus, Czech Republic, Denmark, Ecuador, Finland, France, Hungary, Iceland, Ireland, Italy, Luxembourg, Malta, Netherlands, Norway, Peru, Poland, Portugal, Republic of Korea (South), Russian Federation, Senegal, Slovak Republic, South Africa, Spain, Sweden, The former Yugoslav Republic of Macedonia, Ukraine, Uruguay and Yugoslavia.

S. No.	International Instruments (Date of Entry into Force)	Total No. of State Parties	Total No. of Asian States	Ratification, Accession, Notification of Succession, Acceptance by Asian States
				Iraq, Israel, Japan, Jordan, Kazakstan, Kuwait, Kyrgyzstan, Laos, Lebanon, Maldives, Mauritius, Mongolia, Nepal, Pakistan, Papua New Guinea, Philippines, Republic of Korea (South), Saudi Arabia, Solomon Islands, Sri Lanka, Syria, Tajikistan, Tonga, Turkmenistan, United Arab Emirates, Uzbekistan, Vietnam, Yemen.
8.	UNESCO Convention Against Discrimination in Education (22nd May, 1962)	89	20	Armenai, China, Cyprus, Indonesia, Iran, Iraq, Israel, Jordan, Kuwait, Kyrgyzstan, Lebanon, Mauritius, Mongolia, Philippines, Saudi Arabia, Solomon Islands, Sri Lanka, Tajikistan, Uzbekistan, Vietnam.
9.	Convention Relating to the Status of Refugees (22nd April, 1954)	137	18	Armenia, Azerbaijan, Cambodia, China, Fiji, Iran, Israel, Japan, Kazakstan, Kyrgyzstan, Philippines,

S. No.	*International Instruments (Date of Entry into Force)*	*Total No. of State Parties*	*Total No. of Asian States*	*Ratification, Accession, Notification of Succession, Acceptance by Asian States*
				Papua New Guinea, Republic of Korea (South), Samoa, Solomon Islands, Tajikistan, Turkmenistan, Yemen.
11.	Convention Relating to the Status of Stateless Persons (6th June, 1960)	53	4	Azerbaijan, Fiji, Israel, Republic of Korea (South).
12.	Convention on the Reduction of Statelessness (13th December, 1975)	23	2	Armenia, Azerbaijan.
13.	Convention on the Political Rights of Women (7th July, 1954)	115	27	Afghanistan, Bangladesh, Fiji, ***India,*** Indonesia, Israel, Japan, Jordan, Kazakstan, Kuwait, Kyrgyzstan, Laos, Lebanon, Mauritius, Mongolia, Nepal, Pakistan, Papua New Guinea, Philippines, Republic of Korea (South), Solomon Islands, Tajikistan, Thailand, Turkey, Turkmenistan, Uzbekistan, Yemen.

S. No.	*International Instruments (Date of Entry into Force)*	*Total No. of State Parties*	*Total No. of Asian States*	*Ratification, Accession, Notification of Succession, Acceptance by Asian States*
14.	Convention on the Nationaliy of Married Women (11th August, 1958)	70	12	Armenia, Azerbaijan, Cyprus, Fiji, Israel, Jordan, Kazakstan, Kyrgyzstan, Malaysis, Mauritius, Singapore, Sri Lanka.
15.	Convention on the Consent to Marriage, Minimum Age for Marriage and Registration of Marriages (9th December, 1954)	49	8	Azerbaijan, Bangladesh, Fiji, Jordan, Mongolia, Kyrgyzstan, Philippines, Yemen.
16.	Protocol Amending the Slavery Convention (7th December 1953)	59	12	Afghanistan, Azerbijan, Bangladesh, Fiji, ***India***, Iraq, Isreal, Myanmar, Solomon, Islands, Syria, Turkey, Turkmenistan.
17.	Slavery Convention of 1926 as Amended in 1953 (7th July, 1955)	40	13	Bahrain, Cyprus, Jordan, Kuwait, Mongolia, Myanmar, Nepal, Philippines, Papua New Guinea, Pakistan, Saudi Arabia, Sri Lanka, Yemen.

S. No.	*International Instruments (Date of Entry into Force)*	*Total No. of State Parties*	*Total No. of Asian States*	*Ratification, Accession, Notification of Succession, Acceptance by Asian States*
18.	Supplementary Convention on the Abolition of Slavery, the Slave Trade and Institutions and Practices Similar to Slavery (30th April, 1957)	118	28	Afghanistan, Azerbaijan, Bahrain, Bangladesh, Cambodia, Cyprus, Fiji, ***India***, Iran, Iraq, Israel, Jordan, Kuwait, Kyrgyzstan, Laos, Malaysis, Mauritius, Mongolia, Nepal, Pakistan, Philippines, Saudi Arabia, Signapore, Solomon Islands, Sri Lanka, Syria, Turkey, Turkmenistan.
20.	International Convention on the Suppression and Punishment of the Crime of Apartheid (18th July, 1976)	101	26	Afghanistan, Armenia, Azerbaijan, Bahrain, Bangladesh, Cambodia, China, ***India***, Iran, Iraq, Jordan, Kuwait, Kyrgyzstan, Laos, Maldives, Mongolia, Nepal, Oman, Pakistan, Philippines, Qatar, Sri Lanka, Syria, UAE, Vietnam, Yemen.
21.	Convention on the Elimina tion of All Forms of Discrimi nation Against Women (3rd September, 1981)	167	40	Armenia, Azerbaijan, Bangladesh, Bhutan, Cambodia, China, Cyprus, Democratic Peoples Rep. of Korea (North), Fiji, ***India***, Indonesia, Iraq,

S. No.	*International Instruments (Date of Entry into Force)*	*Total No. of State Parties*	*Total No. of Asian States*	*Ratification, Accession, Notification of Succession, Acceptance by Asian States*
				Israel, Japan, Jordan, Kazakstan, Kyrgyzstan, Laos, Lebanon, Malaysia, Maldives, Mauritius, Mongolia, Myanmar, Nepal, Pakistan, Papus New Guinea, Philippines, Republic of Korea (South), Samoa, Saudi Arabia, Singapore, Sri Lanka, Tajikistan, Thailand, Turkey, Turkmenistan, Uzbekistan, Vietnam, Yemen.
22.	Convention Against Torture and Other Cruel, Inhuman or Degrading Treatment or Punishment (26th June 1987)*	124	28	Afghanistan, Armenia, Azerbaijan, Bahrain, Bangladesh, Cambodia, China, Cyprus, Indonesia, Israel, Jordan, Japan, Kazakstan, Kyrgyzstan, Kuwait, Lebanon, Mauritius, Nepal, Philippines, Qatar, Republic of Korea (South), Saudi Arabia, Sri Lanka, Tajikistan, Turkey, Turkmenistan, Uzbekistan, Yemen.

S. No.	*International Instruments (Date of Entry into Force)*	*Total No. of State Parties*	*Total No. of Asian States*	*Ratification, Accession, Notification of Succession, Acceptance by Asian States*
23.	International Convention Against Apartheid in Sports (3rd April, 1988)	58	13	Dem. Peoples Rep. of Korea (North), ***India,*** Indonesia, Iran, Iraq, Jordan, Kuwait, Mauritius, Mongolia, Nepal, Philippines, Qatar, Syria.
24.	Convention on the Rights of the Child (2nd September, 1990)	191	51	Afghanistan, Armenia, Azerbaijan, Bahrain, Bangladesh, Bhutan, Cambodia, China, Cyprus, Dem. Peoples Rep. of Korea (North), Fiji, ***India,*** Indonesia, Iran, Iraq, Israel, Janpan, Jordan, Kazakstan, Kuwait, Kyrgyzstan,

*Following 44 State-parties have so far made declarations recognizing the competence of the Committee Against Torture (CAT) under Article 21 of the Convention (to examine communication by one State party against another or on behalf of individual): Algeria, Argentina, Australia, Austria, Belgium, Bulgaria, Cameroun, Canada, Croatia, Cyprus, Czech Republic, Denmark, Ecuador, Finland, France, Greece, Hungary, Iceland, Italy, Japan, Liechtenstein, Luxembourg, Malta, Manaco, Netherlands, New Zealand, Norway, Poland, Portugal, Russian Federation, Senegal, Slovak Republic, South Africa, Spain, Sweden Switzerland, Togo, Tunisia, Turkey, United Kingdom (Article 21 only), United States of America, Uruguay, Venezuela, Yugoslavia.

S. No.	*International Instruments (Date of Entry into Force)*	*Total No. of State Parties*	*Total No. of Asian States*	*Ratification, Accession, Notification of Succession, Acceptance by Asian States*
				Laos, Lebanon, Malaysia, Maldives, Mauritius, Mongolia, Myanmar, Nauru, Nepal, Oman, Papua New Guinea, Pakistan, Philippines, Qatar, Republic of Korea (South), Samoa, Saudi Arabia, Singapore, Solomon Islands, Sri Lanka, Syria, Tajikistan, Thailand, Tonga, Turkey, Turkmenistan, UAE, Uzbekistan, Vietnam, Yemen.
25.	Optional Protocol to the Convention on the Rights of the Child on the Involvement of (banning the use of) children in Armed Conflicts (12th February 2002).	14	3	Bangladesh, Sri Lanka, Vietnam.

Index